THE AMERICAN PURITAN ELEGY

Jeffrey Hammond's study takes an anthropological approach to the most popular form of poetry in early New England – the funeral elegy. Hammond reconstructs the historical, theological, and cultural contexts of these poems to demonstrate how they responded to a specific process of mourning defined by Puritan views on death and grief. The elegies emerge, he argues, not as "poems" to be read and appreciated in a postromantic sense, but as performative scripts that consoled readers by shaping their experience of loss in accordance with theological expectation. Read in the framework of their own time and place, the elegies shed new light on the emotional dimension of Puritanism and the important role of ritual in Puritan culture. Hammond's book reassesses a body of poems whose importance in their own time has been obscured by almost total neglect in ours. It represents the first full-length study of its kind in English.

JEFFREY A. HAMMOND is Professor of English at St. Mary's College of Maryland. He is author of *Sinful Self, Saintly Self: The Puritan Experience of Poetry* (1993) and *Edward Taylor: Fifty Years of Scholarship and Criticism* (1993).

CAMBRIDGE STUDIES IN AMERICAN
LITERATURE AND CULTURE

Editor
Ross Posnock, University of Washington

Founding editor
Albert Gelpi, Stanford University

Advisory board
Nina Baym, University of Illinois, Urbana-Champaign
Sacvan Bercovitch, Harvard University
Ronald Bush, St John's College, Oxford University
Albert Gelpi, Stanford University
Myra Jehlen, Rutgers University
Carolyn Porter, University of California, Berkeley
Robert Stepto, Yale University

THE AMERICAN
PURITAN ELEGY

A Literary and Cultural Study

JEFFREY A. HAMMOND

CAMBRIDGE
UNIVERSITY PRESS

PUBLISHED BY THE PRESS SYNDICATE OF THE UNIVERSITY OF CAMBRIDGE
The Pitt Building, Trumpington Street, Cambridge, United Kingdom

CAMBRIDGE UNIVERSITY PRESS
The Edinburgh Building, Cambridge CB2 2RU, UK   http://www.cup.cam.ac.uk
40 West 20th Street, New York, NY 10011-4211, USA   http://www.cup.org
10 Stamford Road, Oakleigh, Melbourne 3166, Australia
Ruiz de Alarcón 13, 28014 Madrid, Spain

First published 2000

Printed in the United Kingdom at the University Press, Cambridge

Typeface Monotype Baskerville 11/12¹/₂ pt.   *System* QuarkXPress™ [SE]

A catalogue record for this book is available from the British Library

Library of Congress Cataloguing in Publication data
Hammond, Jeffrey.
The American Puritan elegy: a literary and cultural study /
Jeffrey A. Hammond.
p.   cm. – (Cambridge studies in American literature and
culture 123)
Includes bibliographical references.
ISBN 0 521 66245 1
1. Elegiac poetry, American – History and criticism.   2. American
poetry – Colonial period, ca. 1600–1775 – History and criticism.
3. American poetry – Puritan authors – History and criticism.
4. American poetry – New England – History and criticism.
5. Literature and anthropology – New England – History.
6. Christianity and literature – New England – History.   7. Puritans –
New England – Intellectual life.   8. Death in literature.   9. Grief
in literature.   I. Title.   II. Series.
PS309.E4H36   2000
811.009′3548 – dc21   99–16898   CIP

ISBN 0 521 66245 1 hardback

For my parents

Jeanne Weldon Hammond
and
Evan Ronald Hammond

The hand of the Lord was upon me, and carried me out in the Spirit of the Lord, and set me down in the midst of the valley which was full of bones,

And caused me to pass by them round about: and, behold, there were very many in the open valley; and, lo, they were very dry.

And he said unto me, Son of man, can these bones live? And I answered, O Lord God, thou knowest.

Ezekiel 37:1–3

Contents

Preface

Like many books, this one began in frustration. A few years back, while pruning the bloated first draft of a study of American Puritan poetry, I removed a three-chapter section dealing with the funeral elegy. It pained me to do so: I was pursuing a cultural reading of Puritan verse, and regretted omitting a full discussion of the most popular poems of the era. Still, I couldn't get these strange old poems out of my mind. There remained something more compelling about them than their wooden surfaces could explain, and since they both repulsed and attracted me, it seemed important to understand why. Accounting for the repulsion was easy enough. Like others of my professional generation, I had been trained to value poems that differed radically from these repetitive, predictable laments for the Puritan dead. Accounting for my attraction took more probing, but three reasons finally emerged. First, the Bible-centered Protestantism that stamped my earliest years probably made these poems less alien to me than they seemed to other readers, at least if the commentary surrounding them was any indication. Second, these poems, for all their deviation from modern taste, articulate the larger relationship between language and loss, between words and the absence that their use inevitably invokes. Nowhere does the issue seem more real – less glibly theoretical or aridly intellectual – than in elegiac texts, which exist precisely because their human referents are gone. Third, I believe that an important function of literary history is to recuperate neglected or misunderstood texts, an impulse that David Perkins has called "chivalrous" (33). There are worse labels, certainly, for a literary historian to bear. Moreover, chivalry toward the dead is a familiar impulse among early Americanists, veterans of a longstanding struggle to get our period and our writers taken seriously. Puritanists in particular have come to know what it is like to root for underdogs. Critics often judge Puritan poetry by postromantic artistic, psychological, and moral standards, and even though Anne Bradstreet and Edward Taylor seem marginally able to hold their own in the face of anachronistic readings, such has definitely not been the case with other seventeenth-century New England poets, especially the elegists. Indeed, no other form of Puritan poetry seems more in need of historical and aesthetic contextualizing.

Given current constructions of art and mourning, it is difficult to approach Puritan elegies without expecting a type of literary performance in which the poets themselves – and the mourners they sought to comfort – had little interest. In this study I have tried to describe another kind of performance that the poems embodied, a ritual performance consistent with how they were experienced by their original writers and readers. What Puritans experienced in elegy was, at root, the power of a cultural myth and the satisfactions of a verbal performance that allowed them to enter that myth. The central trope of the Puritan elegy, when read in light of the literary codes of its time and place, is not the enduring monument, the treasured urn, or nature weeping in sympathy with survivors. The central trope is resurrection – a trope that emerges perhaps most clearly in the unforgettable image of a regathered and revivified Israel set forth in Ezekiel's vision of the valley of dry bones. When the divine voice asks the prophet, "Son of man, can these bones live?" Ezekiel replies, "O Lord God, thou knowest" (Ezek. 37:3). Speaking resurrections for the dry bones of the Puritan dead was central to a verbal ritual that early New England's elegists repeatedly and tirelessly performed. The image also suggests what a literary historian faced with the dry bones of forgotten poems might hope to achieve.

Acknowledgments

I have been assisted in this book by my English Department colleagues at St. Mary's College of Maryland, whose varied reactions and diverse enthusiasms kept me trying to make these old poems as interesting to them as they are to me. In particular, Andrea Hammer led me toward deeper insights into the cultural and historical implications of what I was trying to do; Sheila Sullivan helped me clarify my methods and theoretical positions; and Michael S. Glaser gave a poet's critique, at once sharp and kind. Elizabeth Bergmann-Loizeaux of the University of Maryland offered thoughtful responses to the project in its earlier stages, as did David Kuebrich of George Mason University, a good friend whose example continually reminds me of the moral dimension of our teaching, writing, and lives. Edward Lewis, former president of St. Mary's College, and former provost Melvin Endy granted a sabbatical in which I wrote the first draft. Edward A. Strickland of Catholic University kindly checked my renderings of Latin poems and saved me from several gaffes; because I occasionally gave my rusty Latin free rein despite his advice, he is not responsible for any slips that might remain. I am also grateful to Anne Sanow, Terence Moore, Robyn Wainner, and Raymond Ryan of Cambridge University Press, who saw possibilities in what might strike some as an unappealing subject, and to the anonymous reviewers for their helpful comments and suggestions.

I especially thank Norma Tilden of Georgetown University. Although she has encouraged me to seek new ways to make scholarship matter, her support has always gone far beyond professional limits. Finally, I acknowledge with deep gratitude the continued support and friendship of Thomas M. Davis, recently retired from Kent State University, and William J. Scheick of the University of Texas at Austin. Nobody ever had better mentors, and if my attempts to please them here fall flat, it wasn't for lack of trying.

Introduction

Stephen Greenblatt once justified his attraction to the past by confessing a "desire to speak to the dead" (*Shakespearean Negotiations* 1). If Greenblatt's motives appear morbid or nostalgic, mine will seem more so. In this book I have wished to speak to the dead *about* the dead, and in so doing to try making sense of a body of poems whose importance in their own time has been obscured by their nearly total neglect in ours. Although historians have traditionally justified their obsessions by claiming to explain the present or anticipate the future, the simple wish to connect with those who have gone before seems as valid and honest a reason as any for writing literary history. I do not deny that history can teach us something about ourselves by proposing the origins of current social and cultural practice and thereby shoring up – or perhaps debunking – our collective and individual place in the world. These high-sounding goals, however, nearly always mask something far more basic and even selfish in studying the past: the pleasure of hearing old stories and telling them back to life as fully and convincingly as we can. The historical impulse is, at root, a desire to tell stories about people who can no longer speak for themselves.[1]

Like all history, this book tells a story about a story. The first story comprises what Puritans told each other about death and commemoration. The second story is my interpretive shaping of their story – my hearing of it. In telling this second story, I have replaced the validation of formal beauty that underlies traditional literary history with a focus on the utility of texts within their cultural and historical moment. Instead of the usual praise for the poem on the page as an isolated and supposedly timeless object, I describe the role that elegies played within a framework of literary practices defined by culture, psychology, religion, and other texts. Although this book does not enact a search for well-wrought urns, I in no way dismiss the importance of poetic form. Early New Englanders thought of their elegies as "poems" and read them as such, even though the surviving texts break nearly every modern rule surrounding the poetry of mourning. As I discuss specific textual traits in light of their functional significance for Puritan readers, I am playing the admittedly impossible role of a sympathetic ethnographer who tries to see another world through its inhabitants' eyes. David Perkins is surely right when he asserts that "sorting by genre is valid if the concept of the genre was entertained by the writer and his contemporary readers" (115). Puritans certainly recognized a "successful" elegy, by their lights, when they saw one. This book attempts to describe exactly what they understood a successful elegy to be.

In trying to illuminate a Puritan aesthetic of commemoration, I have tried to resist the usual belief that the judgment of early New Englanders was "wrong" or, more basically, that the present is somehow superior to the past. I do not approach early New England's elegies as primitive harbingers of a later "America" or as repressed foils to later expressions of loss that we find more beautiful or sincere. For me, the past does not exist to validate who we are or how we do things, including how we mourn and how we write our way through it. Mine is, in essence, an anthropological approach, and I take it in part as a practical necessity: the traditional questions posed by literary historians have not worked with these poems. If we read them according to our notions of selfhood and mourning, they seem like affronts to the fact of loss, heartlessly reductive in their dismissal of the survivor's agony. Modern notions of how skill and sincerity should intersect in elegy do not apply to these poems, at least not in obvious or predictable ways. Once we ask what the elegies did for their initial readers and hearers, we can avoid simply lamenting, once again, what they fail to do for *us*. That case has already been made too frequently to bear repeating, and not just about these poems but about Puritan verse generally.[2]

Asking certain questions about texts always entails the decision, conscious or otherwise, not to ask others. The most important lesson of literary theory for the literary historian is not that there are right or wrong questions, but that we must be aware of the kinds of knowledge that can be generated – or not – by the questions we choose. The questions asked in this book embody my belief that texts embody authorial intentions which are partly recoverable, and that recovering such intentions is indispensable to historical criticism. When seen from a discursive standpoint, of course, intentionality encompasses a great deal more than a writer's deliberate choices. An author's decisions are profoundly shaped by extrapersonal factors that are often felt as idiosyncratic and deeply "personal." The postromantic aesthetic has mystified the artist's role to such a degree that any author's awareness of the extent to which his or her goals are *not* freely chosen is always problematic. The interplay between what is written and what must be written – between text and context, expression and ideology – is so extensive and complex that the traditional line between the "literary" foreground and the "historical" background cannot stand.[3]

Unlike other Puritan poems that hold greater appeal for modern readers, the elegy has consistently been pushed into the furthest recesses of its historical "background." Early New England's most ubiquitous form of popular verbal art, apart from the sermon, has been virtually forgotten in our nearly exclusive focus on a relatively small canon of poems restricted mainly to Anne Bradstreet's reflective lyrics and Edward Taylor's *Preparatory Meditations* and *Gods Determinations*. This selective sampling is unfortunate, not least because popular art often reveals more than critically accepted works about the interplay of text and context. This is true not because poems like Bradstreet's and Taylor's are any less firmly bound to their time and place, a view encouraged by the traditional search for timeless "masterpieces," but because the continuing power of older constructions of "literature" makes such ties harder to discern in works that seem to satisfy modern aesthetic criteria. I thus approach New England's elegies not as a collection of finished textual products to be assessed according to their capacity to provoke appreciation, but as scripts that organized a cluster of social practices surrounding a specific process of mourning. Ironically, early New Englanders intuitively grasped a truth that modern critics have only recently rediscovered: texts do powerful cultural work in addition – and often in opposition – to encouraging their appreciation as "art." Given the Puritan use of texts as indispensable aids to salvation, the notion of literary experience as an ongoing and often volatile interplay of text and reader was far less alien to seventeenth-century New Englanders than it is to many of us today. We can access that notion only through our deliberate effort, prodded by the remorseless probings of theory, to break reading habits associated with the appreciation of literary masterworks. Puritans, by contrast, participated in a dynamic model of reading as a potentially self-altering process every time they opened a Bible, attended a sermon, and read or heard a pious poem, hoping that the words would transform the very root of their being.[4]

To say that texts and selves interact doesn't tell us much about what a "self" is. The irresistible imperatives of culture refute the naive conviction that human nature is in all respects constant and immutable, that it always manifests itself in the same manner regardless of time and place. There is no need, however, to push this useful truth to the opposite extreme of denying that certain emotions and impulses are indeed universally "human," and that they find analogous forms of expression in all historical and cultural settings. One such emotion, I believe, is the anxiety that results from loss, and one such impulse is to relieve this anxiety through the performance of ritual action, usually involving ritual speech. Despite radical claims that all human experience is linguistically and culturally constructed, I thus accept the traditional anthropological assumption that certain patterns of grief and mourning are transcultural and transhistorical. If social "power" is a cultural universal, then it surely follows that its inverse – a sense of impotence in the face of death – is also universal. While the impulses informing and sustaining these rituals are universal, the forms that the rituals take are decidedly culture-specific, often to the point of being unintelligible to outsiders. This is why we cannot simply read Puritan poems of loss and directly intuit their deeper significance. Moreover, although ritual practices from other times and places – and the ideologies they embody – are certainly not beyond our criticism (indeed, we often cannot help it), all such objections naturally derive from values appropriate to our time and place. Objections of all sorts leap to mind quickly enough when we consider the ideology of the American "Puritans," whose very name has come to mean something largely malevolent in our popular culture and collective memory. For this reason, it seems especially important that critiques of Puritan culture start from a rigorous effort to understand and empathize with the people who inhabited that culture. Failure to do so will produce easy answers, a short-circuiting of historical understanding, and even worse, the literary historian's chief occupational hazard: a sense of superiority to the people whose writings are providing his or her livelihood.[5]

William Empson once remarked that "the central function of imaginative literature is to make you realize that other people act on moral convictions different from your own" (*Milton's God* 261). To forget this is to reduce literary history to romantic self-inscription, recasting the dead as primitive versions of ourselves and thereby begging the question regarding the past's relevance to the present. While such models can make the past more appealing, they invoke historical sameness prematurely and thus obscure the past's fundamental and inescapable alterity. In countering the tendency to refigure the past as a mere proto-present and to wrench the dead into validating conformity with – or damning opposition to – current values and tastes, literary historians must try to read against their own grain. The elegies of early New England virtually compel us to do this: in their stubborn resistance to current conceptions of art and loss, there is much that these poems force us *not* to take for granted. Their longstanding critical dismissal is based on an aesthetic program so powerful that we forget that it is neither absolute nor universal, but the product of an institutional history in which we are all situated. To try reading these poems as Puritans once read them requires us to pretend that the subsequent "history" of poetry – the evolving construction of what good verse is and how one should read it – never happened. To be sure, such forgetting is something to attempt rather than achieve. This is why historical criticism can never be truly "objective," perhaps especially when it deals with a people so freighted for modern Americans as the Puritans. We can never efface our own preferences, biases, and identities when we try to read historically. It might even be argued that the decision to read against those biases is itself a bias, one that produces merely a differently romanticized past, antiquarian and even exotic in its strangeness. I understand this risk but am willing to take it here. For a literary historian, having too much sympathy for the dead is better than having too little.

The critical neglect of early New England's elegies has been reinforced, ironically enough, by a poet who not only wrote his share of them but stimulated a new understanding of the Puritan imagination. Since the rediscovery of Edward Taylor's verse in the 1930s, the enormous scholarly attention he has received grew out of the premise that he wrote good poems. In the frenzy of this work, what "good" really meant – why we prized Taylor's verse to begin with – was rarely questioned. He was, we knew, a bit like Donne and even more like Herbert – and *they* were good poets, weren't they? I like Taylor immensely, and don't for a minute think that the time and energy spent on him have been wasted. My point is simply that a reorientation of literary historiography around cultural practices has helped me understand more clearly *why* I like him. It also clarifies the extent to which this "good" Puritan poet has ended up making his contemporaries seem even worse. For years Taylor's canonical status has kept us from coming to terms with those other poems that bore and puzzle us as much as his verse – some of it, anyway – excites us. While Taylor's poetry has always seemed good enough for critics to read him in ways consistent with modern notions of poetic success, and

even at times to refashion him into an artistic or national forebear, we
have had almost nothing to say about the more "typical" poems issuing
from seventeenth-century New England. Even Taylor has been distorted
by his success. For all our excitement about *Gods Determinations* and the
Preparatory Meditations, we have remained virtually silent about those
poems which seem disappointingly "typical" of his time and place –
roughly three-quarters of his extant work.[6]

At the center of this neglected body of Puritan poems is the funeral
elegy. New England's elegies underscore, with unusual clarity, theoretical problems surrounding the role of artistic assessment in literary
history. How is the historical critic to redeem poems like these without
either sealing them within their unfamiliar world or bending them to fit
aesthetic categories emanating from our familiar world? How can these
contrasting aesthetic horizons be negotiated without ignoring or violating either one? The answer informing this study is that such poems confront the modern reader with a dialectic of sameness and difference, a
dialectic reflected in Louis Montrose's comment that reading past texts
"always proceeds by a mixture of estrangement and appropriation"
("Professing the Renaissance" 24). The Puritan elegy, issuing as it did
from a culture that differed in many ways from our own, presents us
with many points of alienating difference, puzzling features whose function and significance the literary historian must reconstruct. Yet because
the poem was written from human impulses that have not changed
beyond recognition in three centuries, it also offers points of similarity
that are frequently obscured by its distracting surface. While poems
from so remote a culture inevitably exhibit traits that frustrate our
expectations, such differences conceal an element of sameness: an articulation of recognizable anxieties and satisfactions that lie beneath
formal and ideological features reflective of the text's cultural and historical moment. Puritan elegies, for instance, routinely convey an
intense longing for heaven. Most late-twentieth-century academics consider this belief to be hopelessly naive, and thus find it difficult not to
infantilize it when we encounter it in others, including historical others.
But if we make no attempt to suspend – or at least adjust for – our disbelief in this most basic of Puritan reading and writing premises, the
resulting interpretation will be profoundly off point, anachronistic at its
very core.[7]

By the same token, to historicize such texts need not result in arid
detachment or bloodless antiquarianism. Perkins is surely right when he
remarks that it would be "paradoxical" and "dismaying" to literary his-

torians "if, after they had related texts to their time and place, the texts left them cold" (39). Alien texts can still speak to us if we translate their ideologically bound features into affective terms accessible to modern readers. Although most of us no longer hope for heaven, we still know what hope is – along with sadness, anger, fear, envy, disappointment, joy, and, to cite an emotion particularly central to the poems considered here, anxiety at the prospect of dying. By recovering the basic emotions that underlie the explicit formal and ideological features of a text, we can rediscover that text as a human expression without insisting that the expression assume the forms that we would choose. Although early New England's funeral elegies do not speak easily or directly to modern constructions of death and commemoration, it is possible to probe the contrast between off-putting embodiments of ideological difference and those fundamental samenesses by which modern reader and older text can unite. By clarifying how the poem articulates emotions that find expression in all cultures, including ours, we link the elegist's choices not to the conventions of modern poems of loss, but to deeper impulses that Puritan verse and "our" verse – the postromantic elegiac canon – were both written to express. In this way it is possible to explain, and even defend, textual features of the Puritan elegy without either ignoring the historical terms of its production or denying the modern reader meaningful access to the poem as a document shaped by human need. If the poems are read in light of this dialectic of sameness and difference, their more puzzling features become legible as confirmations of historical and cultural particularity, as reminders of the simple fact that early New Englanders did many things differently than we do, including the writing and reading of elegy.

With this recognition, deeper impulses with which modern readers can identify are allowed to break through the text's unfamiliar surface. The personal link with these distant poems emerges once we see that they have far less in common with "poetry," as we usually define it, than with the idealizing impulse of eulogy, and indeed of memory generally. The Puritan elegy gains significance not as a mere historical document or a failed attempt at poetic craft, but as a ritual script designed to bring comfort to people within a particular culture – the same sort of comfort, fundamentally, that ritual texts still provide, through less frequently and conspicuously. Within this realigned perspective, the most interesting questions about these maligned poems are the simplest ones. Why did Puritans write them? Why did they write so many of them? Why are the poems so much alike? Why are the commemorated dead variations on a single personality? What responses, satisfying or otherwise, did these poems probably generate? And finally, how do these responses differ from "modern" readings divorced from the mourning ritual in which the poems were originally embedded?[8] In practical terms, the anthropological approach requires that we suspend some of our deepest assumptions regarding the nature and uses of poetry. It forces us, most basically, to think of a poem in premodernist terms: as something that *does* rather than something that *is*. It forces us to confront a notion of artistic performance that does not center on original thought or expression, and thus does not foreground the professionalism and virtuosity of "authors." Finally, it asks us to resist the patronizing uses that the present often makes of the past. I have no interest in arguing for the quaintness of the Puritan elegy or describing it in ways that make modern attitudes toward poetry and grieving seem contrastively more sophisticated. There will be no confirmations of literary, cultural, or national progress here, no affirmations of how far we have come as poets, readers, or mourners. By the same token, I have no interest in theorizing the Puritan elegy to the point of claiming for it a modernity that anticipates our notions of linguistic or psychological complexity. Too much theory, like too little, can become yet another means of marginalizing the past as periphery to our center.

In basing my discussion of these poems on models and mentalities prevalent in Puritan culture rather than on those privileged by my own time and place, I am aware that I am substituting one "fiction" with another, replacing an essentially postromantic artistic model with an alternative built up from early New England statements on art, death, grieving, and religious experience. This is, of course, my construction of a Puritan construction – an inevitable and necessary falling away from "truth" inseparable from the fact that nobody writes or reads or even sees "pure." The most we can hope for is plausibility, a goal that becomes more attainable if we try to inhabit the mindset of the people whom we study rather than willfully or unwittingly imposing our own. The major drawback of failing to resist our own preferences, of course, is that the results are not very interesting: the highly predictable "knowledge" of our disappointment at the failure of the Puritan elegy to meet our aesthetic demands. A better, though imperfect, alternative is to attempt a reconstruction of the cognitive and affective terms in which these poems were experienced by their initial audience. There's no avoiding the conclusion that Puritan readers drew strength and consolation from the didacticism and conventionality of their elegies – the very qualities that distance the poems from us. If we wish to understand and appreciate the Puritan poetry of loss, we must learn another way of reading.[9]

Although my primary aim is to describe a decidedly alien mode of commemoration, anyone who sees the past chiefly as difference must answer an important question: what's the point? If literary history has so little to do with *us*, why bother with it at all? The answer lies, once again, in the recognition that we are only partial outsiders to the past, that older texts embody transhistorical sameness as well as historical difference. In the points of sameness we find reasons to read that transcend merely professional motives or antiquarian obsessions, provided we dig deeply enough to get beneath the distractingly alien surface that these poems present to us. Although the bulk of this study insists on the otherness of Puritan commemoration, significant spiritual and psychological continuities rooted in the experience of loss underlie and counter the alterity inscribed in the contrasts between Puritan and modern verbalizations of grief. I hope that these subtler continuities pulse just as strongly, if less explicitly, throughout this book. I believe that behind the forbidding otherness of these poems, modern readers will find much that is recognizable and even familiar.

Because literary historians tell stories that they cannot help telling, they must be aware, as Perkins states, "of whatever desires motivate them" (31). Hans Robert Jauss correctly observes that historians must bring their "own experience into play" when they confront the past (*Toward an Aesthetic* 34). In fact those experiences come into play whether we want them to or not. Even an excursion into seventeenth-century funerary poems reveals the truth of Marianna Torgovnick's observation that "The 'I' is a heady release conflicted by a potent nostalgia" (153). I have come to see that much in my personal history prepared me to respond sympathetically to the Puritan elegy, despite the fact that my professional training pushed me in the opposite direction. The extent to which my Protestant upbringing preconditioned a sympathetic response to Puritan poems of loss has made this book a far more personally engaging project than I ever suspected it would be. Although this study stresses the suspension of current subjective and aesthetic values, it also demonstrates the usually latent truth that historians are, as Montrose puts it, "historical subjects" whose positioning shapes the stories we tell ("Professing the Renaissance" 23). In the end, any desire to speak to the dead is both subverted and enabled by who we are. Their voices achieve coherence, finally, only in relation to ours, as Greenblatt discovered when he learned that "if I wanted to hear the voice of the other, I had to hear my own voice. The speech of the dead, like my own speech, is not private property" (*Shakespearean Negotiations* 20). Although Greenblatt gives up on historical objectivity in anything like an absolute sense, his concession is perhaps as close as we can come to achieving it. This dilemma makes for bad history only if we ignore it. And it makes history unwriteable only if we insist on standards of theoretical purity that can be imagined, perhaps, but not achieved. Like most human activities, the practice of literary history is inherently and inescapably paradoxical: we accept contradiction and impurity as preconditions for doing it at all.[10]

"Historical writing," as Brian Stock has aptly remarked, is "an apologetic whose moral is coherence" (84). Perkins puts this another way when he states that the ultimate criteria for assessing such writing are not empirical but "aesthetic" (110). In this rage for order, the literary historian, like any other storyteller, cannot keep from fitting the materials at hand into a scholarly narrative that creates an illusion of control and even mastery over the past. If I had not closed one eye and pursued that illusion, there would be no book here – and probably not even this sentence. But the uses that historians make of the dead as a matter of professional course need not reinforce the accompanying illusion – one that is far more destructive – that we are somehow superior to those distant voices we are straining to hear. Having once lived inside a twentieth-century version of the Protestant Christianity that animated Puritan elegists, I have probably erred too far in the direction of sympathy for these forgotten poets. But even though traditional Christian responses to loss no longer hold personal meaning for me, I cannot fault people who lived three centuries ago for making choices different from what mine would be today. By resisting the urge to fault them for not "escaping" certain ideological strictures, as on good days I like to think I did, I hope that early New Englanders emerge here as neither devils nor angels, but simply as human beings who coped with loss as best they could, who struggled to allay familiar fears with tools that have become alien to us.

CHAPTER I

Monuments enduring and otherwise

The simple funeral took place late in the afternoon on a gray Monday, the first day of December, 1712. As the seventy-year-old minister walked slowly toward the burial ground, leading the wagon that bore the plain coffin, he found comfort only in his belief that David Dewey's passing played some part, as yet unknown, in God's plan. On his arm leaned the widow, Sarah, closely followed by the four Dewey boys, ranging from four to twelve years old. A two-year-old daughter, gravely ill and being tended to at home, would die within two weeks. Behind the minister, the family, and the wagon filed about three dozen mourners. The minister patted Sarah Dewey's hand and whispered a few words into her ear. She lowered her handkerchief briefly from behind her veil and nodded.

David Dewey, a leading citizen of Westfield, a small town nestled in the Connecticut River Valley, was dead at thirty-six. A member of the Westfield church for twelve years, he had been ordained as one of the congregation's two deacons only six months earlier. Since arriving as a young man to help his uncles run their sawmill outside of town, he had served as constable, selectman, and schoolmaster. As his recent selection as deacon affirmed, Dewey was also a pious man. Four years earlier he had composed sixteen prose meditations on the faith; additional exhortations to his children were found among his papers after his death. "Are the things that are here," he had written, "all beautiful in their Season; how beautiful then is our Glorious Redeemer? who is altogether Lovely & Beautiful; who is the Head of Excellency?"[1]

By all accounts, David Dewey was the ideal New Englander, a man in whom inner piety and civic duty merged to create a perfect life in the Lord. Among Dewey's writings was the following advice to his children: "You must not Play nor tell Stories on the *Sabbath-Day*: but read your Books, and pray to God, and mind what the Minister sayes" ("Edward Taylor's Elegy" 80). That minister was Edward Taylor, whose

own writings would shed surprising new light on Puritan inner life
when they were rediscovered over two centuries later. As the procession
moved silently along, Taylor stared at the muddy road and carefully
guided Sarah Dewey away from the ruts. Hearing the coffin shift
slightly in the wagon, the old minister reflected on how it rained on the
just as well as the unjust. He and his beloved Elizabeth, now over
twenty years dead, had certainly been witnesses to that. They had made
this same walk together to bury five infants, and then she was gone.
Taylor worked long and hard on her elegy, which he carefully preserved
along with courtship poems he had written as cherished mementos of
their love. Although he dearly loved his second wife, Ruth Wyllys of
Hartford, he could never preside over a burial without thinking of
Elizabeth and the babies. Each new death reminded him of how much
he had trusted in the flesh and how severe a penalty God had exacted.

Ruth had borne him six children, but Taylor, fifty-one when the first
daughter arrived, was not as close to them as he was to Elizabeth's three
surviving children. Moreover, urgent matters had left him little time to
spend with his new family. Solomon Stoddard, minister at nearby
Northampton, continued to press for changes in administering the
Lord's Supper, and was allowing people to participate in the Sacrament
who had not first professed their conversion in Christ. Taylor harbored
no personal animosity against his colleague, whom he knew to be a holy
man, sincere in his beliefs. But he could not fathom how so well-meaning
a shepherd could stumble so badly as to debase the Sacrament, and with
it, nearly every principle that the brethren had struggled to uphold for
nearly a century. Although Taylor had preached tirelessly on the issue,
town after town was adopting Stoddard's open Supper. Not even his old
friends Increase Mather and son Cotton, who shared the powerful pulpit
of Boston's Old North Church, could stem the tide. Some members of
Taylor's own congregation were calling for Stoddard's changes, but
Westfield would not lapse into such error as long as he was in charge. For
three decades Taylor had meditated privately on the sanctity of the
Sacrament, pouring out his love for Christ in impassioned poems written
in spare moments. These private exercises brought him unspeakable
comfort. New England might be sliding into apostasy, but God's garden
could still be firmly paled and lovingly tended in Westfield – and in the
sanctuary of his heart.[2]

David Dewey had been a firm ally on the issue, a stabilizing voice
in a congregation that was often contentious. Now he was dead, and at
the very time when he was most needed. As the procession entered the
burying ground, Taylor suddenly felt very old. Dewey reminded the

minister of his faithful charges during those early years in Westfield, after one of Dewey's uncles had called him to the valley from Harvard. In those days believers longed with all their hearts to make a sincere profession of their faith, and Taylor could remember when many of them were harder on themselves than the Word required. No pastoral duty had given him greater pleasure than offering such souls the encouragement which, in their humility, they so clearly deserved. Some thirty years ago he had even written an examination of conscience in dramatic verse, which he circulated among those believers whose tender scruples held them back from their professions. Some had been converted by that poem, and Taylor took special pride in having used his God-given eloquence to bring them to Christ. The thought that some of those people, now in late middle age, were filing slowly behind him made him smile inwardly despite his dark mood.

As the procession gathered around the gravesite, Taylor nodded to several young men, who slid Dewey's coffin from the wagon and placed it gently on the ropes lying next to the open grave. Although fierce winds and rain had pelted the valley the night before, there had been a recent stretch of unusually warm weather, and the gravediggers had managed to do their work without too much difficulty. The old minister said a few words over the grave, words not so different, really, from those he had spoken dozens of times among these stones over the decades. As at Elizabeth's burial, he knew that he was to proclaim – and to proclaim it so clearly that no hearer in heaven or earth could miss it – that there was but one faith and one salvation. David Dewey had lived a life so clearly stamped with holiness that God's grace could be plainly seen by all who looked upon him.

Taylor concluded with a short prayer. After a few moments of silence he nodded to Thomas Noble, Westfield's surviving deacon, who removed a piece of paper that had been pinned to the coffin and handed it to the minister. Taylor hunched over slightly and began to read from the sheet in a trembling voice as he squinted against the fading glare of the winter sky.

> David by Name, David by Nature, shew
> Thou art Belov'd (if that thy Name say True)
> By God and Christ, who in thee gave a Place
> Unto his Image brightly laid in Grace . . .
> ("Edward Taylor's Elegy" 82)

The elegy, soon published along with Dewey's writings in a commemorative pamphlet, would be Taylor's only complete poem to appear in print during his lifetime. The Westfield minister, who apparently never sought publication for any of the other verse that would make him famous two centuries after his death, must have taken considerable pride in the poem. If he thought that it had not performed its sad task competently, even well, it is unlikely that he would have allowed it to appear in a permanent commemoration of so beloved a citizen as David Dewey, least of all a commemoration that the minister probably guided into publication. Not everyone, even at the time, would have been pleased with Taylor's efforts. Just ten years later, the young Benjamin Franklin would reduce this kind of elegy to a mock recipe in his brother's *New-England Courant*. Writing as Silence Dogood, a perversely Matherian busybody, Franklin purported to answer "the Complaint of many Ingenious Foreigners. . .*That good Poetry is not to be expected in* New-England." Silence selects as her proof-text an "*Extraordinary* Piece" written by Dr. John Herrick of Beverley on the death of Mehitabel Kittel, wife of John Kittel. Herrick's lament for "a Wife, a Daughter, and a Sister," Silence gushes, creates "a Sort of an Idea of the Death of *Three Persons*," which "consequently must raise *Three Times* as much Grief and Compassion in the Reader." Dubbing such verbal performance "a new species of Poetry," Silence places the work in a class by itself. It is, she proclaims, "*Kitelic Poetry*" (19, 21). In an accompanying "Panegyrick" by "Philomusus," Franklin attests that the author of so fine a poem, that "great Bard" and physician who brought "Learned Doggrell, to Perfection," has been blessed with unusual opportunity to exercise his muse: "For if by Chance a Patient you should kill, / You can Embalm his Mem'ry with your Quill." So great a poet could never receive a worthy embalming from another: Dr. Herrick should at the very least "Write your own Elegy against you're Dead" (23).

Franklin's joke was based, of course, on his reader's recognition that "Kitelic" poems were hardly new. They had in fact become the single most popular "species" of verse in New England, having worked their way into an increasingly elaborate ritual of mourning practiced by a people whose outspoken denunciations of ritual would be taken too literally by later observers.[3] The passing of a devout soul virtually demanded a poem, a verbal marker of the deceased's victory and an encapsulation of the Puritan view not just of leaving this world but of living in it. Like all funerary texts, the Puritan elegy extended consolation in part because of its predictability. What made it distinctly "Puritan" was the fervor with which it both reaffirmed the communal mission of God's people and situated individual readers within that mission as a precondition to paying proper respect to the dead. Nor was such an office to be performed in secret. In early New England, as in pre-industrial societies generally, nobody died alone, and Puritan grief was not "private" in the sense that it usually is for us: Puritan mourners could not escape Donne's conclusion that "any man's death diminishes me" ("Devotions" 68). Not surprisingly, the initial impact of a death on these close-knit communities was frighteningly disruptive. Not only had a beloved person been taken, but God's workers in the world, scarce enough to begin with, had been diminished by one. While the elegy gave full voice to this calamity, it also directed its audience toward a deeper and more reassuring reading of the event as a confirmation of saving faith. It was this reassurance that kept early New Englanders writing and reading these poems by the hundreds. Conventions become conventional because they satisfy, and the comfort that these stylized poems brought to Puritan mourners lay in the text's transformation of death's disruption into a reaffirmation of belief. Elegy brought comfort precisely because it did *not* surprise. Nearly every formulaic trait satirized by Franklin made survivors feel like participants in an insistent and ongoing rewriting of death into victory. Although these poems came with greater frequency as the seventeenth century progressed, their underlying form remained essentially unchanged from the first settlement to Franklin's day. Such stability, though it defies modern demands for originality, suggests that the Puritan elegy worked, and worked well, within the ritual of grieving that it was written to demonstrate and encourage. Strip away that ritual, and the life of the text evaporates.[4]

To readers alienated from the original affective contexts of the Puritan elegy – to readers like Franklin and us – it might seem to embody mindless habit, artistic laziness, perhaps even the hypocrisy of writing what one knows to be false. That the commemorated dead in poem after poem are all stamped from the same pious mold was certainly not lost on the young Franklin. "Having chose the Person," Silence Dogood cites from the recipe left by her late "Reverend Husband," "take all his Virtues, Excellencies, &c. and if he have not enough, you may borrow some to make up a sufficient Quantity: To these add his last Words, dying Expressions" and "a Handful or two of Melancholly Expressions, such as, *Dreadful, Deadly, cruel cold Death, unhappy Fate, weeping Eyes*, &c." These "Ingredients" are to be poured into the cauldron, in Franklin's view, of New England's ills: "the empty Scull of some *young Harvard.*" After a liberal sprinkling of "double Rhimes," Silence concludes, "you must spread all upon Paper, and if you can procure a Scrap of Latin to put at the End, it will garnish it mightily; then having affixed your Name at the Bottom, with a *Maestus Composuit*, you will have an Excellent Elegy" (21–22). As a parodic catalog of the elegy's distinguishing traits, Franklin's "Ingredients" were devastatingly accurate. The chant-like reiteration of the loss, the deceased's pious last words, virtues seemingly "borrowed" to depict souls too good to be real, stock "Melancholly Expressions," frequently even the Harvard authorship – all had become indispensable to a "species of Poetry" with which New Englanders had been intimate for nearly a century. Franklin's attack on what he saw as extreme sentimentalism and rote convention, however, bears comic witness to what happens when Puritan verse is isolated from the theology that fueled it and from the psychological processes that it was written to promote. No type of poem, certainly, was more popular among Puritan readers than the elegy, and none offers a better point of departure for reconstructing the experience of poetry as most early New Englanders knew it in their daily lives. As John Draper noted seventy years ago, the public role of elegiac verse makes it "an admirable medium for the study of social ideals" (*Funeral Elegy* viii). Although Draper was apologizing for artistic deficiencies in the poems he was examining, the social and the aesthetic are far more difficult to separate than in 1929. Still, modern critics have joined Franklin – and in his hostility toward Puritan ideology, Franklin *was* a "modern" reader – in forgetting that Puritan elegies were written to formula because the formula helped actual readers cope with actual loss. Indeed, if seen from a critical perspective that incorporates rather than dismisses or apologizes for the "social" functions of art, these poems emerge as models of cultural adaptation, as remarkably successful discursive performances.

The need for frameworks more sympathetic than Franklin's for reading these distant poems would be suggested, if for no other reason, by the fact that early America's finest poet wrote at least ten elegies and, as we have seen, allowed one of them to stand as his only published poem. Modern readers might expect that whenever a poet with Taylor's gifts works within a conventional genre, the outcome will deviate sufficiently from the norm to reveal the stamp of original genius on worn-out clay. But Taylor did not dispense with the elegy's most rigid conventions, however trite they seemed to Franklin and others who have approached these poems as "literary" texts – in the then-new mode of Dryden and Cowley – rather than as ritual texts firmly wedded to cultural practice. For all the inventive power evident in Taylor's better-known poems, the old minister anticipated Silence Dogood's formula almost exactly. Mehitabel Kittel, trisected into wife, daughter, and sister, finds her masculine counterpart in Taylor's Dewey, who is lamented as a father bringing his children "up to Christ," a husband whose grace "drencht" his "Consort's heart," and a citizen whose "Grace did make thy Township Neighbourhood / Among us, very pleasant, usefull, good" ("Edward Taylor's Elegy" 82–83). Also consistent with Franklin's satire, Dewey's inner life is indistinguishable from that of any saved soul. Taylor builds Dewey's weeping on a particular Fasting Day into an elaborate pun on the deceased's "Dewy Tears" of remorse, extending the pun to encompass the deceased's "Dewy Rhymes" of edification to his "Offspring all." Dewey's "Conversation," which "gave a Shine / Of Prudence, Peace, and Piety Divine," meets Silence's Dogood's demand for an elaborate yet generalized listing of the deceased's "Virtues" and "Excellencies." Taylor might even be accused of "borrowing" some of these virtues, as Silence recommends, reaching as he does into an unseen realm to describe Dewey's persistence as a saint who "Cudgeld" his body of sin, never slacking the "raine" he kept on a carnal element portrayed in equally paradigmatic terms. Smaller touches also bear out Taylor's commitment to the formula that Franklin would lampoon. As was mandatory in "Kitelic" verse, Taylor dutifully records the deceased's "last Words, dying Expressions, &c." by reporting Dewey's deathbed wish to "*be with Christ to Morrow*" as well as his prophetic remark on the winds that blew as he lay dying: "*The Wind is high. . .But by to Morrow I'st above it be!*" Although Taylor keeps Silence's "Melancholly Expressions" to a minimum, he concedes at the poem's close that Dewey's survivors must borrow his "Coffin's Cambarick" to "wipe off of our Eyes the Tears of Sorrow." Taylor also manages, as Franklin would soon recommend, to "procure a Scrap of Latin" to "garnish" his poem: his "*Sic flevit mastus amicus*, E. T." is a nearly exact equivalent of Silence's "*Maestus Composuit.*"

Although Taylor was no longer a "young Harvard," he certainly remained an old one. If the aging minister ever chanced upon a copy of issue Number 7 of the *New-England Courant*, Franklin's parody made no impact on how he applied his poetic gifts to the occasion of death. Increase Mather died scarcely a year after the Dogood parody appeared, and during the next two years Taylor carefully worked through four versions of an elegy for his old friend written in the same old style. Taylor saw no need to abandon a form of commemoration that was still vital for him, least of all for such trivial reasons as bowing to literary fashion or heeding the benighted carpings of Boston wits. In elegy, as elsewhere,

Taylor wrote as he saw fit. When Louis Martz warned long ago against seeing Taylor merely as a "burlap version" of George Herbert, he was confirming a simple truth that many critics of the time were ignoring: Taylor's poetry differed from Herbert's for the simple reason that he was not trying to imitate Herbert ("Foreword" xviii). Similar integrity – most would say stubbornness – marks Taylor's elegies. Taylor adhered to a commemorative formula already outmoded in England and ridiculed by urbane Bostonians because he chose to, not because he tried to escape it and failed.

When we say that Taylor had the skill to make the Dewey elegy significantly different from the hundreds of other elegies that New Englanders had been penning for nearly a century, what we are really saying is that he could have written a poem of greater interest to modern readers. Such a poem might have told us more about Dewey the individual and less about Dewey the generic believer, whose carnal element would be raised "at the Resurrection of the Just" to rejoin the soul to sing "with Saints and Angels" in the celestial choir. Such a poem might have contained more philosophical musing and less theological dogma – perhaps some meditating on the cycles of nature or the power of love or memory to conquer time, perhaps even a few lines about the sad permanence of art over the fragile deceased, whose immortality would be ensured by a poetic monument more lasting than bronze. These options were indeed available to a poet whose Harvard schooling had acquainted him with their classical precedents in the poetry of Theocritus, Vergil, and Horace. But Taylor made other choices, and the fact that he did so underscores the challenge of dealing with older texts that violate modern notions of literary worth. The critical dismissal of hundreds of poems like the Dewey elegy illustrates the difficult intersection of historical objectivity and irresistible taste. Most of us would agree that the occasion of death has produced some of the most sublime poems in the canon. These poems embody the faith that language can defeat mutability – that death's sting can be abated by the compensatory power of timeless and universal art. There has always been some truth in William Empson's wry comment that the occasion of death is "the trigger of the literary man's biggest gun" (*Collected Poems* 58–59). Faced with one of the most artistically auspicious occasions imaginable, early America's best poet seems to have let us down.

Our disappointment with Taylor's poem for Deacon Dewey is sharpened, of course, by the enormous and longstanding prestige of the pastoral elegy, a form of commemoration strikingly different from those that issued from New England's pens. One critic writing in the late 1960s put the contrast this way: "To remember that while Puritan Milton was writing 'Lycidas,' his American coreligionists were composing acrostic elegies is to recall how provincial American Puritanism quickly became" (Waggoner 13). The canonical elegy – in practice, the pastoral elegy – has reinforced the critical tendency to divorce the Puritan commemorative poem from its ritual milieu and to read it against an aesthetic agenda shaped by the great poems of mourning in English: Shelley's "Adonais," Tennyson's "In Memoriam," Whitman's "Lilacs," Arnold's "Thyrsis," Yeats's poem for Major Robert Gregory, Auden's poem for Yeats – all of which participate in the pastoral tradition of "Lycidas." An elegiac standard shaped by such poems, seductive as it is, obscures the fact that New England's elegies, including Taylor's, were written for reasons quite different from those imputed to Milton and his successors. At the heart of this difference lies a conflict between formalist and functional approaches to the poetry of mourning – and it is a conflict that is by no means new. Its roots lay in Renaissance England, where Protestant reforms initiated lively debate over what constituted proper mourning. John Canne, an advocate of the newer, plainer customs, urged in 1634 that funerals be conducted "without either singing or reading, yea, without all kind of ceremony heretofore used, other than the dead be committed to the grave, with such gravity and sobriety as those that be present may seem to fear the judgments of God." In 1645 the Westminster Convention endorsed what had become increasingly popular practice by issuing the following directive: "let the dead body, upon the day of Buriall, be decently attended from the house to the place appointed for publique Buriall, and there immediately interred, without any Ceremony." Such Puritan plainness struck some, however, as going too far, even to the point of casting dishonor on the deceased. In 1631 John Weever complained that "wee, in these days, doe not weepe and mourne at the departure of the dead, so much, nor so long, as in Christian dutie we ought" (Stannard 104, 101, 105). It was within this debate, with opinion ranging from disgust at pomp and ceremony as a relic of "Romish" practice to horror at Puritan-inspired funerary rites so plain that they struck many as being disrespectful, that the varieties of English elegy developed. Like so many other aspects of life in early modern times, mourning was enlisted in an ideological war that transcended the immediate occasion. All elegies honored the dead, but the manner in which they did so revealed the living for who they were and where they stood.

The writing of elegies flourished during the Renaissance with the rise of literacy, printing, humanistic individualism, and a growing nationalism that prompted imitation of the great models of antiquity in the service of a literary Albion whose worthies were thought to deserve equal commemoration. Laments at Sidney's death in 1586 stimulated the popularity of elegy, and the raft of poems commemorating the death in 1612 of Prince Henry, son of James I, solidified its status as the era's dominant genre of public verse. A relaxation of traditional strictures on grief and its expression during the later sixteenth century contributed to this popularity (Pigman 3, 126), as did the role played by elaborate funerary rites in shoring up the waning power of the aristocracy (Stone 572–81). In order to understand the verse commemorations that Taylor and his New England contemporaries wrote, we need to remember that many options were available to seventeenth-century elegists, only one of which was subsequently designated as "literary." This, of course, was the highly artificial and elaborate pastoral elegy, shaped chiefly by Spenser's lament for "Dido" in the "November" eclogue from *The Shepheardes Calendar* (1579) and his poems for Sidney, or "Astrophel" (1595). Ironically, especially given its longstanding place in the canon, the pastoral elegy remained relatively rare in the nearly sixty years between the "November" eclogue and the climax of the form in "Lycidas." Most elegists during this period took a more direct approach to verbal mourning, one that drew on Elizabethan patriotism and patronage and, later, Jacobean melancholy and popular devotional traditions. This type of poem, usually called the "funeral" elegy to distinguish it from the pastoral, was frequently incorporated into funerary rituals, with the poem recited at the service and pinned to the hearse during the procession. Many Tudor and Elizabethan funeral elegies consisted of laments for nobility penned for general distribution, as illustrated by the popular poems of Thomas Churchyard and George Whetstone. Initially, funeral elegies reflected all religious persuasions, and ranged from what Draper termed "Cavalier panegyric" to the more theologically oriented "Puritan lament" (*Funeral Elegy* ix), the latter shaped by a turn to piety and introspection influenced by Donne's 1612 "Anniversaries" for Elizabeth Drury and the outpouring of laments at the death in 1646 of the Protestant champion, the Earl of Essex. By this time the Puritans had taken over the more explicitly religious elegy, stylizing its forms, intensifying its millennial fervor during the Civil War, and using it to reinforce the legitimacy of Cromwell's rule. By the early 1650s the funeral elegy had become so closely associated with religious dissenters that the anonymous "J. C." equated "common formall Elegies" with the "Geneva Jig."[5]

The English funeral elegy could scarcely have posed a sharper contrast to the classically based pastoral, in which the frank artifice of a timeless and placeless landscape encouraged a retreat from mutability into the static sanctuary of art. The death of a poet provided a special opportunity for the pastoral elegist to confirm his professional vocation and assert virtuosity as a poet rising to the sad occasion. To write elegy was both to acknowledge the void left by the deceased and to fill it as the rightful successor. The pastoral elegy thus came to play a special role in witnessing the poet's coming of age, and in this, too, the ancients had shown the way: Vergil's pastoral eclogues witnessed the first stage of what came to be seen as the archetypal career of a poet. The vocational theme reached its culmination in "Lycidas": Milton's momentary questioning, in the face of Edward King's untimely death, of his own dedication to the "thankless muse" leads to a recommitment expressed by and embodied in the poem – a recommitment always seen, of course, with hindsight afforded by the later achievement of *Paradise Lost*. To be sure, Milton confirms a Christian apotheosis for Lycidas, "sunk low but mounted high / Through the dear might of him that walkt the waves" (163). What prevails, however, is an elaborately staged threat to – and recovery of – poetic vocation worked out through the key elements of pastoral: the idealized landscape, the nostalgia for better times, the consoling power of nature, the commingling of grief with topical commentary, and the reassertion of continuity and purpose in response to rupture and anxiety. Such conventions effected a distancing from emotion that emulated classical restraint and made poems of mourning easier to write. Discursive indirection, however, enabled not just a muting of emotion but a deflection of emotion, a shift from mourning to other tasks that could be performed *through* mourning. As the interwoven concerns of "Lycidas" reveal, the variety and interaction of these tasks permitted remarkable thematic range.[6]

Puritans who did not share Milton's regard for the ancients or his more optimistic view of human nature took the "functional" side in the mourning controversy, either rejecting the pastoral surface or deflecting it back to what they saw as its theological and soteriological core, as Milton himself briefly did in St. Peter's diatribe against the "Blind mouths" of the corrupt clergy. Consistent with corresponding reforms in preaching, liturgy, and church polity, this more severe elegiac model returned the poem of mourning to its most immediate function. In contrast to the commemorations for "Asphodel" or "Lycidas," funeral elegies openly proclaimed their situational contexts by giving the real names of the deceased. Determined to adhere to what they saw as "real" rather than "fictive" discourse, funeral elegists refused to allow the commemoration of the dead to stray from its theological significance, which was, in their view, a literal significance that transcended artistic representation altogether. As in the plain-style sermon, there would be no mistaking why the poem existed or what it was trying to do.

To be sure, the young Milton possessed Arian tendencies that allowed for a less gloomy view of human potential than that held by his Calvinist contemporaries. A factor more important than theology, however, accounted for the contrast between "Lycidas" and New England's elegies. As Draper points out, that factor was social: the rise of a largely Puritan merchant class to wealth, power, and artistic patronage (*Funeral Elegy* 22). In contrast to aristocratic and academic readers of pastoral, this new audience made more pragmatic demands on art. For them, the ideal commemorative poem was at once less worldly – that is, more directly concerned with salvation – and more practical, in that it framed grief in explicitly religious terms familiar to the majority of actual mourners. Taking to heart Phoebus's lesson in "Lycidas" by shifting elegiac "fame" from the realm of poetry to the realm of piety, funeral elegists were far less indebted to Theocritus and Vergil than to the Bible, homiletic traditions, and the popular iconology of death fostered by funerary art, broadsides, and emblem books. These poets saw themselves as employing an Augustinian "high style" that eschewed ornamentation and was "created," as Ruth Wallerstein described it, "by the ardor of the thought itself, by the ardent contemplation of truths seen as value, as a motive of the will." "In this style," Wallerstein noted, "the Bible abounds" (28). While the occasional image – the weeping willow, the ministerial shepherd, and churchgoing flocks – afforded brief glimpses of a quasi-pastoral landscape, the ur-texts for these poems were the great biblical expressions of loss, especially David's poem for Saul and Jonathan (2 Samuel 1:19–27). Funeral elegists took seriously Paul's admonition to "Rejoice with them that do rejoice, and weep with them that weep," taking care to "Mind not high things" and to "Be not wise in your own conceits" (Romans 12:15–16). Unlike the pastoral elegist, typically a university-trained man of letters speaking as a professional "poet," the funeral elegist emulated Pauline humility by presenting the poem as a frankly amateur performance that repudiated the vocational preoccupations of the pastoral. Ben Jonson, that most insistently "classical" of Renaissance poets, provided striking expression of the aestheticizing of grief when he mourned his son as his "best piece of *poetrie*" (20). For most Puritans, this seemed a tragically wrongheaded reaction to an occasion as momentous as death. Marvell, for instance, was as deeply schooled as Jonson and Milton in the discursive indirection of pastoral, yet wrote his lament for Cromwell in a nontropic manner far removed from his mentor's model in "Lycidas." The funeral elegy succeeded, Puritans felt, only if it was *not* created as art. Indeed, its deeper message and aims, because divine, did not require a poet's skill so much as a prophet's vision.

At first, the plainer sort of elegy assumed virtually identical form in both Englands. A poem written in 1636 by "I. L." for Rev. John Rogers of Dedham, Essex, whose grandson would become president of Harvard, features most of the hallmarks of the New England elegy. Celebrating the "happy change and blessed gain" of a generalized saint, the poet praises "Our faithfull Moses" whose "graces" the reader is urged to "imitate": "So shalt thou live in happy state, / and pleasing in Gods sight" (Draper, *Century* 21). Like many New England commemorations, the poem ends with a call for survivors to repent in the face of a loss that signals divine disfavor with "Our sleepy formall carelessnesse, / in hearing of God's word" (Draper, *Century* 21). As the Rogers family illustrates, dissenting emigrants to the New World came chiefly from the English audience for such poems, and as a result, the plainer style of elegy proliferated there, becoming increasingly codified after the Restoration forced a sharpening of New England's cultural distinctiveness. At this time, too, funerary customs became more elaborate as a means of reinforcing a community of believers whose ties with England had been weakened. As William Scheick points out, the New England elegy in this later form separated from its English precedents by laying greater stress on the commemoration of a "collective self" through which survivors could absorb the saintly traits of the deceased ("Tombless Virtue" 290–96). Replete with predictable forms and conventional structures appropriate to this increased ritualization of mourning, the New England elegy may also have compensated for the liturgical severity of the Puritan service and provided a communal supplement, similar to that offered by the jeremiad, to the lonely rigors of meditative self-scrutiny.[7]

Once established in New England, the funeral elegy achieved remarkable stability, resisting the shift toward neoclassicism and sentimentality, which began to mark the English elegy soon after the Restoration, until well into the eighteenth century. This conservatism points up the elegy's close fit with social realities in early New England, where funeral poems, circulated in manuscript or broadside among members of tight-knit communities, were written for a far more intimate circle of readers than those addressed in the published and more self-consciously "literary" poems of London and the university towns. Even more importantly, the New England elegy, like the English funeral elegy, was written for a very different *kind* of reader than that addressed by the pastoral. Unlike Milton, whose poem appeared in a commemorative volume produced by and for Christian humanists well acquainted with classical discourse, elegists in New England wrote for entire communities. They could not risk undermining the devotional mandates of grief with pastoral conventions which presented a pagan surface that might be taken too seriously by the uninitiated. In keeping with this broader notion of readership, elegies in New England were not written to be "appreciated" as art in anything like a modern sense or even in the sense that Milton's Cambridge readers would have appreciated "Lycidas." Rather, they were written to be *used* in a process of grieving that was as valid for the illiterate farmer as for the university-trained minister. If death was no respecter of persons, death's grim democracy would also be made to hold sway over the poem of mourning by increasing its accessibility. The duty to clarify death's significance for all was too important to squander in mere verbal display.

As O. B. Hardison once observed, criticism has never known quite what to do with the occasional poem (107–8). Indeed, the very conditions of its making have always worked against it, since literary historians have traditionally believed that art transcends historical conditions. No form of public verse, perhaps, has suffered more from unhistorical critical treatments than elegies, especially those poems which insist on grounding themselves as explicitly as possible in specific occasions of loss. The homiletic and situational directness of such poems in both Englands doomed them to subliterary status, especially in light of the subsequent prestige of the pastoral as the only truly artistic poem of mourning. The preference of academic criticism for the self-contained, ideologically "neutral" work of art authorized a certain indirection in the commemorative act. If the occasional poem failed to transcend its specific occasion, the result was obscurity or charges of patent sentimentality. Attracted to the thematic swerve from death to art enacted by the pastoral elegy, critics considered the degree to which a poem may have brought real comfort to its initial readers irrelevant, perhaps even harmful, to its artistic success. This view was nowhere more evident than in the quick and vehement rejoinders to Samuel Johnson's famous attack on the pastoral conventions of "Lycidas" as "trifling fictions" lacking in any "real passion." Thomas Wharton, in his 1791 edition of Milton's minor poetry, made a telling distinction when he conceded that "Lycidas" contained "perhaps more poetry than sorrow. But let us read it for its poetry." In 1818 Hazlitt cited with approval Milton's "tender gloom" in the poem, "a wayward abstraction, a forgetfulness of his subject in the serious reflections that arise out of it." And in 1854 Henry Hallam responded to Johnson's charge by arguing that "many poems will yield an exquisite pleasure to the imagination that produce no emotion in the heart; or none at least except through associations independent of the subject" (Elledge 230–32, 236). We might add "independent of textual function": even if Johnson's insistence on "passion" was naive, he was merely stressing functional rather than formalist standards for the poetry of loss.[8]

The chief factor, however, in our inability to read the Puritan elegy on its own terms may well be the professional critic's traditional preference for secular responses to death rather than theological structures of the sort embraced by most seventeenth-century mourners. An elegy became an "enduring monument" by exchanging religious ideology for a more general framing of grief that proved attractive to later readers and critics who read for art, not solace. The attempt of later readers to isolate an "aesthetic" experience of funerary texts is encapsulated by Wallerstein's comment that Milton "universalizes" his experience by putting it "not in a religious form but in an artistic form" (113). Seen as compelling support for an essentialist notion of beauty and as a witness to art's transcendence of history, the pastoral elegy became the supreme *monumentum aere perennius*. It defined an elegiac ideal that obscured the viability of other poems of mourning that stubbornly resisted the pastoral compulsion to aestheticize loss.

Standards of taste that would make Milton the foundational poet of the British canon were largely in place when the sixteen-year-old Franklin began slipping the Dogood essays into his brother's paper. Given the enormous prestige of "Lycidas," it is no surprise that Silence Dogood's recipe set the tone for subsequent American readings of early New England's popular counterparts of Milton's great monody. In these first looks backward, developing notions of artistic value were reinforced by literary patriotism and a consequent historiography based on the search for national origins. Within this agenda, crude strengths found in the early poems were cast as premonitions of American vigor, while artistic weaknesses underscored how far the new nation had come. Because Puritan verse accorded well with this construction of nationalism, early historians of American literature approached the poetry with an oddly patronizing filiopiety. The New England Fathers were tough but unrefined, and what they lacked was precisely what the subsequent development of American letters had provided. Among "Puritan" traits cited for approval were honesty, practicality, plainness in speech, and a hard-nosed dedication to duty – all of which seemed to find satisfying embodiment in poems that seemed nothing if not artlessly sincere. Late in life Franklin summarized the eighteenth-century retrospective on Puritan poetry when he characterized his maternal grandfather's "occasional Pieces" as having been written "in the homespun Verse of that Time and People." When later critics looked back on the poems of old New England, they agreed with Franklin in finding "a good deal of Decent Plainness & manly Freedom" (1312–13) but very little art.

The disciplinary mandate to construct a "literary" America left scant room for the "homespun," in part because the enterprise depended on a clear distinction between "high" and "popular" art that was becoming crucial to literary studies generally. The Puritan elegy, like most Puritan verse, was relegated to the popular side of the divide, as were later poems that displayed many of its superficial features. Some of these poems, printed as popular ballads in the newspapers, described sensational deaths like murders or executions and continued to thrive well into the nineteenth century (Coffin 29–71). Others, wedded to theological assumptions softer than those held in early New England and sentimentalized beyond recognition, extended the tradition of accessible poems of loss into the domestic sphere as part of the "feminization" of death described by Ann Douglas (240–49). These latter poems, precursors of the obituary verses still printed in today's papers, found their nemesis in Franklin's fellow printer, Mark Twain. Emmeline Grangerford, as Huck Finn solemnly reports, spun out her "tributes" for the deceased so efficiently that she "didn't ever have to stop to think." When a hard-to-rhyme name finally stumped her, Emmeline simply "pined away," a victim of life's messy intrusion into an absurdly rigid poetic (726). In their dismissal of the popular elegy, including its Puritan forebear, romantics and realists found common ground. One belief that Twain and his romantic antagonists shared was the expectation that a poem of mourning be a *poem*, a self-contained object to be savored primarily for its aesthetic effect. If it was not, it was dismissed as a "folk" expression that only reconfirmed the achievement of canonical elegy.

Early readings of New England's elegies fit well into the creation of a coherent national history based on Whig progressivism. Although the underlying impulse was patriotic, critics looked elsewhere – chiefly, to artistic standards of the British privileged classes – for their aesthetic moorings. The first reconstructions of "early American literature" drew largely on British canonical standards that helped seal the critical fate of the Puritan elegy as an expression of cultural primitivism. In 1878 Moses Coit Tyler brought this view into a framework of Victorian positivism that seemed all the more viable because of Tyler's impressive recovery of historical and biographical facts surrounding the verse. Noting the popularity of elegies and epitaphs in early New England, Tyler maintained that Puritan commemorations were burdened with "those literary quirks and puns that were then thought to be among the graces of a threnody" (231). Believing that the artistically successful elegist managed to break free from such devices, Tyler praised John Norton the younger's poem on Anne Bradstreet because it seemed atypical, even though Norton "once or twice slipped into grotesqueness of conceit, and funereal frivolity" (263–64). Urian Oakes's famous elegy on Thomas Shepard II, which Tyler judged an even better poem, revealed a "true imaginative vision" that was nonetheless "blurred" by "patches of the prevailing theological jargon" (270). Such readings underscored Tyler's general belief in an "inappeasable feud" in Puritan culture "between religion and art" (228): art could not emerge until religion had been eliminated.[9]

Historians followed Tyler's lead in romanticizing Puritan verse as the stunted art of a "frontier" people. In 1890 Edmund Clarence Stedman called the "poetical relics" of early New England "the curios of a museum – the queer, ugly specimens of an unhistoric age" (33), "unhistoric" because a truly "literary" history had not yet begun. Such comments fit well with that species of geographical determinism which wedded the Puritan psyche to the flinty land that supposedly nurtured it. In 1903 Julian Abernethy observed that the Puritan "renouncement of all aesthetic influences left an impress upon the character of New England that is even yet visible, like the barren stretches of rock that scar its green-robed mountain sides in summer" (48). The early elegies and epitaphs confirmed a stifled artistry well matched with this rugged proto-America. As Abernethy remarked, "many a lichen-grown gravestone

still testifies to their struggles to express some freak of fancy in punning
rhymes" (48). Of the "thousands of lines" penned by New England's
earliest poets, Samuel Marion Tucker wrote in 1917, there was "scarcely
a line of genuine poetry, or a single poem worth preservation in its
entirety" (153). Read as a halting expression of an embryonic American
character, the New England elegy was granted a certain unpolished
strength. But read within the perspective of the British canon, the source
for Tucker's definition of "genuine poetry," it was merely old-fashioned.
In 1929 Draper saw the American funeral elegy as a fossilized repository
of "archaic characteristics" already abandoned in England, a darkly
Gothic exercise in which "the edifying gloom of the living was seemingly
accounted of more moment than the Salvation of the dead" (*Funeral
Elegy* 176, 163). That same year Trentwell Mason White and Paul
William Lebmann, arguing that Norton's poem for Bradstreet exhibited
"certain characteristic grotesqueries of the period" (144), agreed that
Oakes's elegy for Shepard might have been "beautiful" were it not for
"certain passages filled with the literary and religious hocus-pocus that
dogged so much of the early writers' works" (146). Similar blinders, of
course, affected readings of Puritan verse generally. As Charles Angoff
stated in the early 1930s, "The Puritans were in possession of everything
necessary for the creation of living poetry, with the exception of the most
important thing of all – a free soul" (196). The postromantic expectation
that the serious poem should subvert religious ideology – that it must
articulate the unmediated responses of a "free soul" – rendered historically sensitive readings of the Puritan elegy impossible. Ola Winslow
flatly stated that "American literature could not begin" until the colonists
shifted their interest "from heaven to the thirteen colonies" (xviii).
Puritans could not write true poetry because they were not yet true
"Americans," not yet free from the beliefs that made them Puritans in
the first place.

At the turn of the twentieth century, Barrett Wendell stated that
Puritan writing told "a story of unique national inexperience" (55).
What hampered early New Englanders in their development as
"Americans" was their commitment to a faith that was unapologetically
antidemocratic, anti-individualistic, and anti-aesthetic. Abernethy
agreed that New England's poets would not improve until they had been
liberated from Puritan theology, with "the unshackling of men's minds
in the period of the Revolution" (49). A more positive assessment came
in 1909 from William Bradley Otis, who argued that early American
verse was to be appreciated not because it lacked "American" traits, but

because it exhibited them fully despite the straitjacket of religion: the poetry "is, as a whole, characteristic of the broad, fresh, original, and liberty-loving nature of the land which gave it birth" (ix). Despite his application of later aesthetic and subjective standards, Otis was among the few critics of his time to achieve a measure of historical empathy with the impulses behind the Puritan elegy. In early New England, Otis conceded, "the death of a good man is not only not depressing, but is often even a source of poetic exaltation" (60). To a degree, critics could accept such a statement as historical fact. They could not imagine, however, that the fact had any but the most devastating artistic consequences.

After the Great War shook the easy positivism that had marked Victorian historical writing, a few critics took a more relativist view of the Puritan elegy. Conceding that early New Englanders held very different assumptions about art than those held by modern readers, Kenneth Murdock remarked in 1927 that the elegies preserved in Joseph Tompson's diary "were written not for us but for him" (*Handkerchiefs* xviii). Puritans believed that "If a poem could edify or console," Murdock observed, "it deserved to be brought forth" (xix). In addition, because early New Englanders saw so much premature death, it would be "worse than foolish to read unmindful of their spirit" (xxi). When he assessed the poems, however, Murdock found it difficult to practice the historical relativism that he preached, conceding that John Wilson's anagrams "lack any spark of imaginative fervor to kindle them to poetry" (lix) and concluding that "When all is said and done, the bulk of the world's great poetry is no whit increased by bringing these forgotten works. . .to light" (lxii). Their one merit, Murdock wrote, was that they "ring true" with emotional sincerity (lxiii). The artistic failure of early New England's elegies was attributed not only to the artistic choke-hold of religion, but to situational and social limitations arising from the colonial condition, especially an absence of leisure for writing and the lack of an audience with sufficient literary sophistication. Thomas G. Wright (86–90) and Murdock both argued that Puritan poets should be compared with English poets who wrote for similar audiences of "simpler folk" (*Handkerchiefs* lxxii). Samuel Eliot Morison, agreeing that "Colonial conditions are never favorable to poetry," also tried to approach the verse of early New England "as an expression of the thought, feeling, and emotions of the times" (*Intellectual Life* 210, 211). But the resistance to historical relativism in assessing these poems remained strong. Suggesting that the elegies were a predictable response to a lack of funerary ritual,

Morison concluded that these poems, like most occasional verse, were "indifferent" in quality.

The hardships of colonial life were real enough, and citing them was the first step toward a more meaningful historicizing of a Puritan aesthetic of loss. Most critics, however, refused to acknowledge that art produced within traditional societies might best be judged by standards other than belletristic. Of critics writing in the first half of the twentieth century, only Harold Jantz made any real effort to defend the Puritan aesthetic on historical grounds. Commenting on the standard critical response to New England's earliest poetry, Jantz observed that "One reason for our patronizing attitude has been the misapplication of the critical standards of eighteenth-century smoothness and nineteenth-century romantic lyricism to seventeenth-century Baroque verse which had no interest in being either smooth or romantic." For Jantz, past texts did not exist solely to gratify present taste: "The poetic intent, the artistic will of the time was simply different from our own." Consequently, "poetic techniques were used with which we are no longer familiar" (*First Century* 6–7). To Jantz's "eighteenth-century smoothness" and "nineteenth-century romantic lyricism" I would add twentieth-century formalism as a third blinder. In 1938 Thomas Johnson, Taylor's rediscoverer, observed that while the best Puritan elegies were marked by "dignity and heartfelt simplicity" and "a tender pathos," they failed in terms of poetic form (551). A decade later Stanley Williams agreed that "a touching simplicity and pathos" comprised the Puritan elegy's sole virtues (23). Conceding the sincerity of a poem was, of course, faint praise indeed in an era dominated by formalist aesthetic criteria promoted by Eliot and the New Critics. The "heartfelt simplicity" and "tender pathos" of early New England's elegies only reinforced the status of the laments that followed "Lycidas" into the elegiac canon. By substituting aesthetics for religion, the pastoral seemed to validate ideological constants shared by Renaissance humanism, rationalistic optimism, romantic individualism, Freudian confessionalism, and the high modernist embrace of all these traditions. Great art about death is timeless because it manages to channel grief into the creative act. People die but the ideal elegy remains, monumental and enduring.

Should an elegy offer beauty or solace? While it's easy to say both, this confident answer begs two fundamental questions: whose definition of beauty? and whose definition of solace? To answer these questions is to be pushed inexorably into history. I have recounted the story of the elegy's reception at some length because it illustrates the persistence of factors that continue to impede a fully contextualized reading of the Puritan poetry of loss. Only when the American elegy began to follow pastoral directives and assert itself as an aesthetic object, divorced from the specific occasion of death and its situational demands, did it begin to be taken seriously as literature. Not until the eighteenth century did the American elegy move from Christian affirmation to a secular blend of philosophical reflection and artistic accomplishment. The new thrust was individualistic, reflective, and – from the standpoint of art – professional. In his October 12, 1833 entry of "Table Talk," Coleridge summed up the romantic construction of elegy as "the form of poetry natural to the reflective mind. It *may* treat of any subject, but it must treat of no subject *for itself*; but always and exclusively with reference to the poet himself" (Kay 232). Coleridge articulates what Morton Bloomfield has called a shift from "elegy" *per se* to the "elegiac mode," the latter a product of the reinscription of transcendence from traditional religion to the natural sublime and the prototype for nineteenth- and twentieth-century lyric generally (147–48). Inseparable from this shift is a highly individualized speaker whom, in Gray's terms, "Melancholy marked . . . for her own" in a reflection on the fact that "The paths of glory lead but to the grave." This is the mode of Wordsworth's speaker in the Lucy poems, who finds solace as well as terror in the knowledge that Lucy is now "Rolled round in earth's diurnal course, / With rocks, and stones, and trees." Tennyson gives equally explicit voice to the consolations of nature in his lament for Arthur Hallam: "Tho' mixed with God and Nature thou, / I seem to love thee more and more."[10]

The most famous American echo of these sentiments came from the nineteen-year-old Bryant, who wrote what became the quintessential poem about death for generations of readers. "Thanatopsis," like Gray's churchyard poem, is not an occasional poem: it thus completes the non-situational thrust of the pastoral elegy by divorcing reflections on death from death's actual occurrence. The young Bryant, extolling comforts to be derived from "Nature's teachings," turns the dissolution of a self destined "To mix forever with the elements" into an assertion of fellowship with an "innumerable caravan" that leads to "the pale realms of shade" and, if seen correctly, to "pleasant dreams." The romantic thrill of melancholy, the anticipated participation in natural cycles from which industrial society felt increasingly alienated, the social commonality of the dead, the anticipation of death as peaceful sleep – all would become staples of the canonical poem of loss in the nineteenth and twentieth centuries. "Thanatopsis" became one of the most popular poems in our literature and a classroom staple, as did Whitman's expression of similar views:

> Come lovely and soothing death,
> Undulate round the world, serenely arriving, arriving,
> In the day, in the night, to all, to each,
> Sooner or later delicate death.   ("Lilacs," lines 135–38)

For modern readers, these poems and the sentiments they convey are nearly irresistible. Nor *should* we resist them, whether as sources of consolation or objects of verbal beauty. But if we wish to understand another view of death and another way to mark its occurrence, we need to recognize that our preferences are not inevitable. We live in a culture that is still very much influenced by the romantic aestheticizing of death as a philosophical abstraction. We should remember, too, that this construction has less to do with immediate loss and sorrow than with post-romantic assumptions of a universal human condition – the same universal condition that the canon was staking out as its special territory as elegy criticism developed.

Bloomfield's distinction between the "elegiac mode" and "elegy" corresponds roughly to an experiential contrast between reflection and reaction. A general awareness of death is one thing; the shock of a specific loss is quite another. Given the Puritan compulsion to seek the divine in the local, it is in this latter mode that early New England's elegies are best approached. The privileging of reflection over reaction is a deep-seated critical habit. Over half a century ago Jantz, noting the power of "anachronistic criteria" derived from "romantic or modern standards," commented that "for a person coming fresh from romantic poetry," the anagram-based elegies popular in early New England will seem "dull, monotonous, and repetitious, just as a person acquainted only with melodic music can often derive no pleasure from the old contrapuntal music" (*First Century* 31). Fifteen years later Roy Harvey Pearce argued for a "baroque decorum" in New England's elegies, one based on "a sense, not of what is formally or artistically, but rather personally appropriate" (228). In order to put such recognitions of historical otherness into practice, the necessary adjustments are considerable. The Puritan elegy did not, first of all, assert its autonomy as an artistic product. Written to draw its audience into a specific response to loss mandated by belief, it deliberately undermined its discrete integrity by invoking a network of mutually supportive "texts" – sermonic, poetic, and experiential – that in turn pointed to the Bible as the overriding source of all Puritan textual experience. Second, the Puritan elegy did not seek to ease death's sting by extending art as a compensatory stay. Elegists routinely renounced the claims to professional virtuosity central to the canonical elegy. Deeply suspicious of such claims in the face of the survivor's impulse to speak and write, they tied the efficacy of commemorative poems to a *lack* of poetic skill, an assertion that went far beyond the conventional self-deprecation sometimes voiced by the pastoral elegiac speaker. Third, New Englanders sought to purge the elegiac rite of all conventions, classical or otherwise, that did not contribute directly to what they saw as the actual project of mourning, which was, in their view, a religious and meditative project. Such conventions, they believed, were too likely to arouse appreciation for its own sake. In art as in life, they feared that beautiful surfaces could conceal a rotten core: eloquence could actually impede the spiritual work that mourning demanded.

In rejecting the professionalism of the pastoral elegy, New England's early elegists made a deliberate effort to shift verbal commemoration from the tropic discourse of the classics to what they saw as the truth-based discourse of Scripture. Hardly the biblical literalists that they are sometimes accused of being, Puritans were convinced that biblical discourse left ample room to maneuver. And because they saw the Bible as a divine accommodation to fallen sensibilities incapable of grasping the naked Word in its purity, they elevated biblical figures to a status that transcended the merely metaphorical. God's tropes were inseparable, as far as human perception was concerned, from the ineffable Truth that they conveyed. Biblical metaphors were equivalent, for all practical purposes, to the reality that they set forth, and to use them was to address that reality as directly as language allowed. On this Milton and his New England contemporaries agreed. The radical difference in their approaches to elegy stemmed chiefly from contrasting rhetorical situations, and not from a fundamental disagreement over the uses of Scripture or the theology of mourning. When Milton mixed classical and Christian discourses in "Lycidas," he assumed a readership of university humanists comfortable with the notion that God's great plan encompassed all things under the sun, including pagan texts that presented muted echoes of divine revelation. Milton could make this assumption – and thus enjoy what we would consider allusive luxury – because his university-trained readers were adept at reading classical discourse as a natural prefiguration of Christian truth. There was no

conflict between Orpheus and Christ for those who were accustomed to
seeing the former as a figure for the latter. For such readers, the stoicism
of classical elegy was a fitting precursor to Christian resignation: the
Orphic surface merely offered attractive entry into Christic substance.
The death of such "shepherds" as the young Edward King occasioned
no essential conflict between two discourses that were, at root, saying the
same thing.

Educated New Englanders, especially the ministers, knew the same
classics, and a few elegists did not hesitate to invoke the ancient tropes
when there was little risk that verbal means would distract from redemptive ends.[11] Even here, however, restraint was the rule, and when classical elements occur in New England's elegies, they are markedly general
and accessible. John Saffin, for instance, mourns his son Simon by recalling his aborted climb as a student up the Muses' mountain: Simon's
"pregnant witt, quick Genius, parts sublime / Facill'd his Books, made
him Pernassus clime" (Meserole 197). Nehemiah Walter memorializes
schoolmaster Elijah Corlet of Cambridge as a latter-day Cicero: "Rivers
of *Eloquence* like *Nectar* flow'd / From his Vast Ocean, where a *Tully* might
/ Surfeit with draughts of *Roman* Eloquence" (Meserole 465). And
Benjamin Colman begins Samuel Willard's commemoration with one of
the most striking classical parallels in any Puritan poem, a ringing echo
of the epic invocation of the *Aeneid*. Colman's hero, however, is not a
Prince of Troy who establishes a new Rome, but a "Prince of the
Prophets" who has helped build a New Zion:

> I sing the MAN, by Heav'ns peculiar Grace,
> The Prince of Prophets, of the Chosen Race,
> Rais'd and Accomplisht for degenerate Times,
> To Stem the Ebb with Faith and Zeal Sublime . . . (Meserole 341)

As these examples suggest, classical allusions usually assumed occupational appropriateness, meshing well with the earthly callings of the
student, the teacher, and the preacher. Willard, a minister's minister
whose sermons on systematic theology were collected in the posthumous
Compleat Body of Divinity (Boston, 1726), was especially ripe for epic treatment. As Colman's tribute also suggests, classical references were more
frequent in poems written for circulation mainly among ministers, who
had been initiated into the humanist lore by virtue of their training in
Hebrew, Greek, and Latin.

Not surprisingly, classical echoes are more frequent in elegies written
in Latin. To write in Latin in the first place, as Lawrence Rosenwald

points out, was to address "the learned world of New England" (314) – a world equivalent to a clerical brotherhood who could be expected to decode a pagan surface for its Christian substance. Accordingly, the Latin elegies occasionally invoke the double discourse exemplified by the ambiguous "shepherd" commemorated in "Lycidas." In a joint elegy for Thomas Hooker and John Winthrop, the scholarly Charles Chauncy, soon to be elected president of Harvard, linked the deaths to Pandora's darkness and the Hydra's dangers, and wondered what Trojan Horse of trouble was yet to come (Kaiser 22). Eleazar, a student at Harvard's Indian School, commemorated Thomas Thatcher of Boston's Old South church by proclaiming that Apollo would be powerless for a task requiring such "fitting tears and heavy grief" ("justis cum lacrymis cumque dolore gravi") (Kaiser 34). And William Adams commemorated Urian Oakes as "Uranius," the "heavenly herald" ("caelestis praeco") who prompts storms in sinners' hearts as powerful as Orion's tears (Kaiser 37). Adams puns on Oakes's last name as well, attesting that he was "like an oak in strength and firmness, / prevailing upon men and God with strong prayers" ("veluti quercus pollebat robore firmo, / robustis precibus vincens hominesque Deumque") – an image that Rosenwald links to Vergil's fourth eclogue, in which "strong oaks shall distill dewy honey" ("durae quercus sudabunt roscida mella") (311).

Such approximations of the coded discourse of "Lycidas" offer vivid examples of Puritan "double-talk," the "duality of signification" that William Scheick identifies in the Puritan negotiation of Renaissance and Reformation discourses (*Design* 29, 3). Most striking, perhaps, is the double duty that certain Latin words performed in unifying the Puritan humanists' biblical/classical world. Like Milton's play on the double-sided "shepherd," New England's Latin elegies for ministers frequently invoke the figure of the *pastor bonus*. Chauncy, attesting that flocks will be scattered when shepherds are stricken ("Dispergentur oves pastores per-cutiendo"), commits John Davenport's soul to Christ, the "Shepherd of shepherds" ("Pastorum Pastor") (Kaiser 23). Elijah Corlet similarly laments Thomas Hooker as "friend" and "shepherd" ("amicus. . .pas-torque"), deliberately extending the classical/Christian duality through words like "vota" ("vows" but also "prayers"), "Domus Emanuel" ("Emmanuel College" but also "house of the Lord"), "rostrum" ("dais" but also "pulpit"), and "viator" ("traveler" but also "pilgrim") (Kaiser 17–18). Rosenwald finds in this poem allusions to Ovid's *Metamorphoses*, the *Aeneid*, and the *Iliad* appropriate to Corlet's "variations on the theme of Hooker as Aeneas," the classical precursor of the Christian "viator"

(308). Adams's poem on Oakes also invokes this dual order in its final exhortation to

> Remember your life is short;
> pale death is at the door. Come to your senses quickly.
> Live today, lest tomorrow's life be too late.
> (Rosenwald's translation, 310).

> Memor esto tu brevis aevi:
> pallida prae foribus Mors est. Resipisce repente,
> vive hodie, ne sera nimis sit crastina vita.
> (Kaiser 37)

As Rosenwald notes, Adams repositions the epicurean *carpe diem* within a Christian framework of eternity: "vive" suggests "live in Christ," while "resipisce" echoes the Vulgate's "resipiscant" of 2 Timothy 2:26, which encourages the believer's recovery from the wiles of the Devil (310–11). In addition, learned Puritans would not have missed the macaronic pun in "repente," so "quickly" was repentance needed after so grievous a loss.

Despite the dominant position of classically trained ministers in the textual world of early New England, the body of Latin poems from the period is surprisingly small – only about a hundred extant poems written before 1720 – and of these, only some fifteen are elegies. Rosenwald persuasively argues that these numbers reflect the characteristically democratic Puritan notion of poetic audience (314). The mandate to teach and inspire through pious texts meant that any language known only to university men could play only a limited role in Puritan literary culture. Moreover, although Rosenwald judges the elegies to be the most artistically successful of Puritan Latin poems (306–7), he finds the Latin verse of the period, including the elegies, to be stylistically conservative and "oddly lucid," marked by "inertness" in comparison to the Baroque structures common in Puritan poems written in English (313). Rosenwald attributes this conservatism and clarity to the public and occasional nature of the Latin poetry. In the case of the elegies there was an additional factor, one that was also responsible for the stylized form of elegies in English: the ritual nature and function of these texts as scripts for Puritan mourning. The Latin elegies are thus linguistically exclusive but thematically inclusive. Like the other Latin poems, they recall what Rosenwald calls "trade-jargon, thieves' argot, and the sacred language of priests" – an instance of those *langues spéciales* cited by anthropologist Arnold van Gennep in his work on rites of passage. But as Rosenwald also notes, Puritan poetry in Latin is "chiefly public verse and contains no secrets" (313, 314). Despite their inscription in a learned argot and their occasional allusiveness, the Latin elegies do not differ substantially from the elegies in English. The deaths of Hooker and Winthrop may have seemed like a Hydra of afflictions, but Chauncy makes far more of his assertion that the deceased leaders were like Moses and Aaron, Zerubbabel and Joshua. Moreover, Chauncy's speaker is no proud Roman swelling with nationalistic pride, but a Naomi/Mara who meekly accepts the bitterness of affliction (Ruth 1:20) (Kaiser 22). Similarly, Eleazar quickly drops his allusions to Apollo and the dead Achilles in favor of straightforward praise for Thatcher as a man "of famous virtue and holy faith" ("nota fuit virtus ac tua sancta fides") (Kaiser 34). And Adams, as we have seen, transforms echoes of epicureanism into a damning commentary on sin: "Alas, how vain is mankind!" ("Heu, quam vanus homo!") (Kaiser 37).

Such shifts from the ancients to the Ancient of Days support Rosenwald's view that Puritans saw the classics not as a vital influence or source, as in the humanist tradition, but as a mere "resource" – simply one means out of many to convey their pious message (313). Humanists in England, including the young Puritan humanist who wrote "Lycidas," deliberately set out to imitate specific Greek or Latin poets, applying the antique song to contemporary events. New Englanders, by contrast, approached classical texts mainly as a ready stock of devices useful chiefly for ornamentation (312). When elegists made classical allusions at all, they did not push them to the point of erecting elaborate discursive structures that ran parallel to what they saw as the core of the poem. The occasional ornament from Vergil or Ovid did not obscure the deeper inspiration and affective center of poems that remained insistently biblical in expression and homiletic in aim. Commemoration was too important for a mere display of learning, which explains why there are so few Latin elegies to begin with. In keeping with the Protestant agenda, elegists in New England reconfigured the commemorative genre for the widest possible audience, for whom the redemptive significance of death needed to be set forth as clearly as possible. Abandoning the aristocratic and learned trappings of the pastoral in order to invoke the basic functions and qualities of what we moderns would call cultural narrative, New England's elegists produced social scripts that addressed, far more directly than poems like "Lycidas," the immediate spiritual needs of everyday people facing personal loss. A learned language could not do this work with sufficient scope and directness, nor could verbal and allusive habits inherited from long-dead authors, however revered, who once used it.[12]

When seen within the history of the genre, the Puritan resistance to the classical/pastoral aestheticizing of loss was an innovation. It was Milton who put the oaten reed to time-honored use; New Englanders, by contrast, saw themselves as trying something new, something that would be more consistent with the larger reformist enterprise. Far less optimistic than Milton in assuming that their readers could decode a pagan overlay for what it was, New England's elegists extended the English dissenters' democratizing of the genre. That we can appreciate their efforts only by performing a kind of aesthetic inversion reveals how *un*democratic the canonical aesthetic of loss actually is. "Lycidas" was transported from its original, exclusive cultural setting into the allegedly universal realm of art. It is one of the great ironies of literary history that this highly elaborate poem, a self-conscious verbal performance enacted within a small community of Cambridge intellectuals, became the standard for the mourning poem in English. This irony is compounded by the fact that "Lycidas" is not just about mourning but about making art, and has in fact been praised chiefly to the extent that it refuses to restrict its focus to the expression of personal sorrow. To put this another way, modern predilections for autonomous literary discourse have conditioned us to value "Lycidas" for precisely what is self-consciously "fictive" about it. We assume that the elegiac poem, like all poems, must stand on its own as an aesthetic performance. The more directly it addresses the unmediated emotion of its occasion (as if such emotion were not already mediated), the more we tend to call it "sentimental" and to dismiss it as an interesting barometer of mass taste, unworthy of serious analysis.

When we patronize such texts by conceding their "sincerity" and "heartfelt simplicity," we obscure the fact that New Englanders took a route that was no less complex than Milton's in its articulation of discursive and cultural practices. The Puritan decision to replace the "fictive" with the "real" in the commemorative poem enacted a shift in elegiac focus from earthly fame to eternal salvation, from an idealized past shaped by classical satire to an idealized future shaped by Christian eschatology. In New England's elegies, the pastoral vision played itself out in heaven, not on earth. The goal was not earthly recovery through nostalgia but eschatological hope through repentance. Relocating the pastoral site of desire from a position outside the reader as onlooker to a position within the reader as participant, the poem was offered with the expectation that it would be – indeed, *should be* – internalized as felt spiritual experience. As we shall see, the pastoral elegist's idealization of the world through rustic tropes was ultimately rewritten by New England's elegists into an idealization of the mourning reader, whose interiority was reshaped into an experiential parallel, though vastly inferior, to that of the glorified deceased in heaven. Although the numinous dead had gained their prize, the penitence that helped them gain it remained within reach of survivors. By placing such gain within the mourner's grasp, New England's poets defined the common elegiac connection of the living with the dead in terms of potential and fulfillment, with saving faith serving as the bridge. Despite the modern propensity to find gloom in these poems, the Puritan experience of them was one of optimism – and it was an optimism thought to be firmly anchored in reality. When Puritans applied the discourse of Scripture to the occasion of death, they did not perceive that discourse as tropic in the sense that Milton consciously "invented" his rude shepherd who fumbles with unripe berries. And because the discursive center of the elegy – as of Puritan texts generally – was relentlessly biblical and thus no less the product of God's hand than the awful Truth that the Bible conveyed, there could be little stress on the elegist as an original creator. The poet's induction into an artistic lineage divorced from grace held little appeal for those who believed that the very means and aims of all true art, elegiac or otherwise, came from God. In Puritan poems of loss, as in all elegy, the impulse to reassert continuity was vital. The inheritance at stake, however, was avowedly spiritual rather than artistic.

When Taylor wrote his tribute to David Dewey, he joined his contemporaries in trying to remove elegy from the realm of "human" invention altogether. While the speaker of "Lycidas" is clearly a poet masked as a shepherd, deliberately enacting an easily recognized deception necessary for healing the disruption posed by death, Taylor and other New Englanders spoke in what they and their readers construed as a "real" voice, that of a neobiblical prophet who conveyed divine truth through forms that were perceived as reinscriptions of God's own voice. The Puritan elegist "invented" the poem only in the older sense of the word, by discovering and revealing preexistent truths set forth in the Word. Elegiac performance became, in New England, a deliberate non-performance cultivated through a search for rhetorical selflessness. To be an effective poet of mourning, one had to become not a creator of poems but a receptive amanuensis for the Creator of all true poems. To write elegy was thus construed not so much in terms of *speaking* human words as it was in *reading* and *hearing* the divine Word and conveying it faithfully as the most useful response to loss. The transfer of the pastoral *locus amoenus* to heaven and to the survivor's meditative life encapsulates the prophetic stance of the Puritan elegist. The biblical prophets spoke to effect inner change, interrogating their hearers' relation to the law and urging their realignment with its dictates. Following the prophetic lead, New England's elegists offered the commemorative text not as a mere "poem" for appreciation or judgment – its lofty biblical models precluded that possibility – but as a script whose words were to be internalized as vital redemptive experience. Given the biblical precedent and mandate, elegists tried to instill in their readers the antithesis of what most of us would consider an "original" response to death. They wrote instead to stimulate a process of mourning that was relentlessly predictable, one that was fully consistent with the Puritan theology of death and Puritan definitions of salvific experience, including the salvific response to loss.

For their insistence on defining and pursuing so specific a textual function, early New England's elegists paid dearly. Their commitment to theological clarity, especially in contrast to the deliberate multivalence of poems like "Lycidas," decreased their intelligibility in later eras that valued imagistic concreteness but thematic ambiguity. The Puritan refusal to translate specific cultural attitudes toward death and grief into discourse acceptable to readers situated outside of their culture illustrates a profound irony, rarely acknowledged, at the heart of literary history. The better a text "works" within its culture of origin, the less well it usually works for future readers looking on – or looking back – from the outside. Seen in this light, the critical fate of the Puritan elegy was sealed not because the elegists performed their task so poorly, but because they performed it too well. From Silence Dogood on down, the issue among critics has never really been whether these poems were badly written, but whether there could be any validity to the reasons *why* they were written in the first place. As we have seen, Benjamin Colman felt compelled to "sing the MAN" – to bend Vergil's epic opening to a commemoration of Samuel Willard as New England's kind of hero (Meserole 341). One critic, commenting on Colman's "epic-like treatment," argues that "where the heroic came into conflict with the elegiac, it was the latter that was sacrificed" (Schmitt-von Mühlenfels, "Puritan Society" 31). But this is surely a modern distinction. For Puritans, heroism and piety were virtually interchangeable; moreover, it was piety that mandated elegy in the first place. It makes perfect sense to conclude that Puritan sermons, so rigorous in shaping a specific response to death, were "coercive" and "repressive" (Breitwieser 69), so long as we understand that the judgment reflects modern notions of subjective control. If read from such a perspective, Puritan elegies will seem even more coercive than the sermons. Yet all cultural structures, including our own, enact constraints that an outsider would find coercive, and in times of crisis we, too, are often grateful for the sense of control that limits can bring. For all the apparent gloom of their elegies, Puritans kept on writing them. To explore the satisfactions they derived from such stylized poems is to enter a world in which literary experience was defined in ways largely foreign to us.

As Peter White has observed, the funeral elegy "provided the Puritan with a kind of public entertainment into which he could invest his imaginative, mental, and emotional powers" (*Benjamin Tompson* 41). Reconstructing the Puritan experience of these powers will not, and should not, convince us moderns to adopt Puritan notions of literary entertainment or to "like" the elegies in our usual sense of literary pleasure. It will, however, help us stop subjecting these decidedly preromantic texts to postromantic notions of art and grief. To read the Puritan elegy on its own terms is to accept its irreducible alterity as a starting point for discussion, rather than as an occasion for premature closure. David Hall points out that texts in early New England functioned as "well-charted scripts" that "worked despite their formulaic nature" (*Worlds of Wonder* 245). To this statement I would make an important modification: Puritan poems worked as redemptive scripts *because* of their formulaic nature. As Ellen Lambert reminds us in relation to English elegy, "there is indeed a special virtue in saying what has been said before" (153). W. David Shaw makes a similar case for Donne's lament for Elizabeth Drury as a "pattern of virtue" in the *Anniversaries*: "Since 'discovery' of that pattern is really a kind of 'remembering,' every step forward is like a step backward, as if the mourner were being reminded of something he already knew" (*Elegy and Paradox* 243). These words also describe the special virtue of liturgy, the comfort that comes from an expected message, the predictable rhythms of belief reconfirmed through language. Puritans wrote elegies to tell a single story: the power and rewards of grace. They accepted that story as true, and even if we do not, we can still listen more attentively to these distant narratives of time, art, death, and faith. We can even understand them, in some measure, because we temporarily possess the fragile privilege of the living to do so. Our own vulnerability, if nothing else, should prompt us to temper our judgment and listen more closely to these laments from a different world.

CHAPTER 2

Toward an anthropology of Puritan reading

As Taylor read his tribute, David Dewey's mourners periodically nodded their heads in agreement, some dabbing their eyes with handkerchiefs or mourning gloves. The older people stared at the coffin with blank expressions and tightly pressed lips. Sarah Dewey, listening closely as Taylor recounted her husband's life, found herself nodding in agreement at the minister's proclamation that "Grace's Dew" in David had

> . . .drencht thy Consort's heart
> In influences of an holy Art:
> Whom, with thy little Stems which thou dist leave
> Thou dists, ere thou departst, to Christ bequeath.
> ("Edward Taylor's Elegy" 82–83)

While Taylor was counting the ways in which David's life had been illuminated by the Spirit, Sarah Dewey felt the words giving a shape to things, settling her thoughts into patterns she had known since she was a little girl. In her sadness and shock, it was a blessing to remember how God's people lived and died. She hoped that when her time came she would be worthy of the same embalming – that the Lord would distill her into the essence of holiness that Taylor was lining out under the formless haze of the late afternoon sky. She knew she would remarry, as most everyone did: if people gave up living because of sorrow, life would cease altogether. She would go on, though just now she could not imagine herself being with another man. How could she ignore David's face in the boys' faces, or their awkward aping of his walk? Feeling herself on the verge of anger, she caught herself. How strange, she thought, that Satan could invade her thoughts even now. How easy it was to trust in something so fragile as flesh – and then to chafe at God's loving correction.

The youngest boy tugged at her hand, and as she pulled his head against her hip she refocused on the minister's words, following their rhythms as they built to a conclusion that she knew was coming. It felt almost as if she were speaking the poem, witnessing to David's faith and to that blessed still point toward which she hoped the Lord was also leading her. She felt her composure return as the minister foretold "the Resurrection of the Just," when her husband's purified body would rise

> . . .out of the Dust,
> Transcending brightest Gold, and shining Sun
> In Glory clear; to which thy Soul shall run
> And reunite, and perfectly repair
> Thy Person spoild while 'ts parts asunder are.
> For, both together Serving Christ as one,
> Shall both together reign with Christ in's Throne,
> And pearch with Saints and Angels in the Ring
> Of Everlasting Glory Praise to Sing.
> While we thy Coffin's Cambarick do borrow
> To wipe off of our Eyes the Tears of Sorrow.

When Taylor finished, he straightened up and handed the poem to Sarah Dewey. As the sexton and his helpers took up the ropes and began to lower the coffin into the ground, Taylor squeezed her hand and gently touched the head of each of her sons. His lips forming an inaudible prayer, he glanced at the grave and then, almost involuntarily, squinted at the gleaming winter sunset.

The original textual situation of the Dewey poem – the conditions under which it was written, heard, and read – suggests why New England's elegies have always seemed to reconfirm Moses Coit Tyler's century-old declaration of an "inappeasable feud" between Puritanism and art in early New England (228). As Kathleen Blake once summarized the problem, the poetry is "seen as either too Puritan to be good or too good to be Puritan" (2). An unasked question, of course, is concealed in Tyler's formulation: *whose* art? If we insist on ours, then we are compelled to read these poems in terms of what they lack, as dry bones of artistic failure. But if we try to suspend, for the moment, some of our most deeply held convictions about poetry, it might be possible to recover something of the Puritan experience of elegy. An attempt at this kind of historical empathy requires us to set aside emotion recollected in tranquility, negative capability, barbaric yawps, the top of one's head coming off, old medallions dumb to the thumb, and a dozen other postromantic characterizations of good poetry. We must forget MacLeish's classic dictum that a poem should not mean but be. Poems like the Dewey elegy did not *be* so much as *do*: they existed not as stable artistic objects, but as spiritual workbooks designed to be used up in an assimilation of the perspective they offered. Deliberately bending to this purpose Horace's advice to mix the useful with the sweet, the Puritan poet tried, as Jonathan Mitchell described Michael Wigglesworth's verse, to roll "Truth in Sugar." "No cost too great, no care too curious is," Mitchell declared, "To set forth Truth and win men's Souls to bliss" (Meserole 412).

This raises another concealed question: what "men's Souls" is Mitchell talking about? Puritan elegists did not write for the university-trained readers of "Lycidas." Educated New Englanders had no quarrel with Milton's desire to wed the faith to classical forms, a project whose fruition in *Paradise Lost* might be useful in conveying the scope and dignity of God's great plan to readers whose learning had swept them into a secular Arcadia. Such efforts might even succeed, as Michael Drayton had hoped seven decades before Milton's epic appeared, in luring poetry lovers from "Tales" to "Truethes," from "Toyes in Mount *Ida*" to "triumphes in Mount *Sion*" (1:3). We have seen, however, that New England's poets had less learned and more diverse fish to catch than Milton did. Committed to a democratization of reading based on universal access to the Word, whether read or preached, they aimed at an audience defined less by social standing and education than by spiritual attitude. The only literary competence they assumed was familiarity with Scripture, a familiarity ensured even among the illiterate by their constant exposure to the Bible-based sermon. Although literacy rates in early New England were relatively high for the era, most poets tried to engage hearers as well as readers: children, slaves, Indians, and unlettered adults to whom poems were read aloud as vital sources of edification and, given the values of the culture, of compelling entertainment. The line between literacy and orality is often blurred in traditional societies: those "double Rhimes" that Franklin ridiculed in the Mehitabel Kittel elegy (22) become more defensible in light of the oral dimension of literary experience in early New England. The ballad meter of *The Day of Doom*, to cite the most famous example of popular verse, was fully appropriate for a poem designed to be read aloud in families as a kind of catechism. Indeed, people were still living at the time of the American Revolution – over a century after the poem appeared – who had memorized its 224 stanzas as children. Like most Puritan ministers, Wigglesworth was familiar with classical poetry through his training in Greek and Latin, and even owned an edition of Horace, the prosodic virtuoso of antiquity (Dean 16). But when he set out to justify the ways of God to New Englanders, he did not follow Horace's lead or even Milton's in using blank verse, a flexible vehicle suited to the elaborate verse sentence. Instead he chose the familiar "fourteeners," the most popular metrical form conceivable and one that ensured maximum accessibility and ease of memorization.[1]

Wigglesworth's choice was typical in its practicality. In poem as in sermon, the Puritan aesthetic was militantly functional: the beauty of words, whether as images or sounds, mattered less than their capacity for moving readers further along the *ordo salutis* or renewing their sense of having been there before. In contrast to – and perhaps as unconscious compensation for – their vocal iconoclasm, bare-bones liturgy, and fear of an unbridled fancy, Puritans exploited a discourse of ritual that leaned heavily on the conventional, the expected, and the repetitive. Denying themselves overtly sensory aids to worship which they associated with Roman Catholic practice, they restricted themselves to the medium of words in their pursuit of the traditional Christian use of the senses to transcend the senses. Their overriding metaphor for salvation was not seeing the light but hearing the Word, and if they shut their eyes to the seductions of stained glass, statuary, and paint, their ears were all the more attuned to the experiential possibilities of language. God, after all, had not given them an icon or an altar screen but a Book, and they were determined, in their spiritual and homiletic exercises, to stick as closely as possible to the medium that God had sanctioned. Not surprisingly, Puritan biblicism had an enormous impact on notions of poetic originality. Not only did sublime verbal catalysts to inner change already exist, and in ample supply, in the pages of Scripture, but considerable risk lay in trying to invent new ones. For the Puritan poet, *inventio* retained its older sense of "discovery," of recovering sacred truths already embedded in the Book of Scripture and its lesser mirror, the Book of Nature, as separate but unequal texts inscribed by God's hand. Puritans believed with Augustine that the Bible set forth a grand design also revealed, though on a shadowy level, in created things. Its pages offered a rich storehouse of tropes and images that poets could exploit without risking the error that was inevitable whenever fallen humans, unaided by grace, tried to see into the life of things. Puritans experienced this belief in language-as-discovery as a kind of liberation, as a participatory means of breaking through the banal mask of created things in order to decipher divine handwriting legible only to the spiritually attuned. To be an "original" poet in anything like the modern sense was

counterproductive to why one wrote poems to begin with. Like all discourse, poetry was meant to draw readers into Scripture, not to pull
them away from it in a perusal of merely human texts no better than the
writings of benighted pagans.

Nowhere was the mandate to stay within biblical lines stronger than at
times of loss, when even the most pious had difficulty seeing the wisdom
of God's ways. Puritan elegies repeatedly countered the anxiety posed by
death with scriptural reassertions of divine order. Given the poem's role
as a mediator between Scripture and self, the more predictable and recognizable its biblical underpinnings, the stronger its impact on a greater
number of readers. Nor was the appropriation of biblical discourse seen
merely as a matter of rhetorical choice. Such language, when warmly
assimilated, evidenced nothing less than right seeing and thinking. This
belief emerges in the routine elegiac practice of comparing the dead to
biblical heroes, as Taylor did when he extolled David Dewey's civic
virtues. Although the name "David" gave Taylor an easy choice, any
prominent person could, when considered in spiritual terms, be seen as
a David, a Solomon, or a Moses – parallels that reminded readers of the
ultimate source not only of wise leadership but of all good things under
the sun. Puritans saw these analogies as reiterations of eternal truths that
resonated more deeply with each repetition. Poets did not resort to stock
figures because they could not come up with better ones, but because they
were convinced that better ones could not possibly exist. Puritan literary
culture thus operated through an ongoing interplay of all texts with the
great Text that lay at the center of a discursive nexus comprised of
sermons, poems, histories, wonder stories, exemplary biographies, conversion narratives, captivity narratives, devotional books, and theological tracts. Each text reinforced the others, and all connected finally with
the Bible as the supreme Metatext inscribing a faith that was itself experienced as a "text" based on the Christic *Logos* spoken by the Father and
extended to humanity through God's two-part "poem," the Old and
New Testaments. Devotional texts also helped readers assess the relation
of the great Text with the "text" of the self. The spirit of God, as Paul
had insisted, was written not "in tables of stone, but in fleshy tables of the
heart" (2 Cor. 3:3). Reading and hearing helped believers pursue an
ongoing self-examination for signs of grace – and the texts they used gave
definition and order to what they found within. With the sermon and the
Bible serving as oral and written centerpieces, this complex of texts
offered a variety of performative scripts that encouraged an engaged
response to the great message that they jointly offered.[2]

Taylor's elegy for Dewey entered this intertextual mix well before its appearance in the commemorative pamphlet, and in the same way that most poems were "published" in early New England. Oral presentation and the circulation of poems in manuscript played vital roles in the literary culture, and apart from the sermon, the elegy was the most common vehicle for this exchange. Verse commemorations were read aloud within grieving families and communities, read silently in acts of private devotion, circulated among the bereaved, and copied into diaries and commonplace books as permanent memorials to the deceased's faith. Taylor sent a poem on the deaths of two infant daughters to former college roommate Samuel Sewall, who in turn gave a copy to Cotton Mather, who reprinted two of its stanzas at the end of a sermon on the proper handling of grief (Johnson, "Seventeenth-Century Printing"). Taylor kept copies of two Latin elegies on John Davenport written by Harvard President Charles Chauncy, himself the subject of a Taylor elegy that the poet preserved among his papers (Kaiser and Stanford). John Saffin entered numerous elegies, his own as well as other poets', into his commonplace book. Joseph Tompson's diary preserved elegies by several poets, including his brother Benjamin and John Wilson. Many poems, such as Harvard president Urian Oakes's elegy on Thomas Shepard II, were well known and widely quoted years after their initial occasion. Despite their occasional origins, elegies achieved a measure of permanence, though more as pious gestures than as "poems," within the collective memory. In his elegy for Oakes, the young Cotton Mather was able to cite a list of elegists extending back over thirty years as he took his own place in the commemorative chain (*Verse* 51). Although a significant number of elegies did achieve formal publication, mostly as broadsides, the hundreds of poems that survive in manuscript reveal that most elegies found their readers in other, more intimate ways.

For all their debates surrounding church polity, theology, and the Sacraments, the New England Puritans were of a mind regarding the uses and practice of poetry, especially elegy.[3] Their artistic assumptions were based on four unshakable convictions. First, the value of a poem lay not in its formal beauty but in its affective power to convey religious truth. This is, of course, to state the point in modern terms. For Puritans, divine truth *was* beauty, and they defined aesthetic pleasure as both stimulus and product of the spiritual message that poems helped them grasp. Second, because these truths were considered to be universally applicable, poets usually addressed readers not in terms of distinctions of

social class, political standing, and education, but in terms of their presumed spiritual condition and their relation to specific communities of
belief – the town, the congregation, or New England as a whole. Third,
poets did not strive for original sentiments, but sought to confirm eternal
principles prewritten in the Bible. It was futile to try outdoing the Word
– and more than futile, it was dangerous. Finally, no poem was an island,
not even when it responded to a particular occasion. Each poem drew
on associations invoked and reinforced by a complex web of other texts,
all of which pointed toward the Bible as the ultimate literary source and
arbiter. The Puritan commitment to this fourfold poetic resulted in a
body of verse designed to align readers with that source, to make them
feel that the act of reading had helped them achieve greater conformity
with salvific patterns extended by that source to all who had ears to hear.
The elegy assumed a critical role – more critical, perhaps, than any other
species of poetry – in a textual system designed to usher readers into a
direct and engaged apprehension of the Word in all its force.

Milton's famous repudiation of rhyme in the preface to *Paradise Lost* as
"the Invention of a barbarous Age, to set off wretched matter and lame
Meeter" spoke to the self-altering experience that Puritans on both sides
of the Atlantic defined as the ideal result of true poetry (249–50). In
place of verbal surface, Milton and his coreligionists sought to provide
the solid substance of Christian experience. Cotton Mather, one of
Milton's most vocal admirers in the New World, reiterated this function-
alist view of art by deciding, when translating the Psalms, not to take lib-
erties with the Hebrew "meerly for the sake of preserving the *Clink* of
the *Rhime*." Mather's view that rhyme was "of small consequence unto
a Generous *Poem*" prompted him to use blank verse in his American
psalter. What made a poem truly "Generous" was "The *Sublime Thought*,
and the *Divine Flame*." These alone were sufficient "to challenge the
Character of *Poetry*" for such "Holy Composures" as the Psalms
(*Psalterium Americanum* vii, xiii). But when it came to elegies written to
convey the "*Divine Flame*" to a broad readership, Mather followed
Wigglesworth's lead rather than Milton's, rejecting both the blank verse
of *Paradise Lost* and the prosodic variety of "Lycidas" for straightforward
laments delivered in rhymed couplets. As we have seen, Milton's underlying construction of mourning was not terribly at odds with that of his
New English contemporaries. But the form of commemoration that he
chose in "Lycidas" precluded its use in New England – and not just for
reasons of prosody. "Lycidas" conveys a Protestant humanist's faith in

the compatibility of biblical and classical discourses unified in Edward King's apotheosis as a "shepherd" who embodies two senses of a "pastoral" ideal. In its discursive doubleness, Milton's poem replicated the classical elegy's dual stress on nostalgia for a lost past and the satirical interrogation of a corrupt present. Developing negatively the more immediate sense of "pastoral" as the work of ministerial shepherds, Milton invokes the elegiac formula of "what he was not" through Peter's thundering denunciation of those who preach only "for thir bellies sake" (161), who "scarse themselves know how to hold / A sheephook" (162). Not surprisingly, the defining deficiency of such ministers is a failure of right utterance. Indifferent and greedy clergy are "Blind mouths" whose "lean and flashy songs," issuing from "scrannel pipes," leave the "hungry sheep" unfed and flatulent from deprivation of the Word.

There was nothing un-Puritan about all this. Still, Peter's intrusion into an otherwise classical landscape underscores the frankly allegorical nature of the scene, its referential doubleness clarified by these relatively plain words on what God's shepherds are all about. The ancient tropes, ushered into the ecclesiastical turmoil of England in the 1630s, worked because Milton deliberately manipulates them *as* tropes. A student named King has drowned, but the poem calls him "Lycidas" and thus underscores the very fact that it *is* a poem, a representation of one scene in terms of another. Like all fictions, the monody of the mourning swain, who skillfully weaves his lament despite "forc't fingers rude" (158), asserts a reality that hinges, paradoxically, on its frank *un*reality. Although Milton's discursive vehicles were openly tropic, his commemorative aims were serious enough: the game of pastoral mourning was no less important to him and his readers simply because they knew its rules. Milton's Puritanism emerges, however, in his decision to make the game and its rules even more legible than usual. Unlike the classical elements in the poem, Peter's speech on ministerial "shepherds" was not offered as metaphor. Nor was the concluding resurrection of Lycidas/King, effected "Through the dear might" – a wonderfully Puritan oxymoron – "of him that walkt the waves" (163). King's apotheosis reasserts an interpretive baseline for the meadows, the allegorical mourners, the flowers, and the rest of a scene grounded in Christian redemption. It's fine to mourn like a pagan, such a poem proclaimed, so long as we understand that what we're actually doing is applying pagan tropes to an act of Christian mourning that reflects who we *really* are. The pagan surface was, of course, enormously attractive – a fact not lost on Milton and his university readers, who were committed to redeeming the

ancient books they loved for edifying spiritual use. There was no need to
follow Jerome in rejecting the wisdom of the ancients altogether.
Instead, one could change how one *read* the ancients, thereby rendering
pagan tropes safe as prefigurations of Christian revelation. The Greeks
and Romans, unaided by the Spirit, had reached the peak of "natural"
human potential. What they had achieved, if read rightly, only deepened
one's respect for Scripture by confirming that the best and the brightest
among the ancients had shadowed, however dimly, what was fully
revealed only in God's Word. For the intended readers of "Lycidas," it
went without saying that Jove was simply a name that educated men
used for God when they were writing for the ages in a particular type of
language that had survived the test of time. In light of Milton's learned
audience, what is most remarkable about "Lycidas" is not that a Puritan
poet could invoke a pagan landscape, but that he would bother to spell
out its Christian import as fully and explicitly as he did. Peter is, after all,
an odd personage to be found wandering through the meadows of
Arcadia, and it is to Milton's credit that the apostle seems almost –
though not quite – at home there as spokesman for the social commentary central to classical elegiac precedent.

As *Paradise Lost* would more fully demonstrate thirty years later, the
struggle to negotiate the ostensibly competing discourses of the classics
and the Bible was tantamount to replicating the inner battle between
human darkness and divine light. William Scheick has described similar
"double-talk" among New England's Puritans as they struggled to negotiate the twin discourses of Renaissance and Reformation, matter and
spirit, earth and heaven, and time and eternity (*Design* 19–23). Read as
an exercise in this spiritual and hermeneutic negotiation, "Lycidas" is
indeed a fully "Puritan" poem. Death's inevitability, immediately linked
to natural cycles by the speaker's determination to sing "Yet once more"
(158), is contrasted with *this* death as a disruption of the natural expectation of a full lifespan for a shepherd "dead ere his prime" (159). As in
New England's elegies, the duty to mourn – a "Bitter constraint" –
"Compells" the speaker to grieve for a soul who "hath not left his peer"
and whose idealization is indispensable to the commemorative rite. Nor
is the poem devoid of theological musings that would receive more
explicit statement in New England's laments. Milton hints at Job's classic
articulation of grief – why does God let such things happen? – in the
speaker's gentle berating of the "nymphs" for not preventing King's
drowning (160). Like his New England counterparts, Milton counters the
human propensity to blame God for loss by reiterating the divine decree

that all must die, even the very best. Not even the supremely gifted Orpheus – a faintly Christic allusion that reappears near the poem's end – could escape a horrible dismemberment suggestive, like King's ship-wreck, of postlapsarian chaos. For Puritans in Old England as in New, death posed an insurmountable affront to human reason, but Milton framed death's challenge squarely in terms of his educated readers. "What boots it" to "strictly meditate the thankless muse" – to study and write in hope of "Fame" – when "the blind *Fury*" comes and "slits the thin-spun life?" Immediately, however, the speaker stands corrected by Phoebus's warning that "Fame is no plant that grows in mortal soil." At this point, eulogistic "fame" shifts from earth to a heaven that lies far from "broad rumor" and is answerable only to the "all-judging *Jove*" (161). This corrective, echoed in the New England elegist's call for survivors to redirect their sorrowful gaze from earthly loss to heavenly gain, initiates the "higher mood" that holds sway in the last part of the poem. Milton, like his American counterparts, confirms that merely human gifts are sufficient neither to explain the death nor to achieve genuine resignation to it. Triton, who ducks responsibility by blaming King's ship as an emblem of humanity's best-laid plans rather than the waves or "fellon winds," dramatizes nature's inability to frame a definitive explanation for loss. Nor can human learning, in the guise of old Camus, provide an explanation: all Cambridge personified can do is lament the death of its "dearest pledge." Not even Peter, with his "massy keys" to heaven, can explain *why*, in human terms, Lycidas was taken. Instead, he merely underscores the cruel loss of so pious a "young swain" while others continue to tempt God's enigmatic "two-handed engine," poised to punish them for their clerical abuses.

The poignancy of "Lycidas" arises mainly from the speaker's tacit awareness of the inadequacy of his tropes. The referential duality of pastoral commemoration indeed poses a kind of interpretive game, but finally, Milton concedes, the game will not save us. Peter's tirade and Phoebus's reorientation of "fame" underscore the self-conscious artifice of the ceremonial laying of flowers on the (empty) bier, a functional microcosm of the poem as a whole. Milton confirms the cosmic significance of the loss by invoking the traditional *natura plangens*, the sympathy of "the woods and desert caves." But "nature," which Milton and his New World counterparts saw as fallen, could not save Lycidas. Nor, finally, can nature console his survivors. Although the flowers "interpose a little ease" (163), they are part and parcel of a created realm whose end is foreshadowed in Lycidas's death. Placed within a ceremony construed as a pathetic stay against despair, the flowers fulfill a merely *human* need. As countless New Englanders would also proclaim, the very existence of sorrow witnessed the need to be reminded, "yet once more," of a truth that sinful humanity repeatedly forgot: death was the only passage to eternal life. "Weep no more," trumpets a voice, perhaps Michael's or perhaps the speaker's. Death, seen in redemptive terms, becomes a source of joy and not a terror reflective of worldly sensibilities. Like David Dewey, whose sharp division into the "Nadir" and "Zenith" of body and soul echoes the sin/grace dichotomy that defined the inner life of all true believers, Lycidas is both "sunk low but mounted high." With this recognition, Milton distracts his reader from the body's death to the soul's marriage with Christ, as Lycidas "hears the inexpressive nuptiall song / In the blest kingdoms meek of joy and love" (164).

As we shall see, New England's elegists would endorse the same relation between the living and the dead posed in "Lycidas." Like them, Milton asserts King's exceptionalism as a soul with "no peer," but the poem's affective power depends on reconnecting King with his survivors, and not just in a future reunion in heaven. However peerless, Lycidas is also the speaker's twin, a spiritually perfected version of the rough swain who sings the obsequies. Although that speaker celebrates Lycidas's apotheosis, "we were nurst upon the self-same hill" and "Fed the same flock by fountain, shade, and rill" (159). In keeping with classical convention, the bond invokes poetic lineage, a passing of the artistic torch from dead to living suggested in the speaker's hope to be similarly commemorated by "som gentle muse" whose "lucky words" might "favour my destin'd urn." The transfer of poetic inheritance is paralleled by a spiritual inheritance asserted in the speaker's hope someday to join Lycidas and "all the Saints above" in heavenly song (164). It is in heaven that Milton anticipates a reunion of the pastoral "sweet societies" shattered by King's death. In heaven, too, King's survivors can now claim a spiritual helper, a "Genius of the shoar" who stands ready to aid all who "wander in that perilous flood." Like his New English contemporaries, Milton begins the poem in earthly loss and ends in celestial gain. In the concluding scene, the "uncouth swain" – now described in a third person suggestive of the speaker's transcendence of a fledgling poetic self who, like so many others, has cut his poetic teeth on elegy – rises to face "fresh woods and pastures new." Faith in heaven makes life on earth possible, including the performance of elegy. As the poem closes, the speaker reenacts the Christic pattern of death and resurrection that brought Puritans, English and American alike, their deepest consolation in the face of loss.

The basic themes inherent in the Puritan construction of death are all here. But by applying classical discourse so fully to Christian mourning, Milton made a decision that his counterparts in New England would not follow. Although Lycidas winds up in a Christian heaven, this is not primarily what the reader takes away from the poem: as Jahan Ramazani observes, the poem's "frame of fictionality encompasses even that supreme action" (116). New England's elegists seem to have recognized that the insertion of the pastoral element as an extra interpretive level between grieving reader and redemptive message would surely muddle death's significance. Milton found the classical/biblical tension useful for reminding his readers that divine truths were indeed concealed within the literature he loved. For New Englanders, however, Milton's choice risked stressing artistic ingenuity over salvific resignation. While the lineage of grace – the transfer of sanctity from the deceased to the survivor – got full play in New England's elegies, the accompanying focus on poetic professionalism did not. Within the pastoral swerve from loss to art, nature's flowers might seem to "interpose a little ease" (163). But in New England, elegists believed that readers needed something clearer than Milton's subtle denigration of nature's balm. And what they needed, above all, was a sharp reminder that loss, especially when experienced and construed in "natural" ways, was *supposed* to hurt. If commemorative poems merely dulled one's sensibilities to death's corrective lessons, why write them at all? Death, after all, was sin's wages – and to mourn was to be reminded, once again, of the dark heritage of Adam, Eve, and Cain. Joshua Moody gave the expected shock vivid form at the death of John Reiner of Dover. Moody claims that when he heard the news, his "Lips quiver'd, Belly trembled, / My Spirits fail'd, Corruption seiz'd my Bones, / My Face grew pale, my heart as cold as Stones" (Jantz 151). The living, no less than the dead, lay under the bondage of sin, and accordingly, Moody articulates a sympathetic "death" in imitation of Reiner's. A saint has died – and his commemorator, equally subject to the "Corruption" of the grave, must figuratively die if he is to follow the deceased into glory.

Moody's mock death is a far cry from Milton's humanist belief that the ancients had modeled a stoicism akin to Christian resignation. But New England's elegists were not writing to console Cambridge classicists imbued with these traditions. Seventeenth-century Harvard was a tiny college by English standards, and Boston's population at the turn of the eighteenth century was only around 7,000, hardly sufficient to sustain large literary circles of the type found in London, Cambridge, and Oxford (Bridenbaugh 143). Moreover, pastoral – whether in Elizabethan England or Augustan Rome – is a decidedly urban mode. Its radical idealization of country life can work only among city-dwellers, whose distance from the actual countryside permits such representations and the nostalgia that fuels them. The Renaissance English pastoral consistently invoked a sharp contrast to the social realities that defined its production and consumption: the world it depicted was antithetical to the social spaces – the court, the city, the university – where it was most popular. It may be too obvious to note that one cannot wax nostalgic about that which is glaringly present, especially in poems designed to convey divine "truth" at times of affliction. For members of the farming communities of early New England, the blatant idealization of nature central to a poem like "Lycidas" would have seemed not just theologically suspect, but representationally ludicrous. If anyone in the first generation was equipped to embrace the artificial surface of the pastoral, it was Anne Bradstreet, whose wide reading is fully evident in her *Quaternions*. But when Bradstreet belatedly joined the ranks of poets commemorating her famous kinsman Sidney, many of whose poems followed Spenser in adopting the pastoral mode, she rejected that mode and registered distaste for Sidney's secular verse by projecting her own repudiation of such wit onto her subject: "His wiser days condemned his witty works, / Who knows the spells that in his rhetoric lurks, / But some infatuate fools soon caught therein" (189).

Bradstreet's reaction will no doubt strike modern readers as extreme. After all, Sidney and Milton were no pagans. But more to the point, they were not farmers or tradesmen either. Milton's embrace of classical discourse, however appropriate for old Cambridge, left far more interpretive and affective space than was appropriate in poems written for popular edification at an occasion of loss: a self-consciously artistic performance is even encoded in Milton's labeling his poem a "monody." In New England, elegy became a ritual performance enacted not through the monodic voice of the poet, but through a triadic relation of poem, reader, and deceased that was more consistent with a small and cohesive readership. New England's elegists wrote in the belief that mourning could not succumb either to a mere venting of "natural" emotion or to a prideful cultivation of poetic virtuosity. Death was too important to be given over to a poetry of fictions and false hair, and elegists could no more restrict themselves to a coterie of educated readers than preachers of conscience could withhold the Word on the basis of their hearers' education or social standing. Despite this social broadening of elegy, it would be wrong to romanticize the New England elegist's aims as either a foreshadowing of "American" egalitarianism or an anticipation of modern notions surrounding the liberating potential of texts. For Puritans, the democratized aesthetic of loss held the opposite significance. They believed in the clarity of all texts, including elegiac texts, for a darker reason: people, if left to their own devices, were no more inclined to read rightly than to act and think rightly. Sin's stain ran far too deep for that.

The rejection of "Lycidas" as a model for elegy reflects larger aesthetic choices made in early New England, choices that have always seemed clear enough in the aesthetic pronouncements of the day. The famous dictum in the preface to the *Bay Psalm Book* that "God's altar needs not our pollishings" (**3v) seems to square well with Cotton Mather's recommendation, nearly a century later, that candidates for the ministry make only "a little *Recreation* of *Poetry* in the midst of your more painful Studies." Clearly, there were more important things to do than to "be always poring on the *Passionate* and *Measured* Pages" (*Manuductio* 42). Such statements, read in light of modern tendencies to project nineteenth- and twentieth-century constructions of "Puritan" onto seventeenth-century Puritanism, have prompted many critics to overlook the fact that early New Englanders were more far indulgent as moral critics than Plato, who excluded poets from his ideal republic because they lied. Most Puritans persisted in believing that a poet did not have to lie, and their determination to reform rather than reject poetry out of hand would be clear, if from nothing else, from how much of it they read and wrote. The number of poems that survive from early New England is less surprising when we recall that Puritanism arose within Elizabethan culture, at a time when, as Samuel Eliot Morison pointed out, "almost everyone who could read at all, read poetry, and many attempted to write it; when all grammar-school boys were taught to write Latin verse, and almost everyone sang the songs that are found in the countless 'garlands' of the day" (*Intellectual Life* 210). Also consistent with Renaissance literary culture was the Puritan acknowledgment of the power of language. Thomas Wilson's popular *Arte of Rhetorique* opened with vivid witness to the irresistible charm of words: the tale of the orator Cineas, a former student of Demosthenes who persuaded the Romans to surrender to Phyrrus (5). Wigglesworth's college declamation on eloquence similarly underscored the power of speech to "secretly convay life into the hearers understanding rousing it out of its former slumber, quickning it beyond its naturall vigour, elevating it above its ordinary conception." So great was the potency of artful speech, Wigglesworth insisted, that it was "as if the oratour together with his words had breathed his soul and spirit into those that hear him" ("Prayse of Eloquence" 674, 675).

Like their Renaissance contemporaries, Puritans on both sides of the Atlantic saw poetry as an especially potent form of language, "a maner of utterance more eloquent and rethoricall," as George Puttenham's *Arte of English Poesie* affirmed, "then the ordinarie prose, which we use in our daily talke" (8). All texts could change the self, but poetry's special capacity to do so meant that it could not be given over to unregenerates without a fight. Nor was the impulse toward artistic reform, an enterprise dedicated to convincing readers that spiritual betterment *was* aesthetic pleasure, the exclusive property of Puritans. Early in the seventeenth century George Herbert had asked the divine Muse whether poetry could only "Wear *Venus* Livery? only serve her turn? / Why are not *Sonnets* made of thee?" (206). In later life Donne turned to topics that the more radical reformers would also embrace. Milton also counted himself squarely within this movement when he invoked the "Heav'nly Muse" for help in his ambitious desire to "assert Eternal Providence, / And justifie the wayes of God to men" (251, 252). As was so often the case, however, New Englanders were determined to go further. The battle for readers' hearts found more direct expression in Wigglesworth, who complained that many so-called "Christian Poets" committed "Blasphemy, / And Heathenish Impiety" by making

> . . . Jehovah to stand by
> Till Juno, Venus, Mercury,
> With frowning Mars, and thundering Jove
> Rule Earth below, and Heaven above.

Wigglesworth practiced what he preached, rejecting even the traditional invocation of the Muses as "th' Unchristian use, and trade / Of some that Christians would be thought" (*Poems* 9). His example was not ignored. We have seen his tutor at Harvard, Jonathan Mitchell, agree that good versifying, like good preaching, worked "To set forth Truth and win men's Souls to bliss." In this, the true poem was not so different from the effective sermon. Quoting Herbert's dictum that "A verse may find him who a sermon flies," Mitchell maintained that the true poet rejected "Toys" and "Fables (Poets' wonted crimes)" in favor of rolling God's truth in verbal sugar (Meserole 412). The feeding trope, common in Puritan descriptions of sacred discourse, reveals that poets, no less than preachers, were to heed Christ's command to "Feed my sheep" (John 21:7), a mandate that Peter passed on in his exhortation to "Feed the flock of God which is among you. . .not for filthy lucre, but of a ready mind; / Neither as being lords over God's heritage, but being ensamples to the flock" (1 Pet. 5:2–3). The truly pious would recognize solid spiritual nourishment when they found it. "If thy taste be good," Mitchell tells his reader, poems like Wigglesworth's will yield sufficient delight even if they violate the standards of literary London. God himself had authored poetry in Scripture, but the gift of rich words had been sadly abused. Weren't Job, the Psalms, and the Song of Songs a far cry from the ballads and sonnet sequences that were so much in vogue? Puritans were convinced that literary taste, like every other human trait, needed to be channeled into proper directions.[4]

Paradoxically, Puritan art embodied the practical pursuit of what can only be called mystical ends. In this goal, criteria for the effective poem were nearly indistinguishable from those for the effective sermon. As a Harvard thesis of 1643 put it, "Eloquentia naturalis excellit artificialem": the "natural eloquence" of a spiritually enflamed heart far surpassed the "artifice" of mere verbal technique (Morison, *Harvard College* 584). William Ames, commenting on the demands of successful preaching, could just as easily have been describing the Puritan ideal for verse: "The sum of the matter is that nothing is to be allowed which doth not contribute to the spiritual edification of the people, and nothing omitted by which we may surely reach that end" (196). Conceived as an extension of the sermon, the popular poetry of early New England was written, read, and heard for much higher stakes, in the Puritan view, than an appreciation of a poet's skill. These artistic aims, which make Puritan poetry so hard for *us* to hear, manifested themselves in a profoundly conventional and even ritualistic mode of discourse. No Puritan, of course, would have agreed with this characterization as I have stated it. Ritual, after all, was the Papist curse. Hadn't the clean line that the reformers redrew from the Word to the heart freed saints, once and for all, from such monkish practice? Still, the sharp contrast between Puritan aesthetic theory and Puritan poetic practice – between the severity of what early New Englanders said about poetry and the ritual complexity of the poems that they wrote – illustrates a truth that literary theorists have been telling us for some time now: the scripts by which people actually operate are precisely the ones that they cannot recognize, truths considered so self-evident that their alternatives lie beyond comprehension. Such structures are usually not "felt" at all, let alone felt as restrictive. Indeed, full awareness of their directives, whether limiting or enabling, would rob them of their power.[5]

Reading in early New England entailed what Wolfgang Iser calls a "dynamic happening" (*Act of Reading* 22), a process defined by the reader's interaction with the text's salvific message. In their conflation of religious and literary response, Puritans considered devotional reading – whether in the Bible itself or in texts designed to mediate between Scripture and self – to be a vital help along the redemptive path, an ordinance nearly as valuable to the soul's progress as hearing the Word preached. As David D. Hall points out, the slow, intense reading of devotional works played a central role in the "traditional" literacy of early New England. Hall's assertion that "The distance between books and life was very short" ("Uses of Literacy" 35) goes far beyond modern constructions of didactic texts as agents of coercion, as ideological impositions from without. From the Puritan standpoint, the distance between pious texts and pious readers was ideally almost nonexistent. The Puritan poem was fully "self-consuming" in the sense that Stanley Fish used in describing seventeenth-century English devotional texts. A poem existed for the reader's assimilation of its message, which in turn effected a subjective realignment with extrapersonal patterns that defined the saved soul. Nowhere was this inner realignment more relentlessly pursued than in the funeral elegy, and on no other occasion did Puritans consider the self-regulation provided by texts to be more welcome. This regulation, effected by a triangulation of deceased, speaker, and reader within the paradigm of the saved soul, accounts not only for the nonspecific elegiac portraits that Franklin lampooned, but also for the power that such idealized portrayals held for Puritan readers. Elegists routinely reinscribed the dead as saintly ideals to which the mourner could aspire, and as Scheick observes, the reader of elegy was reshaped in accordance with the pious example ("Tombless Virtue"). To speak the process was to participate in it. Just as Taylor's David Dewey is virtually indistinguishable from all other saints, Taylor's voice echoes the speakers of countless other poems that lamented them. Speaking for the ages and beyond, the elegy, like most Puritan poems, was neither written nor read as a vehicle for what we would call "personal" expression. New Englanders devalued that mode of speaking and writing because they devalued the mere self, one's particularity as a fallen individual. The unique, personal voice traditionally valued by literary critics was something that Puritans sought to confess in order to transcend. And because confessing a sinful self was indispensable to salvific progress, even the most intense revelations of personal sin assumed highly conventional form. The wretched worldliness that preachers and elegists railed against was routinely encountered whenever believers looked within and conveyed what they found there, especially in contrast to the glorious dead whom grace and death had perfected.[6]

Ideal selfhood assumed full coherence only in relation to the pages of Scripture. This represents a decidedly preromantic view of tradition, one based on reverent emulation rather than artistic transcendence. Wigglesworth studded the margins of his doomsday poem with references to his biblical sources – a pious precursor to Eliot in *The Waste Land*. But while Eliot's notes reinforced his ironic authority as a Myth-Redactor whose individual talent was revitalizing the Tradition, Wigglesworth's notes enhanced the poet's textual role as a mere instrument, a conduit of words authored by God himself. "Nor is it I that thee reproove," Wigglesworth proclaimed elsewhere, "Let God himself be heard" (*Poems* 89). Puritan poets, including elegists, assumed authorial power by repudiating it, consistently assuming neobiblical identities as contemporary extensions of the Word. Verse historians like Wigglesworth in "God's Controversy with New-England" and Benjamin Tompson in *New England's Crisis* spoke as latter-day prophets reading out the moral significance of events and reconfirming the hand of Providence behind them. Authors of homiletic poems designed to ease readers through cases of conscience, like Taylor in *Gods Determinations* and Wigglesworth in *Meat Out of the Eater*, spoke as latter-day Pauls articulating the redemptive turmoil set forth in Romans. Poets who turned personal events into edifying vignettes, like Bradstreet in the house-fire poem or the elegies for her grandchildren, spoke as latter-day Psalmists who modeled the varying moods of the earthly pilgrim. Even private, meditative poets, like Taylor in the *Preparatory Meditations* or Bradstreet in "As Weary Pilgrim" and "Contemplations," absorbed neobiblical identities, often speaking as the allegorical Canticles Bride in anticipation of their celestial union with Christ. There was also, as we shall examine more fully in subsequent chapters, ample biblical precedent for an elegiac voice, not only in David's lament for Saul and Jonathan, but in the elegist's role as a latter-day apostle spreading the "gospel" of the holy dead who had recently entered into celestial glory.

Readers confronted with such texts were "biblicized" as well, drawn by the poet as seer – a neobiblical "Pen-man," as Puritans called the various amanuenses of Scripture – into full engagement with Scripture not simply as a holy book but as the ground of perceptual reality. Historical and biographical verse, including the elegy as a conflation of both, remapped the reader's world along biblical lines: New England became the New Israel, Boston the New Jerusalem, the Atlantic a Red Sea of deliverance, the Indians Philistines and Amalekites, the forest a Wilderness of Sin, the magistrates new Moseses and Davids, the militia captains new Joshuas, the ministers new Melchizedeks, Aarons, and Elijahs. The parallels were endless – and Puritans never tired of reflecting on them. Readers, textualized as experiential antitypes of repentant Israelites, were repeatedly warned to melt down their golden calves, eat their manna, and persevere. Elegies reminded them that the places where they lived were neobiblical sites, ideal jumping-off points for heaven. Look at our holy dead, elegists repeatedly proclaimed. They were once *here* – members of our families, congregations, and towns – but now they are *there*, in the heavenly Jerusalem toward which all of Scripture and history pointed. It was within experiential patterns defined by the Bible and embodied in the deceased that poet and reader found common ground. Like all Puritan poetry, the elegy stimulated a particular subjectivity, one that manifested itself in the struggle between a sinful dimension born to this world and a saintly dimension born to the next. Refashioning mourners in accordance with redemptive psychology, the elegy offered regulating comfort to poet and reader alike. The private experience of loss, which would become central in romantic and postromantic modes of elegy, was expressed only to effect its transcendence. Puritans saw *that* kind of experience as damning, and the Puritan elegy sought a very different response in which the extrapersonal could be felt as personal – could indeed *become* personal through an engaged act of reading. Given the task at hand, the reader's aesthetic judgment was neither cultivated nor sought. There was, instead, a sense in which the reader was being judged by the *poem*, by the spiritual orientation that it articulated.

From a modern perspective, this seems an intolerably passive approach to texts. But Puritan reading, in its receptivity to textual directives, was construed as an echo of the experience of grace itself. To read was to be led through the story of salvation. Although one's final share in that story had to remain inconclusive, its stages were clearly defined. Having first attained an "historical" faith, the mere knowledge of salvation available to all and usually characterized by lukewarm belief, the saved soul would sooner or later be "convicted" in sin, humbled by what Thomas Hooker called an abject "levelling" of carnal identity (146). This was the wound that only Christ could heal – the dark night of the Puritan soul that convinced believers of their need for a Savior. The consequent repentance – the "broken heart" of sincere contrition – made an efficacious conversion possible, and with conversion came the will to combat one's carnal leanings and a capacity to experience what William Ames called the "double form" of the saint, "that of sin and that of grace" (170). Seeking ever stronger assurances of salvation, the believer began the oscillation between fear and hope that Puritans called "growing in grace" or sanctification, an ongoing replication of the initial conversion that continued until the saint's death and subsequent glorification. The believer's postconversion life offered repeated confirmations of an inner doubleness reflective of the Psalmist's declaration that "The Lord beholdeth all that fall, and raiseth up all those that be bowed down" (Ps. 145:14). This doubleness effected an internal replication of the two covenants, with the saint's gradual weaning from a law that could not be performed to a gospel that had been freely given.

Guided by the dispensations as a macrocosm of identity, believers tracked, with endless fascination, an ongoing struggle between the sinful self of the first birth and the saintly self reborn in grace. If sanctification were complete in this life, Thomas Shepard confirmed, "we should war and wrestle no more" (*The Sound Believer* 256). Ames attested that "a spiritual war is continually waged between these parts" in "a daily renewal of repentance" (170, 171). In the midst of this war, postconversion believers ideally enjoyed moments of assurance that confirmed their ability to see with a perspective renewed by grace. Gradually, they could see like a "meditating Christian," whom Edmund Calamy called "a man full of eyes, that doth not only know God, but sees much of God" (Brumm, "Meditative Poetry" 331). There was only one way to achieve such vision. The Christians at Rome received Paul's congratulations for obeying "from the heart that form of doctrine which was delivered to you" (Rom. 6:17). Seventeenth-century New Englanders sought, no less fervently, to conform their hearts to the Word as it had been delivered to them. As Ames insisted, "Inasmuch as faith is in each believer individually it is in the form of those that are called" (176). Edward Taylor similarly told his congregation that the redemptive process was "the Same in one and in all, and the Same in all as in thee" (*Christographia* 229). The Bible had clearly lined out the interiority to be sought, the "form and pattern," in Ames's phrase, that animated every saved soul (256). Texts could intensify a sense of this identity by forcing readers to make what Puritans saw as the central decision of life. It was not the choice to believe, an option precluded by the soul's passive reception of grace, but the choice to *want* to believe. By re-creating within themselves salvific patterns extended in poems like Taylor's elegy for David Dewey, readers could obtain clearer glimpses of the self of their desires.[7]

The more afflictive the event occasioning a poem – a dark night of the soul, a lapse in communal piety, and especially the mourning of a loss – the more welcome the experiential regulation that texts provided. To read properly, in the Puritan view, was to feel the salvific hope that Ames called "Christian confidence," the habit of "looking to the good which is to come" and feeling one's "hope confirmed." Such "hope is strengthened by all evidences which assure us that the good hoped for belongs to us. Rom. 5:4, *Experience produces hope*" (247, 248). It was saving faith, Puritans repeatedly insisted, that made such hope possible. John Davenport explained that "Reason of itself, in this corrupt state of fallen man, cannot teach men to hope in God. But when God hath in the word of promise given himself to us to be our portion, and faith hath closed with him, as our portion; and the word telleth us it is our duty, and for our good to hope in him, then faith seeth good reason that we should hope in him." As Davenport insisted, "what faith believes, hope expects" (148). For Puritans, striving for Christian hope was the best possible reason to read and write, especially when sorrow made the grounds for such confidence seem especially precarious. If sin and its wages, so clearly illustrated by the loss at hand, bore ample witness to the rigors of the law, faith in Christ's power to save brought home the consolations of the gospel. Through the reading and writing of elegy, Puritans drew from the occasion of death an inner echo of the twofold revelation of Scripture itself.[8]

Puritan discourse drew power from its capacity to make salvation seem more accessible. Writing and reading helped Puritans pursue a meditative *kenosis*, a self-emptying that echoed Christ's humility in assuming "the likeness of men" when "he humbled himself, and became obedient unto death, even the death of the cross" (Phil. 2:8). While the Son had divested himself of a measure of his divinity in order to become human, believers were encouraged to divest themselves of a measure of their humanity as a prelude to becoming divine. And insofar as being human meant being sinful, the meditating Puritan was encouraged to repudiate the very element that Christ had assumed at the Incarnation. In *The Soules Humiliation* Thomas Hooker thus urged believers to "loose your selves, and all ordinances, and creatures, and all that you have, and do, in the Lord Christ" (Miller and Johnson 1:60). Cotton Mather introduced his *Magnalia* with a couplet that encapsulates the ideal of self-emptying: "Quid sum? Nil. – Quis sum? Nullus. – sed gratia *CHRISTI*, / Quod sum, quod vivo, quodque laboro, facit" ("What am I? Nothing. Who am I? No one. But the grace of Christ makes what I am, how I live, and what I do") (1:38). Puritan poets enacted artistic parallels to redemptive selflessness by emulating, always in affect and often in form, the biblical "psalms, hymns, and spiritual songs" (Eph. 5:19, Col. 3:16) that God had provided as helps to a vivid, active faith. To find the self one had to lose it, and as Paul attested, the true believer's reliance on divine power stemmed from Christ's promise that "My grace is sufficient for thee: for my strength is made perfect in weakness." "Most gladly therefore," Paul concludes, "will I gather glory in my infirmities, that the power of Christ may rest upon me. Therefore I take pleasure in infirmities, in reproaches, in necessities, in persecutions, in distresses for Christ's sake: for when I am weak, then am I strong" (2 Cor. 12:9–10). By confirming the value of affliction "lest I should be exalted above measure through the abundance of the revelations" (2 Cor. 12:7), Paul modeled a redeemed subjectivity in which suffering became a precondition for Christian hope.

The death of a loved one posed a particularly jarring test of this subjectivity, and New England's elegists worked to make the test as explicit as possible. Like all Puritan poetry, the elegy was relentlessly performative – and the specific performance it demanded was the reader's realignment with the perspective on dying afforded by saving grace. Invoking an aesthetic of response, to use Hans Robert Jauss's distinction, rather than an aesthetic of representation (*Aesthetic Experience* 268), the poem challenged readers to become – and helped shape them into – those whom Fish once called a "fit" audience capable of moving the salvific message from page to heart (*Surprised by Sin* 207). The Puritan manner of "completing" such a text was modeled on an engaged reading of the Bible. Enacting a *mimesis* not of the world but of the Word, elegy presented itself as a subtext of Scripture, the deeper text to which the reader was actually responding. Taylor's generalized description of Dewey's inner life provided experiential room in which readers could assess their own relation to the deceased's piety. By ensuring that the paradigms of belief were active, the text brought a sense of control in the face of life's harshest trial, channeling anxiety into a form that effected both its expression and its containment. Poems like Taylor's countered sorrow with the sense that the sinful self – one's own worst enemy – could be overcome even in this worst of times. The elegiac formula – the biblicized speakers, the repeatable scripts of humility and hope, the constant invocations of redemptive hope – enhanced the ease with which readers could feel that the story of the saved soul was being rewritten not only within the deceased but within themselves. In encouraging such a self-reading, this textual ritual did not rely on literary *personas* in the usual sense of the word, no conscious replacing by poet or reader of a bad identity with a better one. Puritans did not believe, even secretly, that they could write or read their way to heaven through willed rhetorical acts. On the contrary, the Puritan elegy helped readers imagine, through the iconized deceased, what they hoped was their deepest and most "real" identity – deepest because it was born of faith and most real because it would outlast the body. Elegy offered an opportunity to assess this self's fit during the meditative pre-death provoked by sorrow.[9]

It might seem that Puritan mourners were placed in a no-win situation, but it is probably more accurate to say that they could not lose. To feel chastened – by the poem, by the loss itself – was the first step toward spiritual renewal. Although it was disquieting for survivors to discover that God had taken a life in order to correct their iniquity, Paul had promised that "Where sin abounded, grace did more abound" (Rom. 5:20). Taylor's elegy might seem to have left its readers horribly confined, presenting them with only the simple choice to "accept or reject" that Iser identifies in all didactic texts (*Act of Reading* 190). The modern preference for textual and psychological open-endedness, however, should not blind us to the fact that the simple decision to accept Christ – the pure "yes" of the renewed will – was the goal of all Puritan reading. For the Puritan mourner, the satisfactions of elegy did not reside in constructing his or her own truths from blanks in an indeterminant text, but in forging stronger and more hopeful connections between a disturbingly volatile identity and a stable truth defined by God's Word. Texts, both oral and written, reduced the ambiguities of being human, and thus fallen, to a choice that most early New Englanders fervently wanted to make. What we would feel as subjective and discursive chains they felt as freedom to become what they most wanted to be.

This literary dynamic operated as a complex of verbal gestures and responses shared, usually unconsciously, by members of close-knit communities. Hall reminds us that Puritan popular religion embraced a "world of wonders," a divinely infused realm whose drama was mirrored in an inner life that replicated the ups and downs of biblical Israel. Elegy helped New Englanders bring the fact of death inside the comprehensible parameters of that world. Elegy's stylized predictability – that which most distances it from modern tastes – was precisely what animated these poems within their hearts. The occasion of death propelled survivors to the center of the world's one story: the struggle of good versus evil. Elegies not only forced mourners to reflect on that story, but helped them feel more prepared as they drew ever closer to the individual crisis of its plot, signaled by their own "Great Change," as they often called it, from earthly sinner to celestial saint.

For those who did not share in this ideological and discursive world, the conventions of Puritan elegy made it ripe for satire long before Silence Dogood's recipe. Thomas Morton's parodic "Carmen Elegiacum," included in his 1637 *New English Canaan*, must have scandalized any first-generation contemporaries who saw it. "Shee was too good for earth, too bad for heaven," Morton concludes, "Why then for hell the match is somewhat even" (275). The subject of Morton's mock elegy escapes to Virginia and recovers from an overdose of New-English zeal, "quite cured of her mellancholly, with the help of the water of Ma-re Mount" (276). Nearly a century later, the young Franklin, dreaming of a life at sea, yearned for just such an escape from a Boston in which Increase and Cotton Mather still wielded considerable power. Morton and Franklin, the cavalier and the deist, were actively hostile to the theology that fueled poems like Taylor's elegy for Dewey. So, too, were later poets and critics, for whom the success of "Lycidas" prompted an equating of pastoral and quasi-pastoral modes with the ideal commemorative poem in English. While it is true, as John Draper noted, that in New England the elegy "retained its most archaic characteristics longer than did the parent stock" (*Funeral Elegy* 176), the term "archaic" is appropriate only if we believe, in accordance with traditional literary history, that literature improves through time as it approaches current values and standards. If we abandon the progressive model, however, and affirm merely that literary codes *change* along with other cultural structures, a less anachronistic view becomes possible. The New England elegy failed to keep pace with English developments not because of colonial stagnation or primitivism, but because it proved a remarkably successful adaptation to the expressive needs of its culture.[10]

In directing the mourner toward inner ceremony, poems like Taylor's were, as Edward Davidson has written of the sermon, "ritual in a serious sense that Puritans would not admit" (504). To read an elegy was to find that it had furthered the self-examination mandated by the theology, not just at times of affliction but as an ongoing habit of mind. This discursive framework fostered what Michael Reed has called "a completely balanced and self generating psychic system capable of producing constant psychic energy for the true believer" (332). New England's elegies, like all elegy, drew heavily on the power of verbal ritual, of speaking in an expected way at the expected times. For the deceased, redemptive energy had reached its desired end in the stasis of eternal peace, and elegy ensured that this energy would not die with the dead – that mourners absorbed it by imagining their capacity to follow them and to walk "by faith, not by sight" (2 Cor. 5:7). Elegists repeatedly transformed the despair and confusion posed by grief into hopeful anticipations of the celestial clarity lined out by Paul: "For now we see through a glass darkly; but then face to face: now I know in part; but then shall I know even as also I am known" (1 Cor. 13:11–12). The poem embodied an act less of art than of faith, not only in the presumption that the deceased had indeed been blessed, but in the conviction that survivors could apply language to the impossible task of commemorating a self who had passed beyond the capacity of language to describe. Strange as it may seem to describe a literary community of anti-ceremonialists in such terms, this was a decidedly *liturgical* use of language. Encouraging redemptive realignment in the face of divine wrath, these poems were not simply texts to read but scripts for what one could become as a result of retracing what they enacted. Puritans did not experience such elegy as "poetry" in our usual sense of the word. Instead, they experienced it – to use a term that would surely anger them – as if it were a Mass. Like the Mass, the elegy addressed an experience of faith that was at once intensely private and richly communal. Like a Mass, too, the poem enacted an ingestive rite, a taking in of the pious dead through the survivor's assimilation of their saintly example. To read such a poem was to heed the deceased as a guide to a transformed identity as Paul's "New Creature," a secret sharer in redemptive mysteries revealed only to Christ's true Brides and internalized by means of right reading and proper mourning.[11]

In performing this office, elegy enacted a more complicated experience of reading than is generally recognized. The chief function of all Puritan poems, including elegies, was not simply to teach the faith – a misunderstanding widespread in the criticism – but to encourage an engaged *response* to the faith by assessing the reader's current relation to it. The self-scrutiny at the heart of Puritan mourning explains why the funeral elegy became the quintessential Puritan poem. The real focus of the poem was not the deceased, for whom God had provided, but the reader whose spiritual fate still hung in the balance. In promoting an ongoing search for personal evidence of extrapersonal pattern, New England's elegists eschewed poetic "originality" in favor of the Bible as an all-encompassing text into which each poem – and each departed saint – was absorbed. Elegiac discourse stabilized in New England because Puritans held stable notions regarding the right uses of poetry and the proper response to loss. As was the case in all Puritan devotional practices, the goal of Puritan mourning was the survivor's transformation from a sinful, indifferent self to a hopeful pilgrim actively engaged in the Pauline struggle against sin. Like all ritual texts, the Puritan elegy imposed order onto chaos as a means of transforming fear into hope. The terrifying prospect of death was made less fearsome through the commemoration of the deceased's life as an orderly pilgrimage to glory. This journey could be proclaimed only if its patterns were set forth with absolute clarity, only if the dead were portrayed in terms of what Scheick has called "the broad configuration of saintliness" ("Tombless Virtue" 296). This pattern is what Taylor encouraged his readers not merely to find in David Dewey but to take from his passing. Death could be rewritten into victory, as Paul promised in Corinthians – or "Made Usefull," as Taylor proclaimed in one of his Meditations (*Poems* 55) – through poems that asserted divine purpose in response to the shock and disorientation of grief. As the deceased was transformed, so was the mourner, both as an individual and as a member of a redeemed community. Modern distinctions between "private" and "public" and between "literary" and "popular" would have meant little to early New Englanders, especially as a basis for judging poems of loss. Equally problematic would be our distinction between the "personal" and the "conventional." Although Taylor speaks the Dewey poem in a voice that we might term prophetic or apostolic, he did not consider that voice to be an artistic, psychological, or theological construction. In his view, it was merely his true voice as mourner, friend, minister, and poet. What we would call the "real" Edward Taylor, the directly expressive, literally autobiographical identity stressed by traditional literary history, has been profoundly shaped by a performative ritual of mourning and writing. While the Dewey poem offers a clear expression of personal grief, we will not find an unmediated, "personal" Taylor in its lines.[12]

Recovering the ritual dimension of the Puritan elegy allows access to these poems as texts capable of moving their initial readers by easing them through the darkest night that life still poses. An anthropology of Puritan reading, one that is sensitive to how early New Englanders themselves experienced their poetry, allows us to locate, in Karl Keller's phrase, "a serious esthetic *within* Puritanism rather than at its limits" (*Example* 1). It also permits a glimpse of what Jane Donahue Eberwein has called "the human experience of Puritanism" (8). However alien or off-putting their theology, New England Puritans were human beings struggling to oppose the pain of loss with the cultural tools available to them. Their experience of language and loss may not have been ours, but it was human nonetheless.

3

Weep for yourselves: the Puritan theology of mourning

What, for early New Englanders, did it mean to die? And what did death's uncertainties mean for those charged with the sad task of commemorating loss? For these as for most questions, Puritans sought answers in God's Word, developing views that they considered to be fully biblical even though the Bible gave mixed messages regarding death's significance and proper observance. Although these varied messages in part reflected broader contrasts between the two Testaments, Puritans harmonized the differences in a manner consistent with their approach to biblical typology. From the Hebrew Bible they borrowed the *how* of mourning, including many of its forms and conventions. From the New Testament they derived the *why* of mourning, the spiritual goals that would justify the use of those forms and conventions. In order to understand the construction of death and commemoration fostered by New England's elegists, we must first consider what they found when they turned to the Scriptures for guidance.

Like all ancient peoples, the authors of the Hebrew Bible pondered the mysteries of death. Unlike many, however, they refused to romanticize it, generally seeing it as a malevolent force nearly equivalent to faithlessness. Life and death were linked in the Law with "blessing and cursing: therefore choose life, that both thou and thy seed may live" (Deut. 30:19). The dead descended into Sheol, a shadowy pit invoked in the recognition that "we must needs die, and are as water spilt on the ground, which cannot be gathered up again" (2 Sam. 14:14). Everyone, regardless of moral or spiritual standing, came to the same end: "the dead know not anything, neither have they any more a reward, for the memory of them is forgotten" (Eccles. 9:5). The Psalmist frequently begged God to effect his deliverance by pointing out that "in death there is no remembrance of thee: in the grave who shall give thee thanks?" (Ps. 6:5; see also Ps. 88). The book of Job gave classic expression to death's oblivion in a passage that Anne Bradstreet would import into

"Contemplations": "But man dieth, and wasteth away: yea, man giveth up the ghost, and where is he? As the waters fail from the sea, and the flood decayeth and drieth up: So man lieth down, and riseth not: till the heavens be no more, they shall not awake, nor be raised out of their sleep" (Job 14:10–12). In Job, as elsewhere, the underworld is a "land of darkness, as darkness itself; and of the shadow of death, without any order, and where the light is as darkness" (Job 10:22). In the face of this inescapable void, the most practical advice seemed to come from Solomon, who counseled that "Whatsoever thy hand findeth to do, do it with thy might; for there is no work, nor device, nor knowledge, nor wisdom, in the grave, whither thou goest" (Eccles. 9:10).

The gloomy silence of Sheol was not to be disturbed. The legal and prophetic books alike forbade contact with the dead as an affront to Yahweh, evidence of an impious trust in necromancy and "an abomination unto the Lord" (Deut. 18:12): "Regard not them that have familiar spirits, neither seek after wizards, to be defiled by them: I am the Lord your God" (Lev. 19:31). Conjuring up the "familiar spirits" of the departed was punishable by death (Lev. 20:27). The most famous breach of this command, Saul's consultation with the witch of Endor (1 Sam. 28:3–20), came to a morally predictable end. Beset by a vast Philistine army, Saul, who had banished keepers of "familiar spirits" and "wizards" from the land, could obtain no divine guidance through ordinary channels, "neither by dreams, nor by Urim, nor by prophets." The witch suspects a trap to expose her, but after Saul promises not to punish her and commands her to "Bring me up Samuel," she sees "gods ascending out of the earth" and the old prophet in a mantle. Samuel's ghost is hardly benign. Before predicting Saul's death in battle, he replies, "Wherefore then dost thou ask of me, seeing the Lord is departed from thee, and is become thine enemy?" Elsewhere we learn that "Saul died for his transgression which he committed against the Lord, even against the word of the Lord, which he kept not, and also for asking counsel of one that had a familiar spirit, to inquire of it; And inquired not of the Lord" (1 Chron. 10:13–14). Isaiah reiterated the logic behind the severity of the injunction: "when they shall say unto you, Seek unto them that have familiar spirits, and unto wizards that peep and that mutter; should not a people seek unto their God?" (Isa. 8:19).

The strict separation of the dead from the living is countered by scattered references to immortality and coming resurrections as expressions of divine power. As the ancient Song of Hannah confirmed, "The Lord killeth, and maketh alive: he bringeth down to the grave, and bringeth up" (1 Sam. 2:6). The Psalmist similarly attested to God's ability to transform grief into joy: "Thou hast turned for me my mourning into dancing: thou hast put off my sackcloth, and girded me with gladness" (Ps. 30:11). Isaiah projects such deliverance into the future, proclaiming that Israel's "dead men shall live, together with my dead body shall they arise. Awake and sing, ye that dwell in dust: for thy dew is as the dew of herbs, and the earth shall cast out the dead" (Isa. 26:19). At the fall of Ephraim, who is cast out from the "children," God promises that "I will ransom them from the power of the grave; I will redeem them from death: O death, I will be thy plagues; O grave, I will be thy destruction: repentance shall be hid from mine eyes" (Hos. 13:14). Ezekiel similarly urges Israel to repent and live: "Cast away from you all your transgressions, whereby ye have transgressed; and make you a new heart and a new spirit: for why will ye die, O house of Israel?" (Ezek. 18:31). Such pronouncements spoke to a communal restoration of God's people rather than individual resurrections. Although Ezekiel's prophecy of the regathering of the "dry" bones in the valley anticipates the collective triumph of a postexilic Israel, the text does not suggest that the pious dead would live again on earth. "Son of man, these bones are the whole house of Israel: behold they say, Our bones are dried, and our hope is lost" (Ezek. 37:11). God pledges that if Ezekiel will spread the divine word, "I will open your graves, and cause you to come up out of your graves, and bring you into the land of Israel" (37:12). Later Jewish traditions laid greater stress on a coming resurrection, though the issue was hotly debated. The Book of Daniel closes with a prophecy that Michael shall rise and destroy all but those whose names are "found written in the book": "And many of them that sleep in the dust of the earth shall awake, some to everlasting life, and some to shame and everlasting contempt" (Dan. 12:11–12). Although some of the Qumran materials corroborate this expectation and intensify it with messianic overtones, not all segments of postexilic Judaism agreed. In New Testament times the Sadducees were prominent among those who denied a future resurrection altogether (Mark 12:18, Luke 20:27, Acts 23:8).

Tentative expressions of a possibility of resurrection were reinforced by three incidents in which faith reversed death's finality. Two of these raisings are deliberate and one is inadvertent, and the deliberate miracles appear to be variations on a single story. When a poor widow of Zarephath obeys Elijah's request to bake him a cake even though her stores are almost empty, he rewards her with a self-replenishing barrel of meal. Soon, though, her son falls ill, "and his sickness was so sore, that there was no breath left in him." After the widow mocks the "man of God" for permitting the death, Elijah lies on the child in what appears to be a ritual exorcism: "the soul of the child came into him again, and he revived." In a reversal so sudden as to be comic, the widow proclaims that "Now by this I know that thou art a man of God, and that the word of the Lord in thy mouth is truth" (1 Kings 17:10–24). A second version of the story involves Elijah's successor, Elisha. A wealthy woman of Shunem gives Elisha food and lodging; a grateful Elisha predicts that she will bear a son. Later the boy is suddenly stricken in the fields. Refusing to call on Elisha's servant Gehazi, the mother insists on speaking to the prophet himself. Elisha sends the servant ahead with instructions to "lay my staff upon the face of the child," but when Elisha and the mother arrive at the house they learn that the surrogate rite has failed. Elisha then repeats the lying-on ritual from the Elijah story. After he performs it twice, "the child sneezed seven times, and the child opened his eyes" (2 Kings 4:8–37). In the story of the accidental resurrection, a prophet's power to raise the dead extends beyond his own demise. A burial party surprised by a "band of men" flees after dropping the corpse into Elisha's grave: "and when the man was let down, and touched the bones of Elisha, he revived, and stood up on his feet" (2 Kings 13:21). While this last story would eventually fuel the veneration of relics among medieval Christians, it had no such impact on ancient Judaism. Indeed, all three stories were isolated as special occurrences whose repetition was not to be expected. Details from these ancient stories would find their way into the miracle narratives of the gospels and Acts, and from there, into Puritan narratives of the soul's passage to eternal life. But Jewish tradition gave the stories little theological import beyond vivid historical demonstrations of a prophet's power.

A theological context for such resurrections emerged, of course, with Christianity, when a relatively minor element in Jewish thought became the central premise of the new faith. Christ promised that "as the Father raiseth up the dead, and quickeneth them; even so the Son quickeneth whom he will." And again: "He that heareth my word, and believeth on him that sent me, hath everlasting life, and shall not come into condemnation; but is passed from death unto life" (John 5:21, 24). Even more famous were Christ's words to Nicodemus: "For God so loved the world, that he gave his only begotten Son, that whosoever believeth in him should not perish, but have everlasting life" (John 3:16). Paul hailed Christ's conquest of death in an early hymn quoted in 1 Corinthians, framed as a fulfillment of Isaiah's prophecy that "He will swallow up death in victory" (Isa. 25:8) and of Hosea's promise that "O grave, I will be thy destruction" (Hos. 13:14): "So when this corruptible shall have put on incorruption, and this mortal shall have put on immortality, then shall be brought to pass the saying that is written, Death is swallowed up in victory. O death, where is thy sting? O grave, where is thy victory?" (1 Cor. 15:54–55). In the next verse Paul theologizes death by asserting that "The sting of death is sin: and the strength of sin is the law" (56). In Romans Paul confirmed the personal resurrection of believers as the chief reward of faith, promising that "if Christ be in you, the body is dead because of sin; but the Spirit is life because of righteousness. But if the Spirit of him that raised up Jesus from the dead dwell in you, he that raised up Christ from the dead shall also quicken your mortal bodies by his Spirit that dwelleth in you" (Rom. 8:10–11). Paul similarly promised the community at Corinth that "God hath both raised up the Lord, and will also raise up us by his own power" (1 Cor. 6:14). For Paul, as for his New England successors, the real enemy was not death but the sin that made humans vulnerable to it: "O wretched man that I am! who shall deliver me from the body of this death?" (Rom. 7:24). Faith would transform utterly the sinful body, "sown in corruption," "dishonour," and "weakness," into a new entity "raised in incorruption," "glory," and "power": "It is sown a natural body; it is raised a spiritual body" (1 Cor. 15:42–44). Through grace, the carnal self would be purified: "But where sin abounded, grace did much more abound: That as sin hath reigned unto death, even so might grace reign, through righteousness, unto eternal life, by Jesus Christ our Lord" (Rom. 5:20–21). Paul repeatedly defined the essence of life and death in terms of belief: "For the wages of sin is death; but the gift of God is eternal life, through Jesus Christ our Lord" (Rom. 6:23).

The chief claim of early Christianity was that what the Hebrew prophets did for a select few, Christ would do for all who believed. A key sign of faith in deliverance from the "body of this death" was a transformed attitude toward death, a readiness to die voiced in Paul's proclamation that "We are confident, I say, and willing rather to be absent from the body, and to be present with the Lord" (2 Cor. 5:8). In a young sect subject to persecution, overcoming the fear of death quickly became a hallmark of true belief. Thus began a tradition of Christian martyrdom first exemplified by Stephen (Acts 7:59–60) and elaborated through Paul's tropes of death and rebirth: "we which live are alway delivered unto death for Jesus's sake, that the life also of Jesus might be made manifest in our mortal flesh" (2 Cor. 4:11). "For if we have been planted together in the likeness of his death, we shall be also in the likeness of his resurrection" (Rom. 6:5). The reward of "dying" in Christ, whether literally or spiritually, was atonement – "For he that is dead is freed from sin" (Rom. 6:7) – and eternal companionship with the Savior. Not even death, Paul declares, "shall be able to separate us from the love of God, which is in Jesus Christ our Lord" (Rom. 8:38–9). The gospels, especially Mark, took up the theme of martyrdom as a portal to glory; the book of Revelation broadened it by linking personal death and resurrection with the fate of the world, transposing the fate of the individual believer into a cosmic framework. "And they overcame him [Satan] by the blood of the Lamb, and by the word of their testimony; and they loved not their lives unto the death" (Rev. 12:11). Thus, early Christians believed, was fulfilled Isaiah's prophecy of a collective redemption in which "the Lord God will wipe away tears from off all faces" (Isa. 25:8). The final reward revealed on Patmos reiterated, on the grandest possible scale, the promised reversal of human suffering: "And God shall wipe away all tears from their eyes; and there shall be no more death, neither sorrow, nor crying, neither shall there be any more pain: for the former things are passed away" (Rev. 21:4). This prophecy of the latter days extended the promise of individual rebirth to an entire redeemed community, a notion vital to the communal exhortations issued by New England's elegists.

Such promises were grounded, of course, in the story of Christ's Resurrection, a narrative prefigured in Elijah's circumvention of death when he mounted up to the skies in a chariot and left his mantle to Elisha. A similar passing of salvific power was stressed in the gospel narratives of the Transfiguration (Matt. 17:1–13; Mark 9:2–13; Luke 9:28–36), in which the appearance of Moses and Elias (Elijah) suggested a transfer of legal and prophetic authority to Jesus, a theme reinforced by the equation of John the Baptist with Elijah as the messianic forerunner (Matt. 17:12–13, Mark 9:13). In the gospels, as in the Elijah/Elisha cycle, three episodes demonstrated this power. In the first, Jesus raises the daughter of Jairus (Luke 8:40–56), usually equated with "one of the rulers of the synagogue" (Mark 5:21–43) and a "certain ruler" (Matt. 9:18–26). The second episode is the raising of the widow's son, the young man of Nain (Luke 7:12–16). The third and most dramatic raising, which we will examine a bit later, occurs only in the Gospel of John: the story of Lazarus. Christ transferred his power to raise the dead to the disciples in his instructions for the mission: "And, as ye go, preach, saying, The kingdom of heaven is at hand. Heal the sick, cleanse the lepers, raise the dead, cast out devils: freely ye have received, freely give" (Matt. 10:7–8). Peter later exercised this sacred power in Joppa by raising Tabitha/Dorcas (Acts 9:36–42). So did Paul, who showed enviable patience as well as piety by raising a young man from Troas who had nodded off during one of his sermons and fallen from a loft (Acts 20:8–12).

From these diverse biblical traditions Puritans developed a theology of death centering on Pauline self-division as an inner recapitulation of the opposition of Fall and Resurrection which they saw as the underlying plot of the two Testaments. Dying occupied the liminal space between carnal and gracious identity; which one would prevail within the believer remained uncertain until the moment of death. Although earthly assurances of salvation could never be total, the optimistic eschatology of the New Testament presented each saved soul as another Lazarus, raised to eternal life by the continuing power of Christ's sacrifice. Puritan mourning focused on witnessing to contemporary reenactments of Christ's Resurrection, celebrating the passage of another graced soul from earth to heaven, sin to perfection, and time to eternity. Old Testament models of verbal mourning were thus placed in a New Testament context as a means of securing the rite's redemptive efficacy.

Old Testament mourning was public and demonstrative, marked by elaborate ritual gestures common throughout the ancient Near East. At the loss of his children, Job "arose, and rent his mantle, and shaved his head, and fell down upon the ground, and worshipped" (Job 1:20). When Jacob thought that Joseph was dead, he "rent his clothes, and put sackcloth upon his loins, and mourned for his son many days" (Gen. 37:34). Jacob was himself mourned for seventy days in Egypt (Gen. 50:3), and Joseph mourned him with "a very great and sore lamentation" for seven more days at his burial in Canaan (Gen. 50:10). Aaron and Moses were mourned for thirty days (Num. 20:29; Deut. 34:8). The ill-fated Amalekite who brought the news that Saul and Jonathan had died came "with his clothes rent, and earth upon his head" (2 Sam. 1:2), and when her husband Manasseh died, Judith remained at home for over three years, fasting and wearing widow's weeds and sackcloth (Judith 8:46). Royal deaths were followed by seven days of fasting (1 Sam. 31:11–13). "All the people wept" for Abner, tearing their clothing and wearing sackcloth and ashes (2 Sam. 3:32). Professional mourners were often engaged: Joab hired a "wise woman" from Tekoah to pose as a mourner

in order to intercede for Absalom (2 Sam. 14:2), and at the death of King
Josiah "all the singing men and the singing women spake of Josiah in
their lamentations to this day" (2 Chron. 35:25).[1]

Curbs were sometimes placed on such excessive mourning practices
as self-mutilation and shaving the head (Lev. 19:28, Deut. 14:1), and
taboos against contacting the dead were reflected in the fact that priests
could not "defile" themselves with the usual rituals of grief, not even for
parents or siblings (Lev. 21:10–11; Num. 6:7). Isaiah mocked the sumptu-
ousness of funerary monuments when he attacked the vanity of Shebna,
a "treasurer" who "heweth him out a sepulchre on high, and that
graveth an habitation for himself in a rock": "Behold, the Lord will carry
thee away with a mighty captivity, and will surely cover thee" (Isa.
22:15–17). Early Christians found further justification for restrained
mourning in Christ's victory over death. To be sure, grieving for the loss
of believers was a duty that began with the faith's first martyr, when
"devout men carried Stephen to his burial, and made great lamentation
over him" (Acts 8:2). But the key word here, as Puritans saw it, was
"devout." Asserting a point that early New Englanders took fully to
heart, Paul argued that excessive mourning obscured the difference
between believers and pagans: "But I would not have you to be ignorant, brethren, concerning them which are asleep, that ye sorrow not,
even as others which have no hope. For if we believe that Jesus died and
rose again, even so them also which sleep in Jesus will God bring with
him" (1 Thess. 4:13–14). Paul recommended a stoic response consistent
with the notion that this world was merely a preparation for the next.
"Rejoice with them that do rejoice," he counseled, "and weep with them
that weep. Be of the same mind one toward another. Mind not high
things, but condescend to men of low estate. Be not wise in your own
conceits" (Rom. 12:15–16). We have heard these words before, as a key
text underlying the Puritan desire on both sides of the Atlantic to write
a plainer sort of elegy, one that spoke to the imperatives of salvation
rather than art. Support for emotional and expressive restraint, however,
came from an even higher authority than Paul. After his sentencing Jesus
turns to a crowd of women "who bewailed and lamented him."
"Daughters of Jerusalem," he warns, "weep not for me, but weep for
yourselves, and for your children" (Luke 23:28). Puritans routinely cited
Christ's words as witness to the absurdity of weeping for a Savior in
heaven and for those who followed him there. When they eulogized their
dead, they felt that they were obeying Christ's command to shift the
focus of mourning from the dead to the living, to survivors whose final

peace was not yet secure. Like Paul, early New Englanders were theological ironists, basing their commemorations on a faith-based inversion of "life" and "death" set forth, among other places, in Romans: "Likewise reckon ye also yourselves to be dead indeed unto sin, but alive unto God through Jesus Christ our Lord" (Rom. 6:11). This inversion was tantamount to a shift from natural to gracious perspectives reflected in the promise that a hearer of the Word "is passed from death unto life" (John 5:24). This promise formed the doctrinal and homiletic core of the Puritan text of loss.

Consistent with the habit of reading the two Testaments as prophecy and fulfillment, Puritans combined outward forms derived from the Old Testament with an inward spirit derived from the New. Old Testament precedents for the duty to mourn included Jeremiah's lament for Josiah (2 Chron. 35:25) and the lament of the daughters of Israel for Jephthah's daughter (Judges 11:40). The chief precursor of the commemorative poet, however, was David, Israel's "sweet singer," especially in such texts as Psalm 38, a brief lament for rival Abner recorded in 2 Samuel, and the famous dirge for Saul and Jonathan. The simple lament for Abner spoke deeply to the Puritan sense of communal loss: "Know ye not that there is a prince and a great man fallen this day in Israel?" (2 Sam. 3:38). The elegiac model that Puritans most frequently cited was the most celebrated funeral poem in the Hebrew Bible: David's song for Saul and Jonathan (2 Sam. 1:19–27). This "Song of the Bow" offered sacred precedent to which New England poets routinely appealed in defense of the elegiac poem. In his elegy for Thomas Shepard, Urian Oakes invokes both of David's laments. While Oakes ends the poem by urging readers to "Mourne that this *Great Man's* faln in *Israel:* / Lest it be said, *with him New-England fell!* (Meserole 220), he opens it by invoking the fuller precedent of that "Elegiack Knell" in which "*Israel's* singer sweet" "Rung out his dolours, when dear *Jona'than* fell" (Meserole 208). In his poem for Samuel Hooker, Edward Taylor declares that it would be "Sacraledge" not to proclaim Hooker's worth: "shall brave Jon'than dy? / And David's place be empty? Sling ly by?" (*Minor Poetry* 116). Elijah Corlet made more oblique reference to David's precedent by calling Thomas Hooker "eagle-like" ("aquilae similis") (Kaiser 17), an echo of David's affirmation that Saul and Jonathan were "swifter than eagles" (2 Sam. 1:23). Puritans saw David's elegy as a poet's poem – the prototype of the highest use to which poetic art could be put. Bradstreet and Taylor both wrote verse paraphrases of the lament, and it was routinely included in the many collections of Old Testament "psalms and hymns and spiritual songs" (Eph. 5:19, Col. 3:16) that appeared during the sixteenth and seventeenth centuries.

For Puritans, the power of this precedent resided in the fact that David linked commemoration to moral commentary. The equation of personal loss with communal tragedy, a link dependent on idealizing the dead as "the beauty of Israel," emerges immediately: "how are the mighty fallen!" David's grief is political – the sad news must not be published to the Philistines, "lest the daughters of the uncircumcised triumph" – but it is also cosmic, as he invokes nature as a symbolic mourner by calling on the "mountains of Gilboa" to withhold dew, rain, and crops in sympathy with the loss. A catalogue of virtues confirms Saul and Jonathan's prowess ("they were swifter than eagles"), bravery ("stronger than lions"), charm ("lovely and pleasant in their lives"), and loyalty ("and in their death they were not divided"). After calling on the "daughters of Israel" to remember Saul's generosity and the prosperity he brought, David acknowledges his deeper and more personal attachment to Saul's son: "I am distressed for thee, my brother Jonathan: very pleasant hast thou been unto me: thy love to me was wonderful, passing the love of women." The entire poem witnesses death's cruel irony. The "mighty" are now "fallen," "slain upon thy high places," and for all their power, the "weapons of war" have "perished." Indeed, the loss seems to nullify God's special regard for his chosen: Saul is dead "as though he had not been anointed with oil." This view of death as the bearer of grim reversals extends to the song's narrative frame. The bringer of the sad news, who had obeyed the defeated Saul's command to kill him, is executed for killing a divinely chosen king. "Thy blood be on thy head," David tells the messenger's corpse, "for thy mouth hath testified against thee, saying, I have slain the Lord's anointed" (2 Sam. 1:15). All of these themes, including the survivor's culpability, were incorporated into Puritan elegy. New Englanders would take the mandate to idealize the dead, however, far beyond David's limits, extending it to encompass resurrection motifs at the heart of Christian belief. Elegists repeatedly confirmed that at death, elect souls had become far more than "mighty" personages. Perfected by Christ's grace, they were nothing less than extensions of Christ himself, heavenly beings whose glory mirrored their redeemer's. The proper commemoration of such souls required something more than the exterior form provided by David's words: it required a gracious spirit, rooted in an artistic humility that was based on the recognition that mere outward imitations of David's elegy would fail utterly. As Paul had said of all such legal performances, "the commandment, which was ordained to life, I found to be unto death" (Rom. 7:10). Like every other duty foreshadowed in the Old Dispensation, the Song of the Bow needed to be performed with a gracious spirit.

While David provided a supreme verbal model for New England's poems of loss, Christ himself lined out the eschatological framework by which that model assumed redemptive force. Christ's own "elegy," a lament for Lazarus reported in the third person, comprises the shortest verse in the Bible: "Jesus wept" (John 11:35). For New Englanders, the full import of the epigram came from what followed Christ's tears: a resurrection that demonstrated the triumphant power of belief. In the story Martha dramatizes the progressive deepening of this belief. Her initial proclamation of faith – "Lord, if thou hadst been here, my brother had not died" (John 11:21) – is followed by an exchange that Puritans considered a defining vignette of redemptive mourning. After Martha states that God will grant Jesus's requests, Jesus declares, "Thy brother shall rise again." Although Martha assumes that he is referring to a general resurrection of the sort prophesied by Ezekiel, Jesus corrects her with an "I am" pronouncement characteristic of the Gospel of John: "I am the resurrection, and the life: he that believeth in me, though he were dead, yet shall he live: And whosoever liveth and believeth in me shall never die." When Jesus asks Martha "Believest thou this?" her response confirms the faith that Puritans believed made all such miracles possible: "Yea, Lord: I believe that thou art the Christ, the Son of God, which should come into the world" (John 11:22–27). Committing himself to the miracle "that they may believe that thou hast sent me," Jesus then cries "with a loud voice, Lazarus, come forth" (John 11:42–43). Staged as a series of deferrals of the central miracle, the story presents the raising as the endpoint of an elaborate confessional process, a gradual movement from shock and doubt – Martha remarks that the body will stink after four days in the tomb (John 11:39) – to pronouncement and deed. The episode begins in tears modeling natural response to loss which Puritan elegists strove to overcome. Martha's sister Mary gives equal witness to such response: "When Jesus therefore saw her weeping, and the Jews also weeping which came with her, he groaned in the spirit, and was troubled" (John 11:33). At this point the reader recalls Jesus's initial reaction to the news of Lazarus's illness, the confident proclamation that "This sickness is not unto death, but for the glory of God, that the Son of God might be glorified thereby" (John 11:4). The deeper focus of the Lazarus story, as Puritans read it, was the one that they brought to the center of elegy: not life and death, but belief and unbelief. Lazarus's raising anticipates another feature of New England's elegies by dividing its witnesses along this line, confirming the faith of Christ's followers but hardening Christ's enemies in their opposition: "Then from that day forth they took counsel together for to put him to death" (John 11:53). In the Lazarus story, the movement from mourning to miracle results in a community of belief – a sequence that Puritans followed in their own texts of loss.

The tension between "groaning in the spirit" and celebrating a holy life; the ultimate conquest of death by faith; the utter dependence on Christ for recovery from loss; the salvific inversion of life and death; the reinscription of mourning as a confirmation of faith; the sense of communal isolation within a scornful world; the power of sacred words uttered "with a loud voice"; the culminating focus not on death but on resurrection – these themes worked their way into a Puritan ritual of mourning that was repeated, without significant variation, at each saint's passing. Christ, not the poet, had uttered the restorative command to "come forth," and it remained to the elegist to bear verbal witness to a neobiblical "raising" that had just occurred. Each elegy offered microcosmic reconfirmation of this optimistic eschatology. Many New Englanders, including the influential John Cotton, echoed the first Christians in expecting the arrival of God's Kingdom within their lifetimes. But even those who looked for a more prolonged coming of the latter days shared the view that death was only a temporary state, even for the physical body. For pre- and postmillennialist alike, the eschatology lined out in the "little apocalypse" of Mark 13, the appearance of the dead at the Crucifixion, and the celestial regathering of the blessed set forth in the book of Revelation proclaimed that even though death had split soul from body, it was only a matter of time before Christ would heal the division and restore the believer, perfectly renewed, to the eternal kingdom. The impact of Christian eschatology on Puritan mourning cannot be overstated. It underwrote the elegist's every verbal choice, including the choice to write a poem in the first place. David had provided the generic model and some of the words with which the miracle of redemption could be celebrated. New England poets indeed followed his words, adding others from Scripture to fill out the structure. It was understood, however, that while the elegist would proclaim the deceased's apotheosis, it was Christ himself who had done the actual work, both in deed and in word, and who was thus, in this ultimate sense, the true author of all elegy.

Because death conferred the believer's entry into the heavenly community envisioned on Patmos, elegy was inseparable from hagiography, an embalming of God's "mighty" who were lamented in the tradition of David but celebrated in the spirit of Christ. But while salvation seemed assured for those demonstrable saints whose passing was being marked, survivors were left with a nagging question. It was not David's question: why have the mighty fallen? It wasn't finally even Job's question: why does affliction come to good people? Convinced that they already knew the answer to these riddles, Puritans instead asked a question that could not be answered definitively except through the intervention of faith and time: what about us? Like Donne, they knew for whom the bell tolled, and they had plenty of opportunities to ask the question. It has become a critical and historical commonplace to assert that early New Englanders were obsessed with death. The grim skulls on tombstones, the concern with mortality that pervades Puritan thought, and the preponderance of explicit death-texts – funeral sermons, meditations on mortality, and elegiac poems – all contribute to the widespread image of a people nearly paralyzed by morbidity, trapped in an ongoing contemplation of death which made them forget how to live. We shudder to hear that young children learning their letters from the *New England Primer* met with such admonitions as "*Youth* forward slips, Death soonest nips," complete with a tiny cut showing a skeleton aiming its arrow at a tiny figure (65). We find it macabre that Anne Bradstreet's father carried around a poem – it was reportedly found in his pocket when he died – reminding him that "A death's head on your hand you neede not weare, / A dying head you on your shoulders beare" (Meserole 505). Puzzled, even disturbed, by the relish with which Taylor seems to anticipate death as a joyous passage to a "Shining Habitation" and by his disappointment that his journey has been delayed, we might well join Peter Sacks in finding "severe rationalization" in Puritan attitudes toward loss (363). "Why comst thou then so slowly?" Taylor asks death, "mend thy pace / Thy Slowness me detains from Christ's bright face" (*Minor Poetry* 241, 264). And when, near the end of her life, Bradstreet called for the celestial Bridegroom to "come away" (295), we can easily see her words as a capitulation to a culture of death, sad evidence that Puritan death-obsession finally conquered her exuberant spirit.

It is easy to forget, however, that Bradstreet had voiced the same readiness to die at nineteen, in her earliest dated poem. Writing before her recovery from a serious illness, she declared that "The race is run, the field is won, / The victory's mine I see" (222). This suggests a certain practicality to Puritan death-consciousness: had Bradstreet actually died at nineteen, the loss would not have been all that unusual. "We are not *Ignorant*," Cotton Mather proclaimed, "that we are every Day *Falling*

Asleep; and that the *Night of Death* is hastening upon us" (*Awakening Thoughts* 1). The contemplation of death became a virtual industry in early New England. Countless warnings issued from pens and pulpits to "prepare" for the "Great Change" that marked the end of any chance to repent. "Dying work," Edward Pearse declared in a popular treatise on preparing for death, "is great work" – and it could not be put off until the last minute. While others are dying all around us, Pearse affirmed, "God spares us time after time, but no provision do we make for a dying hour" (10, 35). Mather, arguing that meditating on death was the greatest spur to repentance, recommended the practice as a useful exercise for the Sabbath. "On the *Lord's-Day evening*," Mather wrote, "we may make this one of our exercises: to employ most serious and awful thoughts on that question: 'Should I die this week, what have I left undone, which I should then wish I had made more speed in the doing of'?" (*Bonifacius* 36). Mather's *memento mori* was hardly an abstract exercise. "My friend," he continued, "place thyself in *dying* circumstances; apprehend and realize thy approaching *death*. Suppose thy last hour come; the *decretory* hour; thy breath failing, thy throat rattling, thy hands with a cold sweat upon them, only the turn of the tide expected for thy expiration. In this condition, *what would thou wish to have done, more than thou hast already done, for thy own soul, for thy family, or for the people of God?*" (36).

Many modern readers will recognize this Puritan urgency to seize the day from the famous Enfield sermon of Jonathan Edwards, with its reminder that "there is no other reason to be given, why you have not dropped into hell since you arose in the morning, but that God's hand has held you up" (164). In our disbelief that anyone would sit still for this, we miss Edwards's point: God's mercy was evident in the fact that his hearers were *not* dead. "Now God stands ready to pity you," he assured them: "this is a day of mercy" (167). Pearse anticipated Edwards's call: "How soon may the Word and Ordinances of God, which you now enjoy, be withdrawn from you?" (45). The mercy of continued life, central to death's cultural significance in early New England, was lost on Hawthorne, who remains the principal lens through which many of us still perceive his Puritan forebears. Hawthorne was as hostile to Puritan theology as we moderns are, and it is difficult to finish *The Scarlet Letter* without feeling a measure of relief at the death of its tortured spokesman, Arthur Dimmesdale. In Dimmesdale, a fluttering ghost for too many pages, Puritan death-obsession receives chilling reinscription as social pathology, as perverse wish-fulfillment. This man, we solemnly agree, practically *wills* himself into the grave. Such response embodies a healthy twentieth-century denial of Dimmesdale's tortured gloom. In making it, however, we forget that Dimmesdale is a romantic reconstruction, a man from one era portrayed in terms of another.

Given the varying situational and expressive needs of different cultures, it seems fair to ask whether early New Englanders were actually "obsessed" with death, or whether we are remarkably *un*obsessed with it. If we examine attitudes toward death and dying through the broader lenses of history and anthropology, we discover that we moderns are the odd ones. In contrast to most peoples in most cultures and most eras, we enact a genial conspiracy to make death more tolerable by hiding it, relegating its practical necessities to professionals and construing it as an aberration, an unfortunate breakdown of "natural" processes. To us, death signifies failure. When someone dies we want to know why and how, as if such knowledge will make the loss easier to accept. In contemporary American culture, death is an embarrassing intrusion into an idealized realm of youth, confidence, and accomplishment in which many of us construct our most basic identities. We see death and dying this way in part because our medical technology permits us to do so. We live longer and better than our forebears, and once we begin to die, we are often separated from families and communities with an abruptness unheard of only a few generations ago, ending our days in hospitals, hospices, or rest homes, tended by strangers who are paid to look after us. Our corpses are frequently prepared to look "natural" – that is, *not* dead – and our obsequies take place in funeral "homes" that imitate Victorian parlors, perfect places for a subdued social gathering. Most basically, the fact of death is an affront to our desire for rational control, our militant individualism, our faith in progress, our boundless confidence. Three factors – the spread of AIDS, the increase in gun-related violence, and the overall aging of the American population – may yet force us to think differently. So far, though, our culture has largely succeeded in repressing the existence of death and dying. Death remains isolated from our daily lives unless, by occupation or temperament, we choose to incorporate it.[2]

Writers ranging from Jessica Mitford to Philippe Ariès have made the modern denial of death well known, and I cite it neither to argue that things should be different nor to invoke nostalgia for an earlier, less anesthetized era. I wish merely to point out how difficult it is for most of us to imagine a different view of death or, more basically, a different way of life in which our elaborate structures of denial would be considered not just impractical but untenable. Puritans were "obsessed" with death, if we wish to use the term, for two reasons. First, like all preindustrial Europeans, they knew death as a constant and unrelenting presence in their lives. They were on intimate terms with it, and made no attempt to create structures by which dying could be isolated from living. Second, their theology invested death with supreme importance as the threshold between the human and divine realms. As Pearse confirmed, the Devil raged most fiercely at two times in the believer's life: "when a Man is going from Sin to Grace" at conversion, and "When a Man is going from Grace to Glory" at death (11). The power of death assumed social as well as theological form – and the two arenas reinforced each other in a symbiosis that intensified their impact for as long as Puritan culture retained its vitality.

In order to imagine historical conditions in which a death-centered ideology might have adaptive utility, we need to remember death's greater visibility in preindustrial times. Although the infant mortality rate was probably slightly lower in New England than in England and Europe, it has been estimated that in seventeenth-century Andover and Ipswich, one out of ten children died at birth or very soon after. In more densely populated areas like Boston, the rate may have been one out of three (Slater 16). As late as 1734 Franklin brooded over a contemporary calculation that "one half of Mankind" did not survive to the age of sixteen, and that another quarter died before reaching thirty (228). Such facts make it seem less odd that although David Dewey died at what we would call a "young" thirty-six, Taylor's elegy does not bother to mention the illness that killed him. Taylor's omission was typical – and telling. Puritans considered "premature" death to be merely an especially poignant demonstration of the normal scheme of things. To die young was not to be cursed; on the contrary, to live long was to be *blessed*. Benjamin Colman, in a 1714 funeral sermon for fourteen-year-old Elizabeth Wainwright, urged parents to prepare their children for the very real possibility that they could die at any time by putting "them betimes on preparing for Death: they will die never the sooner for it, but may much the better, and you'll have the more peace and comfort in their death, if they are *suddenly* taken from you." Early death was not without lofty precedent. Colman reminded his hearers that Christ himself "has *sanctify'd an Early Death*, by dying in the *prime* of the Life of Man" (*Devout Contemplation* 48, 29). The specific cause of death was relatively unimportant to Puritans, who saw death not as a variable but as the constant, both theologically and experientially. In their view, to "explain" it in natural or scientific terms was really to offer no explanation at all.[3]

To be sure, some elegies do state the circumstances of the death. One of John Saffin's poems for his wife Martha records that she died of small-pox (20), and John Wilson notes that Abigaill Tompson froze in a snow-drift on her way to the Braintree church (Murdock 8). Deodat Lawson published a broadside lament for Captain Anthony Collamore of Scituate, whose ship struck a reef in the winter of 1693 (Winslow 19). When Collamore's grandson Isaac Stetson drowned in 1718, Nathaniel Pitcher's broadside elegy not only revealed the cause of death in an anagram – "'Tis Cast on Sea" – but included an engraving of a floundering ship (Winslow 33). A 1667 broadside declared that Lydia Minot of Dorchester had died in childbirth (Winslow 7), and in a pre-elegy for James Bayley of Roxbury, Nicholas Noyes took a singularly unsentimental view of Bayley's agonizing illness by drawing out several pious puns on the soon-to-be fatal "Stone" that was destroying Bayley's kidneys and bladder. Even if "this Stone should do its worse" and "if thou shouldst be Stone'd to Death," Noyes consoles his friend, "Thou wilt like *Stephen* fall asleep / And free from pain for ever keep" (Winslow 21). Such medical specificity, however, was the exception. Most elegists made Taylor's choice in the Dewey poem – and for the reasons Wilson suggests when he cites drowning as merely the "outward cause" of Joseph Brisco's passing (Meserole 384). As for the underlying cause of Brisco's death or anyone else's, Puritans felt that they already knew the answer. It was not because of treacherous seas, inadequate diets, chill winds, hostile Indians, mysterious microbes, poor sanitation, or medical backwardness. While these were among the terrifying and often unrec-ognized forms that death assumed, death's efficient cause was always sin – and its final cause was a God who had given fair warning before car-rying out the promised punishment. On this point early New England's elegists were brutally clear. In a 1717 funeral sermon for Wait Winthrop, Cotton Mather invoked a common theme by chastising "you surviving Friends of the Dead" for forgetting the fundamental axiom of belief, God's omnipotence: "surely you will now see enough to silence all *Murmurs*, all *Complaints* under your Bereavements? 'Tis your SAVIOUR, who has done, what is come to pass" (*Hades* 121). The same lesson held for private losses. In elegies for her grandchildren, Bradstreet reminded herself and her family that children die by "His hand alone" (235). Puritans were not afraid to put Job's great question in its most extreme form: why does God kill us? And when they tried to read the riddle, they found an obvious and ready answer echoing down from Eden. For them, the real mystery was why, given the convicting evidence of human corruption, God allowed them to live. Even more mysteriously, why would he let some of them live eternally, and in bliss?

The Puritan view of death was inseparable from the Puritan view of life, especially inner life. Early New Englanders conceptualized death, along with nearly everything else, in terms of the dichotomous experience of true belief, the ongoing struggle between the sinful self of the first birth and the saintly self born at conversion. The volatile cohabitation of these inner dimensions of identity defined the saint's life in the world, and the struggle ceased only at death, when the gracious soul achieved liberating separation from the sluggish, froward body. This cycle of belief provided the foundation for a theology of death, attitudes toward grief and mourning, and funerary practices. The principal assumption was that in saint and sinner alike, the entity that died was wholly "natural," born to sin and defined by carnal appetites. One such appetite, the human propensity to place love for the creatures above love for the Creator, was exposed fully and tellingly in survivors by the very fact of grief. Indeed, Puritans repeatedly confirmed that a person could die from being the object of too much love. Such a death brought a hard lesson for those whose affections had become so tragically misaligned. To grieve excessively over the loss only added sin to sin, a further witness to the survivor's continued indulgence of carnal preferences. Mather conceded his own need for such correction when he buried his 73-year-old mother. Preaching on the benefits of a mother's love, he nonetheless reminded himself and his hearers that God's blessings were infinitely greater. A caring mother was a marvelous gift, but such *"Temporal Consolations,"* he warned, "must not be too long dwelt upon" (*Essay* 67).

It is on this point, surely, that the Puritan theology of death strikes us moderns as being just plain wrong, its demands hopelessly at odds with the simple facts of being human. Puritans, however, held the opposite view. The despair they felt when tragedy struck only seemed to prove the truth of their convictions. Although they conceded that it was natural to grieve, this very naturalness was precisely what made grief suspect. Sorrow was, by definition, a smarting at God's will, vivid evidence of a disparity between human and divine perspectives on this world and the next. In a 1683 sermon marking the death of mintmaster John Hull, Samuel Willard affirmed that in death's inscrutable timing, God always knew best despite the sting of human tears. God makes certain, Willard insists, "that his people shall alwayes die in the best time for them: it may be a bad time for the World to lose them in, but it is a good time for them to leave it in" (8). God knew best for survivors, too. As Mather attested in a brief essay "Directing Persons under Sadness, what Course to take," "you shall not be kept in your *Sadness* One Moment longer than the *Good State* of your *Better Part* shall require it" (*Cure of Sorrow* 24). To overgrieve was to reject this divine corrective. Moreover, to question God's judgment in this holiest of mysteries was to place one's immediate desires not only above divine wisdom but even above the interests of the dead, whose eternal reward would be delayed if mourners had their way. At the death in 1724 of Harvard president John Leverett, Nathanael Appleton gave Leverett's family the standard advice on handling the human – and thus fallen – impulse toward anger: "Be *dumb*, and *open not your mouths*, in the least murmurings under this severe Correction of your heavenly *Father*." However tragic Leverett's passing seemed, "this whole affair (in the most minute Circumstances of it) was by the order and direction of an infinitely *wise, holy* and *righteous*, yea and *gracious* God." Further, this God "does not *afflict willingly* nor *grieve his Children*, but only when he sees they *need* to be in heaviness, then he corrects them for their *Profit*, to make them *Partakers* of his *Holiness*" (210–11).

A stoic approach to loss central to Reformed thought manifested itself in the austere funerary customs that some observers found so shocking in both Englands during the early seventeenth century. In 1642 Thomas Lechford reported, after touring New England, that "nothing is read, nor any Funeral Sermon made, but all the neighborhood, or a good company of them, come together by tolling of the bell, and carry the dead solemnly to his grave, and there stand by him while he is buried" (Stannard 109). As Lechford suggests, anticeremonialism ran high in New England, at least initially; what we would call "funerals" did not even exist prior to the latter half of the seventeenth century. The dead were buried without ceremony, as quickly as possible, and processions to the burial site were purely functional, with family and close friends bearing the coffin. Ministers were sometimes present, but sometimes not. A few words might be said at the gravesite, but nothing so elaborate as to constitute a ceremony. Although the physical evidence is inconclusive, it appears that graves often went unmarked. A funeral sermon might be preached soon after the death of an especially prominent citizen, especially a minister, but rarely on the day of interment and certainly not at a special service. Instead, the normal rhythms of worship continued uninterrupted: the sermon would be offered at the next Sunday meeting, or perhaps at the midweek teaching service.

All of this soon changed. Before long, as David Stannard observes,

"New England Puritans ritualized death as only the most non-Puritan of pre-Restoration Englishmen would have dared do" (117). Stannard attributes this rapid development of funerary ritual to the same "tribal vulnerability" that gave rise to the jeremiad in the decades following the Restoration (122). By the turn of the eighteenth century funerals had become elaborate and expensive affairs, marked by the exchange of mourning gloves, scarves, and rings, and often followed by feasts at the church or the deceased's home. Embalming became more widespread in order to allow time to prepare for the funeral, and the corpse was often placed on view. Elaborate funeral processions became the norm, with participants dressed in mourning cloaks and lined up according to social standing. The hearse and the horses pulling it were frequently draped with bunting depicting the traditional images of mourning: the death's head, the sharp-angled coffin, the pick and shovel, and the hourglass. Gravesite prayers became increasingly elaborate, and funerary texts of all kinds proliferated to the point where no prominent citizen died without some manner of verbal embalming. Funeral sermons were now preached on the day of burial rather than on regular meeting days, and the sermons themselves became more explicitly situational and eulogistic. As early as 1673, Joshua Scottow criticized the excessive praise offered in these sermons: by "mis-representing the Dead," Scottow complained, overly zealous preachers "have dangerously misled the living, and by flattering corrupted many" (Geddes 161). The old custom of pinning elegies and other tributes to the coffin or hearse also became more widespread, and by 1685 Cotton Mather alluded to what had become ritual mandate when he declared Nathaniel Collins worthy of so many elegies that he needed a "*Paper* winding sheet to lay him out" (*Verse* 64). In keeping with the proliferation of funerary ritual, devotional and consolatory treatises were sometimes distributed as tokens to mourners. On the title page of Pearse's manual on "a Timely and Thorough Preparation for Death," the printer "Recommended" the book as "proper to be given at funerals." Frequently cited as an anomaly in a culture noted for its anticeremonial severity, funerary customs might almost be said to have gotten out of hand by the first decades of the eighteenth century. Such, at least, was the opinion of the Massachusetts legislature, which in 1724 felt it necessary to legislate restrictions in order "to Retrench the extraordinary Expence at Funerals" (Stannard 115).[4]

This dramatic increase in funerary ritual could not have occurred without equally dramatic changes in the ideology of mourning. As Stannard and Ronald Bosco ("Introduction") point out, a key factor in this shift was the increasing prominence at midcentury of jeremiad themes in sermons and other texts. By the 1650s, the gap between the ideal and the real in the New Zion seemed alarmingly wide, and ministers seized on the deaths of first-generation stalwarts as opportunities to voice their growing concern over New England's direction. This concern manifested itself in the jeremiad's dual message of fear and hope. Although God has sent this affliction to punish us for our sins, the preachers argued, the punishment proves God's concern for us because it forces our repentance. If we are sincerely contrite, both collectively and as individuals (and the former is not possible without the latter), we can restore the mission to its former glory and realign our present condition with an eschatological future appropriate to the New Israel. As Bosco notes, the increase in funeral sermons precipitated other changes in mourning ritual ("Introduction" xx). The jeremiad impulse of the sermon, with its tense balance of fear and hope, echoed precisely the sinful/saintly duality of grieving survivors, who found themselves torn between lamenting a loss and celebrating a victory.[5]

The passing of a saint offered a telling instance of God-sent affliction, a corrective all the more sharp because dying lay in everyone's future. As sin's universal wage, death gave concrete urgency to the ongoing call to repent, not least because dying brought an end to all opportunity to do so. The passing of exemplary believers surely signaled what Willard called "evil and calamitous times": God takes such souls away "*When they are despised or undervalued in the world*" (10). In his sermon for Increase Mather, Colman agreed that pious souls are taken because an indifferent people cannot value them sufficiently (*Prophet's Death* 148). Appleton similarly insisted that the deaths of prominent saints offered sure signs that the people were disregarding their examples. Such inexcusable ingratitude presaged even greater afflictions: "God, when he is resolved to bring sore and heavy Judgments upon a People, will take away his eminent Saints, that he might not have the opportunity to reject their prayers, or that his tender Compassions may not be so stirred up by their earnest supplication, as to stay his hand from executing vengeance upon the people" (198). Like the ten righteous persons who could have saved Sodom and Gomorrah (Gen. 18:32), true believers interceded for the rest. Their loss suggested that God was hardening his heart against those who remained. But there was another side to mourning. Countering their thunderings by stressing the continued opportunity to repent, preachers connected the fear/hope duality voiced in the jeremiad and corroborated by redemptive experience with the body/soul separation of the dead. The cessation of saintly turmoil in the deceased thereby became the hopeful precursor to a successful outcome for the mission at large as well as for individual survivors. These deaths, preachers insisted, were sent for our correction – and God would surely not bother to correct us if we did not remain objects of his love. The text with which Appleton closed his sermon for President Leverett said it all: "Come, and let us return unto the Lord: for he hath torn, and he will heal us; he hath smitten, and he will bind us up" (Hos. 6:1). The best response to this death – to any death – was always the same, and it replicated the *kerygma* of the Christian faith: "Repent: for the kingdom of heaven is at hand" (Matt. 4:17). Just how close at hand was evident in death's occasion. As preachers and elegists repeatedly pointed out, didn't one of us just enter the kingdom's gates?

Once a theological reconstruction of loss subsumed grief under the salvific sequence of sin and repentance, mourning could be rehabilitated for redemptive use. Grieving for the saint's fallen body – for the carnal element common to all humanity, whether saved or not – remained suspect because there was nothing distinctively Christian about it. "Death makes no distinction between great and small," Appleton confirmed, "But the high and the low, the rich and the poor, must all lie down in the grave together." Even "righteousness it self, altho' it delivers from the *second*, yet don't deliver from the *first Death*" (194, 195). Not even the prophets lived forever, Colman reminded his hearers, "And we see that *Wise* men die: And your *Fathers* (the *Ancients*) where are they?" (*Prophet's Death* 143). Precisely because it was universal, sorrow was no reliable mark of a chosen people. This was mere "natural grief," the mourning of the "wicked" which, as English divine Richard Sibbes attested, "is little better than frenzy or madness" (283). Such mourning was no better than pagan grief, and an affront to Christian faith and hope. To mourn in the "natural" manner, as Paul had confirmed, was to mourn as if there had been no Resurrection and the deceased were not enjoying its fruits. As Willard proclaimed, "surely these Notes do not suit with an Elegiack train; and yet this is the comfort which is given them to feed upon, whose dead Relations and Friends were Saints upon the earth" (17). Glorified saints, Willard insisted, are not greeted in heaven with doleful dirges, but "are welcomed into the Palace of delight with *Panegyricks*." Was it not a shame, he asked, that saints are "here dismissed with no more but a sorry saying, there is now a good Man gone, and he will be missed in the Family, or the Church to which he once belonged?" (18). Sibbes, in a pair of sermons on the Beatitude extending comfort to "those who mourn" (Matt. 5:4), was especially clear regarding the superiority of what he termed "spiritual mourning," a manner of grieving that led to heartfelt repentance. Not only was repentance the highest honor that one could offer to the holy dead, but it eased the pain of loss by deflecting the mourner's attention to higher things. "The more a man can mourn for his sins," Sibbes explained, "the less he will mourn for other matters" (270).

This was a species of mourning that neither ignored the deceased's presumed bliss nor tarnished the survivor's redemptive hope. Elegists pursued it by trying to imitate the celebratory spirit of the heavenly panegyrics for newly arrived saints that Willard extolled. The key to emulating the celestial songs of welcome, so different from secular elegy and its stress on worldly wit, was to replace the standard lament for the deceased's physical element, now corrupting in the grave, with an insistent focus on a spiritual element that had just gone to inconceivable joy. By stressing the saint's celestial glorification, elegists attempted to move survivors from an unproductive smarting at God's ways to a situational embodiment of Sibbes's "spiritual mourning," the sanctifying grief for sin within the self. Remorse for sin was, in the Puritan view, the only form of grieving that did any good, the only grief that saved. Sibbes explained that "every mourner and weeper is not therein blessed, except his outward losses, and crosses, and occasions, be an occasion through God's blessing and a means to bring him to spiritual sorrow and mourning." Such mourning, Sibbes argued, was actually "an happy estate and condition" because it enhanced one's chances for salvation (268). In taking up this work, Puritans practiced with a vengeance the truism that funerary rites are not for the dead but for the living. The belief in Purgatory had been swept away by the earliest Reformers, along with the attendant practice of praying for the souls of the dead, especially those who seemed destined for salvation (Stannard 99). Why pray for someone, ministers and elegists asked, who is now very probably seated in eternal bliss? It made no sense to "grieve" for souls whose reward was so full. In a rare understatement, Willard proclaimed that "it is no hurt to die if we die Saints." When death, "which is in it self an evil thing," comes to "a Child of God," faith transforms it into "a thing of very great worth" (5). To mourn for those who have passed into glory, Willard concluded, is merely "superfluous" (17).

Appleton agreed that when saints die, "we have no reason to mourn on *their* account: for Death is a happy Change to them." Indeed, the deceased is the only one who was not the victim of death's summons.

"And therefore," Appleton insisted, "we are to mourn on *our own* accounts; for the loss is not theirs, but ours" (200). Grieving for the self – especially the self's culpability for the sin that prompted God to take the dead away – also squared well with Christ's instructions for his own obsequies. Willard invoked these instructions when he warned against *"irregular Mourning"* for saints: "though we are to lament their Death, yet we must beware that it be after the right manner. . .after the same Language that Christ did to those weeping Women" (16–17). Appleton placed Christ's words – "weep for yourselves, and for your children" (Luke 23:27, 28) – in the mouth of the deceased Leverett, who, "if he were permitted to speak to us, it would be to the same purpose with that of our Saviour" (209). Survivors had good reason to weep for themselves. Not only had they not received their reward, but unlike the deceased, they enjoyed no guarantee that they ever would. "Carnal sorrow," Sibbes argued, "leaves a man worse than it finds him. It makes him more sick, and more weak, than it finds him." The "Spiritual sorrow" that led to repentance, by contrast, "leaves him better" (277). In their attempts to help the bereaved become spiritually "better," elegists joined the preachers in channeling the Protestant ambivalence toward mourning into a clear repudiation of weeping for the deceased's carnal dimension. The *other* aspect of the dead – the part that lived forever – could be fully mourned and celebrated. In their pursuit of this goal, ministers and elegists may have made a virtue of necessity. But it was, in their view, the highest possible virtue in response to the most urgent possible necessity. To achieve the proper spiritual frame at times of loss brought incalculable comfort. "Thy sorrow may begin in the flesh," Sibbes confirmed, "but, if it end in the Spirit, all is well" (290).

Puritans did not see themselves as being unrealistically stoic, least of all inhuman, in the face of tragedy. Appleton conceded that "Indeed the death of *any person* ought to affect our hearts" (199). But when saints died, another kind of grief was required, a grief pitched to a higher spiritual plane and issuing from motives purer, in the Puritan view, than mere sadness. As Appleton argued, "the death of *great Men*, Men of great endowments and abilities, and that have actually been of great use and service in the world, ought more deeply to affect our hearts" (200). And the greatest of all persons, Puritans agreed, were persons of faith. Lamenting the loss of their grace as a redemptive force in the world constituted mourning worthy of their spiritual stature. This begins to explain why the eulogized Puritan dead all seem alike. A broad pattern of sanctity, not the deceased's fallen individuality, comprised the ideal focus of mourning. Preachers and elegists invariably celebrated the deceased's translation from sinful particularity to the fruition of a gracious personality shared by all true saints. A recurring trope in funeral poem and sermon alike, as we will see, was the duty of embalming the dead. This is, on the face of it, an unexpected image, given the Puritan mistrust of corporeality and loathing of superstition. Puritan death-texts made it clear, however, that what was being embalmed was not saints' bodies but their souls, the receptacles of those virtues that defined them as saints in the first place. This is also why Puritans disdained any artificial eulogizing, banning gratuitous intrusions of conscious "art" from the commemorative act. As Willard affirmed, all that was needed was simply to recount the saint's virtues: "we should embalm the memory of the Saints with the sweet smelling Spices that grew in their own Gardens, and pick the chiefest Flowers out of those Beds to strew their Graves withal" (18). Sanctified mourning, appropriately enough, centered on that which was saintly – and what marked blessed souls for gracious commemoration was the simple fact, as Willard stated it, "that they lived and died Saints": "this onely will endure and be fresh and Flourishing, when Marble it self shall be turned into common dust" (18).

A question that Puritans repeatedly asked themselves at times of loss helped them assess their motives: are we mourning the deceased merely as a beloved person, or as one of God's people? The choice, framed as simply as possible, was whether to mourn the deceased as a sinner or as a saint. "*When the Saints die let us mourn,*" Willard proclaimed, "And there is no greater Argument to be found that we should excite our selves to mourn by, then the remembrance that they were *Saints*" (16). Puritan death-texts repeatedly challenged survivors to choose whether to grieve by the flesh or by the spirit, whether to cling to carnal ties or to emulate Christ's preference for a community defined by belief. "Who is my mother? and who are my brethren?" Jesus asks when his family comes to call him home. "And he stretched forth his hand toward his disciples, and said, Behold my mother, and my brethren!" (Matt. 12:48–49). Willard echoed the Christic reinscription of community by insisting that "it should more effect our hearts at the thought of this that they were *Saints*, then that they were our Father, or Mother, or Brethren, or nearest or dearest Friends" (16). At Increase Mather's death Colman cited the same biblical precedent: "has not Christ taught us to value a Relation in Grace, even more than one in the flesh only?" (*Prophet's Death* 159). Although parents brought us into this world, only a true saint could help bring us into the next. "To whom do we owe more," Colman asked Mather's mourners, "to the Fathers of our flesh or unto these?" (158–59).

The real object of Puritan mourning was not the deceased but the deceased's faith, not the individual but God's work in and through that individual. This response to loss articulated the conviction that at death, elect souls underwent a perfection of their graces. As Dickran and Ann Tashjian have observed, the central theme of the Puritan iconography of death was "metamorphosis" (17), the transformation wrought at death's great change by the miracle of salvation. "There is nothing," Appleton declared, "that *inlarges* the Soul, like true Grace. It is this that renders us the most like to the great GOD himself" (188). Spiritual mourning witnessed the survivor's esteem not simply for departed souls, but for Christ's spirit in them. As Colman explained, "the love that pious People bear them while they live, and the tears with which they mourn their decease, are a respect paid unto *Christ* himself." What was truly worthy of commemoration was Christ's "*Name* on the persons, his *Spirit* in them, his *Work* committed to them" (*Prophet's Death* 157). Grace and death had refashioned such a person, as Taylor said of Samuel Hooker, into nothing less than a "bit of Christ" (*Minor Poetry* 123).

What early New Englanders tried to cherish most about their dead was precisely what they wrote into texts that commemorated them. Deceased saints were repeatedly depicted as pure vehicles of grace, pointers to God as the source of the faith that had ripened within their souls. In this manner, physical death was transformed from a source of disruption into yet another sign of spiritual continuity. The holy dead are gone, elegists repeatedly conceded, but the God that made them holy still lived. The Psalmist had confirmed that "They shall perish, but thou shalt endure" (Ps. 102:26) – the text that Appleton cites when he argues that God takes great souls to show "that altho' *they perish, yet He endures*" (197). In the Puritan view, each saint's departure opened up a void that Christ himself stood ready to fill. Appleton was typical in counseling President Leverett's family to submit to a love transcending what they had felt for their husband and father: "And then the *Widow's Heart may and will rejoice, because the Lord her Maker is her Husband: With him also will the Fatherless find mercy*" (211). Appleton at this point appropriates Isaiah's words of solace to a desolate Zion: "for thou shalt forget the shame of thy youth, and shalt not remember the reproach of thy widowhood any more. For thy Maker is thy husband; the Lord of hosts is his name; and thy Redeemer the Holy One of Israel" (Isa. 54:4–5). In a prose meditation Bradstreet internalized Isaiah's promise of divine intimacy, connecting her hope with a resolve to "be no more afraid of death, but even desire to be dissolved and be with thee, which is best of all" (250). It was this desire to be with God, a desire exemplified by and fulfilled for the deceased, which sanctified commemoration as a holy rite. By focusing on the paradigm of the saved soul, mourners could redeem the impulse to mark loss with language. By channeling raw emotion into vital spiritual work, they translated the grief that they could not help feeling into a realignment with larger redemptive patterns. "God complains of this," Appleton declared, "as one of the Sins of his people of old, that *when the righteous perished, no man laid it to heart*" (see Isa. 57:1). Surely, Puritans reasoned, members of the New Zion, who enjoyed the light of faith, could do better. God's complaint "implies," Appleton explained, that it is "our *duty* to lay to heart the death of such" (200).

"Holy tears," Sibbes maintained, "are the seeds of holy joy" (279). Once tears were redefined as holy, strictures on praising the dead, stemming in part from disgust at the hyperbole and insincerity that Puritans found in the secular elegy, could be relaxed. A proper commemoration praised a gracious personality authored by God himself; indeed, not to praise such a self as fully as language allowed was to denigrate God's work. Nor, given the transformative power of grace, was there any danger of going too far, as secular elegists often did. How, Puritans asked, could one possibly overpraise a self that had so recently been God's instrument in the world? The Puritan distrust of hyperbole was thus answered at the level not of style but of perception. The glory that elegy attributed to the holy dead was not a matter of earthly "realism," but of the survivor's capacity to see grace at work in the deceased. As in David's lament and in the crowd's reaction to Lazarus's raising, the death of a saint divided survivors into those who cherished his or her faith and those who could not – or would not – see God's work for what it was. Bradstreet drew this line at the death of her father, Governor Thomas Dudley: "The good him loved, the bad did fear, / And when his time with years was spent, / If some rejoiced, more did lament" (203). In the response to a death, whether pious or dismissive, an inner "elegy" had already been written, one that exposed survivors for who they were. Willard confirmed that although "Wicked men" habitually slander God's people, "in the hearts of the faithful they have an honourable esteem, a worthy monument" (11). Reading and writing a proper commemoration brought this inner elegy to the perceptual surface, refashioning personal grief – the private pain of loss – into "spiritual mourning" whose redemptive value could be shared for the common good. The poem on the page tested – and shored up, if necessary – the deceased's salvific impact on those who had been left behind. On this point Willard cited Solomon's promise that "The memory of the just is blessed, but the name of the wicked shall rot" (Prov. 10:7). When saints died, Puritans made every effort to see that Solomon's words were fulfilled. As Appleton affirmed, "we should think and speak respectfully of them; and must carefully avoid every thing, that will cast the least dishonour upon them, or detract from their just Character: but instead thereof we are to bury all their defects, failings and infirmities with them" (202).

Puritans never denied that even the most pious believers had faults. Indeed, as Appleton insisted, "There is no man that passes thro' the world without them" (202). Why these faults rarely got into Puritan funerary texts is clear, however, from Appleton's use of the phrase "just Character." The term "character" did not connote idiosyncratic personality, as it does for us, but something like its opposite. The Puritan goal was to embalm the dead as edifying "characters" of the saved soul, in the Renaissance sense illustrated by the popular character books of Theophrastus, Sir Thomas Overbury, and Bishop John Earle. As Appleton's insistence that the character be "just" suggests, Puritans saw no falsehood or deception in such portraits. It was the survivor's faults, not the deceased's, that were relevant to spiritual mourning. The deceased's failings had nothing to do with the commemoration because those failings had been fully and finally pardoned by a merciful God. Moreover, God was not responsible for human failings – and Puritan mourning was nothing if not a determined search for resignation to that for which God *was* responsible. The saintly "character" repeatedly lined out in New England's funerary texts reflected what Puritans considered to be the deceased's truest identity: an essence defined wholly by faith and fated to outlast the ephemeral traits of the worldly self. Puritans reasoned that God had surely fashioned such glorious selves, like other embodiments of his Word, to be *used* – and perhaps especially at their deaths, when their graces had been perfected. As Willard said regarding the holy dead, "Never doth the Box of their sweet Ointments give a better savor, than when the Case is broken" (14). The key to releasing this savor for the comfort and benefit of the living was to set forth the deceased's piety as clearly as possible, to frame a legible "character" that could be read and imitated by all who aspired to the same path.

Like the jeremiad, elegy confirmed what John Weemse recommended as the proper sequence in preaching: "the gift of thundering must come first, and then comes the gift of consolation" (284). However numinous the pious dead had become, they had completed a pilgrimage that was still accessible to the living. For all their glory, the dead offered immediate and compelling examples of how grace could irradiate a human life. Like the drowned Lycidas, poised as the "Genius of the shoar" to aid "all that wander in that perilous flood" (164), the Puritan dead were textualized as spiritual guides for the living, as personified exhortations to persevere in the piety they exemplified. "We should be so affected with the death of such," Appleton urged, "*as to be more careful than ever, to imitate all that we saw great & excellent in them*" (202). As the sole point of entry into such perfection, death invested such souls with enormous exemplary status. Appleton remarked that "The thoughts of their being *dead* should make so deep and strong Impressions of their vertues upon our minds, as to make us more ambitious than ever, to be like them, and more carefull and resolute to tread in their steps, and imitate them in all that was imitable in them" (203). In their perceived capacity to interpose between survivors and divine wrath, the holy dead were eulogized as liminal straddlers of the "potent fence," in Philip Pain's phrase (Meserole 287), that separated earth from heaven. Willard neatly catalogued the images appropriate to the loss of such souls, images common in sermon and elegy alike: "When a *Saint* dies," he affirmed, "there is manifold ground of Mourning; there is then a Pillar pluckt out of the Building, a Foundation Stone taken out of the wall, a Man removed out of the Gap" (16). The gap to which Willard refers was the frighteningly narrow space between God's people and God's wrath. Interceding as pleaders for divine mercy, "gap-men" were hailed as heroes of what Edwin Bowden aptly calls a spiritual Thermopylae (5). "MEN of knowledge, wisdom, and grace are *gap-men*," Appleton explained, "that are oftentimes the means of keeping off the Divine Judgments. They by their vigilance, prudence, and prayers are the means of lengthening out a peoples tranquillity" (198). As Colman attested at Increase Mather's death, the immediate question to ask was "who shall *fill up* their place? Are there *many* rising up to do it? how many, or how *few*, remaining in the good Spirit of *the Deceased*"? Even worse, "what if Death should return and *take away the rest?*" (*Prophet's Death* 148). God's anger could be contained only if new gap-men emerged among the living, and if mourners absorbed the redemptive model that the deceased held out to them, they could be made ready to rush into the breach. Appleton declared that "the death of such ought to affect us as to put us upon the Imitation of them, *that so the loss & damage* sustained by their death, may in some measure be *repaired* in and by *us*" (203). By encouraging this reflection, efficacious mourning stimulated a transfer of sanctity from the dead to the living, a heartfelt internalizing of virtues whose clear portrayal in the funerary text made them that much easier to assimilate. As Appleton maintained, "we should endeavour that altho' *they* die, yet their vertues and graces may not die with them, but may live in *us*; that the same excellent Spirit, that dwelt in them, may dwell in us; and that we may be so under the influences of it, as to make good their ground, and fill their places" (203).

This was New England's version of the continuity reasserted by all elegy. Appleton declared that if the "Virtues and excellent Endowments" of the dead "live in *us*," then "the Loss" sustained through their passing "will be the less" (210). Puritan mourning helped survivors gain a sense not just of recovery but improvement. Through the proper channeling of grief, the deceased's virtues not only lived on but were diffused even more widely than before, in all who marked the loss. Appleton insisted that God called saints home in part to show that "he is not confin'd to particular Instruments, for the carrying on his purposes; but that, if the present Instruments imployed, are removed, he can raise up and qualify others to carry on the Service" (197). Colman issued the same hopeful challenge at Increase Mather's death: "So when *Moses* was dead, God said to *Joshua, Arise thou*: Take and fill his place, and go on where he left" (*Prophet's Death* 149). This characteristic blend of Old Testament story and New Testament interpretation reinforced New England's antitypical relation to ancient Israel, a comforting bond in light of the perceived declension. We have seen that the great biblical expressions of loss, particularly David's lament for Saul and Jonathan, were often cited as precedent for funeral poems and sermons. Colman cited Psalm 38 (*Prophet's Death* 160), a wrenching song of supplication in which the Psalmist complains that "my sorrow is continually before me" (Ps. 38:17). Modern readers might classify this as a Psalm of repentance rather than a true lament, but in the Puritan view, repentance was precisely where lamentation should lead: "For I will declare mine iniquity; I will be sorry for my sin" (Ps. 38:18). As situational models for proper grieving Appleton recited a short list of biblical commemorations: "When *Aaron* the high Priest died, *all Israel mourned for him*, Numb. 20.29. And *they wept* in their mourning for the death of *Moses*, Deut. 34.8. And they lamented the death of *Samuel*; and all *Judah* mourned for *Josiah*. And this was not only an external mourning, but real and hearty. Even so ours ought to be, when God removes such from the midst of us" (201). "Real and hearty" mourning, like any other gospel rite, derived its power not from rote performance but from the informing presence of saving faith. Puritans believed that those women who followed Jesus to Golgotha, thereby enacting a centuries-old tradition of demonstrative grieving, had the right idea but the wrong motives. When Jesus corrected them he was calling for something new, replacing secular tradition with the sin-searching introspection that was central to New England's commemorations.

As Colman pointed out (*Prophet's Death* 155), Christ had provided two other demonstrations of the saints' obligation to mourn properly. The first occurred at the death of John the Baptist, when Jesus was "moved with compassion" for the multitude "because they were as sheep not having a shepherd" (Mark 6:34). This text, which underscored the communal and dehortative dimensions of Puritan elegy, was immediately followed by the miracle of the feeding, a biblical analogy to the elegiac swerve from death to renewed life. Christ's second endorsement of sanctified mourning occurred at Lazarus's death, when he "groaned in his spirit, and was troubled." "Jesus wept. Then said the Jews, Behold, how he loved him!" (John 11:33–36). And, of course, the resurrection that followed Jesus's tears was seen as the prototype of a victory repeated at all pious deaths. In both incidents, Puritans found what they considered to be a manner of weeping that invoked hope over loss. The Baptist completes his work as the forerunner, and his death prompts a necessary passing of the torch to a greater prophet who feeds the multitude. Mourning also leads to an improbably joyous conclusion as a bound and dazed Lazarus stumbles forth from the grave. When Martha focuses on the body's corruption, Jesus replies, "Said I not unto thee, that, if thou wouldest believe, thou shouldest see the glory of God?" (John 11:40). Puritans took this rebuke to heart. Convinced that Christ's Resurrection gave elect souls resurrections of their own, they marked these passings in a spirit ascribed in the book of Acts to the earliest Christians, who mourned Stephen with proper honors and "made great lamentation" over him (Acts 8:2). Puritans saw this first Christian burial as the start of a redemptive history in which they could situate their own losses. After Stephen came the endless parade of martyrs, an unbroken chain that extended, as John Foxe's fervent accounts attested, nearly to the Puritans' own day.[6] An honorable passing was not, of course, restricted to literal martyrs, such as those who had been killed during the Marian persecution, but included all believers who "only stand and wait," in Milton's phrase – all whom faith had made dead to the world long before they physically left it. This was, for early New Englanders, a history well worth telling, a holy procession that survivors longed to join even as they lamented the fact that one of their own had just done so. The pain of loss, however sharp, made such joinings possible. "Consolation," wrote William Ames, "is an easing of fear and oppressive grief." "Yet it sometimes," Ames explained, "contains by synecdoche the beginning of all salvation" (174).

Why do we die? For early New Englanders, the question made better sense as it had been phrased in Ezekiel: "Why *will* ye die?" (Ezek. 33:11). Thomas Shepard gave the standard Puritan answer: "The great cause why so many people die, and perish everlastingly, is because they will; every man that perisheth is his own butcherer or murderer" (*Sincere Convert* 68). Old Testament prohibitions against contacting the dead survived in the insistence that the earthly shell of the deceased was not to be lamented excessively. There was, in the Puritan view, no theological justification for it: dust to dust and ashes to ashes. But where theology closed one door, it opened another. Inevitable emotions received validation in the elegiac shift from body to soul, from corrupt particularity to saintly paradigm. Through this paradigm, the living could not only maintain their connection with the dead, but absorb a measure of their sanctity. Death could thereby be rewritten into victory, sinful grief into saintly celebration. The tension between weeping and rejoicing, between Hebraic resignation and Christian resurrection, defined the crux around which New England's dead could be lamented. Puritan mourning found a place for both the human and the extrahuman, for David's dirge for the mighty as well as for Mary and Martha's astonished joy at having a brother, four days dead, restored to life. The grace displayed in the dead was sufficient to ensure that such victories would continue, provided that survivors heeded their saintly model. As in the classical and pastoral elegy, life would go on, but it would not do so because of continuities provided by the permanence of art or the heritage of offspring or any of the other standard tropes of recovery. Life would go on because of faith. As the dead took their leave, their textualized identities remained to point survivors to God as the source of all deliverance. Heeding the directives provided by such souls might even avert further losses. "Let us account the *Saints* precious whiles they live," Willard urged, "and God will not begrutch them to us" (20).

4

This potent fence: the holy sin of grief

Dying assumed geometric clarity as the great divide not just between the living and the dead, but between the potential for salvation and the end of all redemptive opportunity. Edward Pearse declared in his treatise on preparing for death that for the unrepentant, dying marked the irreversible step "from Hope to Despair." It brought the great "Change from fair probabilities to utter Impossibilities of Life and Salvation" (56). As Roy Harvey Pearce has aptly described it, "the occasion of a death, the point just before final proof of election or damnation, gave the Puritan poet his greatest opportunity. Now a man, newly dead, would really *know*. And the poet would bear witness to that knowledge, if only he could work out the way of getting it" (25). Fear of dying did not speak well to one's readiness for this final test. "O where's the man or woman," Philip Pain asked, "that can cry, / *Behold I Come, Death I desire to dye?*" What was it, exactly, that made death so terrifying? Nothing, Pain insisted,

> . . .but the sense
> Of *guilt* and *sin*: Break down this potent fence,
> And then be sure for aye you shall enjoy
> Joyes everlasting, Everlasting joy. (Meserole 287)

The most daunting barrier stood not between the dead and the living, but between those destined to remain caught in sin's snares and those whom faith would set free. The surest way to "Break down" the "potent fence" that separated the self from salvation was to learn to perceive the grave as a site of release rather than terror. With proper meditative preparation, Pearse maintained, death "will not appear half so terrible; yea, thou wilt find it to be not so much an Enemy as a Friend, not as a King of Terrors, but rather as a King of Comforts" (149).

A fully redeemed perspective – an ability to see the grave as Bradstreet's "silent nest" (294) or Taylor's "Down bed" (*Poems* 55) – was possible only for elect dead who had broken through the barrier. Still, the living were challenged to replicate their view through an ongoing *memento mori* by which earthly life could be seen, in Bradstreet's words, as a "bubble" that is "breaking, / No sooner blown, but dead and gone, / ev'n as a word that's speaking" (222). No believer, not even the very young, could presume upon unlimited time to acquire this perspective. As Grindall Rawson tersely confirmed at the death of John Saffin, Jr., "Sculls of all Sizes lye in Golgotha" (Meserole 477). This lesson came with literacy itself, driven home not only by the alphabet couplets in the *New England Primer*, but by "Verses" designed to be absorbed into the young reader's consciousness:

> I in the Burying Place may see
>   Graves shorter there than I;
> From Death's Arrest no Age is free,
>   Young Children too may die;
> My God, may such an awful Sight,
>   Awakening be to me!
> Oh! that by early Grace I might
>   For Death prepared be.   (80)

Particular losses became situational pointers in a lifelong preparation for death that Charles Hambrick-Stowe has called "the culminating exercise of the entire devotional system" (*Practice of Piety* 229). As Pearse confirmed, "*The meditation of Death* (saith one) *is Life*; it is that which greatly promotes our spiritual Life; therefore walk much among the Tombs, and converse much and frequently with the Thoughts of a dying hour" (65). At times of warm religious assurance, the otherworldly take on death seemed within reach. Bradstreet's brief letter "To My Dear Children" is typical in its confident projection of the meditating speaker beyond this world. "I have sometimes tasted," Bradstreet asserts, "of that hidden manna that the world knows not . . . and have resolved with myself that against such a promise, such tastes of sweetness, the gates of hell shall never prevail" (243). Bradstreet's resolving "with myself" articulates the ideal outcome of all Puritan meditation: a self-division in which a saintly identity prevails over a carnal identity soon to be abandoned. In keeping with the Puritan conviction that a soul poised between heaven and earth could see the pilgrimage more clearly than someone still mired in this realm, Bradstreet speaks just this liminality as a means of helping her children "gain some spiritual advantage by my experience" (240).

The importance of a proper preparation for death accounts for the popularity of self-elegy, which projected the meditating speaker beyond physicality altogether. In its didactic and communal aims, self-elegy recalls Moses's lament that the people have strayed from God's ways: "O that they were wise, that they understood this, that they would consider their latter end!" (Deut. 32:29). In its private dimension as a vehicle of the poet's consolation, self-elegy replicated Paul's affirmation that "I am now ready to be offered, and the time of my departure is at hand. I have fought a good fight, I have finished my course, I have kept the faith" (2 Tim. 4:6–7). Edward Taylor followed Paul's example in the two versions of "A Fig for thee Oh! Death" and the three versions of a full-scale farewell to earthly life, "A Valediction to all the World preparatory for Death." The first poem voices the religious assurance of a speaker who has already hopped the fence of guilt and sin. "Why comst thou then so slowly?" Taylor asks death: "mend thy pace / Thy Slowness me detains from Christ's bright face" (*Minor Poetry* 264). For Taylor, Pearse's meditative transformation of the King of Terrors into the King of Comforts has already occurred. "Thou'rt not so frightful now to me" (263). In the last Canto of the final version of the "Valediction," Taylor speaks as a Pauline pilgrim who has fought the good fight and is ready to cross over:

> While to this durty Vaile I here abide,
> Strange Fogs & damps loosen my Viol strings
> And rust my Golden wyers, I'm hoarse besides,
> My Melody's too mean for thee my King,
> My Musick's harsh, & jars, yea dumpish dull
> To Saints not pleasant, now in glory full. (*Minor Poetry* 240)

The liminal self contemplating its own image in death recurs in "Upon my recovery out of a threatening Sickness." Complaining that the "golden Gate of Paradise" is once again "Lockt up," Taylor struggles to accept God's will in keeping him "quartering" on earth (*Minor Poetry* 219). As in "A Fig for thee," he is not just ready but eager to die. Nor was a position half in and half out of the world confined to the poetry of Taylor's later years. The *Preparatory Meditations*, which he began at the age of forty, start with the voice of a paradigmatic saint who strains to glimpse a Savior knowable only in the next world even as he acknowledges a sin-clogged body that he consistently opposes to his essential identity.

The quintessential vehicle for preparing to die, the self-elegy enacted a discursive pre-death, a trying on of mortality appropriate to the Puritan disdain for the flesh. As Judge Sewall wrote in his letter-book and inscribed in a gift copy of a commentary on Job, "While ear, mind, eye, hand, mouth, and foot continue to function, it is better to learn to wish for death" ("Auris, mens, oculus, manus, os, pes munere fungi / dum pergunt, praestat discere velle mori" (Kaiser 39). To wish for death was to transfer one's allegiance from this world to the next, and thus to speak the eschatological identity that one most desired. Through self-elegy, Puritans also recast themselves into edifying texts for others. Speaking as selves fully used up by the world, self-elegists encouraged the reader to use *them* up as well, to apply the patterns they embodied to his or her own journey to bliss. In effect, self-elegists spoke their own discursive martyrdom, a willed self-emptying enacted so that others might live. In the Puritan view, such a voice did not suggest pride or arrogance, but indicated a warm assurance of faith as "the substance of things hoped for, the evidence of things not seen" (Heb 11:1).

The self-elegy was also common among English Puritans (Draper, *The Funeral Elegy* 157–58); indeed, a poem attributed to a revered English dissenter probably encouraged the popularity of the form in New England. The *New-England Primer* contained an "Exhortation to his Children" supposedly authored by Marian martyr John Rogers shortly before he was executed. Asserting an identity as a man already dead, as he would actually *be* in the reader's present, the speaker leaves his children "a little Book" in verse

> That you may see your Fathers face,
>   when he is dead and gone.
> Who for the hope of heavenly things,
>   while he did here remain,
> Gave over all his golden Years
>   to Prison and to Pain.   (89)

Paul Leicester Ford's comment that the poem is "nothing but a piece of sectarian garbling and falsehood" reflects an anachronistic expectation of literal "truth" in Puritan elegiac texts (33). Objecting that "all the pity spent upon it by millions of readers was no more deserved than that lavished upon the unfortunate heroes and heroines of fiction," Ford overlooked the paradigmatic thrust of most Puritan poems. The selves that Bradstreet and Taylor speak are scarcely any less "fictive" – that is, framed in accordance with cultural and theological expectation – than the speaker of the "Rogers" poem. Puritans, of course, did not feel such identities as mere constructions. Self-elegists articulated what they considered to be their deepest and most significant selves, not from self-deception or smugness but as acts of hope for themselves and gestures of support for others. Anticipations of celestial peace were no more taken as boasts than were the admonitions of a godly sermon. In the last sentence of his *Sincere Convert*, Thomas Shepard tells his reader that he has tried "to lead you so far as to show you the rocks and dangers of your passage to another world" (109). This was the guidance that self-elegists offered as well.

Self-elegy reduced a life – or from the Puritan point of view, elevated it – to its essence as a vehicle of pure edification. Most early New Englanders worked to absorb this mode of self-experience from an early age. While we might expect this perspective in poems written late in life, like Bradstreet's "As Weary Pilgrim" and Taylor's "Valediction," we have seen that Bradstreet's earliest dated poem, written while she was suffering "a Fit of Sickness" at age nineteen, also projects a speaker whose "race is run, my thread is spun, / lo, here is fatal death" (222). The appropriation of so conventional a stance was not a consciously "artis- tic" decision on Bradstreet's part. On the contrary, it was the expected result of an effective preparation for death. Governor Bradford adopted the same weary stance when he presented a life already best described in the past tense: "In *Fears* and *Wants*, through *Weal* and *Woe*," Bradford asserts, "As Pilgrim past I to and fro" (Meserole 389). Shifting to the present tense to confess current weakness, Bradford speaks as a self emptied of all human gifts and thus ready for the identity that Christ will form in him.

> My dayes are spent, *Old Age* is come,
> My *Strength* it fails, my *Glass* near run:
> Now I will wait when work is done,
> Untill my *happy Change* shall come,
> When from my labours I shall rest
> With Christ above for to be blest. (Meserole 390)

Bradford textualizes himself as a human *ars moriendi*, a meditative object for generating an expectation of the "happy" transformation for which all believers yearned. While the eschatological Bradford voices the end- point of true belief, the earthly Bradford confesses the weakness that was indispensable to getting there. When he counsels his soon-to-be survi- vors to fear God "in *Truth*, walk in his *Wayes*, / And he will bless you all your dayes," he asserts faith in his reward as well as theirs by speaking the Christian hope that the saintly self – the identity to which his readers also aspired – would prevail in him.

Another governor, Bradstreet's father, articulated a similarly general- ized self wrought by grace. By depicting his life as having already ended, Thomas Dudley voices the perspective of all souls whom carnal weari- ness had reduced to abject dependence on divine strength:

Dimme eyes, deaf ears, cold stomach shew
My dissolution is in view
Eleven times seven near lived have I,
And now God calls, I willing dye. (Meserole 365)

A human zero poised to be filled with God's infinity, Dudley invokes the
desired subjective vacuum with particular clarity: "My life is vanish'd,
shadows fled," he asserts, "My soul's with Christ, my body dead."
Jonathan Mitchell ascribed the same liminality to Michael
Wigglesworth, whose chronic ill health has allowed him to "send thee
Counsels from the mouth o' th' Grave. / One foot i' th' other world long
time hath been, / Read, and thou'lt say, His heart is all therein"
(Meserole 413). Wigglesworth asserts liminality for himself throughout
Meat Out of the Eater and in such lyrics as a Latin poem "On His Misery":
"Sick, helpless, orphaned, weary with heavy cares, / listless in body and
failing in soul, / I am overwhelmed by adversities" ("Aeger, inops, orbus,
curarum pondere fessus, / corpore languescens, deficiens animo, /
obruor adversis") (Kaiser 30). In its fervent anticipation of release from
this life, self-elegy confirmed the pre-death resulting from all successful
meditation. The extent to which Wigglesworth's speaker seemed already
dead added to his credibility as a subjective model.

The liminal stance enabled self-elegists to offer their lives as guides to
redeemed experience, as witnesses that salvation *felt* exactly as readers
had been told in sermons, treatises, and pastoral conversations. This
inner story was endlessly retold. The corporeal element stood in constant need of conviction, and physical death was to be welcomed
because it made possible the unimpeded flowering of a Christ-fashioned
identity in heaven. Mather clarified the disembodied ideal when he
joined Mitchell in spiritualizing Wigglesworth's feebleness: "His *Body*,
once so *Thin*, was next to *None*; / From Thence, he's to *Unbodied Spirits
flown*" (*Verse* 95). Peter Bulkeley, meditating on old age on his seventy-
second birthday, marked the passing of another year by wishing for the
"new mind and new life" ("mens nova, vita nova") that only dying could
bring (Kaiser 26). Three years later he again scorned his languishing corporeality, the "dead weight" ("pondus iners") of physicality. Begging
death to come quickly that he might sing heavenly songs all the sooner,
Bulkeley anticipates his end as a debt that he yearns to pay (Kaiser 26).
The same eagerness is voiced by the aging Taylor, who performs, with
unsettling relish, a verbal self-autopsy in his "Valediction" to the world:
"Fare well my Vitall Spirits all of Which / You have in my Flesh Camp
your abodes pitch. / You've nigh worn out your Nerves" (*Minor Poetry*
236). For Taylor, death will change saintly potential into actuality by

giving access to the "New Heart, New thoughts, New Words, New wayes likewise" for which he had asked more than thirty years earlier (*Poems* 49). Samuel Arnold of Marshfield left a "last FAREWELL to the World" similar to Taylor's, though shorter and far less elaborate. Praying for God to "bend / My Soul" "to Thy Self" "that it may soar and mount aloft," Arnold underscores the role of the self-elegy as a didactic as well as a meditative text with a closing request: "When I translated am with Thee to sing," he hopes that his family might "'Mongst them that fear thee. . .find a place" (Winslow 15).

The Word fully and resolutely lived, conceived as a particularized embodiment of the Word read and preached, was a reliable source of assurance. New Englanders agreed with Bishop Wilkins, though he was no Puritan, that "consolation" in preaching "may be amplified" by "the promises that are made in Scripture" and "the experience of others" (18). The value of other believers' experience explains the Puritan fascination with spiritual biography and autobiography. The highest use to which a life could be put was as an aid to others in their own preparation for death. Bradstreet embraced this ideal in "As Weary Pilgrim" when she encouraged her readers to persevere so that they might receive the "lasting joyes" that she anticipates (295). Her father's words to his "dear wife, child[re]n and friends" similarly embody the near-death self who guides those who will remain behind: "Hate heresy, make blessed ends, / Bear poverty, live with good men, / So shall we meet with joy agen" (Meserole 365). By exploiting the regulating function of texts, self-elegists gave a positive shape to Puritan death-consciousness, constructing it in ways that were assuring and even invigorating. To write such a poem was not only to become more nearly the person one wished to be, but it was also to expose one's own weaknesses for the betterment of others. In its blend of the confessional and the didactic, self-elegy enacted an especially efficacious conviction in sin. Self-elegists transformed themselves into living – or barely-living – homilies of salvific hope: follow me, they write, and my reward will be yours. Puritans did not associate pride with this rewriting of identity into an edifying text for others. Rather, in the discursive rush toward selflessness the speaker was appropriating a dead or dying identity so that others might live.[1]

To speak as all saints spoke was not simply a technique employed to enhance a poem's didactic impact, but a mode of self-perception indicative of a vital faith. In keeping with the expected patterns of that faith, saintly humility often tempered the speaker's spiritual boldness. However exemplary Bradstreet seems in "As Weary Pilgrim," for instance, she begs simply to be made "ready" for the Judgment (295). And Taylor, in his most elaborate self-elegy, faces carnal doubts head-on even as he asserts his identity as a soul destined for bliss. Responding to "Churlish Clownish" thoughts that "Chide" his faith with accusations of "gross Presumptions," he proclaims that "I'm resolvde, my Faith shall never Crickle / It on Christs Truth & Promises relies" (*Minor Poetry* 239, 240). Such modesty could be relaxed when someone else became the meditative object, as witnessed by the many encomiastic poems that circulated in early New England. Nicholas Noyes's poem congratulating Cotton Mather on the *Magnalia*, for instance, offers praise as rarified as that set forth in any elegy (Meserole 275). Noyes wrote another "living elegy," or more accurately, a pre-elegy, to his friend James Bayley, "Living (if Living) in *Roxbury*" and suffering from "that Disease that plagues the Reins." Noyes confirms Bayley's heavenly reward even though Bayley had eight more months to live. Although Noyes begs his addressee to "Excuse me, though I Write in Verse, / It's usual on a Dead mans Hearse," such praise of the living was more common than he suggests (Meserole 278, 279). Most of the "memorials" in Edward Johnson's *Wonder-Working Providence* are in fact living elegies, exhortations to contemporaries to keep up the good fight in the here and now.

Holiness perfected in death could be celebrated with even less restraint, which suggests why Franklin's comic objection to the undifferentiated deceased in the Mehitabel Kittel poem was beside the point. The central goal of elegy, as of the funeral sermon, was not to frame a literal biography of the dead or even to lament an individual death, but to identify and celebrate the effects of grace on yet another pilgrim life. Taylor, we recall, proclaimed David Dewey's translation from an earthly being whose body was once "a Seat of Sin" into just such a "noble Soul refin'd, all bright," swimming in "fulgent Glory" and "fill'd with Bliss to th' brim" ("Edward Taylor's Elegy" 83). Although "[I]t's easier to bring / Bears to the Stake" than it is to make the body "cease to Sin" (83–84), death and grace had *made* Dewey perfect in a passage from sin to glory that was considered the same for all elect souls. John Fiske thus extolled Nathaniel Rogers as the archetypal pilgrim whose life, backread in light of his election, evinced a steady walk toward heaven:

> In this worlds wildernes no Rest He found
> But heavenly Canaans Rest his hope it was
> His weary Travells now dispatcht hath He
> And by our Josua that Rest He has. (Jantz 127)

Urian Oakes's reading of Thomas Shepard II reiterates the pilgrim pattern. Shepard "Fears, he Cares, he Sighs, he Weeps no more: / Hee's past all storms, Arriv'd at th' wished Shoar" (Meserole 211). Elijah Corlet similarly attests to Thomas Hooker's safe arrival at "his heavenly home-land" ("coelestem patriam. . .suam") (Kaiser 18), and Benjamin Tompson has Edmund Davie speak to his own successful pilgrimage through the world: "I'm now arriv'd the soul desired Port / More pleasing far then glories of the Court" (Meserole 223). When any saint died, spiritual accuracy demanded a depiction not of the dead so much as of the identity that faith had fashioned in them. In the Puritan view, por-traits of perfected faith could not possibly be hyperbolic: how could the impact of God's work on a life be overstated? Mather joined Edward Johnson in asserting the saint's life as redemptive history in microcosm when he devoted two out of seven books of the *Magnalia* to exemplary biographies of New England's worthies, both civil and ecclesiastical. This Puritan version of "great man" historiography was preceded, of course, by John Foxe's *Acts and Monuments*, which presented the lives and deaths of Protestant martyrs as episodic centers of church history. Ultimately, the Puritan impulse to conflate biography and history went back to Luke, whose stories of Peter and Paul in Acts placed salvation history squarely in the hands of those who did God's work in the world. In the great pilgrimage to heaven, it was the pious dead who could best lead the living.

By celebrating individual pilgrimages as expressions of God's larger plan, the elegy became the most characteristically "Puritan" of all Puritan verse. New Englanders were convinced that there was no wor-thier poetic task than to recount these parables of divine agency in exemplary lives. Oakes calls Shepard's death "a subject for the loftiest Verse / That ever waited on the bravest Hearse" (Meserole 209), and Cotton Mather, alluding to such biblical precedent as David's lament, asserts in a collective elegy for young ministers that "Smooth Numbers first were form'd for Themes like these; / T'immortalize deserving *Memories*" (*Verse* 83). What gave elegy its consolatory power was the fact that it seized upon the ideal opportunity for reasserting faith-based con-nections between the seen and the unseen. What better revelation of redemptive continuity – of the ties uniting this world and the next – than someone who had just leaped Philip Pain's "potent fence" and crossed over to the other side? As a marker of such crossings, elegy presented death as a situational intersection of fear and hope. On the one hand, the death of a saint posed a grim reminder that earth was not heaven.

On the other, it proved that the terrifying space between the two realms could be bridged – that it indeed *had* been bridged, and by someone who once walked among us. An anonymous elegist depicts the venerable John Alden of Plymouth and Duxbury, who died at eighty-nine, in just such terms, underscoring Alden's liminality as a latter-day Moses who stood on Pisgah "and *Canaan* view'd, / Which in his heart and life he most pursu'd." The poet also situates Alden on Tabor by having the deceased echo Peter's remark at the Transfiguration: "*'Tis good being here.*" After a lifetime of soaring "on wings of Contemplation" and sending "up many a dart," the old man truly "desir'd to die" (Winslow 13). Such a figure offered a gauge, at once intimidating and encouraging, by which survivors could measure their own spiritual condition. By urging a redeemed perspective on the deceased's life, elegy, like the funeral sermon and the jeremiad, indicted readers for such declension as the death witnessed even as it reinforced their identification with a holy people destined, like the deceased, to transcend such affliction. Further, by urging readers to assess their faith in light of the saintly self who had just gone to glory, the elegy offered a situational replication of the convicting and consoling properties of Scripture itself. Like the law and the gospel, the dead – and the texts that presented them for contemplation – simultaneously condemned and encouraged survivors. Although elegists repeatedly told survivors that they were not at all like this saintly soul, a comforting message was just as clear. If mourners persevered in their efforts to pass death's test by emulating the deceased, they and the commemorated saint might well turn out, like Milton's "uncouth swain" and Lycidas, to be gloriously twinned in heaven.[2]

Seen from an unregenerate perspective, death was a devastating victory of flesh over spirit. For the redeemed, however, death precipitated a still greater victory of spirit over "nature," including the natural inclination to cling to what flesh loved. Each pious death brought the world one step closer to the final dissolution set in motion by the Fall and its legacy of returning "unto the ground" (Gen. 3:19). Agreeing with Milton that the death of the good was "As killing as the canker to the rose" (160), Puritans marked such losses with a biblical version of the ancient trope of *natura plangens*, thereby stressing an identification of saved with Savior, at whose death "the earth did quake, and the rocks rent" (Matt. 27:51). The trope of nature in mourning was especially common in elegies for prominent New Englanders. At the death of Governor Leet of Connecticut, Samuel Stone II proclaimed that "The earth's now clad in sable Gown" (Jantz 155), and when President Chauncy of Harvard died, John Saffin confirmed that "Soll, and Luna and the fermament / Seeme to Instruct us how we Should Lament" (14). In a late example, an anonymous elegist mourned Thomas Bridge by issuing a similar call: "Let the earth, air, and sky lament, let the sea and heavens groan, / and let all things filled with streaming showers weep" ("Aer terra polusque gemant, gemat aequor et aether, / imbribus effusis omnia plena fluant") (Kaiser 41). And in a poem for Jonathan Mitchell, Harvard student Francis Drake proclaimed that when Mitchell fell ill, "the *Air* a *Feaver* took"; when Mitchell died, "the *Spheres* in *Thunder, Clouds, & Rain* / Groan'd his *Elegium*, Mourn'd and Wept *our Pain*" (Meserole 459). Such invocations of a weeping world strengthened the identification of sin with the physical realm in which survivors were still mired. Sensing its own fragility, the created world weeps for itself – or should, as David suggested when he called for the "mountains of Gilboa" to join the threnody: "Let there be no dew, neither let there be rain, upon you, nor fields of offerings" (2 Samuel 1:21). New Englanders followed David's lead more selectively than Milton did in his personification of "nature" as a complex of sympathetic forces. For them, nature was a realm of created and thus fallen entities. This was the inescapable lesson of mutability, as Bradstreet suggested when she set "Contemplations" in the waning hours of a day at the end of a year. Elijah Corlet made this point in his poem for mintmaster John Hull, whose passing was mourned as yet another sign of the relentless movement toward decay. "God did not want there to be a perpetual spring or perennial summer," Corlet claims, but expressed his will by "binding all things in snowy chains in sad winter" ("Nec ver perpetuum voluit Deus esse, perennium / noluit aestatem. . .cumque nivali / vinclo ut tristis hyems constringeret omnia"). For Puritans, the challenge of elegy, as of all devout texts, was to escape the temporal cycles of the fallen world in which constant divine intercession was necessary if believers were to be "kept perpetually healthy and pure by the grace of Christ" ("sed nobis gratia Christi / perpetuo servet sanas atque inviolatas!") (Kaiser 19).

This is one reason why nature imagery, when it appears in Puritan elegy, usually takes biblical form. The most frequent cosmic image appears in Taylor's description of Samuel Hooker of Farmington as "a bright Star / That never glimmerd" (*Minor Poetry* 123), an image that strengthened the deceased's neobiblical identity by recalling the "star in the east" of the Nativity (Matt. 2:2), the Old Testament prophecy that "there shall come a Star out of Jacob" (Num. 24:17), and Christ's apocalyptic manifestation as "the bright and morning star" (Rev. 22:16). The falling of a saintly star, a trope that Hawthorne borrowed to mark the passing of Governor Winthrop in *The Scarlet Letter*, lent biblical support to the deceased's role as harbinger of an astrology of potential doom. The prophecy that stars would fall at the "tribulation" (Matt. 24:29, Mark 13:25) and at the opening of the sixth seal (Rev. 6:13) prompted elegists to depict the passing of a saint as yet another sign that earthly time and redemptive opportunity were running out. Tompson refers to the death of the younger John Winthrop, governor of Connecticut, as "the setting of that Occidental Star" (Silverman 145). Another, anonymous elegist calls the governor a "Star of such resplendent glorious Light, / Whose Fellow never yet approacht our sight" (Winslow 9). John Saffin, whose standard elegiac phrase is a "Star of the first Magnitude" (22), applies the image to Thomas Willett, Governor John Leverett of Massachusetts, and Judge Thomas Danforth (22, 117, 139). And Cotton Mather tells "rash *Astronomers*" that they must correct their star-charts now that Sarah Leverett has become "the brightest of them all": "Your *Sirius* now shall be a LEVERET" (*Verse* 82–83). The image suggested the leaders' cosmic impact as bearers of gospel light to New England's wilderness. Benjamin Woodbridge describes John Cotton as "A *Star* that in our Eastern *England rose*" and moved "on Earth from East to West; / There he went down, and up to Heaven for Rest" (Meserole 411).[3]

Cotton's setting star, "hurry'd" out of Old England by religious persecution and out of New England by death, gives grimly oracular significance to the saint's passing. As Francis Drake noted at the death of Jonathan Mitchell, "*Stars falling* speak *a Storm*: when *Samuel* dies, / *Saul* may expect *Philistia's* Cruelties" (Meserole 458). At Shepard's passing Oakes spells out the import of the image with particular clarity:

> As when some formidable Comets blaze
> As when Portentous Prodigies appear,
> Poor mortals with amazement stand and gaze,
> With hearts affrighted, and with trembling fear:
> So are we all amazed at this blow,
> Sadly portending some approaching woe. (Meserole 212)

There is no need, Oakes claims, for "bold Astrologers, / To tell us what the Stars say in the case." The proper reading of the event, as for all afflictions, could be found in the "sacred Oracle that says, / When th' Righteous perish, men of mercy go, / It is a sure presage of coming wo" (Meserole 212). The text behind these lines is Isaiah 57:1: "The righteous perisheth and no man layeth it to heart: and merciful men are taken away, none considering that the righteous is taken away from the evil to come." The younger Samuel Stone echoed Isaiah's warning by claiming that the "sad Catastrop[h]e" which "Astrologers" had predicted for that year had just occurred in the death of Governor Leet of Connecticut: "Already Fatal it hath been / To us" (Jantz 155). And at the death of schoolmaster Ezekiel Cheever, Mather proclaimed that while the ancients knew only a thousand stars and "later Globes" identified nineteen hundred, "Now such a CHEEVER added to the Sphere, / Makes an Addition to the *Lustre* there" (*Verse* 91). Greater luster *there*, of course, meant less luster *here*. With each death a bit of gospel light had been extinguished from an unworthy realm, returning to its divine source and leaving the mission and the survivors darker in its passing.

Other, equally conventional images underscored the cosmic significance of the loss. The portrayal of the deceased as a plant that God has moved from the earthly garden to the heavenly invoked biblical allusions to the believer's grafting into Christ, the "root and the offspring of David" (Rev. 22:16). An anonymous elegist confirmed John Alden's identity as a newly pruned "branch" of the "*choice Vine*" that God brought "to this desart land" (Winslow 13). Mather, in a collective elegy for seven ministers, places the standard interpretation of the image into the mouth of God, who answers human anxiety with the directness of a laconic gardener:

> Lord, Why so soon, such Fruitful Trees cut down!
> No Wood of Such, was on the Altar known.
> Trees not cut down, (the Glorious Answer is,)
> But all Translated into Paradise.   (Verse 87)

Even though mourners could take pride that God had chosen these fruits of the New English Eden, garden imagery also held darker meanings. Chiefly, the spiritual maturity of the dead underscored the stunted spirituality of the living. When "E. B." (perhaps Edward Bulkeley) called John Norton and Samuel Stone "our Beauties" and "Two choicest *Plants*," he forced readers to wonder whether they would ever achieve equal ripeness. Moreover, continued conditions for spiritual growth could not be guaranteed. Although John Fiske describes John Cotton as a branch securely knotted in "a plant of Gods owne hand," the loss of the "Hony sweet" that he dispensed causes Fiske to "feare a famine" (Meserole 188–89). Finally, the trope of God's harvest reinforced the mourner's confrontation with the sheer power of the divine will. In her

poem for granddaughter Elizabeth, Bradstreet cites the premature harvesting of "buds new blown" as a humbling reminder that God will
decide who is ready for glory and when, human expectations notwithstanding (235). Taylor voiced this hard lesson at the deaths of two daughters in "Upon Wedlock, & Death of Children": "I joy, may I sweet
Flowers for Glory breed, / Whether thou getst them green, or lets them
Seed" (*Minor Poetry* 107). As Bradstreet and Taylor suggest, the consolation to be had from natural cycles was, at best, severely limited.

Because nature was incapable of fostering a redeemed view of the
loss, it was social and not natural entities – congregations, towns, colonies – that wept loudest in New England's elegies. While garden imagery
portrayed a ripening of faith within individual souls, images derived
from building and construction spoke more directly to the collective
mission.[4] We have heard Samuel Willard's funeral sermon for John Hull
striking the expected notes: "When a saint *Dies*, there is a manifold
ground of Mourning; there is then a Pillar pluckt out of the Building, a
Foundation Stone taken out of the wall, a Man removed out of the Gap"
(16). Images of disrepair are especially common in poems for prominent
clergy or political leaders. An unsigned elegy mourned Governor
Winthrop of Connecticut as a "pretious Pillar in his earthly station"
(Winslow 9). Fiske laments John Cotton's passing as the loss of a "Father
in our Israel" who "in the Church a pillar was" (Meserole 187). "E. B."
exploits an inevitable pun by proclaiming Samuel Stone a foundation of
right religion: "A *Squared Stone*, became Christs Building rare; / A *Peter's
Living lively Stone*, (so Reared)" (Silverman 143). The image confirmed
Stone's apostolic status: in Hartford, at least, Christ had anointed him
"Petrus" (Matt. 16:18). Charles Chauncy similarly hails John Davenport
as a "strong pillar" ("validam. . .columnam") that has fallen (Kaiser 23),
and Taylor mourns John Allen as a supporting beam in New England's
garden and temple: "And hearing something Crash, there's cause to
doubt / Another Stud is broke, or Stake pluckt out / Out of its place"
(*Minor Poetry* 30–31).[5]

In characterizing Zecharia Symmes of Charleston as a "Pillar, & a
Builder" who had "laid down his Square," Taylor invokes elaborate
images of disrepair to underscore the dire implications for those who
remained to tend New England's *hortus conclusus*:

> Altho' the Doors be firm, & would abide
> Rift off the bars, & down the boards will Slide
> When Posts do faile, the Pales & Rales down fall
> And Vinyards so ly common unto all.

Alass! alass! our Wall grows small, & weake:
Wherein, say you? Our golden Studs do breake,
Altho' the Watlings last, the hedge, I take
Is very feeble losing of its Stake.   (*Minor Poetry* 21)

Such images highlight the sense of fragility with which many elegists
depict the mission. As Oakes suggests in the Shepard poem, the loss of
so many pillars, stakes, and fenceposts threatened to return God's plantation to a wilderness state.

When such a Pillar's faln (Oh such an one!)
When such a glorious, shining Light's put out,
When Chariot and Horsemen thus are gone:
Well may we fear some Downfal, Darkness, Rout,
When such a Bank's broke down, there's sad occasion
To wail, and dread some grievous Inundation.
                                    (Meserole 212–13)

The "Inundation" that Oakes fears, with its echo of biblical destruction,
reaffirms the deceased's role as catalyst for a renewed conviction in sin
within speaker and reader alike. The dead saint's iconic status, reinforced by stylized images of holy plants, falling stars, and fallen pillars,
invoked a disturbing contrast between dead saint and living reader. As
John Wilson proclaimed at John Norton's death, "they [the survivors]
had grief, but he [the deceased] had the highest glory" ("his dolor, ast illi
gloria summa fuit") (Kaiser 14). Merely to outlive such a person was to
have one's sinful nature exposed. As Chauncy pronounced at
Davenport's death, "how unworthy we are to enjoy so great a light!" ("O
nos indignos, qui tanta luce fruamur!") (Kaiser 23). Taylor proclaimed
the diminishing of survivors even more directly when he commemorated Francis Willoughby: "Unworthy We, oh Worthy he!" (*Minor
Poetry* 22).

This dehortative function of elegy was not unique, of course, to New
England. In his popular *Arte of Rhetorique* Thomas Wilson described a
view, standard in both Englands, that the dead "were taken awaye from
us for our wretched sinnes, and mooste vile naughtines of life, that
therby we being warned, might be as readie for God, as they nowe pre-
sentlie were, and amend our lives in time" (151). But because Puritans
conceived of sin and grace as absolute polarities, each of which effected
a discursive heightening of the other, the presumed perfection of the
dead enabled New Englanders to push the reformist agenda to the very
center of elegy. "See," Oakes proclaims, "what our sins have done!":
"Our sins have slain our *Shepard!* we have bought, / And dearly paid for,

our Enormities" (Meserole 219). Fiske levels similar blame at the death of John Cotton, who has been sacrificed for the neglect of a sinful people who thought themselves too good for the plain "Cotton" gospel-wear he provided (Meserole 189). Shame at not having sufficiently heeded the dead was a common theme. Like the preachers, who claimed that God carried off saints in order to block his own tendencies toward mercy, elegists repeatedly portrayed ministers and magistrates as prophets without honor in their own country. When Theophilus Eaton died, Abraham Pierson proclaimed that "our wicked deeds robbed us of him" ("Hunc nostrae nobis noxae eripuere") (Kaiser 28). Daniel Henchman similarly scolded readers for squandering Governor Phips's usefulness:

> But Thou Chief looser Poor New England, speek
> Thy Dues to such as did thy Welfare seek.
> The Governour, that Vow'd to Rise and Fall
> With Thee, thy Fate shows in his Funeral.
> Write now his Epitaph; 'twill be thy own:
> Let it be this; A PUBlick Spirits gone. (Silverman 162)

Henchman's warning encapsulates the elegy's function as a jeremiad against personal and collective sin. The greatest threat to the New English garden was God's wrath, the terror of abandonment that Winthrop had voiced aboard the Arbella, when he warned that "if wee shall neglect the observacion of these Articles" and "fall to embrace this present world and prosecute our carnall intencions seekeing greate things for our selves and our posterity, the Lord will surely breake out in wrathe against us" (198). Elegists addressed this fear most directly in an image we have encountered before: the deceased as a "gap-man" whose piety held off divine anger against less worthy souls. Oakes applied the title to Shepard, "Our wrestling *Israel*, second to none, / The man that stood i' th' gap, to keep the pass, / To stop the Troops of Judgement[s p]ushing on" (Meserole 212). Saffin similarly described John Hull as a "Gap-man" made "t'avert Heavens Rod" (Meserole 201), while Mather proclaimed Shubael Dummer of York, Maine, "The Countreyes *Gapman*" (*Verse* 94). Here, too, the precedent was biblical: the image ultimately derives from Ezekiel's thundering dehortation against negligence: "O Israel, thy prophets are like the foxes in the deserts. Ye have not gone up into the gaps, neither made up the hedge for the house of Israel to stand in the battle in the day of the Lord" (Ezek. 13:5).

Oakes attests that Shepard "the honour had to hold the hand / Of an incensed God against our Land" (Meserole 212). God's wrath could not be held off unless others were prepared to fill the void left by the deceased, and any commemoration that failed to prepare survivors for this role, Oakes suggests, was useless.

> In vain we build the Prophets Sepulchers,
> In vain bedew their Tombs with Tears, when Dead:
> In vain bewail the Deaths of Ministers,
> Whilst Prophet-killing sins are harboured. (Meserole 219)

The killing of a "prophet" – and, transparently, of New England's "profit" – offered a timely occasion for condemning indifference, especially among clergy. As we have seen, Milton made this theme prominent in "Lycidas" by contrasting Edward King's ministerial promise with those who preached "for thir bellies sake" (161). Drawing the same conclusion from the loss of the seven young pastors, Mather proclaimed "*What they were not*": lukewarm ministers and hypocrites "who to *Pulpits* hop Unfledg'd and there / *Talk* twice a *Week*, and *Preach* not once a year." Such clergy were "*Snuffs*, instead of *Stars*" (*Verse* 84). Echoing David's complaint that the wicked prospered, elegists routinely invoked the "what they were not" formula in poems for persons who had broad societal influence. Benjamin Colman praised Samuel Willard for his attacks on Quaker thought. The "Courageous" Willard "dar'd Alone to stand the Shock, / Of num'rous *Priests* of *Baal*, and to deride their *Stock*" (Meserole 341). Taylor uses Samuel Hooker's passing as an occasion to attack a "Pinfeathered Prelacy" seemingly strengthened by Hooker's leaving. "Where," Taylor asks, is the deceased's "Strenth, & Potency? / And Congregationall Artillery?" Clearly, this was no time for such a man to die. "We need the Same; & need it more & more," Taylor laments, "For Babels Canons 'gainst our Bulworks roare" (*Minor Poetry* 116). Bradstreet, as we have seen, saw the death of her father as effecting a sharp division between piety and indifference: "If some rejoiced, more did lament" (203).

Such contrasts stressed the deceased's incompatibility with a fallen world. As Nicholas Noyes confirmed at the death of Cotton Mather's wife, sinners felt threatened whenever due praise was given to an elect soul. Noyes presents Abigail Mather as a personified sermon against a realm grown too corrupt to contain her sanctity:

> Say *little* of her *Inside Grace*;
> For this World is a Spiteful place;
> And takes it self for Injured
> If Saints are Prais'd, *Alive* or *Dead*;
> And they for *Witts* are in Esteem,
> That *Heavens Dwellers* do blaspheme. (Meserole 283)

The natural world was no better than the social world at containing such piety. Cotton Mather claimed that Sarah Leverett had "grown for *Earth* too Good, on *Earth* she grew / *Heav'n* claim'd her then: and then to *Heav'n* she flew" (*Verse* 82). John Wilson has the deceased Joseph Brisco celebrate the God who "from nature drew me into Grace, / And look'd upon me with a Fathers face" (Meserole 385). Nehemiah Walter similarly attests that "*Natures* Tree" has "Too feeble grown to bear" the "ponderous fruit" of Elijah Corlet's spiritual graces (Meserole 466). And Mather hints at something *un*natural – that is, something divine – about old Ezekiel Cheever's boundless energy: "*America* a *Wonder* saw: *A Youth in Age*, forbid by *Natures* Law." In Mather's hands, Cheever becomes an icon of spiritual patriotism, powerful enough to reverse natural expectations held by "You that in t'other Hemisphere do dwell" regarding the "*Winter of Life*, that *Sapless Age* you call" (*Verse* 91). This was biography recast as embodied theology, a confirmation that salvation was a cheat on postlapsarian nature. It was a typically Puritan move to use poems of death to proclaim God-given escapes from the slide toward death shared by all created things.

Still, such deaths seemed to signal the victory of darker forces in the world. It was a matter of simple arithmetic: the loss of a saint increased the sum total of sin in a world that was dark enough already. As an anonymous poet has Lydia Minot tell her survivors, "In leaving your Dark world, I left all Night" (Winslow 7). The saint's gracious light underscored the spiritual darkness of all who were still mired in the here and now. In his poem for Thomas Shepard I, John Wilson lamented that without such example, "neither learned men nor writings can cut sinful errors to pieces" ("Qua sine doctores non ulli, scripta nec ulla, / errores possunt carnificare malos" (Kaiser 13). Taylor similarly depicted Increase Mather as a fallen warrior who left the field precisely when he was most needed. The pulpit of Boston's North Church is "empty," Taylor laments, "now thy guides not there" (*Minor Poetry* 246). Wilson has the deceased John Harvard warn his students to stick to their studies and to sound doctrine, lest they anger God all the more ("atque magis summo displicatura Deo") (Kaiser 12). Chauncy calls on God to spare John Davenport's congregation "if you have pity on the flock" ("si miserere gregum") (Kaiser 23), and Fiske portrays Cotton's survivors as heartbroken children crying for the spiritual nourishment of a lost parent: "But now o and alasse to thee to call / In vayne tis thou no Answer give or shall" (Meserole 187). At the death of Samuel Sharpe, Fiske drives home the precarious state of the living in halting rhythms that replicate the anguish of a genuine conviction in sin.

oh! who shall us! us! comfort, hope, helpe, give?
who shew shall what hath us of him depriv'd?
where may supply? how may the worke be done?
our safety peace, tell us, which way contriv'd[.] (Silverman 139)

The loss of saints threatened a depletion of sanctity itself. As Oakes
declared, Shepard's death severed one more tie to the divine:

What! must we with our God, and Glory part?
Lord! is thy Treaty with New-England come
Thus to an end? And is War in thy Heart?
That this Ambassadour is called home. (Meserole 213)

Time and redemptive opportunity were slipping away as the great
exempla of the faith were being "called home" one by one. "Thus God
Decrees," lamented Grindall Rawson at the death of John Saffin II,
"minutes" to some and "Degrees" to others: "So Irrisible is this our
Doome, / That in our Loftiest hopes we find our Tombe" (Meserole
476). As Fiske conceded, the only remedy for "a stroke so greate" was to
entreat "Mercy alone" (Silverman 139).

As the first- and second-generation stalwarts passed away, God's
anger seemed to be prompting a mass exodus of the godly out of New
England. At Oakes's death, William Adams urges readers to "bewail the
hot anger of the offended divinity" ("Laesi ferventum plangamus
numinis iram") (Kaiser 36). Saffin makes the same point at the death of
Jonathan Mitchell: are New England's "Enormities" and "provocations"
so "augmented" and "unrepented / That the Most High in fury takes /
His jewels hence such breaches makes?" (112). If Governor Leet's death
does not prompt repentance, Samuel Stone II warns, "we are in greater
danger, / Of overtures and changes here" (Jantz 155–56). And Taylor
asks, at the death of John Allen, "Shall none / Be left behinde to tell's
the Quondam Glory / Of this Plantation?" (*Minor Poetry* 31). In his poem
for Zecharia Symmes, Taylor seems to give the question the most pessi-
mistic answer possible:

Hereby our Israels glory waxeth thin;
Compared now to what it once hath bin.
Our Motto write in teares, that all may View it,
That Predicates our Glory greate is FUIT. (*Minor Poetry* 21)

Taylor was surely aware of the dismissive effect of the Latin verb (*fuit* –
"it was") if read as an English pun. With Symmes's passing New
England's glory had receded one saint deeper into darkness. In the otherness of his piety, Symmes embodied a success story authored and
enabled by God's mercy, taking his place on the safe side of the "potent

fence" that separated the victorious dead from their brooding survivors. The deceased had found bliss, but who could say when God's anger might suddenly close the gates forever? As elegists and their readers celebrated these victories, they could not help asking what is perhaps the one inevitable question of elegy: what about us?

The challenge of elegy placed Puritans in a double bind, a no-man's land between callousness and hysteria. On the one hand, biblical precedent made it clear that a failure to mourn revealed a shameful indifference to God's people. As the young Cotton Mather asked at the death of Urian Oakes, "what *Man* won't a *Mourner* now become?" (*Verse* 52). On the other hand, to grieve according to one's natural impulses revealed a misguided compulsion to lament what should be celebrated as a saint's final victory. Mather clarified the dilemma in a sermon based on Paul's admonition not to forget those who "sleep in Jesus" (1 Thess. 4:14). "To have no *Sorrow at all*, Or to be *without Natural affection*," Mather concedes, "is to be *worse than Infidels*." But "To indulge *too much Sorrow*, and to fall into *Extravagant* and *Exorbitant* Ejaculations, this is to be *as bad as Infidels*" (*Awakening Thoughts* 4–5). Why does so glorious a fulfillment of God's plan as a saint's victory leave us stunned and fearful? Mather framed an answer by having the deceased Nathanael Collins dismiss the outpouring of grief: "FOND *Mortals*; wipe your eyes (said he) pray keep / That *liquor* for your selves" (*Verse* 72). Mather's Collins might just as well have asked, "Woman, why weepest thou?" (John 20:15) – the words of the risen Jesus to Mary Magdalene in the garden. When Puritans asked the question of themselves, they concluded that God had sent them a humbling lesson. The settled state of the dead pointed up the *un*settled state of survivors forced to examine their real motives for grieving. Often the answer was not comforting. Mather's Collins speaks the needed correction by accusing his mourners of bad faith: "poor *Envy* 'tis / Which prompts your *Threnodies* for me. To weep / For *my Sake*, is but to Ignore *my Bliss*" (*Verse* 72). We have seen that overdeveloped carnal love was frequently suspected as lurking among the motives for sorrow. There might even be, as Mather hints, a trace of envy or resentment. Why was *I* not worthy to be taken? What lessons have I not learned that *my* peace has been deferred?

Because the fact of grief evidenced damning self-centeredness, elegy was unsingable unless the survivor could be deflected from natural mourning to what Richard Sibbes called "spiritual mourning," sorrow not for the loss so much as for the sin that caused the loss. For such difficult work, Puritans acknowledged the useful regulation provided by poetic form. As Mather stated in his poem for Urian Oakes, "A *Verse* our *Custome*, and thy *Friends* will have: / And must I *brue* my Tears? ah! shall I *fetter* / My Grief, by studying for to *mourn* in *Metre*?" (*Verse* 53). Given the natural propensities of the bereaved, to have one's grief fettered "in *Metre*" was far preferable to letting it run an unrestrained course. Like every other rite under the New Dispensation, commemoration demanded a gracious spirit – and the challenge of summoning up such a spirit at times of loss was formidable. The process necessarily started from multiple convictions in wickedness: original sin and its debt, which had just been paid by the deceased; the sin of grief as a sign of excessive love for the creatures; the sin inherent in the fact of remaining alive in a world unworthy of the deceased's piety. There were, in addition, the performative dangers inseparable from elegy. Poets acknowledged not only a mismatch between fallen language and sacred task, but the irony of using human speech to praise a now-divine self. There was the danger of hypocrisy if poets wrote what was untrue or what they did not feel, and thus reproduced the wretched excess and hollow rhetoric of secular elegy. A related danger lay in taking pride in the results, the poet's occupational curse and a negation of why elegy existed in the first place. Finally, and always, there was the danger of failing to perform the inner ritual that the poem was written to stimulate. If the poet was unable to transcend the natural sorrow common to believers and unbelievers alike, the poem could not move readers beyond what Taylor called mere "blubbering," that profitless species of grieving which not only rejected the consolations of faith but made loss even harder to bear.

As we have seen, most Puritans were convinced that the "literary" elegies of the day offered little help in avoiding these pitfalls. The pastoral elegy in particular encouraged a suspect blend of *thanatos* and *eros* in worldly panegyric that merely extolled profane virtues. Puritans countered this deadly conflation with their own blend of *thanatos* and *caritas*, conceived and rendered in terms of the spiritual marriage between Christ and the believing Bride. John Danforth biblicized the traditional elegiac conflation of love and death when he confirmed that Anne Eliot now possessed "*Heav'n's* Richest Spices" and "Choice Graces," which were "[*Queen Esther* like,] allotted to *Thy Share*, / For to *Prepare* Thee for Thy KING" (Meserole 321). The dead had entered into an eternal marriage – and the goal of pious mourning was not simply to untangle the intertwined threads of earthly love and death, but to subordinate both to the spiritual love shared by Christ and the deceased. The

ancients' priorities in grieving, though fully human, were all wrong for
the simple reason that they *were* fully human, devoid of the benefits of
such love. Cotton Mather agreed that without a moderating of sorrow,
"We render our selves too like unto the *Hopeless Pagans*, who did on such
Occasions abandon themselves unto hideous and endless Lamentations" (*Awakening Thoughts* 3). Why write elegy at all if it merely
heaped spiritual harm on top of natural sorrow? Mourning without
repentance was deadly, and excessive grief suggested that true repentance had not yet been achieved. Such mourners, as Sibbes declared,
"must unweep this weeping" (270).

The challenge of finding a right way to weep placed the elegist at the
center of some difficult dichotomies: between strong emotion and a
need for restraint, between anger at the loss and faith in the rightness in
God's ways, between the mysteries of death and the directives of theology, between love for the deceased and fear for the self, between stunned
passivity and a need to *do* something in the face of loss. For Puritans, the
elegist's bind had a familiar, biblical feel. Scripture contained hundreds
of stories in which God required the impossible but provided the means
to do it. Like salvation itself, the truly efficacious elegy lay beyond mere
human agency. But what divine power did for the deceased it might also
do, on a smaller scale, for a poet who took up the sad duty with a pure
heart.

It should be clear by now that elegies were high-stakes poems in early
New England. There is little wonder that elegists often framed the act of
writing as a burden nearly equal to that posed by grief itself. Proper
verbal mourning did not require a skilled poet so much as a sincere
believer – and who could make that claim? "Reader," Urian Oakes conceded in his poem on Thomas Shepard II, "I am no Poet: but I grieve!"
(Meserole 208). When Oakes died, William Adams asked in turn, "Who
among us" can write a poem "worthy of our departed President?" ("quis
nostrum poterit defuncto Praeside dignum?") (Kaiser 36). The elegist's
dilemma was more than merely artistic, though the impossibility of
finding the right words became its most explicit trope. Sincere and vehement grief offered a measure of vindication by certifying the elegist as
someone who cared deeply for God's people. But grief exposed another,
darker dimension within the mourner, and many elegiac speakers
confess an inability to achieve the resignation urged by their own words.
Especially in the opening lines, the speaker often concedes to having
been caught off guard by the loss, exposed in an unregenerate forgetting
of the fact that everyone dies.

On a rational level (Puritans would call it a "notional" level), New England's elegists certainly understood that each saint was, as Oakes called Shepard, "a Loan / Of Heaven" (Meserole 212). Bradstreet similarly described her granddaughter as a "fair flower that for a space was lent" (235), and Benjamin Tompson confirmed that his sister-in-law Mary Tompson was but "a stock in hand only on trust, / Which to Returne upon Demand is just" (Murdock 4). As Tompson reaffirmed when his niece Elizabeth died, Christ "takes no more than what he lends or gives" (Murdock 10). But even as they voice these theological truisms, elegists frequently acknowledge their need for the strictures of verse in order to say anything at all. The issue recalls Mather's comment about being fettered in meter. Confessions of grief that cannot, in Oakes's phrase, be "Curb'd, and rein'd-in by measur'd Poetry" (Meserole 208) create a double tension: first, between how the speaker feels about the death and how he knows he *should* feel about it; and second, between the strong emotion that the elegist confesses and the stylized structures in which that emotion was insistently embedded.

Such dichotomies, which echoed the deceased's splitting into body and soul, clarified the opposition of sinful and saintly tendencies within the mourner. A struggle suggestive of the redemptive turmoil thought to occur within all believers thus receives situational restatement in the poet's attempts to write while ostensibly being scarcely in control. Taylor begins his poem on his wife by conceding a human inability to accept what God has wrought:

> Some deem Death doth the True Love Knot unty:
> But I do finde it harder tide thereby
> My heart is in't & will be Squeez'd therefore
> To pieces if thou draw the Ends much more. (*Minor Poetry* 110)

Taylor refers to the poem as "this little Vent hole" designed "for reliefe," an image he also used over thirty years later at the death of Increase Mather: "Should silence now be hid our sorrows big / To get a vent would breake thy Coffin lid" (*Minor Poetry* 246). To "vent" grief was to confess a sinful opposition to God's will – but failing to acknowledge grief was dishonest, a denial of the sin that godly mourning was supposed to expose. By freely confessing to a self stung by God's will, the elegist dramatized the need for divine help in moving beyond unchecked lamentation, those "Streams of bitterness" that Samuel Danforth II cites in a poem for Thomas Leonard (Meserole 489). As in all Puritan confessions, the only solution was to tell a theologically explicit version of the truth – to transcend immoderate response by stating it as emphatically as possible. "Grief will find Vent," Danforth declares, "and Fulness of affection / How to express our selves will give direction" (Meserole 489)."Next to the Tears our sins do need and crave," Oakes states, "I would bestow my Tears on *Shepards* Grave" (Meserole 211). Conceding that it is "our sins" which "need and crave" such expression, Oakes presents himself as someone laboring under a grief that is neither reducible to the usual constraints of poetry nor appropriate to the duty at hand. By repudiating the "celebrated Sisters," the poet demeans elegiac convention even as he exploits it as the best available expression of – and restriction on – his grief:

> We need no *Mourning Womens* Elegy,
> No forc'd, affected, artificial Tone.
>   Great and good *Shepard's* Dead! Ah! this alone
>   Will set our eyes abroach, dissolve a stone.   (Meserole 210)

To grieve falsely, whether immoderately or mechanically, was to betray a lack of faith. Set within a commemorative rite expressive of such faith, poetic virtuosity was as dangerous as hypocrisy or indifference. In his elegy on John Hull, Saffin similarly refuses to invoke the Muses "To screw my Muse up to a Mournfull Straine." Reality is sad enough, and Hull's death will, in itself, provide whatever eloquence the poet can muster: "this, this, is cause alone, / The Dove-like Meek-Beloved John is gone" (Meserole 200).

The only honest response to a death was a Puritan version of "look in thy heart and write." But what did elegists say they found there? Most often, they voiced an all-too-human tendency to let immoderate emotion cloud the wisdom of God's ways, even to the point of weeping at a fellow believer's victory over the flesh. Benjamin Colman, consoling "Urania" on the "Death of her first and only Child," applies Christ's question in the garden – "Why weepest thou?" – to a mother's loss:

> Why mourns my beauteous Friend, bereft?
> Her Saviour and her Heav'n are left:
> Her lovely Babe is there at Rest,
> In Jesus' Arms embrac'd and blest.   (Meserole 337)

Bradstreet poses the same question at the death of granddaughter Elizabeth: "why should I once bewail thy fate, / Or sigh thy days so soon were terminate, / Sith thou art settled in an everlasting state?" (235). In a brief poem on William Tompson, Samuel Danforth puts the question on the lips of the deceased: "Why wepe yea still for me, my Children dear? / What Cause have ye of sorow, grief or fear?" (Murdock 19).

Saffin has the spirit of John Hull issue similar advice derived from Jesus's admonition to the weeping women of Jerusalem: "Mee thinkes I heare his blessed Genious say / Weep not for me, but for yourselves aright" (Meserole 201). Taylor imagines his wife Elizabeth issuing a gentle reprimand from beyond the grave (*Minor Poetry* 111). To grieve excessively was not only to ignore the deceased's victory, but to forget that the death was caused, as Bradstreet reminds herself, "by His hand alone that guides nature and fate." The motto to Francis Drake's elegy on Jonathan Mitchell gave the same blunt truth: "Whatever we do, whatever we suffer, comes from above" ("Quicquid agimus, quicquid Patimur venit ex Alto") (Meserole 457).

Sin caused death, death brought grief, and grief exposed sin – and nobody still in the world could escape, or forget, this endless cycle. As Philip Pain attested, "Alas, what's Sorrow? 'tis our portion here; / The Christian's portion, Trouble, Grief, and Fear" (Meserole 289). To grieve excessively was to forget that each deceased saint was, like Bradstreet's granddaughter, someone's "heart's too much content" (235), another example of the human compulsion to place earthly love above heavenly. Not even Cotton Mather was above this lesson. Nicholas Noyes warned him, at the death of his wife, against singing "*Threnodies* that are unjust": "Let not cross'd *Nature* now repine; / Sir, *Grace* hath taught you to resign / To *Christ*, what *Nature* called, *Mine!*" (Meserole 282). Mather the minister knew this, of course, but Mather the earthly pilgrim was still struggling against his fallen "Nature." Placing too much affection on souls on loan from God was an inevitable part of being human, a point that John Danforth makes while consoling Samuel Gerrish on the death of his wife Mary: "You grieve, the Time's so short; but yet / had you Enjoy'd her longer, / The Bands of Love had Faster grown, / and Bands of Grief much stronger" (Meserole 318). At the death of her child, Colman reminds "Urania" that God had every right "The Loan at Pleasure to resume, / And call the pretty Stranger Home" (Meserole 338). For Colman, as for other elegists, tears merely exposed an unbowed will: "Learn hence, *Urania*, to be dumb! / Learn thou the Praise that may become / Thy lighter Grief; which Heaven does please / To take such wondrous Ways to ease" (Meserole 339). Dead saints had learned this lesson, and elegists showed them standing ready to teach it forcefully to survivors. The deceased Mary Tompson, Benjamin Tompson confirms, would "Chide those teares of, & make you refrain" (Murdock 5). In a poem for his mother, Tompson has Abigaill Tompson tell her husband that if he truly loves either her or Christ, "do not thou my Death too much deplore" (Murdock 8). Elijah Corlet states that Thomas Hooker's survivors would gladly have pursued their own selfish ends and blocked his path to heaven, trapping his soul in "snares of endless prayers and tears" ("insidias precibus lacrymisque perennibus") (Kaiser 18).

The dilemmas posed by death and articulated in elegy made it clear that grief was a holy sin, the paradoxical response of an equally paradoxical self in which the sinful and saintly tendencies were inseparably mingled. As Ruth Wallerstein once remarked in reference to "Lycidas," "In the Christian experience of death as it was early formulated, there were two griefs, the personal grief which kills, [and] the grief of repentance leading to God" (110–11). Confessing the former in order to promote the latter, Puritan elegists linked both to the conviction and consolation central to redeemed experience generally. Being human, one had to grieve. But grief also exposed a fallen perspective in the mourner's sadness over an act of God. In his poem on Samuel Hooker, Taylor makes the paradoxical essence of Puritan mourning explicit:

> Griefe sometimes is a duty yet when Greate
> And geteth vent, it Non-Sense sobs doth speake
> Cutting off Sentences by Enterjections
> Made by the force of hard beset Affections. (*Minor Poetry* 116)

When mourners turned from loss to language, from sorrow to commemoration, unchecked words were not just sinful but unintelligible, a Babel of nonsense that contrasted sadly with the calm majesty of the Word. As Taylor confirmed in the Hooker elegy, tears are "Becoming" provided they come "not to excess. / Then keep due measure. Should you too much bring, / Your too much is too little far for him" (*Minor Poetry* 122). Taylor tells Hooker's children that "Weeping for him is honour due from you. / Yet let your Sorrows run in godly wise / As if his Spirits tears fell from your eyes" (123). Don't just grieve *for* Hooker, Taylor insists. You must try to grieve *like* him, like someone who has attained the celestial perspective on death. As Taylor conceded in "Upon Wedlock, & Death of Children," "nature fault would finde" (*Minor Poetry* 107) with God's decision to take the lives of loved ones. The natural impulse to grieve, however, could neither explain nor console. "Nature" had to be transcended.

This ambivalence toward grief accounts for the pervasive tension in Puritan elegy between emotional chaos and rhetorical control. Even as the poets denigrate the conventions of verbal mourning as inadequate expressions of their loss, they seize upon them as the most reliable means to achieve a pious if shaky stoicism. In a late example, Thomas Bridge's anonymous elegist frames the poet's search for verbal decorum as a check on the mourner's worst self: "You, who possess a more restrained grief and a Muse suited to learned writing – say what kind of man he was" ("Vos quibus est luctus moderatior, aptaque doctis / Musa vero scriptis, pangite qualis erat") (Kaiser 42). Oakes voices a similar opposi- tion of natural grief and restrictive form:

> He that his crosses wailes
> Indeed, would vent his griefs without restraints.
>   To tye our grief to numbers, measures, feet,
>   Is not to let it loose, but fetter it. (Meserole 208)

Oakes makes full use of the very conventions he disdains as a matter of theological necessity. Pearse's handbook on holy dying assured pious readers that death would carry them "from a strange Land to thine own Home, and Father's House" (150). Still, natural love would beg for a delay – just this once – in a beloved soul's return to the heavenly mansion. Natural sorrow, unaided by grace, could produce only a futile wailing that demonstrated the need for a manner of grieving superior to that pursued by nonbelievers and pagans. Puritans accepted the inevita- bility of sadness, pain, and even anger at the loss of a loved one. They were equally certain, however, that mourners who overindulged such feelings would suffer even greater anguish when death came for them.

Puritan commemoration began in a dual act of faith and confession: faith that the dead had attained the greatest reward conceivable, and confession that their sanctity seemed hopelessly distant. In contrast to the ethereal Shepard, transformed by death and grace into a pure, Christic spirit, Oakes underscores the corporeal sluggishness of survi- vors, who remain "clogg'd with sin and clay" (Meserole 220). An expli- citly theological framing of this contrast came from Nicholas Noyes, who urged Mather at the death of his wife Abigail to "Grudge not her *Happiness* above; / You live by *Faith*, and she by *Love*" (Meserole 282). Building on the biblical paradox of losing one's life in order to save it, the Puritan elegist consistently reminded survivors that it was they who were truly "dead" in their corporeality. Noyes voiced a common theme in asserting that "To *live* is *Christ*" – that is, to suffer like the earthly Christ – and "to *Dy* is *Gain*" (Meserole 282). Mather similarly claimed that Nathanael Collins "changed Death for *LIFE*" (*Verse* 63). The inversion of life and death, central to the resurrective core of the New Testament, was one of the paradoxes that Wigglesworth examined in "Riddles Unriddled." Christ's sacrifice, Wigglesworth declares, has made death into "a Bridge whereby / We pass to Heavenly Rest." If this were fully understood, "Who would not then be willing, / *When* Christ him calleth hence, / To lay aside this sinful Flesh" (*Poems* 251, 254)? The saintly reversal of life and death, also central to English funeral elegies (Bennett 118, 123), was the principle theme of Pain's *Daily Meditations*, an extended self-elegy reiterating the promise that "By death I live if that I live to Christ" (Meserole 288). Samuel Torrey turned William Tompson's chronic melancholia into an emblem of the passage to true life undergone by all elect souls: Tompson was "By Death deliverd from yt liveing grave. / By this thine epitaph, now thou art gon: / Thy death it was thy resurrection" (Silverman 144). An anonymous poet has Lydia Minot claim that "Life unto Life is gone, through th' Living way": "When Breath expir'd, my Life came flowing in; / My Soul reviv'd, made free from th' death of Sin" (Winslow 7). At John Norton's passing, John Wilson began his elegy by insisting that "God himself crowns his servant, when he dies, with deathless honor" ("Deus ipse coronat honore / servum, cum periit, non pereunte suum") (Kaiser 14). Eleazar, a student at Harvard's Indian school, made the same point about Thomas Thatcher in an echo of Paul's celebration of Christ's victory over the grave in 1 Corinthians: "Now the Cross stands empty: his bones rest in the grave, but death is dead; blessed life returns to life" ("Crux jam cassa manet; requiescunt ossa sepulchro; / mors moritur; vitae vita beata redit") (Kaiser 34).

These sentiments echo Paul's theology of the "body of this death" (Rom. 7:24): to be still in the flesh was to be slain in sin and the law. It was also, Puritans believed, to live with a frustrating separation from God. Of this, too, the holy dead provided humbling reminders, as John Fiske makes clear in an address to the deceased Anne Griffin:

> What thou heere soughtst, pray'd for, hop'd for, desir'd
> Which heere is not our portion to Enjoy
> That there Thou hast more fully then requir'd
> Or understood could bee whilst sin annoy[.] (Meserole 191)

Griffin's spiritual fulfillment reminds Fiske that such joy is not the "portion" of the living. Edward Johnson similarly complains, at the death of Thomas Shepard I, that "hee's in Heaven, but I one Earth am left: / More Earthly, 'cause of him I am bereft" (Meserole 151). Elegists repeatedly confirmed that the deceased's escape from physicality under-scored the "More Earthly" situation of those left behind. Fiske insists that the one soul *not* to be pitied at Samuel Sharpe's death is Sharpe, who enjoys "An Ample-share in the Reward he has / which layd up is in Heaven" (Silverman 139). The real objects of pity, as we saw in Wilson's elegy on Norton, were not the dead but the living: they had "grief, but he had the highest glory" ("his dolor, ast illi gloria summa fuit") (Kaiser 14). Edward Taylor agreed that Richard Mather's glorification pointed up the fallen condition of his survivors. Indeed, Mather's loss "would sinke us if [w]e did not spie, / That whilst we drown in griefe he swims in Joy" (*Minor Poetry* 20).

For perfectly human reasons, such intense concentration on someone else's joy was more easily sought than achieved. Taylor finds himself unable to assume the role of a soul outstripped in glory by the deceased without a measure of irritation, as his closing words to President Chauncy of Harvard suggest:

> Well, Chauncey, well, thou, where thou wouldst be, art.
> We Sink in Sorrow, judgment, & the Darke.
>   In middst of all the Combat pray do we
>   Inable us, oh Lord, to Shine as Hee. (*Minor Poetry* 35)

Because we remain mired in the "Sorrow, judgment, & the Darke" of earthly "Combat," Taylor concedes, Chauncy's rest makes our *unrest* more poignant (*Minor Poetry* 35). We have heard Cotton Mather's Nathanael Collins accuse the living of "poor *Envy*" in their inability to celebrate "*my Bliss.*" Envy for the dead highlights the deceased's role as a convicting text, an authoritative source of correction. When Mather has Collins attest to his current enjoyment of the "ever-glorious Face of the GOD-MAN," the deceased's words sound almost like a boast: "I *Know*, I *Live*, I *Love*; but *How?* forbear / To be inquisitive: It can't be told / To *You*" (*Verse* 73, 72). In John Wilson's poem on Abigaill Tompson, the deceased tells her husband that for all his ministerial experience, he cannot begin to know what heaven is like. "And i believd," she says, that

> . . .if any knew, twas thou
> That knewest what a thing it was; but now
> I se thou sawest but a glimps, and hast
> No more of heaven but a little tast,
> Compared with that which hear we see & have,
> Nor Canst have more till thou art past the grave. (Murdock 8)

The boasts of the dead are a common feature in Puritan elegy. Samuel Stone has William Leet attest to a heavenly joy so great that readers could not help but feel deprived: "Well I am now, my Christian Friends

beleive it / In Joy so great, you cannot well conceive it" (Jantz 156).
Samuel Danforth has William Tompson claim that he is "With rarest
pleasures the highest heavens aford, / Feasted, refresh'd, beyond
exp[e]rienc glad" (Murdock 20). Simply to remain alive was to be denied
such vision, a humbling lesson that Benjamin Tompson stressed in his
tribute to Samuel Sewall's granddaughter, six-year-old Rebekah, by
asserting her celestial wisdom: "Could She, from her New School,
obtain the leave, / She'd tell you Things would make you cease to
grieve" (Winslow 27).

As I have suggested, the sin-drawn line between the dead and the
living found a discursive parallel in the contrast between the celestial
object celebrated by the poem and the fallen language in which the
poem had to be written. Elegists routinely made a sharp distinction
between the grief they felt and the poem itself as a second-rate expression of that grief. In this they echoed Donne, who questioned, at the
death of the fifteen-year-old Elizabeth Drury, the efficacy of "Carkas
verses, whose soul is not shee": "Can these memorials, ragges of paper,
give / Life to that name, by which name they must live?" (*Complete Poetry*
286). New England's elegists frequently registered similar shame at the
predictable direction that their grief, once verbalized, had to take. They
defended their efforts, however, by appealing to the depth of a sorrow
that could not otherwise find expression. "Reader! I am no Poet,"
exclaims Oakes, "but I grieve!" Oakes's apology is really an assertion.
After all, it was sincere grief and not verbal skill that determined an
elegist's fitness. Whether the elegy stands or falls will depend on whether
sorrow finds its proper reinscription as piety – and in this, the poet

> . . .wisely doth perform his mourning part
> In Verse, lest grief should time and measure miss.
> But griefs unmeasurable would not be
> Curb'd, and rein'd-in by measur'd Poetry. (Meserole 208)

Here we return to the Puritan elegist's rage for order. New England's
elegists invoked the conventions they disdained in order not to "miss" the
"time" and "measure" of commemorating God's people. Without
recourse to the verbal formulas of "measur'd Poetry," a potent opportunity for furthering God's work might evaporate in compulsive babble
or mute despair. "Behold here," Oakes warns, "what that passion can
do! / That forc'd a verse, without *Apollo's* leave." Yet the very fact that
Apollo had little to do with it was what would save the poem from hollow
virtuosity:

Could I take highest Flights of Fancy, soar
Aloft; If Wits Monopoly were mine:
All would be much too low, too light, too poor,
To pay due tribute to this great Divine.
    Ah! Wit avails not, when th' Heart's like to break,
      Great griefs are Tongue-ti'ed, when the lesser speak.
                              (Meserole 210)

Heartfelt grief covered a multitude of artistic sins, but it also exposed spiritual sins that were far more threatening. The value of confessing to a broken heart lay in its capacity to lay bare those sins, and many others, with glaring clarity. "Fancy" and "wit" became the elegist's worst enemies because they worked to dull the poem's force as an act of contrition.

Ultimately, the poet's confessed inadequacy was symptomatic of deeper unworth. In his poem for John Hull, Saffin asserts that despite the weakness of his "Punie Muse," he is determined to bring his widow's mite of praise: "Such as I have my humble Muse here brings / As a free offering" (Meserole 200). Grindall Rawson, confessing a similar inability to eulogize Saffin's son with any hope of success, echoes Oakes in claiming that Apollo himself could not help a poet so wracked with grief:

> But ah! my Simple muse, what flattering smile
> Drawn from Apollo's face could so beguile,
> Thy feeble hopes to think thou couldst acquitt
> What's Due unto his Learning, vertue Witt. . . (Meserole 478)

A poet's muse, "Simple" or not, could not possibly pay "What's Due" a glorified saint. The result was an inversion of the professionalism associated with the pastoral elegy – a *loss* of control that provided, paradoxically enough, conventional justification for the poet's right to write. A professed loss of words makes words possible. At Jonathan Mitchell's death, Francis Drake complains that "*Sighs* diffuse / *Convulsions* through my language, such as use / To type a *Gasping Fancy*" (Meserole 458). John Danforth approaches the obsequies of Hannah Sewall, Judge Sewall's wife, with a "*Ruffled Mind*" and a "Trembling" pen. To extol such a saint with poor words, Danforth concedes, would be an impertinence: "Shall We adventure these Unpolish'd Lines? / *Lucina*'s Dust deserves far Richer Shrines" (Winslow 31). An anonymous poet interrupts his "mournful Muse" to complain that he could praise Governor Winthrop of Connecticut adequately only if "I had / *Briarius* hands to set his virtues forth, / And *Argus* Eyes to weep his golden worth" (Winslow 9). John Norton similarly ends his tribute to Anne Bradstreet by claiming to be unable to continue because there is simply too much that could be said: "Who undertakes this subject to commend / Shall nothing find so hard as how to end" (Meserole 463).

Such confessions of emotion may indeed "force" a poem, as Oakes conceded (Meserole 208). But as Mather admitted in his elegy for Oakes, "From first to last, *Grief never made good Poet*" (*Verse* 54). At the death of Ezekiel Cheever, Mather attested that the holy dead lay beyond any poet's capacity to describe them. "*Ink* is too vile a Liquor" for Cheever's praise: "*Liquid Gold* / Should fill the Pen, by which such things are told" (*Verse* 89). The deceased's glory has raised the challenge of elegy to impossible levels. At times, elegists protest that the shock of death has rendered them incapable of using language at all. At John Allen's death, Taylor claims to have received the news like a watchman whose breastplate has been pierced with bullets, and like a rose that is "All barbd, & Shrivles up its leaves" from a lightning stroke (*Minor Poetry* 30). Word of the death of John Reiner similarly incapacitates Joshua Moody, who responds, as we have seen, by imitating the dissolution of a dying person: "I heard, Lips quiver'd, Belly trembled, / My Spirits fail'd, Corruption seiz'd my Bones, / My Face grew pale, my heart as cold as Stones" (Jantz 151). Eleazar confesses to stunned silence when Thomas Thatcher dies: "The mind staggers and mouths are stopped" ("Mens stupet, ora silent") (Kaiser 34). At Oakes's death, Adams claims that "unexpected death strikes my ears with wondrous blows" ("miris ferit ictibus aures / mors inopina meas"): "a trembling seizes each limb, stunning the stricken soul" ("totos pavor occupat artus, / attonitum reddens animum") (Kaiser 36). And at the death of Elijah Corlet, Nehemiah Walter claims that grief "presses hard our tim'rous heart whence flows / A Torrent of amazing Fears, whose *Waves*" threaten to bring "Universal *Deluge* to that Verse / That dares pretend to equalize his *Fame*" (Meserole 465).

With faculties so incapacitated, how could anyone possibly write a poem worthy of the occasion? As Thomas Bridge's anonymous elegist asks, "Woe is me: what tears shall I pour from my eyes, what laments from my mouth? / To what end this my elegy?" ("Hei mihi quas oculis lachrymas, quas ore querelas / fundam? quis elegis terminus iste meis?") (Kaiser 41). And if uncontrolled tears were an inadequate response to sacred duty, grief-wracked silence was worse. John Danforth opens his lament for Peter Thatcher and Samuel Danforth II by complaining that his grief has left him "Dumb": "and would we be press'd to Death as Mutes? / Angels use speaking Arts: but rarely Brutes" (Meserole 310). In his poem for Oakes, Cotton Mather graphically conveys the stunned silence of a speaker shocked out of speech by the very event that he must commemorate:

> The wrath of the Eternal wields a blow
> At which my Pen is gastred —
>
> ————————————————
>
> But up! — Lord! wee're undone — Nay! Up and Try!
> Heart! Vent thy *grief*! Ease *Sorrow* with a *Sigh*! (*Verse* 57)

Bringing the silence of conviction into the poem as a series of visual blanks, the sullen beats of a broken heart, Mather confirms that language can express neither Oakes's glory nor a godly response to his loss. Acutely aware of the feebleness of their words, elegists approached the glorious dead with extraordinary reverence. In his elegy on Elijah Corlet, Nehemiah Walter invokes the image of a scared rabbit to convey the intimidating inequity of poem and subject:

> *Creep* then, poor *Rythmes*, and like a *timid Hare*
> Encircle his rich Vault, then gently *squatt*
> Upon his Grave the Center there proclaim
> Tho' he *subside*, yet his abounding Worth
> Does infinitely *supersede* thy *Layes*. (Meserole 465)

We cannot help but smile at Walter's image, so determined he was to voice a humility appropriate to the saint's apotheosis. But in his view, Corlet had become nearly as difficult to portray with words as Christ himself. Walter's self-deprecation was surely intended — and given the gap between medium and message, the humorous description of his efforts may have been intentional as well.

The insistence on the insufficiency of language assumes real poignancy in poems in which elegist and deceased shared an intimate relationship. In his poem for first wife Elizabeth, Taylor disparages the sadly conventional form that he knows his speech must assume, conceding that his best efforts will produce only "a mournfull Song," "blubber'd Verse / Out of my Weeping Eyes Upon thy Herse" – a mere "Weeping Poem" that "Cramping Griefe permitts to Stut" (*Minor Poetry* 111). Elizabeth's death must have posed as difficult a challenge as Taylor could imagine – a brutal juxtaposition of the sin and the piety that were inseparable from grief. Taylor tells his wife that his "mournfull Poem may / Advance thy joy, & my Deep Sorrow lay," but only if "Some Angell may my Poem Sing / To thee in Glory, or relate the thing" (111). Here, the performative pressure of elegy is at its highest: not only does Taylor need an angel's help to write, but he assumes that "Bright Saints, & Angells," including his beloved wife, will be among his readers. Elizabeth was now celestial, and his sad task was mandated by heaven itself. Taylor, of course, was still earth-bound, and probably never felt more so than when he was writing this poem.

The truly worthy elegy was, in the Puritan view, impossible to write. Speech was deeply suspect, and the occasion of death forced the poet to choose between using a corrupt medium or maintaining a sullen, disrespectful silence in the face of God's will. The stunned silence reflected in *not* writing was a far cry from the silence of pious resignation. The latter was a "Silence" that "becomes us, and Submission," as Nicholas Noyes stated in his poem for Mary Gerrish, "For we should come to this; *Thy Will be Done!*" (Winslow 29). But if silence could have convicting or consoling implications, depending on the mourner's motives, so could artful speech. Could an elegy be too well-made for its own good? How was one to reconcile rhetorical *inventio* – a poet's discovery of the right words – with the belief that the most sublime models for verbal mourning already existed in Scripture? How, in short, could one write an occasional poem with the humility that the occasion demanded? As we will see, the problems of elegy could not be resolved if poets insisted on seeing it in terms of writerly authority. The only chance for success, in the view of New England's elegists, was to work though a process by which one's gaze shifted from the grieving self to the commemorated other. Through an unblinking focus on the grace revealed in the deceased, a prideful writer could be refashioned into a selfless "reader" of piety. Only then, with a reorientation of poetic vocation around its more literal sense of a believer's "calling," could these unsingable songs be sung.

5

Lord, is it I?: Christic saints and apostolic mourners

The occasion of death forced New England's elegists to choose between facility and honesty, between writing an aesthetically assertive poem or a poem that spoke more directly to the sin that grief exposed. This was not an especially difficult decision: to choose properly was to align oneself with Puritan attitudes toward poetry generally. The deeper dilemma of elegy stemmed from the mandate of rigorous self-examination in the face of loss – and it centered on the poet's motives for writing. The holy sin of grief created an uneasy space between incoherent babbling and rueful silence, between giving free rein to sorrow and not writing at all. Poets caught in this disturbing position registered ambivalence toward the limitations imposed by elegiac conventions. We have seen that even though they complained at being "Curb'd, and rein'd-in by measur'd Poetry," in Urian Oakes's phrase (Meserole 208), they accepted such restrictions as necessary vehicles for fulfilling the resurrective mandate of a truly Christian lament. In this, too, lay a submission of will. Elegies were written not just to honor the dead but to make mourners more *like* them, and to translate human tears into a vehicle for furthering God's work in the world was to imitate the piety of the souls being commemorated. The spiritual and the artistic problems of elegy thus found identical resolution in a repudiation of self, both as worldly mourner and as professional poet.

The work of elegy had to be done from evangelical and not legalistic motives, a stance consistent with how Puritans saw the performance of all pious duties foreshadowed in the ceremonial types of the Old Testament. Baptism enacted a spiritual recapitulation of circumcision and the Lord's Supper did the same for Passover – but only if these rites were observed as expressions of faith and not works. This stress on intention over outcome was extended beyond the Sacraments to encompass all sorts of religious activities. Edward Taylor, contemplating the morning and evening Temple sacrifices described in Numbers 28, found typological precedent for his daily prayers and meditations: "The Ceremonies cease, but yet the Creede / Contained therein, continues gospelly" (*Poems* 129). John Weemse clarified how the ceremonial types could continue "gospelly," free from legalistic demands. "The Saints are judged," Weemse explained, "*in foro novae obedientiae, non stricti iuris*" – not by the rigors of the law, but in accordance with a new obedience defined by faith rather than performance. When judging Christian acts of worship, God "accepts the will for the deed": the "end" will find approval "although the meanes oftentimes bee defective" (302). Just as Taylor connected private prayer with the Temple cult, poets found what Oakes called "Diviner Warrant" for elegy (Meserole 209) in texts like David's lament, appropriated as precursors of a species of mourning that linked grief to repentance.

To perform elegy "gospelly" was to pull it safely within this "new obedience," to write from a humility appropriate to repentance and not from habit or artistic pride. For this the facility of the professional poet and the unfelt cries of the professional mourner were equally unsuited, as Oakes confirmed in his poem for Thomas Shepard:

> Away loose rein'd Careers of Poetry,
> The celebrated Sisters may be gone;
> We need no *Mourning Womens* Elegy,
> No forc'd, affected, artificial Tone. (Meserole 210)

What "tone" should one strike? As with all Puritan textual performances, the answer lay less in the product than the process, less in the artistic outcome than in the spirit in which the poem was written and the impact it had on mourners. Percivall Lowell voiced this attitude when he pledged "*Lowells* loyalty" to Governor John Winthrop in verses "Pen'd with his slender skill / And with it no good poetry, / Yet certainly good will" (Winslow 3). Once "loyalty" and "good will" – the equivalents of the pure heart of an efficacious ceremony – were firmly established as the motives for elegy, poets were free to develop a pointedly ritualistic discourse that seems, at first glance, sharply at odds with New England's antinomian strain. John Saffin, for instance, does not hesitate to create an elaborate funeral procession consisting of Thomas Danforth's "Offspring," "Senators," clergy, academics, and finally, "all the People" (137). "Lo! how they Muster and in crowding turn / To pay their Duty to his silent urn" (137). As in Milton's "Lycidas," the mourners include cosmic agents: "The Constellations of Benigne Starrs. / Conjoyn their Influences without Jarrs: / To Grace his Herse, and Phoebus (shineing clear) / Makes warm the Weather in our Hemisphere. . .In honour of his mournfull Obsequies. . ." (137). At the death of Governor John Leverett, Benjamin Tompson invokes a procession that includes the "Grand matron" Harvard, the "Infant schools," and the "Regiments, professours of the time" (Jantz 159). Such self-conscious invocations of ceremony helped create the perception of a common fate and a shared responsibility for the sin that took the deceased away. At the death of the elder Samuel Stone, E. B. (perhaps Edward Bulkeley) was typical in calling upon the towns of New England to "Come bear your parts in this *Threnodia* sad" (Silverman 142). By extolling such commonality and urgency of purpose, the elegy helped make public and mythic – and thus salvifically useful – a death that might otherwise remain private and anecdotal. Through elegy, the pure intentions of an acceptable sacrifice could be extended to an entire community.[1]

The predominant voice of Puritan elegy is thus a generic voice that coaxes readers toward a "we" expressive of collective response. And the pattern of that response is the same fear/hope cycle articulated in the jeremiad sermon and in redemptive experience generally. As Oakes makes clear, "we" have been singled out for divine punishment, but "we" are also the recipients of God's loving correction:

> Ah! but the Lesson's hard, thus to deny
> Our own dear selves, to part with such a Loan
> Of Heaven (in time of such necessity)
> And love thy comforts better than our own.
> > Then let us moan our loss, adjourn our glee,
> > Till we come thither to rejoice with thee. (Meserole 212)

As in the jeremiad, the deferral of "glee" chastens mourners with a harsh conviction in sin. But if they repent they can expect to "rejoice" with the dead in the next world. To struggle with grief was to renegotiate the most basic – and familiar – mandates of the faith, "to deny / Our own dear selves" and to "love" Shepard's "comforts better than our own." Elegy thus reconstructed mourning as a progression from randomness to order, from shock at a particular affliction to the recognition of an ongoing redemptive process that encompassed individual and society alike. Societies could repent – hadn't Nineveh turned at Jonah's preaching? – and such public events as days of fasting and humiliation encouraged New England to do so. But communal reform hinged on individual acts of penitence.

Elegists extolled the deceased as proof of the rewards of this process.

Commemorated as an embodiment of its conclusion, the dead saint was represented as a completed version of an inchoate self that survivors struggled to glimpse in private meditation, an "after" to their "before." Subsumed under a single subjective paradigm that was fully manifest only in the dead, speaker and reader focused on this deeper "self" as the true object of commemoration. Franklin was right when he observed that the Puritan dead are essentially interchangeable from poem to poem. But he missed why they had to be so, and how Puritan readers derived satisfaction from meditating on idealized figures who embodied a process by which all saints were saved.[2] The dead, elegists confirmed, were both different from and similar to the living. Because they had achieved a glory that contrasted sharply with earthly weakness, elegists were careful, as Kenneth Silverman notes, to portray them in distant terms (126). But the dead also embodied the fruition of patterns identifiable within the mourners' contemplative lives, especially at moments of warm religious assurance. Elegy helped readers feel the difference and sameness between living self and dead saint as an oscillation of sinful and saintly tendencies within themselves – an oscillation which suggested gracious activity. The result was an explicitly theological version of the twinning motif that appears in "Lycidas." Just as Milton's speaker and Lycidas were "nurst upon the self-same hill" (159), the living and the dead were linked by patterns of salvific experience. Merely to contemplate the holy dead – to absorb the fear and hope prompted by their pious example – was to replicate the process by which they had been tempered for heaven.

For Puritans, Christian hope resided in the ability to imagine such a self. But elegy, like the sermon, could not console until believers had been sincerely convicted in sin. The glorious otherness of the dead, which threw the contrast between sin and grace into high relief, was enlisted to this end. As Taylor reminded himself after a meditative struggle with earthly limitations, "Earth is not Heaven: Faith not Vision" (*Poems* 255). By reasserting this distinction through their otherworldly perfection, the dead offered a condemnation of the living. Cotton Mather thus asserts, in a convention also found in English elegies, that John Clark was too good for earth: "So must the Tree / Too rich for *Earth*, to *Heav'n* transplanted be" (*Verse* 86). Nehemiah Walter's elegy on Elijah Corlet makes the point by confirming that "*Natures* Tree" has grown too feeble "to bear such ponderous fruit" (Meserole 466). His piety having expanded beyond the capacity of a fallen world to contain it, Corlet has outgrown "nature" itself. Elegists repeatedly maintained that the best die so that the worst may be corrected. Oakes, warning that when "men of mercy go, / It is a sure presage of coming wo" (Meserole 212), declared that the sins of Shepard's survivors necessitated his sacrifice just as surely as original sin necessitated Christ's:

> See what our sins have done! what Ruines wrought
> And how they have pluck'd out our very eyes!
> Our sins have slain our *Shepard!* we have bought,
> And dearly paid for, our Enormities. (Meserole 219)

The deceased's now-Christic status invested each loss with neobiblical urgency. Every saintly death recapitulated and intensified guilt accruing from the Crucifixion. Addressed as participants in ongoing, localized reenactments of the Fall which necessitated that supreme sacrifice, New Englanders were killing off the very souls who could best lead them to heaven.[3]

With the withdrawal of the holy dead from a corrupt world, the simple fact of being alive became an indictment. The inequity of earthly loss and celestial gain seemed insurmountable, as John Saffin suggested at the death of John Wilson: "Great is our Loss in him but his gaine more / Who is Exalted to augment Heavens Store" (115). John Danforth insisted that Mary Gerrish, Samuel Sewall's daughter, died at nineteen "to her Profit, and our Loss" (Meserole 316). John Fiske similarly called the deceased Samuel Sharpe the real "Gayner," "changd" as he was "for ample-share of Blisse you see" (Jantz 125). Dead "gainers" made for living losers, and to survive was most assuredly to be punished. But for what? This was what readers were urged to discover for themselves. As Wilson proclaimed at the passing of John Norton,

> Oh! let us all impartially
>   our wayes and spirits search;
> And say as the Disciples did,
>   Lord, is it I? is't I? (Murdock 96)

Wilson's anxious question, an echo of the disciples' response to Christ's prediction that "one of you shall betray me" (Matt. 26:21), articulates the self-examination central to Puritan mourning. Was it my sin that killed the deceased? Although this seems a harsh question to ask mourners, Puritans were convinced that they could not hope for the glory attained by the dead unless they acknowledged a share in the sin that drove them off. Faced with the task of marking a neo-Christic sacrifice, elegists

offered their readers one more chance to profit from the deceased's
example – to heed in textual form those correctives which they had
rejected in the flesh.

Wilson's question also suggests the deeper strategy of Puritan elegy:
reshaping survivors into imperfect copies of the dead. In this, New
Englanders followed the New Testament call to believe and repent, a
kerygma at once proclamatory and dehortative. In seeking to praise the
dead and reform the living, elegy reproduced the eschatological urgency
of the gospels, especially Mark: the kingdom of God was at hand, and
the saint's passing proved that the time of entry – or exclusion – could
come at any time. Expressions of anguish over inadequate words and
vehement grief, however standardized, enacted Christ's command to
"weep not for me, but weep for yourselves" (Luke 23:28), and thus provided a foil to the presumed tranquility of the deceased. The fact that
pious mourning demanded repentance went far in easing the performative pressures of elegy. Repentance, after all, could not be achieved alone.
As Thomas Hooker advised spiritually downcast readers, "I do not say
thou canst do the work, but do thou go to him that can do it" (448).
Although Hooker was referring to Christ, elegy offered the deceased,
represented as Christ's emissary, as the figure who could "do" what the
poet could not. It was, finally, the dead saint and not the grieving speaker
who validated the poem as an instrument for transcending self-indulgent
sorrow. Whoever looked *only* in the heart and wrote found a spirit stung
by God's will, but whoever turned from wounded self to the saintly
pattern revealed in the deceased would discover, as Oakes called
Shepard, "A Monument more stately than the best," one that reflected
grace back into the "gratefull Breast" of those who cherished the
deceased's example (Meserole 211). The elegiac confrontation with sin,
though the indispensable first step of all repentance, was thus transcended through a contemplation of the *imitatio Christi* manifested in the
pious life that was being celebrated in the poem. This stands in sharp contrast to the classical tradition, which, as Eric Smith observes, extended
the poem itself as a stay against mutability: because the "finding of form
coincides with the defeat of grief," "the finished work is in some sense a
triumph over time" (21). New England elegies did not assert such permanence. Instead, the poem served as a transparent pointer toward the real
monument: the glorified saint. And *that* monument, objectified as a catalyst for spiritual renewal, would outlast not only the occasion of loss but
the poem itself, which dissolved as an artifact in its own redemptive use.

Ultimately, as William Scheick has observed, the elegiac monument embodied in the deceased was transferred to survivors, absorbed through a contemplation of the saintly dead and an assimilation of their gracious pattern ("Tombless Virtue" 296). The "fame" so prominent in "Lycidas" was thus redirected to the salvific instruction of the living – and it remained within reach of all who persisted in the path that the dead had blazed. As Benjamin Colman attested in a poem for Samuel Willard, "A *Name imbalm'd* shall be the *Just* Mans lot, / While vicious *Teeth* shall *gnash*, and *Names* shall rot" (Meserole 344). Cotton Mather, in his collective elegy for seven young ministers, demanded "*Eternity* for them; / And they shall Live too in *Eternal Fame*" (*Verse* 85). What Mather is actually commemorating is the saintly essence which defined all such souls – the piety that mandated a poem in the first place.

In this sense, elegy was enabled not by *writing* so much as by *seeing*, by bearing witness to a transformation into pure spirit that had already been effected by God himself. Because faith had carried the dead to glory, they needed only to be preserved "with the sweet smelling Spices," as Willard phrased it, "that grew in their own Gardens" (18). The dead saint, as John Fiske proclaimed of John Cotton, was already "Embalmd with grace" (Meserole 188): all that remained was to seal with words what grace had already accomplished in fact. When Mather lost his wife Abigail, Nicholas Noyes reminded him that there was no need "to Embalm her Memory; / She did *That*, e're she came to dy; / 'Tis done to long Eternity!" (Meserole 282). Once personal grief was suppressed in favor of a steady focus on the deceased's holiness, elegy would virtually write itself. As Oakes attested,

> Here need no Spices, Odours, curious Arts,
> No skill of *Egypt*, to embalm the Name
> Of such a Worthy: let men speak their hearts,
> They'l say, He merits an Immortal Fame. . . (Meserole 210–11)

The elegist's spiritual and artistic problems were thus partially resolved in a shift from sinful self to saintly other, a movement that mirrored the deceased's translation from corrupt flesh to pure spirit as well as the poet's shift from human gifts – mere "Arts" and "skill" – to a passive gaze on the dead as pure embodiments of grace. As Taylor conceded at Increase Mather's death, the embalming would succeed not because of his gifts as poet but because of Mather's virtues as saint: "When many left Christ's holy word thou stoodst fixt to 't / Which makes my gray goose quill commence thy poet" (*Minor Poetry* 248). Poetic skill could not, by itself, generate heartfelt reverence for the dead. Instead it was the other way around: heartfelt reverence would produce an acceptable poem.

The elegiac impulse to "embalm the Name" became, in Puritan hands, a desire to effect the survivor's progress from despair to hope. Despite a stifling of eloquence brought by remorse, this was a duty that could not go unperformed without squandering the pious example of the dead. As Taylor asks Samuel Hooker,

> Shall thy Choice Name here not embalmed ly
> In those Sweet Spices whose perfumes do fly
> From thy greate Excellence? It surely would
> Be Sacraledge thy Worth back to withhold. (*Minor Poetry* 116)

With the alternatives so framed, the mourner's choice was easy. To enact the discursive antithesis of "Sacraledge," the elegist needed only to proclaim an honor that had already been bestowed onto the dead as an embodiment of God's Word. The key to commemorating one elect soul was to remember – and bring into focus – promises that Scripture had made regarding all elect souls. The commonality of all saints also made it possible to bring pride of place into the commemorative act. Mather, reprinting in the *Magnalia* two poems for Jonathan Mitchell, one by Francis Drake and one by an English elegist, boasted that New England was fully capable of harvesting its own gracious fruits: "Let it be known, that America can *embalm* great persons, as well as produce them, and New-England can bestow an *elegy* as well as an *education* upon its heroes" (*Magnalia* 2:113). Such defensiveness hints at Mather's awareness of how far the elegies of "our little New-English nation" had strayed from British taste (2:112). But the disparity was apparent only if one made the mistake of judging them as if they were *merely* poems and not proclamations of holy victories. The essence of a godly embalming, elegists repeatedly confirmed, was not to write well but to *see* well – to perceive and then to convey, as legibly as possible, what faith had wrought in the deceased's soul. Grace would provide the means as well as the mandate to embalm. Taylor, like other elegists, can obtain what Oakes called the necessary "Sweet Spices" only from the "greate Excellence" of Hooker himself. To embalm Hooker properly, Taylor needed only to consider the saint *as a saint* and to declare what he saw.

From the Puritan perspective, it was the dead themselves who solved the artistic problems of elegy. To embalm them properly, the poet simply needed to describe them – to confirm their essence as found poems of redemption. The natural impulse to mourn could thus be folded into a salvific process thought to be authored by God himself. Poets who eschewed self-reliance by confessing their inability to mourn properly could transform a static fixation on sinful grief – John Saffin called it the "Shackles" of his "Contemplation" (Meserole 199) – into verbal activity indicative of warm belief. To write elegy, as Peter Sacks has observed, is to put into motion a necessary adaptation to the shock of death, to perform an act of concession in which "the mourner must prevent a congealing of his own impulses" (22). For Puritan poets this meant breaking through the initial shock at God's harsh will, thereby exposing mourners in the paralysis suggestive of a fallen perspective in order to take them beyond it. Saffin thus urges his muse to "Rouse up thy droop-ing Spirits, dull invention / That the most unconcern'd may give Attention." Like a latter-day Jeremiah at the death of "Pious King Josiah," he encourages himself and his readers to seize the redemptive day posed by the saint's passing, to "Deplore" and "Lament" the loss "or never Speak no more" (Meserole 200).

As we have seen, the fact of death underscored a sharp contrast between earthly turmoil and celestial peace. The insistent focus on the deceased's glory not only helped keep emotions in check, but ensured the avoidance of insincere hyperbole. Ironically, hyperbole might well seem the signature trait of these poems if we read them divorced from the experiential ritual in which they were embedded. But seen within that ritual, the elegist's elaborate praise for the dead reflects the demands of a hagiography that was considered to be quite real. The chief trap of secular elegy, Puritans insisted, was to exaggerate virtues not directly traceable to God. This disdain for rhetorical excess is especially clear in Nicholas Noyes's elegy on Joseph Green:

> God Hates a Lye, my muse well knows,
> Whether it be in Verse or Prose.
> His praise was in the Church before,
> He needed not a Gilding o'er.
> By over-praising of the Dead,
> Nor they or we are Bettered. (Silverman 126)

The contemplation of saints removed any risk of "over-praising." The pious dead had already received a "Gilding o'er" through faith: how could a poet possibly gild a saintly lily that grace had already perfected? By wedding panegyric to piety, the elegist avoided two additional risks: stimulating the unproductive sorrow that the poem was trying to allay, and discouraging survivors from imitating the deceased's intimidating example. Noyes articulated both dangers when he confirmed that

> Poetic Raptures Scandalize,
> And pass with most for learned Lies:
> Whilst others are discouraged,
> And think Saints can't be Imited. . . (Silverman 126)

Moreover, a focus on saintly essence ensured that the deceased's piety would not be isolated. It was praise for *in*imitable virtues – virtues not potentially available to each saved soul – that risked leaving survivors overawed, with nothing to apply to themselves. Such redemptive work could not be furthered by "poetic Raptures" that drew undue attention either to the deceased's unique qualities or to the poet's skill. The focus had to remain squarely on divine power.

> Such high Flights seem Designed to raise
> The *Poet's*, not the Person's praise.
> Whereas Plain Truth gives no offence,
> And doth effect the Conscience;
> To Imitation doth excite,
> Unflorished Copies Teach to Write.

For New England's elegists, an "Unflorished" copy was a legible copy – a portrait free from all elements that might distract mourners from internalizing the deceased's piety. The goal of recounting the "Plain Truth" about that piety – of showing the effects of grace on the deceased's life – squared well with the Puritan abhorrence of unfelt words and unmerited praise. This was, in their view, a species of "Truth" that removed the possibility of hyperbole altogether.[4]

Ultimately, the key to a proper commemoration was not to look into one's heart and write except to assume one's culpability in the loss. Rather, the poet tried to see into the hearts of the holy dead and to describe the faith that resided there. This was the deepest sense in which the deceased provided all the matter necessary for a sublime poem, more than even the most eloquent poet could possibly handle. As Oakes declares in the Shepard elegy,

> Poetick Raptures are of no esteem,
> Daring *Hyperboles* have here no place,
> Luxuriant wits on such a copious Theme,
> Would shame themselves, and blush to shew their face
> > Here's worth enough to overmatch the skill
> > Of the most stately Poet *Laureat's Quill*. (Meserole 210)

A departed saint, if seen rightly, offered all gold and no dross, a "copious Theme" inexpressible by any but the artlessly pure of heart. In his poem for Jonathan Mitchell, John Saffin agreed that it was impossible to over-praise a soul whom grace had purified: "Angells may Speak him, ah! not I! / (Whose worth's above Hyperboly)" (113). Joshua Moody similarly proclaimed John Reiner to be a perfect work of God's art, a saint whose "words and heart in one did well agree. / Study what should or we would wish to be, / And say 'twas here, fear no Hyperbole" (Jantz 153). And John Norton II, in his elegy on Anne Bradstreet, insisted that true piety removed all need for mere invention: "whoso seeks to blazon thee, / Needs not make use of witts false Heraldry" (Meserole 462). Because elegists were convinced that no art could do full justice to the dead, they framed the ostensible results of craft and custom as discoveries whose sameness from poem to poem confirmed the unchanging realities of sal-vation. Norton's real focus as pious embalmer was not the human Anne Bradstreet, but the "Pattern and Patron of Virtue" who journeyed through the world in her form (Meserole 460). In a borrowing from Francis Beaumont's 1618 encomium "Ad Comitissam Rutlandiae," Norton concedes that

> To write is easie; but to write on thee,
> Truth would be thought to forfeit modesty.
> He'l seem a Poet that shall speak but true;
> Hyperbole's in others, are thy due.
> Like a most servile flatterer he will show
> Though he write truth, and make the subject, You. (Meserole 462)

No praise was too high for a "pattern" of sanctity fashioned and per-fected by saving grace. Such a self, after all, was nothing less than God's greatest work in the world, a "Treasure," as Saffin called Samuel Lee, "Which none Can Estimate by weight or Measure" (47).

In the struggle to move from sorrow to edification, elegists repeatedly confirmed that the highest honor one could pay the dead was to profit from their spiritual example. Cotton Mather attested that "when any Person known to me *Dies*, I would set myself particularly to consider; *What lesson of goodness or Wisdom I may learn from any thing that I may observe in the Life of that Person*" (*Christian Funeral* 27). Such lessons applied even in times of intimate sorrow. How, Taylor asks in his poem for first wife Elizabeth Fitch, would their children and grandchildren ever know her "Vertuous shine" "unless I them define" (*Minor Poetry* 111)? So preserved and heeded, the Puritan dead could achieve a form of earthly immor-

tality far superior to that perpetuated by secular elegists: textual permanence as ongoing spurs to their survivors' spiritual health. It is "proper,"
Samuel Danforth II asserts at the death of Thomas Leonard,

> . . .that to mind we call
> The Greatness of our Loss; the qualities
> And Usefulness of our deceased Friend,
> Whose Pilgrimage on Earth is at an end. (Meserole 488)

The elegist's focus on the saint's "Usefulness" – a word also used in
Samuel's embalming by brother John (Meserole 312) – required that the
deceased be distilled to the "Pattern and Patron of Virtue" that Norton
finds in Bradstreet (Meserole 460). As Mather declared, "He that
Remembers well / The *Use* and *Loss* of *Oakes*, will grieve his fill" (*Verse* 53).
And in his poem for Charles Chauncy, Taylor reaffirmed that the greatest value of the dead, and the true justification for elegy, lay in Chauncy's
fulfillment of the holy paradigm: "Unto the Hive of Piety he drew /
Diffusing all by Pattern, Preaching clear Rich Pray'res, & such like thro'
his Practice heer" (*Minor Poetry* 33). Poets undertaking to diffuse the
deceased's "Pattern" stressed what was universally applicable in the
dead, rather than the merely personal or idiosyncratic. All departed
saints were, in Mather's phrase, "*Mirrours of Piety*" (*Verse* 84); each was, as
Saffin called John Wilson, a "Mirrour of Transcendent Love" (116).
Ultimately, the Puritan belief, as William Ames put it, that faith "in each
believer individually" assumed "the form of those that are called" (176)
virtually mandated such generalized elegiac portraiture. In a poem for
Nathaniel Rogers, John Fiske asserts that

> The way of Rest but One, this way He found
> this way He preach't, by Christ, by Grace alone
> by such a holy Righteous Life as Hee
> hath led the way, and now to Rest is gone. . . (Jantz 129)

The title of Benjamin Tompson's poem on his sister-in-law – "A short
memoriall & Revew of sum Vertues in that examplary Christian Mary
Tompson" – articulated the elegiac goal of reviewing the "Vertues" that
defined the deceased as the "examplary Christian" (Murdock 3). What
was reflected in one saintly mirror was reflected in all.

I have already suggested that these portraits owed much to the
Theophrastian and Overburian characters popular in early seventeenth-century England. When Puritans turned their hand to elegy, they
focused squarely on the character of the Holy Man or Woman. Saffin's
poem for John Wilson presents "His Charracter / Which is much like

him yet falls Short / of what of him I might Report" (115). As late as 1729, an anonymous elegist could assure William Burnet that "The faithful Muse shall raise thy Honours high; / In her just Lines thy Character be read, / And o'er thy Tomb this Epitaph be laid" (Winslow 34). That such generalized types persisted in New England's elegies long after character books had passed out of fashion in Old England suggests how closely they matched Puritan rhetorical and affective needs. Moreover, biblical precedent seemed to reside in David's idealized depictions of Saul and Jonathan as the "beauty of Israel," the fallen "mighty" who were "swifter than eagles" and "stronger than lions" (2 Samuel 1:19, 23). New Englanders who followed David's lead believed that in the task of celebrating the dead as characters of piety, strictly personal details were of limited usefulness. Such souls, after all, had been fashioned by grace and not works, by divine template and not human agency.[5]

Elegists repeatedly trumpeted those holy "qualities" which had the greatest spiritual "Usefulness" for mourners. Benjamin Tompson claimed that in Mary Tompson "A Choicer spirit hardly Could be found / For Universall virtue on the ground" (Murdock 3). Taylor's description of Mehetabel Woodbridge similarly lined out a pattern as applicable to the "Inward man" of any redeemed soul as to the poet's sister-in-law:

> Her Inward man a Storehouse of rich ware.
> Of Sanctifying Grace, that made all fair.
> God-Glorifying Shines hence role in Christ.
> Adorning of her Life all over spic'd
> With Grace, Prayre, Holy Reading, Meditation,
> Rich Good Discourse. Of Holy Conversation,
> An Humble Soule, a Gracious Christian. (*Minor Poetry* 125)

Taylor enacts a mimesis of spiritual rather than physical reality: his list of abstractions underscored Woodbridge's redemptive movement beyond human particularity as the "Gracious Christian." Woodbridge's individuality, how she differed from other saints, had little bearing on her redemptive essence, and Taylor accordingly foregrounds traits that established her similarity to other pious souls, especially pious women. Such catalogues of general piety made the dead more imitable. "Let *ALDEN*'s all their Father imitate," writes John Alden's anonymous embalmer, "And follow him till they come to death's state" (Winslow 13). Mather makes the purpose of such portraiture even more explicit. Putting words of encouragement into the mouth of the now-celestial Nathanael Collins, Mather has the deceased urge his survivors to "follow me":

Be *glad* that I am here, and after hye,
Your selves with diligence, all *posting* hither,
Precepts and *Patterns* left, my *Counsels* eye,
And *Copyes*, so we shall be soon together. (*Verse* 73)

Such "copies" of the dead permitted a redistribution of their piety. For
this reason, elegists regularly brought personal or occupational details, if
they mentioned them at all, under the broader rubric of the saint-in-the-
world. These portraits were neither written nor read as literally biographical. Like the gospels, the elegies were intended not to record
worldly fact but to proclaim gracious truth. Nor, despite the encomiastic excess that modern readers inevitably find in these portraits, did
Puritans consider them to be in any sense "false." As reflections on a life
seen in light of the deceased's presumed glorification, such depictions
were taken as spiritually "real," and were, as such, considered to be more
accurate and useful than a literal depiction could ever be.

The underlying commonality of the dead had obvious social as well
as representational implications. By collapsing distinctions of class, age,
gender, and occupation into nonspecific portraits of sanctity, elegy
turned a grim democracy of death inherited from such popular traditions as the medieval Dance of Death into an effective instrument of
social control. Neither death nor grace was a respecter of persons, as
Nicholas Noyes suggested when he drew from the death of Samuel
Sewall's daughter Mary the lesson that the "bare-bones Scithe Cuts with
Impartial Stroke / The Tender Lily, and the Sturdy Oake" (Winslow 29).
At an occasion of loss, social distinctions and hierarchies were reinscribed as confirmations of a unity of belief, evidence that faith could
make saints of all sorts of persons.[6] The most striking distinction that
elegy effaced, as we will discuss in greater detail in the next chapter, was
the very line that it most explicitly invoked: the difference between the
living and the dead. In a society configured in opposition to God's
enemies, dead and living saints were on the same side. While their clear
differences gave elegy its convicting force, their mutual inclusion under
the expected patterns of redeemed experience brought considerable
consolation. This perspective allowed Edward Johnson, in his *Wonder-
Working Providence*, to treat the living, dead, and near-dead worthies of
New England in a virtually identical manner. For Johnson, all would
receive crowns of glory: it was simply a question of when. Such historio-
graphic dismissal of any significant difference between dead saints and
living saints illustrates an axiom central to elegy in early New England.

The regathering of the Invisible Church in heaven would signal the final victory of faith over death and sin.[7]

Elegists insisted that faith also surmounted the blood-ties that prompted the deepest sorrow, thereby constructing a grieving "family" of belief in imitation of Jesus' rejection of his physical family for a community of disciples: "For whosoever shall do the will of God, the same is my brother, and my sister, and mother" (Mark 3:34–35; cf. Matt. 12:46–50 and Luke 8:19–21). Wigglesworth dramatized this redefinition of social allegiance by underscoring the separation of families at doomsday, when the "tender Mother will own" none of her children except "such as stand at Christ's right hand" (*Poems* 60). This perspective served to diminish the distinction between private and public loss by assimilating the former to the latter. Survivors were frequently urged to put aside private grief for the spiritual benefit of others – in effect, to share their dead with the "Huddling Crowd" of believers that Oakes invokes at the end of the Shepard elegy (Meserole 220). After lamenting the death of Captain Anthony Collamore as husband, father, and gentle master to his servants, Deodat Lawson extends the impact of the loss beyond the grieving family: at the death of "such a *Usefull Man* . . . / A deep *Affecting* and *Afflicting* sense / Is well becoming each one that is left" (Winslow 19). Such reiterations of the deceased's import for "each one" minimized the importance of social distinctions by reinforcing the reader's place within a community defined by faith. As Lawson proclaims, "Let then both *High* and *Low* the *Rich* and *Poor*, / Lament the DEATH of Captain Collamore" (Winslow 19).

In their construction of a community united by loss, elegists repeatedly portrayed New England as a supreme jumping-off point for heaven. As Mather tells New England in his elegy for the seven young ministers, "*Zion*, Thy *Sons* are gone; Tho' men might see / *This and that Man*, brave Men, were *born in thee*" (*Verse* 83). By redefining sorrow as social unity, elegists made mourners feel that their fate, personal as well as communal, was linked to the deceased's triumph. When Taylor asks, at the death of John Allen, "Shall none / Be left behinde to tell's the Quondam Glory / Of this Plantation?" (*Minor Poetry* 31), his ostensible pessimism is tempered by an answer implicit in every Puritan elegy: "we" are indeed telling that glory even as we write and read. Catalogs of place-names, actual towns rather than fictive groves reminiscent of "Lycidas," had the same effect. When Oakes urges his readers to "See where our Sister *Charlstown* sits and Moans!" (Meserole 217), he turns the mere fact of residence into an affirmative spiritual orientation. Taylor similarly begs Connecticut to "Mourn, mourn" for Samuel Hooker: "Alas poor Farmington" (*Minor Poetry* 120). At President Chauncy's death he urges Harvard to "mourn" (34); and at Francis Willoughby's death Taylor urges the school to "rise, Stand up with Watry eyes" (22). As E.B.'s elegy on Samuel Stone demonstrates, the list of grieving places could expand into an incantatory roll call:

> Dame *Cambridge* Mother to this darling Son;
> *Emmanuel, Northampt'* that heard this one,
> *Essex,* our *Bay, Hartford,* in Sable clad,
> Come bear your parts in this *Threnodia* sad. (Silverman 142)

Here lies the deeper significance of Mather's claim that "America can *embalm* great persons, as well as *produce* them" (*Magnalia* 2:113). What greater proof of the mission's viability could there be? Someone who was once here is now *there*, basking in a celestial glory for which all believers yearned. Redemptive possibility was thereby immeasurably enhanced: despite the pain of sorrow, the best of all possible worlds was the mourner's here and now.

Gender was another distinction subsumed under the unifying ideal of sanctity. In the Mehetabel Woodbridge elegy, Taylor moves easily and inevitably into a broad portrayal of the paradigmatic saint-as-wife whose outer calling mirrors inner grace. As in all such portraits, abstractions prevail in his assertion that Woodbridge was "Meek" in her roles as

> A Loving Wife, a Tender Mother Sweet,
> Obedient Daughter Sister very Deare
> A Prudent Mistress, Good Neighbor here.
> An Huswife very good, & very neate
> In all Relations comely, & Compleate. (*Minor Poetry* 125)

Bradstreet extolled the same paradigm in her mother as "A worthy matron of unspotted life, / A loving mother and obedient wife" (204). Benjamin Tompson framed sister-in-law Mary Tompson as an embodiment of the claim in Proverbs that there is "None to be found like to a Vertuous wife" (Murdock 3). When she married, she faithfully attended her marital "Dutyes": "With lovely Clusters Round on every side / The house of god, & hers, she butified" (Murdock 3–4). John Saffin honors Sarah Leverett, wife of the former governor, in equally nonspecific terms: she was "zealiously Devout" and "Examplarie," and her "Reall worth" deserves "the Essayes / Of men or Angells" (93). Saffin commemorates Elizabeth Butler as "Zealously pious, Sweet in Conversation" and of "humble minde, yet kept her Thoughts on High" in a perfect balance of womanly "Modesty" and "Majesty" (34). And Saffin praises Mary Willett as a "Peereles Parragon of fame" who might well have been "Adored as A Deitie" had she lived in "the Dayes of yore" (19). In keeping with Willett's superiority to "Venus, Pallas, Diana, and the Graces," Saffin celebrates the triumph of spiritual over physical beauty: "now She's Parradiz'd Tryumphantly, / Where She shall live unto Eternity" (20). For Cotton Mather, Mary Brown was a woman equally endowed with both, "A *Soul* of *Heav'nly Lustre* Shining thro' / An *Earthly Lanthorn* of a Glorious hue. / A *Body* of a Frame so *fine* and *Rare*" (*Verse* 77). In a rare approach to biographical specificity, Mather carefully adds that Brown spent her spare time reading "A *Bible*, not *Romance*" (75).

It would be natural to assume that such impersonal portraits were limited to public tributes, such as those which a minister would write for a congregation member, but this is not the case. Taylor, for example, invoked a fully generic character of the woman-as-saint in his poem for his first wife Elizabeth Fitch. Saffin spoke in equally nonspecific terms when commemorating his wife Martha, whom he describes in formulaic terms as "Zealously Pious, Sweet in Conversation," dedicated to her "Childrens Education," and "Good to the poor Comiserated all / That were Afflicted, whether great or Small" (21). Twenty-five years later Saffin again described her as "The Paragon of vertue. Loyall Duty / The Cabinet of Graces, Seat of Beauty" (83). In this later, fuller commemoration, Saffin praises Martha's spiritual life, her domestic life, and even her business prowess in terms consistent with the Puritan ideal: "All I have Said; or can in words Comprise, / Her true Perfections but Epitomise" (85). However intimate the loss, the hymn to womanhood in the Book of Proverbs provided the poet's template: "a woman that feareth the Lord, she shall be praised" (Prov. 31:30). Solomon's praise for "a virtuous woman" whose "price is far above rubies" defined an ideal extolled perhaps most fully in Cotton Mather's *Ornaments for the Daughters of Zion*. Describing the virtuous wife, Mather states that "her *Fear* of displeasing her Husband, most remarkably appears in the *Peace that* she preserves with him; and her *antipathy* to all *Contention*, unless it be that of *provoking one another to Love and good Works*" (91). Nicholas Noyes praised Mather's wife Abigail in terms of the same figure of the pious woman as peacemaker:

> How *Frugal*, yet how *Generous!*
> How *Modest*, yet how *Courteous!*
> How *Silent*, yet how *Affable!*
> How *Wise*, how *Pure*, how *Peacable*. (Meserole 283)

Commemorating Abigail Mather in light of her presumed faith, Noyes portrays her as the Holy Woman in an unambiguous demonstration of how grace had pervaded her life. Because elegy ratified a change effected by death and glorification, any contrast that Noyes's readers perceived between the woman they had known and the woman in the poem merely underscored faith's transforming power. Convinced that whatever flaws Abigail Mather exhibited in life had been pardoned at death by Christ, Noyes preserves her memory in precisely these terms. For Noyes's readers, the poem did not effect Abigail Mather's apotheosis; it merely proclaimed an apotheosis that God had wrought.

As these "characters" of the virtuous woman suggest, the family offered a frequent site in which the fruits of grace could be dramatized. Women were most often depicted in these terms, but elegists also showed faith manifesting itself in idealized fathers and husbands. Although Bradstreet commemorated her mother as a type of piety, she depicted her father in equally generalized terms as a "guide" and "instructor" (201). And while Taylor celebrated Mehetabel Woodbridge as the female saint, his poem for Samuel Hooker extolled the male counterpart: a "Loving Husband" and "tender Father" who overflowed "With Pious, Rich Discourse, that was well Spic'd / With Gospell Grace, to bring them up to Christ" (*Minor Poetry* 119). We even find a paradigmatic saint-as-child. John Cotton depicted his daughter Sara, dead of smallpox at fourteen, as just such an embodiment of precocious piety: "*Pray, my Dear Father, Let me now go Home!* / Were the Last Words thou Spak'st to me Alone" (Meserole 382). John Saffin similarly presents son Simon, dead at thirteen, as a fully matured saint made wise by grace. Simon's

> . . .Heaven-born Soul in full ripe fruit appears
> Wherein he liv'd an age above his years.
> Whose pregnant witt, quick Genius, parts sublime
> Facill'd his Books, made him Pernassus clime. . . (Meserole 197)

When Simon's brother John died that same year at the age of sixteen, Saffin sent another son, with equal confidence, "to take his Right / Of Heritance among the Saints in Light" (Meserole 199).[8]

The social sphere provided another arena in which faith's impact could be witnessed. Elegists frequently asserted, for example, that good saints made good neighbors. We recall that Taylor attested to Dewey's benign presence in the township, and according to the unidentified G. H., Richard Dummer was an earthly peacemaker whose "last work was to make his Neighbours even / Who were at Odds, before he went to Heaven" (Jantz 169). The deceased's occupation offered additional evidence of a saintly victory. As Charles Lloyd Cohen has observed, Puritans believed that the importance of one's earthly calling resided in "its relationship to one's general vocation in Christianity; the ultimate end of labor is to serve and glorify God" (117). Elijah Corlet thus embalmed John Hull as a pious merchant and patron whose generosity kept Corlet's "boat from being sunk by the waves" ("sic cymbam prohibens tenuem mihi mergier undis") (Kaiser 20). Political careers offered special opportunities to link social virtue with inner piety. Benjamin Tompson extolled Governor Winthrop of Connecticut as the prototypical saint-as-magistrate, whose "Councel Balsome like, he poured in, / And plaistred up its Breaches made by sin" (Silverman 146). Governor William Phips received similar treatment from Daniel Henchman: "Our Land saw peace by his most Generous Cares. / The Wolvish Pagans at his dreaded Name / Tam'd, Shrunk before him, and his Doggs became" (Silverman 161). And Samuel Danforth II cited Justice Thomas Leonard's political rise as the inevitable result of divine blessings falling on a pious man:

> G o d bless'd his Care and Pains, that he attain'd
> With little help from others, useful skill
> Wherein he out-shone others, that he gain'd
> Preferment in the Town, Esteem, good Will;
> From meaner Posts made gradual Ascent
> To Offices of Trust, Care and Moment.
>
> (Meserole 489)

When Magistrate Thomas Danforth died, John Saffin adapted David's lament for Abner to equate "a Person Eminent in Grace" with "A Stable Piller in our little State": "A Great man's fallen this Day in Israel; / Lo! how they Muster and in crowding turn / To pay their Duty to his silent urn" (137). Saffin firmly links the traits of such a leader – judgment, memory, wit, and zeal – to Danforth's "Conversation. . .with God": "Let us then who remaine in Earth's Estate / His many vertues Strive to Imitate" (138).

The character of the saintly teacher, an occupation respected nearly as much as the ministry, is painted in especially reverent tones. Taylor's portrait of President Chauncy recalls not only the "light" of prophecy but also the "Sun" of Christ: "Learning," Taylor tells Harvard, "hath left your Hall: Your Sun is Set / Will not Such Words Command your Eyelid Wet?" (*Minor Poetry* 34). Benjamin Colman similarly confirms that Harvard Vice-President Samuel Willard fulfilled the "Office" of the pious teacher, whose students "He did Inspect, / Taught heav'nly Truth, and Errors did correct." Significantly, Colman links Willard's greatness as a teacher not to scholarly knowledge but to Christian virtue: he "searcht out Vice, th' Infection to expel" and "perfected where Goodness was begun" (Meserole 345). Nehemiah Walter's elegy on Elijah Corlet, schoolmaster at Cambridge, effects the same idealization through classical allusions appropriate to Corlet's lessons: "Rivers of *Eloquence* like *Nectar* flow'd / From his Vast Ocean, where a *Tully* might / Surfeit with draughts of *Roman* Eloquence" (Meserole 465). And Cotton Mather embalms Ezekiel Cheever, master at Boston Latin, as someone "Prais'd, and Lov'd, and wish'd to *Life* again. / Almighty *Tribe* of Well-instructed Youth / Tell what they owe to him, and Tell with Truth" (*Verse* 88).

Not surprisingly, the fullest invocations of piety in action occur in poems for ministers, whom elegists consistently portrayed in terms of a heroic ideal central to Protestant culture. William Perkins's influential preaching manual, *The Arte of Prophecying*, defined the godly minister as a "Prophet" who mediates between earth and heaven. "Every Prophet is partly the voyce of God, to wit, in preaching: and partly the voyce of the people, in the act of praying" (2:646). William Ames agreed that the minister served as a conduit between God and believers: he "must do those things which he does for the people in the name of God" and "he must do those things which he does for God in the name of the people" (190). The character ultimately derived from Paul's description of the good "bishop," "Whether he be Pastor or Elder," as the Geneva Bible glossed the term. "A bishop then must be blameless," Paul insisted, "the husband of one wife, vigilant, sober, of good behaviour, given to hospitality, apt to teach" (1 Tim. 3:2). Protestants on both sides of the Atlantic revered contemporary embodiments of Paul's description wherever they found them. As we have seen, Milton extolled the *pastor bonus* by memorializing Edward King's devotion to "the faithfull herdsmans art" (162), and Herbert drew upon this ideal for his portrait of the "Country Parson" in *A Priest to the Temple*. The lives and deaths of godly ministers offered especially legible confirmations of a salvation history lined out in the book of Acts – a history reasserted in Johnson's *Wonder-working Providence* and in Mather's decision to retell New England's story through the *"chosen company"* of "ministers and Christians by whom New-England was first planted" and who were inspired "as *one man*, to *secede* into a wilderness" (*Magnalia* 2:240). Mather's wording echoes the elegist's conviction that it was "as *one man*" that God's workers labored – and it was as one man that they were to be mourned. The single ministerial personality at the center of all such poems is underscored by the fact that Mather had no difficulty commemorating seven young ministers in a single elegy. In their collective mission as savers of souls, Mather proclaims, the seven "shall Live too in *Eternal Fame*" (*Verse* 85). Taylor's Samuel Hooker, whose prayers brought "Celestiall Wealth unto the Earth," fully manifests this single personality. Hooker, Taylor attests, was

> A Rich Divine: a Pastour very choice
> Dispensing Grace, with a Sweet piercing voice
> [(]Like to the Still Small Voice Elijah heard)
> That rended Rocks, & Satans Intrest marr'd.
> In Prayer Sweet, the musick of which String
> Celestiall Wealth unto the Earth would bring
> Like little Paul in Person, Voice, & Grace
> Advancing Christ & Sinfull things out race. (*Minor Poetry* 118)

The real object of the panegyric – what Taylor is actually commemorating – is not so much Hooker the individual as it is the Reformed ministry as a whole. If any loss could prompt repentance, the death of a godly minister could be expected to do it. The idealized minister, as Scheick has observed, functioned as the reason and will of the collective identity repeatedly invoked in New England's poems of loss ("Tombless Virtue" 291). Such figures provided the ideal of an ideal: they lay at the affective core of Puritan notions regarding what sort of people deserved the fullest commemoration.

Ministers were routinely portrayed as personalized embodiments of biblical action and belief. Taylor depicts Hooker as a "little Paul" working apostolic wonders in New England, a pure conduit of the Word: "The Sacred Writ with joy he did attend. / And Scriptures dropt even at his fingers end" (119). The biblical and homiletic duality of legal admonition and gospel comfort are verified in Hooker's "knack of Preaching": he could send "Christs fiery Shafts into the flinty heart; / Till it was broken: Then the Smarting wound / Would dress with Gilliads Balm to make it Sound" (*Minor Poetry* 119). Johnson invokes the same duality when he describes Thomas Shepard's ability to disturb and soothe his charges: "Thy lovely speech," Shepard's survivors cry, "such ravishment doth bring; / Christ gives thee power to heale as well as sting" (Meserole 151). John Danforth celebrates pulpit eloquence in Peter Thatcher and Samuel Danforth as examples of all "Shepherds" possessing the power of gospel preaching: "Most bounteously GOD answered their Desire, / Hard Hearts would melt by their seraphick Fire" (Meserole 313). In its capacity to effect conversions, the deceased's preaching was remembered as a contemporary reassertion of biblical miracle. Through their "Prayers and Prophecyings," Thatcher and Danforth "Rais'd up dead Souls, restor'd the Blind to sight." Johnson attributed this verbal power to Thomas Hooker, whose "Rhetorick shall peoples affections whet. / Thy Golden Tongue, and Pen Christ caus'd to be / The blazing of his golden truths profound" (Meserole 150). Mather's description of Nathaniel Collins's pleas for divine mercy recalls Herbert's description of prayer as an "engine against the almighty": "How *lofty* in his RHET'RIC, when with cryes / To the Omnipotent reduc'd to say / *Let me alone*" (*Verse* 120). Oakes asserts that Thomas Shepard II, "Pow'erful i' th' Pulpit, and sweet in converse, / To weak ones gentle, to th' Profane a Terrour," was an epitome of Paul's "Scripture-Bishops-Character" (Meserole 217). And when it was Oakes's turn to be mourned, Mather attested that "Our *Oakes* the *Double Power* has / Of *Boanerges*, and of *Barnabas*": "When the *Pulpit* had him! there hee spent / Himself as in his onely *Element*: / And there hee was an *Orpheus*" (*Verse* 60).

Elegists attested that such ministers would acquire their real fame not from elegy, but from their salvific impact on others. For Peter Bulkeley, John Cotton was the exemplary saint in the world, whose immortality was assured by a life devoted to redemptive usefulness: "You were much in study and much in work; the marketplaces, the temples, and your home sought to make use of you" ("Multus eras studiis multusque laboribus: uno / te fora, templa, domus, te cupiere frui") (Kaiser 25). While these multiple sites of impact recall Franklin's comment on the three-faced Mehitabel Kittel, mourned as "a Wife, a Daughter, and a Sister" (20), Bulkeley performs his itemizing deliberately, and makes quite clear his reason for doing so. "You were not one," he tells Cotton, "but many. Many in one, / You were one endowed with the gifts of many" ("Tu non unus eras, sed multi; multus in uno, / multorum donis praeditus unus eras") (Kaiser 25). Part of a Fiske anagram gave similar expression to Cotton's multiple gifts: "So many from one?" ("Tot è uno?") (Jantz 121). E. B. (Edward Bulkeley?) portrays Samuel Stone the elder in terms of the same conflation of singularity and multiplicity: "In losing *One*,

Church *many lost*: O then / *Many* for *One* come be sad singing men" (Silverman 142).

All believers, not just ministers, could be shown as having this multiple impact on others. If Franklin was irked by the Kittel poem and its suggestion of the deaths of three persons, one wonders what he would have thought of Cotton Mather's elegy on Mary Brown, who died in childbirth. As Mather tells Brown's husband, "She felt *Two Death's*, and YOU a *Thousand* feel" (*Verse* 77). The pervasive impact of a saint's death – the loss of one felt as a loss of many – highlights a certain fluidity in the construction of identity enacted by these poems. Indeed, the very notion of individual identity sometimes becomes problematic. Double elegies like John Danforth's poem for Peter Thatcher and Samuel Danforth II were not uncommon. At the death of schoolmaster Ezekiel Cheever, Benjamin Tompson reissued a poem he had written for another schoolmaster, Robert Woodmancy, at least twenty-five years earlier (White, "Benjamin Tompson" 323). The conflation of individual identities through grace is also suggested, as we have seen, in Mather's treatment of seven deaths in a single poem dedicated to the ministerial archetype of "Vigilantius," or a "Servant of the LORD Found READY for the Coming of the LORD" (Meserole 326). William Bradford similarly combines the passing of several first-generation saints into a single lament:

> O New England, thou canst not boast;
> Thy former glory thou hast lost.
> When Hooker, Winthrop, Cotton died,
> And many precious ones beside,
> Thy beauty then it did decay,
> And still doth languish more away. . . (Meserole 387)

In the face of such generalized piety and collective zeal, it's difficult to know where one self ends and another begins. New England's elegists repeatedly enacted this retreat from particularity as a means of effecting a wider diffusion of the deceased's virtues. True to the mandates of elegy, Bradford honors the departed leaders by invoking extrapersonal abstractions – "Love, truth, good-men, mercy, and grace" – in opposition to the "wealth and the world [that] take their place" (Meserole 387). The elegiac diffusion of piety received more explicit statement from Benjamin Woodbridge, who claimed that the location of John Cotton's "Sepulchre is hard to tell, / Who in a thousand Sepulchres doth dwell; / Their *Hearts*, I mean, whom he hath left behind" (Meserole 411). Benjamin Tompson invokes a similar recirculation of piety in a poem for

William Tompson: "the world may know he wants no tomb / Who in ten thousand harts Comanded room" (Murdock 20). And Oakes confirms that the gracious essence of Thomas Shepard will continue to live "in many a gratefull Breast, / Where he hath rear'd himself a Monument, / A Monument more stately than the best" (Meserole 211).

Elegy rendered the piety of the dead into a circulating commodity. Released by death and redistributed by the poet throughout the grieving community, the holiness of the deceased was thereby placed within reach of all who mourned the loss properly. John James attested that the death of John Haynes would have less sting if his piety "did circulate around": "Then with his loss we could dispence, / And deem Ourselves not So bereft, / For one, were thousand Haynes's left" (Meserole 426). This releasing of stored piety, the elegiac diffusion of the deceased's spirit from one to many, marked private as well as public losses. Mather proclaimed for his wife Abigail the same multiple impact that he would confirm for Mary Brown a year later: "Dear *Friends* with whom thou didst so dearly Live, / Feel *Thy one Death* to *Them* a *Thousand* give" (*Verse* 44). The trope of dissolution and release rendered the dead far less intimidating than their rarified portraits might suggest. By separating the sanctity of the dead from their particularity as individuals, the elegist made it seem more likely that survivors would absorb their saintly example. When John Alden died at eighty-nine, his anonymous elegist spelled out the reason for the didactic reduction of personality effected by the poem:

> Let ALDEN's all their Father imitate,
> And follow him till they come to death's state:
> And he will them most heartily embrace,
> When he shall meet them in that blessed place. (Winslow 13)

By internalizing the saintly traits that elegy set forth, the living could, in effect, *become* the dead, appropriating a measure of their piety and thus intensifying their hope for the same reward. As a couplet at the close of Lydia Minot's broadside elegy put it, "We'le wait, (Blest Saint) till this Day break, and th' shadows flee: / So shall our wish be crown'd, to have One Lot with thee" (Winslow 7).

Writing to coax mourners from private sorrow to an anticipation of the "One Lot" that all believers desired, elegists repeatedly extolled the one self capable of achieving this goal. Each poem offered another parable on the power of faith, another example of how grace sanctifies a life. I have suggested that the Puritan elegy, with its insistent stress on saintly pattern over biographical specificity, found biblical precedent in the gospels, in which kerygmatic proclamation assumes the guise of quasi-biographical narrative. New England's elegy pursued an identical mode by idealizing the dead as once-earthy selves whom death and grace had transformed into Christic souls. In their passage to heaven, they were shown to have undergone latter-day resurrections from sorrow to joy and from death to life. Despite the harsh denunciation of the living which marks many of these poems, elegists repeatedly insisted not only that the deceased's victory was still within reach, but that it was the dead who afforded the best models of a way of being that would culminate in the desired outcome. Long before Franklin framed his *Memoires* as a comic parable of how diligence conquers adversity, New England's elegists were offering their own gospels of self-fulfillment, edifying and endlessly repeatable versions of the first American success story.

The evangelists enacted proclamation through biography by searching the Scriptures for prophecies of Jesus's life and mission, and New England's elegists did the same for their heroes. By comparing the worthies of the Old Israel with the fallen mighty of the New, elegy tested whether mourners could grasp the neobiblical significance of the loss. John Alden's anonymous elegist forces the issue by inserting the old man directly into the pages of Scripture: Alden stood "On *Pisgah's* mount," and "On *Tabor's* mount he saw transfigured / Blest Jesus, which within his bosom bred / That *love* that made him say, *'Tis good being here"* (Winslow 13). "With *Moses*," Alden had "such meditations. . .divine, / Which in Saints eyes did cause his face to shine" (Winslow 13). The crucial phrase here – "in Saints eyes" – underscores the gracious perspective required to mourn the dead properly. Only a probable saint was capable of seeing another saint in such biblical terms. When Benjamin Woodbridge similarly described John Cotton as a quasi-Moses, he clarified the homiletic implications of the elegist's biblicizing of the dead:

> Though not (as *Moses*) radiant with Light,
> Whose Glory dazell'd the beholders sight;
> Yet so divinely beautifi'd, youl'd count
> He had been born and bred upon the Mount. (Meserole 410)

Woodbridge plays the perceptual ambiguity to its fullest. Was Cotton Moses or not? If perceived in earthly terms, Cotton was "not (as *Moses*) radiant with Light" but merely a godly preacher who had emigrated from Old Boston in Lincolnshire. But if Cotton's life was revisited in light of his saintly apotheosis and his redemptive impact, he would indeed appear "as *Moses*" to anyone who was, in the popular phrase, a "true Israelite." Perceived through biblical lenses, the graces with which the Boston minister had been "beautifi'd" made him a Moses to his people. Moreover, those sufficiently attuned to that grace would could certainly "count" him as such. This exemplifies the fact that in the Puritan mind, biblical identifications operated on a level higher than that of conscious comparison or analogy. As assertions of spiritual truth, such comparisons were probably not even consciously perceived as metaphorical. On the contrary, Puritans seem to invoke them as procla- mations of a *real* connection, as expressions of a recapitulative typology that defined how early New Englanders saw their actual identities and their actual place in the world.[9]

The biblical parallel often seems to approach total identification, especially in poems for ministers. The deceased preacher not only speaks the Word with supernatural force: he *is* the Word. Woodbridge claims that Cotton's eloquence made it seem "As if *Apollos* were reviv'd in him, / Or he had learned of a Seraphim" (Meserole 411). Taylor simi- larly calls Charles Chauncy a worthy recipient of Elijhah's mantle, a common figure for the authority of a godly ministry (*Minor Poetry* 34). At Samuel Willard's death Colman proclaims, "ELISHA He! The Wisdom of the choice / Applauded with United Hearts and Voice" (Meserole 346). And John Danforth depicts Peter Thatcher and Samuel Danforth not only as Luke and Zenas for their pastoral skill, but as heirs to Elijah's mantle and "good young ABIJAHS" who succeeded Rehoboam (1 Kings 14) (Meserole 312). John Saffin found latter-day Elijahs in Charles Chauncy and John Wilson (15, 116), and in Samuel Lee he could see, pre- dictably enough, "Samuel that famous Prophet" (47). In the variety and resonance of their spiritual gifts, the dead could recapitulate any number of biblical figures, as is clear from Percivall Lowell's description of John Winthrop as a compendium of Old Testament leaders, includ- ing Moses, Abraham, Joseph, Jonathan, and Solomon (Winslow 3). Significantly, such reassertions of the Israelite/Puritan continuum encompassed not just the dead, but the living whom they had served. Oakes thus depicts Thomas Shepard II as "Our wrestling *Israel*, second unto none," who "stood i' th' gap" between New England and God's wrath (Meserole 212). For John Wilson, Thomas Shepard the elder was "like *David*" as a shepherd to his flock (Murdock 88). Wilson describes William Tompson as a latter-day Paul in one poem (Murdock 12), a New

English Jonah in another (Murdock 15). Benjamin Tompson proclaims sister-in-law Mary "a Dorcas in our israell" (Murdock 4), while Saffin compares the love of John and Elizabeth Hull to that of "Holy Zachary, and Elizabeth" (Meserole 201). Taylor encapsulates the significance of such parallels when he refers to his wife as "a Reall, Israelite indeed" (113). As "real" Israelites, the glorified dead reconfirmed a redemptive myth that began in Scripture but now encompassed the New English Zion. The implications of that myth were clear: if New England could produce such souls, it must indeed be the new Promised Land. What's more, there must be true Israelites still among the living. By asserting the deceased's neobiblical status, the elegist drew readers into a chosen community of holy survivors whose deeper identities, like that of the object of commemoration, were also foreshadowed in the Bible.

The sense of biblical identity triggered by elegy began with the poet's association with David as the prototypical singer of loss. The elegiac concession to falling short of Israel's Sweet Singer merely underscored how much the poet wishes to emulate him. The intimidating precedent threatens to bring Oakes's attempts to commemorate Shepard to an abrupt, sputtering end:

> Stop, stop my Pen! lest *Israel's* singer sweet
> Should be condemn'd, who, in that Song of th' Bow,
> To vent his passionate complaints thought meet,
> And to bewail his great Friends overthrow.
> King *David* in an Elegiack Knell,
> Rung out his dolours, when dear *Jona'than* fell.
>
> (Meserole 208)

But as we have seen, what counted was desire rather than performance. Although Oakes fears sullying the Psalmist's example, he writes anyway – and thereby dramatizes his determination to achieve the purity of heart necessary for performing the rite. However sublime the model, "The Soveraign, Sacred Poet is our guide." Because David "wept his Friend in verse: then let us try, / Now *Shepard's* faln, to write his Elegy" (Meserole 209). The "Diviner Warrant" that will validate the effort is not an assumption that Oakes can write with David's eloquence, but that the sincerity of his desire to mourn one of God's people will allow him to fulfill the spiritual duty that David had typified. In other words, Oakes must strive for neobiblical selflessness equivalent to Shepard's. If the poet's spirit and intent are pure, he will be *as* David, just as John Cotton could be *as* Moses to those whose perspective was animated by faith. In its performative dimension, elegy, like all Puritan poetry, was construed as a verbal sacrifice to the divine. And as in all sacrifices performed in an evangelical and not legal spirit, it was not the quality of the performance but the purity of the motives behind it that mattered. This was the great lesson of Samuel's rebuke of Saul: "Hath the Lord as great delight in burnt offerings and sacrifices, as in obeying the voice of the Lord? Behold, to obey is better than sacrifice, and to hearken than the fat of rams" (1 Sam. 15:22). The gospel reiteration of the lesson occurs when the scribe agrees that love of God and neighbor "is more than all whole burnt offerings and sacrifices." Seeing that the scribe answered "discreetly," Jesus replies: "Thou art not far from the kingdom of God" (Mark 12:33–34). New England's elegists hoped to write poems "not far from" the elegiac ideal, even though they were convinced that achieving the ideal was out of the question. The elegiac stress on the sincerity of love for God's people – and thus on a sincere desire to mourn them properly – helped Puritan poets negotiate the need to commemorate the dead with their distrust of the efficacy of all human performances. A pure heart and God's help, they believed, would see them through.

Oakes can thus plead for "the Raptures, Transports, Inspirations / Of *Israel's Singer*" (Meserole 213) because the poetic results, like any other well-meaning act of piety, would not be subject to legal demands for perfection. As Cotton Mather assured mourners in his poem for the seven young ministers, it was Christ who provided the gospel justification for David's poetic precedent, and who thereby made elegy possible: "Your *Tears* Allow'd, yea, *Hallowed* now become, / Since *Tears* were drop't by JESUS on a *Tomb*" (*Verse* 83). Mather alludes to the scene in which "Jesus wept" for Lazarus (John 11:36) – a scene that not only justified the elegist's actions, but reinforced elegy's role as a situational echo of Christ's ability to join tears with resurrection. Like Jesus's tears for Lazarus, the poem would fulfill its office not as a dirge but as a song of resurrection – and Christ would help the poet to sing it, to be like David and perhaps even to *be* David, at least "in Saints eyes." This, of course, gave readers – the recipients of a new David's message – neobiblical identities as well, a status that Percivall Lowell makes explicit at the death of Governor Winthrop. Since "The Jews did for their *Moses* weep / Who was their Gubernator," how could the new Chosen do less? "Let us for *Winthrope* do the like, / Who was our Conservator" (Winslow 3). Urging readers to "weep with us for *Joshua* / The Loadstone of *America*," Lowell confirms the redemptive power of tears shed for neobiblical saints. To mourn a mythic self was to become a mythic mourner.

The biblicizing of mourners gets its fullest play in the elegist's call to imitate the Bible's stoic sufferers. At the death of "Urania's" child, Benjamin Colman offers the example of Abraham, whose willingness to sacrifice Isaac revealed his humble willingness to be "but Earth and Dust, / Before the Will of God most High" (Meserole 338). In a second poem Colman extends the model of the "gracious *Shunamite,*" whose faith in Elisha's powers brought about the resurrection of her son (2 Kings 4:8–37) (Meserole 339). In addition to Abraham and the Shunammite, praised because she "went to God for Ease," Colman invokes a Puritan version of the *stabat mater*: "Think, how the Bless'd of Women stood, / While impious Hands, to th' cursed Wood / Nail'd down her only Son and God!" (Meserole 339). Benjamin Tompson cites the most common biblical prototype of proper mourning, however, when he compares Humphrey Davie, grieving for his wife and son, to the long-suffering Job:

> A spouses Death, so wise, so Chast, so fair,
> Would bring a Job himselfe next Door Despair:
> Soon after that, the First fruits of your streangth;
> I fear your patience will you fail at length. (Meserole 225)

Tompson insists that Davie would experience Job's story in full measure, by sharing in Job's deliverance as well as his affliction. "Who tends the Furnace," the poet proclaims, "sure will helpe you out." John Wilson offered John Norton's survivors the same model:

> An unexpected death did seize
>   on *Jobs* posteritie
> But in the Heav'ns a glorious Lot
>   for them prepar'd did lie. (Murdock 92)

In a poem for Joseph Brisco, Wilson draws from the anagram "Job cries hope" the consolation available to mourners who relied on divine support: "There is no *Job* but cries to God and hopes, / And God his ear in Christ; to cries he opes" (Meserole 384). Wilson also counsels William Tompson's mourners to "be not like" Job's "unfriendly friends," who urged a false repentance (Murdock 16). Elegists offered many other examples for imitation. Wilson's poem for Norton provides a catalog of deaths and deliverances, from Moses and Aaron to John the Baptist and Stephen (Murdock 92–93). In the Brisco elegy Wilson urges his readers to remember, in addition to Job's grief, "What was the end of good *Josiah's* life, / And how it fared with *Ezekiels* Wife" (Meserole 385). And in his poem for Tompson, Wilson cites Paul and Jonah, both delivered from the sea, though "If paul & ionah will not serve / To satisfie your mind, / Concider job" (Murdock 16). While Job exemplified the ideal individual response to loss, Jeremiah offered a fitting communal model. As Saffin confirms in the John Hull elegy, not to take up the prophet's lament for the sins of survivors revealed a damning disregard for God's people. "Rouse up thy drooping Spirits," Saffin urges his "dull invention," "That the most unconcern'd may give Attention / And Eyes burst out with teares like Jeremiah" (Meserole 199). No elegist could afford to leave readers "unconcern'd." Without the pain of loss, there could be no love for God's people – and without such love, there could be no hope for divine forgiveness.

All such examples of biblical grieving reinforced Christ's command to "weep not for me, but weep for yourselves" (Luke 23:28). By directing sorrow toward the mourners' sin, elegy projected its readers directly into Scripture as apostolic witnesses to another victory for the faith. As we have seen, Wilson articulated the apostolic role when he urged John Norton's survivors to ask themselves, "as the Disciples did, / Lord is it I? is't I?" (Murdock 96). By internalizing the disciples' stunned response to Christ's prediction of betrayal, mourners accepted their share in the depravity that killed Christ and, by extension, his servant Norton. The question, most immediately, was this: "Is it I" who have betrayed the deceased? But Wilson's question also bore a comforting significance. "Is it I" who am destined to follow the deceased into glory? The convicting and consolatory dimensions of the question were not contradictory but sequential, just as they were in redeemed experience generally, which posed an acknowledgment of sin as the indispensable prelude to the consolations of faith. "Lord is it I? is't I?" While the New England elegy forced its readers to face this ambiguous question head-on, it also made them feel that the answer, in both of its senses, was yes.

The objectification of the dead as embodiments of the Word reinforced the simultaneously harsh and consolatory thrust of elegy. The textualized deceased promoted an inner reenactment of the two dispensations, convicting the living through the otherness of their glory but consoling them by means of the redemptive bond that they potentially shared. Believers who could "read" the saint correctly – who identified fully with the elegiac "we" – were thereby drawn into a ritual that transformed affliction into affirmation and legal warning into evangelical comfort. A widespread assumption regarding Puritan elegy, voiced long ago by John Draper, holds that "the edifying gloom of the living was seemingly accounted of more moment than the Salvation of the dead" (*Funeral Elegy* 163). Edification was indeed central to these poems, but the deeper response was anything but gloomy for mourners who were reminded by the poem that the success story of the dead might also be their own. In this sense, New England's elegies conformed fully to Thomas Wilson's definition of elegiac rhetoric as "An example of comforte" (147). The "comforte" they offered, however, was insistently theological, and it was based on the belief that affliction could be reinterpreted as a sign of divine approval if the lessons of the dead were taken to heart. Near the end of his poem on the seven ministers, Mather invoked divine help in achieving this percep-tual transformation: *"Help me, my God, at Work like them to be; / And take their Deaths as Watch-words unto me"* (*Verse* 87). Mather's plea invokes the same consolation offered by the jeremiad. God would surely not waste his breath issuing "Watch-words" to people who were incapable of reform. As William Bradford assured those who would outlive him,

> Faint not, *poor Soul*, in God still trust,
> Fear not the things thou suffer must;
> For, *whom he loves he doth chastise,*
> And then *all Tears wipes from their eyes.* (Meserole 390)

By opposing fear and sadness with salvific hope, elegy reassured survi-vors that the transcendence of death was still up to them – that it depended on their willingness to heed all such watch-words as God pro-vided. This message must have struck early New Englanders as immensely empowering. "Mourn that this *Great Man's* faln in *Israel*," Oakes proclaimed in the Shepard poem, "Lest it be said, *with him New-England fell!*" (Meserole 220). The warning sounds grim, but the ritual of mourning that elegy enacted made it seem all the more certain that the "Lest it be said" would never happen, that New England would not fall. Indeed, the poem's very existence – and the reading experience that it generated – suggested otherwise.

For all the thundering and tears, the deepest assumptions of Puritan elegy were profoundly optimistic. Fear could be transformed into hope if readers worked to absorb the essence of the holy dead textualized as a poem. John Fiske made it clear that although it was impossible to follow John Cotton into glory now, readers were fully capable of realign-ing themselves, however imperfectly, with the path that got him there. If so heeded, Cotton's passing only strengthened the survivor's chances for equal success:

> . . .Hee hath gayn'd his prize
> His heavenly mansion 'bove the starry skie
> Returne thee home and wayle the evills there
> Repent breake off thi sins Jehovah feare
> O Jehovah feare: this will thi wisdom bee
> And thou his waies of mercy yet maust see.
> Returne thou mee;   And turned bie
> Lord unto thee: even so shall I. (Meserole 189–90)

Cotton's survivors may "yet" see mercy, and the ambiguous pronoun shifts in the final lines underscore the potential transfer of the deceased's grace to those who remained behind. Taylor's elegy on Samuel Hooker spells out the precise action – indeed, the only action – by which such a transfer could occur: "Watch, Watch thou then: Reform thy life: Refine / Thyselfe from thy Declentions. Tend thy line" (*Minor Poetry* 120). The call to "weep thy Sins away, lest woe be nigh" reappears in Taylor's poem for Increase Mather: "repent then e're it be too late / Less thou eternally smart in the horrid Lake" (247). In his elegy on Peter Thatcher and Samuel Danforth, John Danforth reiterated the "wounding-Warning" sounded by all saintly deaths: "Portended Ills Prevent! most gracious GOD! / Make all take Warning, by thy speaking Rod!" Mournful repentance, Danforth affirmed, offered ready escape from such portents: "May Heav'ns kind Ears receive their Lamentations! / Give, LORD! Their weakned Hearts strong Consolations" (Meserole 314). Puritans were convinced that God never refused a heartfelt plea: to beg sincerely for divine help was nearly tantamount to receiving it. The challenge, of course, was to make certain that one's pleas *were* heartfelt. As Thomas Hinckley conceded to the deceased Thomas Walley, "God's will is done my loss they [sic] gain; / Which doth or may asswage my pain" (Jantz 148). The conditional result underscored the possibilities of right mourning and right reading. Whether the deceased's gain "doth" or "may" comfort survivors depended on how sincerely they sought the redemptive reinscription of loss embodied in the poem.

However harsh Taylor's call to "Tend thy line" might seem, such admonitions brought a measure of control to the heartbreak of loss by making readers feel more in command of their spiritual fate. Repentance was something that one could *do*, a productive alternative to the stunned impotence of grief. Moreover, repentance renewed the mourners' recognition of what they could *not* do: reject God's help in getting them past the pain of sorrow. Finally, elegy made mourners feel less alone by situating them securely in a community of belief defined in opposition to those unaffected by the death. At the level of explicit statement, elegy forced the reader to choose between standing with unregenerate souls unmoved at the loss, or joining a community of believers – Oakes's "Huddling Crowd" (Meserole 220) – who have learned from affliction to seek divine mercy. At the level of reading experience, however, the poem made this decision for the reader – and the choice was deeply reassuring. Fiske's description of John Cotton's worst survivors effects the characteristic separation of the grieving reader from those *other* people, the ones who don't care whether Cotton lived or died:

> Woe they who doe his Truthes dispent exclude
> And woe to them that factions there contrive
> Woe them whose wayes unrighteous survive
> Woe they that by him warning did not take
> Woe to us all if mercy us forsake[.] (Meserole 189)

By distancing such ingrates through the "they" and "them" of the third person, Fiske safely detaches the reader from those to whom Cotton had no value. Fiske's "us," by contrast, incorporates the reader into a group whose real sin lay not in devaluing the saint, but in not trusting sufficiently to God's mercy as the source of recovery. Such statements of "Woe" were undoubtedly less menacing to Puritans than they seem to us moderns. Fiske's warning occurs, after all, in a text that generated the reader's assent to its redemptive message. By performing – by *becoming* – precisely what was required for an assimilation of the deceased's saintly traits, Fiske's readers were led to embrace the very "Truthes" that defined them as Cotton's ideal mourners.

Through the repentance both encouraged and enacted by elegy, the daunting otherness of the deceased could be diminished. Fiske thus encourages his readers, even as he berates them, to "Try" the holy path taken by Nathaniel Rogers:

> Mind we the name of this our Dearest Freind [sic]
> Mind we the Truth He taught Evinceingly
> Mind what Experiences He had: and Now
> That Onely way of all true Rest doe Try. (Jantz 129)

The potential identification of mourners with the "Experiences" of the glorious dead seemed to diminish the convicting gap between earth and heaven. To our shame, elegists repeatedly lamented, we are not like the holy dead. But faith may yet make us exactly like them, however numinous and remote they have become. Oakes is especially clear in underscoring the promise of such continuity when, after protesting that his praise cannot do justice to Shepard, he pulls himself up short:

> I say no more: let them that can declare
> His rich and rare endowments, paint this Sun,
> With all its dazling Rayes: But I despair,
> Hopeless by any hand to see it done.
>   They that can *Shepards* goodness well display,
>   Must be as good as he: But who are they? (Meserole 217)

Oakes's question cut two ways. Nobody could "declare" the fullness of Shepard's spiritual gifts because, as the stanza most immediately suggests, nobody was "as good as he." Yet the ostensibly damning question – "who are they?" – occurs in the middle of an extended and elaborate celebration of Shepard's piety. Oakes's protestations notwithstanding, the saint's glory *is* being displayed, and speaker and reader are united in a sustained ritual by which the saint's "rich and rare endowments" are indeed being lined out.

In light of the performance scripted by the poem, the final answer to Oakes's question was clear: "they" who can declare Shepard's glory are equivalent to the "we" of the text, to those who stand willing to apply the lessons of his saintly character to their own lives. It is, finally, the *survivor's* life that is rewritten in conformity with the life of the deceased. As textualized demonstrations of Paul's promise that "Death is swallowed up in victory" (1 Cor. 15:54), the Puritan dead were made to perform their last and best service: generating apostolic successors to their piety. By rewriting the fact of death into a sign of divine mercy, elegy helped Puritan mourners judge the extent to which the story of the dead was also *their* story, an optimistic narrative of their own best selves. If the answer was yes, readers found that the sting of loss had been eased considerably. If the answer was no, the poem provided them with yet another opportunity to appropriate the saint's story. The chance to revise one's own inner story was, for Puritans, the most wondrous gift that a merciful God could extend to poor doubting souls, whether during the sad duty of lamenting a loss or in the broader errancy through the world's wilderness. When John Allen died and Taylor asked, "Shall none / Be left behinde to tell's the Quondam Glory / Of this Plantation?" (*Minor Poetry* 31), the poet answered his own question through the act of writing elegy.

6

Diffusing all by pattern: the reading of saintly lives

Puritans brought death and commemoration into the legal and evangelical dispensations of Scripture, with Christ as an articulating center. Grief, like the Word itself, invoked a dichotomy of fear and hope that was reinforced by the deceased, commemorated as a double icon of mortality and glory. Proper mourning was also twofold, a process that led from self-centered tears to a selfless witnessing to the deceased's victory. Elegy regularized this process by offering a textual template, in the deceased as well as in the poem, capable of containing death's disruption. By assimilating the dead to the story of salvation, the elegiac ritual transformed them into permanent "texts" of piety that were, like all Puritan texts, inseparable from the defining metatext of Scripture. Commemorated as anthropomorphic extensions of the Word, departed saints performed the same work as the two Testaments, encouraging the same interplay of text and reader that characterized an engaged reading of Scripture. As embodiments of the biblical text, the dead were subsumed within the text of the poem, which was in turn assimilated by readers who thereby learned to see themselves in biblical terms. With this redistribution of the deceased's piety throughout the community, personal loss was rewritten as redemptive gain.

As Increase Mather proclaimed in a biography of his father Richard, "The Writing and Reading of *the Lives of Worthy Ones*, hath been by some accounted amongst the most profitable works of men under the Sun" (1). Elegy intensified this practice by linking the reading of saintly lives to the liminal occasion of death. By presenting the dead as easily grasped paradigms of holiness, elegists encouraged mourners not simply to imitate them but to imagine themselves facing the great test that they had just passed. "Consider," Cotton Mather urged, "What would a *Dying* man chuse to have *Avoided*? And Avoid those things. Consider, What would a *Dying* man chuse to have *Practiced*? And *Practice* those things. Consider, What sort of *Life* will be most approved in a

Dying Hour. And Lead such a *Life*" (*Awakening Thoughts* 16). Elegists
enhanced the didactic possibilities of the dead by grounding them
firmly within the larger text of Scripture. When Benjamin Tompson
called his father a thundering "Textman" (Silverman 145), a term
describing someone especially conversant with Scripture, he suggested
the deceased's role not only as an advocate of the Bible but as its personalized restatement. Ichabod Wiswell similarly called Samuel Arnold
"a Text-Man large and ready" (Winslow 15) – "ready," presumably, for
the mourner's consultation and profit. Cotton Mather extended the
trope to encompass other, Bible-based texts when he embalmed John
Clark as "A *Living Sermon* of the Truths he *Taught.* / So all might *See* the
Doctrines which they *Heard*, / And way to *Application* fairly clear'd" (*Verse*
85–86). Mather also commemorated John Hubbard as an anthropomorphic text of piety: "His *Life* a *Letter*, where the World might Spell /
Great *Basils* Morals, and his Death the *Seal*" (*Verse* 86). Dying sealed the
saint's identity as a particularized embodiment of the Word: it was the
elegist's task to make such souls readable by unlocking their biblical
essence for survivors.[1]

John Saffin gave Samuel Lee explicitly textual status by confirming
that "within his Head & heart did Lye / Even a System of Divinity" (48).
Repeatedly exposing such systems in the dead, elegists reframed mourning as an act of explication, a situational opening of the Word. As
Mather proclaimed in his poem for Ezekiel Cheever, "The *Bible* is the
Sacred Grammar, where / The *Rules of speaking well*, contained are" (*Verse*
90). Christ as *Logos* or divine utterance comprised an additional "text"
embedded within the text of Scripture. As Wigglesworth affirmed,
"Christ's Sufferings are our Copy-Book, / Whereon we often ought to
look" (*Poems* 121). The dead saint, eulogized as a local *imitatio Christi*,
offered yet another text that was all the more accessible because the
redemptive story could be read in someone whom mourners had actually known. As Francis Drake proclaimed, Jonathan Mitchell's heart
contained "The *Scripture* with a *Commentary* bound" (Meserole 459).
Saffin asserted a similarly textualized identity for his wife Martha, whose
virtues "written are allmost in Every Breast" (20). Benjamin Tompson
called for the survival of his sister-in-law Mary as a pious text: "Let her
example as a Coppy stand / To Childrens Children upon every hand"
(Murdock 5). Mather attested that Sarah Leverett's good works offered
a virtual "*Gloss*" on the law (*Verse* 82). And Joseph Capen gave the trope
occupational appropriateness when he confirmed that although printer
John Foster's body had been "laid aside like an old Almanack,"

Yet at the Resurrection we Shall See
A fair Edition & of matchless worth,
Free from Errata, new in Heav'n Set forth:
Tis but a word from God the great Creatour,
It Shall be Done when he Saith IMPRIMATUR. (Wright 163)

An especially full expression of the textualized deceased occurs in Benjamin Woodbridge's poem for John Cotton. Making explicit a performance central to all Puritan commemoration, Woodbridge anatomizes Cotton as

A living breathing Bible: Tables where
Both Covenants at large engraven were;
Gospel and *Law* in's Heart had each its Colume
His head an Index to the Sacred Volume.
His very Name a *Title Page*; and next,
His Life a *Commentary* on the Text.
O what a Monument of glorious worth,
When in a *New Edition* he comes forth
Without *Errata's*, may we think hee'll be,
In *Leaves* and *Covers* of Eternitie! (Meserole 410–11)

This is a striking example of the Puritan tendency to equate an experience of the faith with reading. Words, the unrelenting medium of inner life, provided sequence and order to what was otherwise unfathomable, and the Puritan conviction that all such language was finally traceable to God eased the performative pressures of elegy considerably. As Dickran and Ann Tashjian aptly observe, "the iconic power of words meant that the poet was not in complete control of the direction that his poem would take" (41). The Tashjians also note that in elegy the line between true poetry and true piety was so thin as to be virtually nonexistent: "the powers of Christian metamorphosis were closely associated with the dynamics of poetic metaphor" (43). If the words deciphered in the holy dead echoed the eternal Word, mourners could feel the plotless void of loss being filled by an endlessly repeatable story authored by God himself.

The elegist's retelling of the deceased's gracious story allowed readers to imagine themselves as products of God's authorship as well. Stanley Fish's comment that Herbert sought "the involvement of the reader in his own edification" also describes the goal of New England's elegists (*Living Temple* 27). Joshua Moody confirmed that the preaching of John Reiner of Dover had evinced just this sort of affective power: "His Sermons were Experiences, first wrought / On his own Heart, then lived what he taught" (Jantz 153). By making the faith of the dead clearly legible, elegists sought to transfer their "Experiences" to living hearts. The deceased-as-text offered a compelling trope – so powerful, in fact, that it outlived its original theological context. Franklin adapted it to more worldly ends in the "errata" confessed in his autobiography and in his "Printer's Epitaph," where he expected to "appear once more, / In a new & more perfect Edition, / Corrected and amended / By the Author" (91). Franklin and his Puritan forebears agreed that the successful life was an open book, even if they differed utterly in their reasons for writing and reading it.

The line between the New England dead and the poems that commemorated them was as thin as the line between self and Scripture. In keeping with the Puritan assumption that careful reading was a precondition for proclaiming the saint's glory, the elegist became a decoder of secrets not unlike a minister explicating the "darker" portions of Scripture. The most common site for such decoding was the deceased's name. New Englanders saw the ability to decipher the messages embedded in names as a divine gift, like wit and eloquence generally, and took great satisfaction in exercising this facility in all sorts of situations, not all of them serious. When applied to elegy, such devices as puns, acrostics, and anagrams were thought to be considerably more than mere ornament. Puritans saw them as extensions of the deceased's textual legibility, and the verbal ingenuity required to discover them was equated with the spiritual insight demanded by proper mourning.[2]

The acrostic, with the deceased's name or an epigrammatic message revealed in the beginning letters of the lines, found precedent in the alphabetical verses of Lamentations and in nine Psalms in which each line begins with the succeeding letter in the Hebrew alphabet (Psalms 9, 10, 25, 34, 37, 111, 112, 119, and 145). An anonymous poet appended an "Accrosticon" to a poem for Governor Winthrop of Connecticut; another poet closed his elegy for Jonathan Marsh with an "Acrostick-Epitaphium" (Winslow 9, 23). Samuel Stone II appended an "Acrosticon" to his elegy for William Leet, Governor of Connecticut (Jantz 156), and John Saffin wrote two acrostic epitaphs for Samuel Lee (48). Taylor's poem for Francis Willoughby, deputy governor of Massachusetts, is a triple acrostic, with Willoughby's name running down the beginning, the center, and the end of the lines that comprise the poem's middle section (*Minor Poetry* 23). Taylor's elegy for President

Chauncy of Harvard is even more elaborate. Arranged in the form of a tombstone, the poem presents what Taylor calls "A Quadruble Acrostick whose Trible is an anagram." Its acrostic messages – "Charles Chauncy," "president dyed," and "a cal in churches" – are followed by a chronogram that spells out the date of Chauncy's death in Roman numerals (*Minor Poetry* 32–34).

Although the severe formal challenge of acrostic reflects the Puritan regard for the regulatory function of elegy, acrostic elegies were too technically demanding to become truly widespread. It was the anagram, the unscrambled message latent in the deceased's name, that became the signature formal device of New England's elegies. The results are fascinating in their ingenuity. Thomas Hinckley found in Thomas Walley's name the anagram "O Whats my all" (Jantz 148), and Samuel Stone turned William Leet into "I tell I am well" (Jantz 156). Samuel Danforth anagrammatized William Tompson into "lo, now i am past ill" and "now i am slipt home" (Murdock 19). Benjamin Tompson turned Edmund Davie into "AD Deum veni" ("I have come to God") (Meserole 223), and Elizabeth Tompson into "o i am blest on top" (Murdock 9). At the death of Mary Sewall Gerrish, John Danforth borrowed a simple anagram from Herbert, who had applied it to the Virgin: "Army" (Meserole 316). Ichabod Wiswell teased "Leave old Arm's" from Samuel Arnold, and Nathaniel Pitcher found "'Tis Cast on Sea" and "A! Son it's Ceast" in the name of Isaac Stetson, who was lost at sea (Winslow 15, 33). Taylor turned Charles Chauncy's name into "Such a Royal Chance" and "Such a Chancelry"; in its Latin form it became "Caelo Charus Canus" ("dear heavenly Dean") (*Minor Poetry* 33, 35).

John Wilson of Boston became famous for his ability to find anagrams, as Nathaniel Ward attested in his mischievous comment that Wilson, "the great Epigrammatist / Can let out an Anagram / even as he list" (Meserole 368). A glance at Wilson's output reveals the truth behind Ward's joke. Wilson turned Joseph Brisco into "Job cries hopes" (Meserole 384), Abigaill Tompson into "i am gon to all bliss" (Murdock 7), and William Tompson into "most holy paule mine" and "Lo my ionah slumpt" (Murdock 12, 15). In Wilson's hands, the Latin form of John Norton's name yielded no fewer than three anagrams: "Nonne is honoratus?" ("is he not to be honored?") (Kaiser 14), "Jesu! Annon Thronos?" ("Jesus! Is not [yours] the throne?"), and "Annon Jesu Honor Sit?" ("Is there not to be honor to Jesus?"). Wilson's English anagram for Norton was "Into Honnor" (Murdock 90–91). When Thomas Shepard died, Wilson also devised four anagrams: "Paradisus hostem?" ("[does] heaven [have] an enemy?") (Kaiser 13), "o a map's thresh'd," "More hath pass'd," and "Arm'd as the Shop" (Murdock 85–87). John Fiske's anagrams showed equal inventiveness: "O, Honie knott" (on John Cotton) (Meserole 187); "Charus es, promat" (on Thomas Parker: "let it be said, you are dear"); "He is in a larg Rest. No" (on Nathaniel Rogers) (Jantz 127); "All mine will sing" (on William Snelling); "In't rar' Angells – Gem" (on Margaret Snelling); and "Sr, Grant mee all: I am willing" (an anagram that commemorates both Snellings) (Jantz 123–24). Another elegist especially fond of the form was John Saffin, who devised anagrams for his wife Martha ("In hart am Saff [safe]" and "Ah! firm an fast") (11), Jonathan Mitchell ("can't I the holy man" and "the holi man it can") (111), and John Wilson ("wish no on, ill") (115).

Once discovered, the anagram functioned like the biblical text of a sermon in suggesting the central theme or image of the poem. Wilson developed each of his Shepard anagrams into a complete poem with the anagram as the initial line. "More hath pass'd," for instance, leads to Wilson's declaration that more has "pass'd" from Shepard's "holy pen" to defend a true baptism than "any *Anti-baptists* can / with solidness confute" (Murdock 86). Saffin, having found an easy anagram – "Sel grace worth" – in the name of his mother, Grace Ellsworth, builds it into a meditation on the pricelessness of election: "Sel grace worth money; more worth one little graine / then all the Incomes of the King of Spaine" (15). Fiske, who was particularly adept at expanding anagrams into complete poems, drew Wilson's anagram – "W'on Sion-hil" – into a proclamation that "Him tho translated hence, yet heere we still" (Murdock 122). From "O, Honie knott," Fiske derived a characterization of John Cotton as "A gurdeon knot of sweetest graces as / He who set fast to Truths so clossly knit / As loosen him could ne're the keenest witt" (Meserole 187). Fiske turned a second anagram of Cotton – "Canon sis: Tot è uno?" ("are you to be the standard? so many from one?") – into a Latin poem that he loosely "Englished" as follows:

> Tho death him seas'd yet hath he left
> Canons so many heere
> as scarce from any one to flow
> doth yet to us appear. (Jantz 121)

Nor did Fiske's decoding of Cotton's redemptive significance end there. In a third poem he based each of two stanzas dealing with the transitory nature of life upon two additional anagrams: "Thô onc', I not" and "O onc', thô not" (Jantz 122). Equal ingenuity is evident in an elegy for Anne Griffin. After teasing "In Fanne: Rig" from her name, Fiske framed the poem around the conceit of earthly life as a threshing of the soul's wheat (in a fan) while the ship of the soul is moored (in rigging). At death, the soul sails to heaven's "haven": "We must the Fanning heere expect till done / Hye Time, when once in Fanne, thinke thence to Trudg[e]" (Meserole 191). A similar theme emerges from Fiske's decoding of Thomas Hooker into "A Rest; oh com'! oh" (Silverman 138), and at the death of Samuel Sharpe, Fiske turned "Us! Ample-share" into a meditation on the "Ample share" of comfort to be found in "those Relicts which hee hath left behind" (Silverman 140).[3]

Puns on the deceased's name offered further clues to the redemptive significance of the loss. Edward Johnson invoked the obvious pun on Thomas Shepard I: "Oh Christ, why dost thou Shephearde take away, / In erring times when sheepe most apt to stray" (Meserole 151). So did John Wilson: "This holy *Shepard* is like *David*, / From Lyon's mouth and Beare's who saved / That *little Kid*" (Murdock 88). Urian Oakes followed suit at the death of Thomas Shepard II: "Our sins have slain our *Shepard!*" (Meserole 219). When Oakes died, William Adams punned on both of his names by proclaiming him "Uranius," the herald of heaven ("caelestis praeco"), and an "oak" of stability: "and he was like an oak tree in strength and firmness" ("Ac veluti quercus pollebat robore firmo") (Kaiser 37). Fiske embalmed Cotton with an equally predictable pun, complaining that some Bostonians "in thi Cotton clad" had begun to "count't too meane a dresse and sought / Silk Velvetts Taffeties best could be bought" (Meserole 189). Elijah Corlet played on John Hull's occupation as a merchant and, more subtly, on his name by remembering that "he lightened the heart of one in need of clothes and money, / and thus kept my little boat from being sunk by the waves" ("vestibus et nummis animum relevavit egentis, / sic cymbam prohibens tenuem mihi mergier undis") (Kaiser 20). John Norton II declared that Anne Bradstreet's "breast was a brave Pallace, a *Broad-Street*, / Where all heroick ample thoughts did meet" (Meserole 462). In addition to proclaiming David Dewey "David by Name, David by Nature," Taylor went on to cite the deceased's "Dewy Tears" of repentance, the "Dewy Rhymes" with which he had instructed his children, and the "Grace's Dew" that had "drenched" the hearts of the deceased and his wife ("Edward Taylor's Elegy" 82). Taylor also punned on Samuel Hooker's name and occupation as a ministerial fisher of men: "Shall angling cease? & no more fish be took / That thou callst home thy Hooker with his Hook?" (*Minor Poetry* 121). In his poem for John Allen, Taylor rang multiple changes on the deceased's name: "The GRACES ALL ON Allen showing bright / Are calld ALL IN to bed, & bid Good night." At the poem's end, "ALL END in ALLEN, by a Paragoge" (*Minor Poetry* 31). For E. B. (perhaps Edward Bulkeley), the possibilities posed by Samuel Stone's death proved even more irresistible. The poet equates Stone with Samuel's Ebenezer of victory, a diamond, a cordial stone, a whetstone, a loadstone, a "*Ponderous Stone*" for sounding the bottom of "Scripture-depths," a sharp stone to remove gangrenous sin, a dividing stone, a "*Squared Stone*" fit for "Christs Building," and the "*Peter's Living lively Stone*" on which was built the church at Hartford (Silverman 143).[4]

When applied to the work of mourning, such devices reflected wit put to its highest possible use: wresting purpose from affliction by discovering the sacred messages embedded in names. In his encomium to the living Mather, Grindall Rawson clarified the point of the exercise: "My Muse will now by Chymistry draw forth / The Spirit of your Names Immortal Worth" (Meserole 478). Discovering the "Immortal Worth" of a name – the equivalent of a saint's "Spirit" – took on special urgency at the occasion of death. A comment on John Wilson's anagrams, made in a poem that Mather printed in his *Magnalia* thirty-five years after Wilson's death, spelled out the significance of decoding the deceased's name. Wilson's "care to guide his *flock* and feed his *lambs*," the elegist maintains, manifested itself in "*words, works, prayers, psalms, alms*, and *anagrams*":

> Those *Anagrams*, in which he made to start
> Out of meer *nothings*, by *creating Art*,
> Whole *words* of counsel; did to *motes* unfold
> *Names*, till they Lessons gave richer than gold. (*Magnalia* 1:320)

Mining "Names" for "*words* of counsel" and lessons "richer than gold" was only a more pointed form of the ritual of reading the dead enacted by elegy generally – and it was not limited to well-known poets like Wilson. An anonymous elegist, for example, found three anagrams in Lydia Minot – "I di to Al myn'," "I di, not my Al," and "Dai is my Lot" – and then proceeded to build a short poem from each of them, the last being an acrostic on her name (Winslow 7). The rage for order reflected in this kind of ingenuity exemplifies the Puritan determination to apply wit to the regulating of emotion. Given their cryptic form, their salvific revelations, and the mental concentration necessary to find them, puns

and anagrams virtually forced the contemplation of the textualized dead
demanded by elegy.

At root, elegy presented mourners with situational reenactments of the
broader story of Scripture. The law reasserted itself in the occasion of
death as a debt even the best of saints had to pay. The prophets received
restatement in the elegist's call for repentance and renewed commitment
to the Puritan mission. The "writings," especially Job and the Psalms,
reasserted themselves in the elegiac stress on affliction and deliverance.
The gospels and Acts anticipated the poem's diffusion of the deceased's
gracious essence. Paul's letters found their parallel in the elegist's insistent bonding of the living with the dead under the cycles of redeemed
experience. Finally, the book of Revelation lined out the eschatological
underpinnings of elegy, justifying both a reassertion of the provisional
nature of earthly life and a stress on the deceased's glory as a goal held
out to survivors.

Death seemed to concentrate the grand narrative of Scripture into a
single event, and elegy intensified the survivors' hope to internalize this
narrative as witnesses to a holy life. Readers who managed to absorb the
deceased's lessons could themselves become embodiments of the Word,
participants in an active redistribution of his or her sanctity. We have
seen Taylor praise President Chauncy for "Diffusing all by Pattern,
Preaching clear / Rich Pray'res, & such like thro' his Practice heer"
(*Minor Poetry* 33). What better goal for elegy, in the Puritan view, than to
imitate the grace-diffusing activity of the dead? As John James states in
his poem for John Haynes, it would be "better" if the deceased's "goodness could in all be found, / And that did circulate around" (Meserole
426). By proclaiming this "goodness," elegists produced miniature
gospels that diffused the glory of a saint who had just received, as
William Ames described it, "the bestowal of total perfection" which
occurred "immediately after the separation from the body" (174). The
poet would bear apostolic witness to another soul who had joined "the
spirits of just men made perfect" (Heb. 12:23). The apostolic impulse of
elegy emerges most clearly in repeated confirmations of a redemptive
legacy being passed down from the dead to the living. The young Mather
invoked this lineage of faith when he situated himself in a line of
embalmers extending back through Oakes, Shepard, Jonathan Mitchell,
John Wilson, John Norton, and John Cotton to Thomas Hooker (*Verse*
51). The apostolic impulse also receives explicit statement in one of the
poems in Mather's textual chain, Wilson's elegy on Norton. We have

seen Wilson tracing the elegiac succession back to its biblical roots, to the disciples' panicked response – "Lord, is it I? is't I?" (Murdock 96) – when Christ predicts his betrayal at the Last Supper. Urging Norton's survivors "impartially" to search "our wayes and spirits," Wilson alludes to the gospel episode as evidence that efficacious penitence was indeed possible. Faith, after all, had transformed these anxious disciples into dedicated apostles who overcame their shame at abandoning Jesus to promulgate the message "in Jerusalem, and in all Judaea, and in Samaria, and unto the uttermost part of the earth" (Acts 1:8). For Puritans, the propagation of the gospel anticipated the preservative goal of elegy, providing New England's answer to the continuity sought by Milton's "uncouth swain," who hopes that "som gentle muse" might someday favor his "destin'd urn" with "happy words" (159). Through a proper embalming, the "Apostolicall" identity that Oakes celebrates in Shepard (Meserole 216) became transferable from Shepard to his survivors. In this the elegist practiced the sincerest form of flattery, imitating the dead by "diffusing" the gracious "Pattern" of the deceased, to use Taylor's words, throughout the grieving community.

Writing to confirm a victory for faith, elegists portrayed their subjects as no longer merely human – the precise result, Puritans believed, of glorification. Even Mather's appropriation of the biblical *ecce homo* was insufficient to describe what Urian Oakes became by dying: "see the *Man* / (Almost too *small* a word)!" (*Verse* 59). Oakes had made the same claim when he recounted something of Thomas Shepard's manner. His real focus was not on Shepard so much as on the fruits of grace in any saint:

> His Look commanded Reverence and Awe,
> Though Mild and Amiable, not Austere:
> Well Humour'd was He (as I ever saw)
> And rul'd by Love and Wisdome, more than Fear. (Meserole 215)

Oakes's Shepard, a compendium of traits favored by the "Muses, and the Graces too," models godly balance as an equivalent of the classical *nihil nimis*: "Wise He, not wily, was: Grave, not Morose: / Not stiffe, but steady; Seri'ous, but not Sowre" (Meserole 215). A similar *via media* of sanctity occurs in Joshua Moody's depiction of John Reiner, who was "not old but sage," "Chearful but serious, merry too but wise" (Jantz 153). The idealized dead frequently went beyond human specificity altogether, as in Benjamin Colman's poem for Samuel Willard. We have seen Colman finding in the classics a model for his opening, the self-conscious invocation of a gospel hero to replace pagan warriors like Aeneas. As a result, Willard's life emerges as a manifest epic of the spirit:

I sing the MAN, by Heav'ns peculiar Grace,
The *Prince of Prophets*, of the *Chosen Race*,
Rais'd and Accomplisht for *degenerate Times*,
To Stem the *Ebb* with Faith and Zeal Sublime. . . (Meserole 341)

Colman's Willard strides through – and beyond – the world like a colossus whom faith made capable of feats every bit as dramatic as biblical miracles:

He *Pray'd*, the *Sealed Heav'ns* withheld their *Rain*:
He *Pray'd*, the op'ned Clouds discharge again.
Provokt, *He* askt; *strange* blazing show'rs of *Flame*
Stream down, and *Sodoms Day* renewed came. (Meserole 342)

Puritan readers understood that the poem was not celebrating Willard so much as God-in-Willard. Although they knew full well that Willard did not literally control the rain, they believed that he had indeed offered special access to divine blessings and warnings. This, for Puritans, was the real miracle, and Colman sought to convey it with whatever resources language allowed. The poem celebrated Samuel Willard as seen through the eyes of faith, a Willard whom Christ had just welcomed to bliss as a Bride made "all fair" and spotless (Cant. 4:7).

Puritans justified such portrayals in their belief that at death the saint became more like Christ than like the carnal individual who had just left the world. As Ames attested, conversion had initiated this gradual coming together of saint and Savior: "The receiving of Christ occurs when Christ once offered is joined to man and man to Christ. John 6.56, *He. . .abides in me, and I in him*" (158). Death completed the believer's Christic refashioning by eliminating the fleshly barrier that kept the two from full communion. In elegy as in salvation, individual particularity fell away to reveal the saint's redemptive essence. We have seen Taylor articulate this dismantling of worldly identity through self-elegy, in a jubilant contemplation of his soon-to-decay body: "my vessell soon / Would Taint, tho' all your Love, & skill should bloom" (*Minor Poetry* 236). Saffin more subtly de-fleshes the celestial John Hull, whose transcendence of carnal selfhood has made him too glorious to describe:

My lowly Muse now takes her flight on high
I am Envellop'd in an Extasie
As one Surrounded with some Dazleing Ray,
Mee thinkes I heare his blessed Genious say
Weep not for me, but for yourselves aright
I'me fixed in an Orbe at glorious Light
I'me Paradiz'd in unconceived Joy
Above the pitch of Envy or annoy. (Meserole 201)

Even though a Miltonic "blessed Genious" seems to speak to Hull's survivors, the words come directly from Christ – from Jesus' commandment
to "Weep not for me, but for yourselves" (Luke 23:28). Like Christ's
warning, Hull's words framed a sweeping denunciation of the human
perspective. To weep for someone who had moved beyond "Envy, or
annoy" was to forget that the survivor was a far worthier object of pity.
John Danforth's depiction of Anne Eliot, now scarcely recognizable as
a person, conveys similar numinosity: "Haile! *Happy Soul!* In Luster
excellent / Transcending far the *Starry Firmament* / Which is thy *Footstool*
now become" (Meserole 320). Eliot has become a "*Sagacious* and
Advent'rous Soul," an "*Amazon!* Created to Controll / Weak Nature's
Foes" (Meserole 321). And in a tender ode to his wife, Cotton Mather
forces himself to acknowledge Abigail Mather's translation from intimate spouse to austere saint. As Mather concedes, "my Dove" is "now
no longer *Mine!*": she must "Leave *Earth*, & now in *Heavenly Glory* Shine. /
Bright for thy Wisdome, Goodness, Beauty here; / Now *Brighter* in a more
Angelick Sphaere" (*Verse* 44). Like other elegists, Mather turns the rebuke
and consolation of mourning onto himself. Although he has lost a wife,
he has gained a new celestial object, more Christic than human, on
which to fix his meditative gaze.

   This was, in the Puritan view, a concession to theological accuracy: in
shedding a carnal identity that impeded the perfection of grace, the
dead simply *were* no longer human. As Mather's poem for the seven ministers also suggests, the holy dead had been transformed into radically
dehumanized form. John Clark, one of the seven, has become a heraldic
emblem of celestial grace, a dead saint reduced – or, from the Puritan
perspective, elevated – to verbal stained glass. We have already seen
Mather's textualizing of Clark as "A *Living Sermon* of the Truths he
Taught" (*Verse* 85). A few lines later, when Mather makes the short leap
from verbal to visual icon, Clark emerges as a graphic image of the
Saved Soul as stylized as any tombstone angel:

> *Painter*, Thy Pencils take. Draw first, a *Face*
> *Shining*, (but by himself not seen) with *Grace*.
> An Heav'n touch'd *Eye*, where [what of *Kens* is told]
> One might, MY GOD, in *Capitals* behold.
> A *Mouth*, from whence a *Label* shall proceed,
> And [O LOVE CHRIST] the *Motto* to be Read.
> An *Hand* still open to relieve the Poor,
> And by *Dispersing* to *increase* the Store.   (*Verse* 86)

By extending a heraldry of grace, Mather opposes the "false Heraldry"
of wit scorned by John Norton in his tribute to Anne Bradstreet

(Meserole 462). Mather adopts the same strategy in his poem for Sarah Leverett. After lamenting the fact that portrait painting had not been invented in time to record the faces of biblical women, Mather declares that in Leverett "there is an end of all complaints; / ONE Matron gives a sight of *all* the *Saints*." Leverett, "a curious Draught," is "what an one! by what fine Pencil wrought" (*Verse* 80).[5]

Such frank acknowledgments of representation constitute an open concession to the inadequacy of language to describe the celestial state of the dead. John Wilson clarified the theology behind this assumption when he portrayed John Norton as a self defined solely in terms of Christ: "Such was our John, sincere of heart, / who held nothing dear but what belonged to Christ" ("Qualis erat noster syncero corde Johannes, / cui, nisi quae Christi, chara fuere nihil") (Kaiser 15). To be perfected in Christ was very nearly the equivalent of achieving identification *with* Christ. When Taylor celebrates Samuel Hooker's translation from believer to icon, from fallen flesh to pure spirit, he portrays a saint whose glorification has all but extinguished his once-human self. Piling up metaphors in an attempt to approximate what God has wrought, Taylor commemorates Hooker as

> A Turffe of Glory, Rich Celestiall Dust,
> A bit of Christ here in Deaths cradle 's husht
> An Orb of Heavenly Sunshine: a bright Star
> That never glimmerd: ever shining fare,
> A Paradise bespangled all with Grace:
> A Curious Web o'relaid with holy lace
> A Magazeen of Prudence: Golden Pot
> Of Gracious Flowers never to be forgot
> Farmingtons Glory, & its Pulpits Grace
> Lies here a Chrystallizing till the trace
> Of Time is at an end & all out run.
> Then shall arise & quite out shine the Sun. (*Minor Poetry* 123)

Like other elegists, Taylor defined his duty as witnessing with words an apotheosis that had already occurred in gracious fact. Grace and death had rendered Hooker into his redemptive essence as "a bit of Christ," a process that Taylor foregrounds by alluding to the "Chrystallizing" of Hooker's body in the grave until the Judgment. Taylor took the ritual of verbal embalming to its theological conclusion. Omit the line "Farmingtons Glory, & its Pulpits Grace" from the passage above, and we would be unable to distinguish Hooker from any other glorified saint. Omit the final four lines and we could scarcely distinguish him from the Christ addressed in the *Preparatory Meditations*. In death, "Farmingtons

Glory" had become much more than human, and Taylor took pains to
mark that change as clearly as language would allow.

As members of a preindustrial society, early New Englanders conceived
of mortality in a manner that Philippe Ariès has described as the
"tamed" death, the "old attitude in which death was both familiar and
near, evoking no great fear or awe" (*Western Attitudes* 13). This does not
mean that Puritans were unafraid of dying, but that death occupied an
acknowledged and explicit place within their cultural landscape. Such a
view contrasts sharply with modern attitudes, in which, as Ariès
observes, "death is so frightful that we dare not utter its name." Puritans
would have agreed with Whitman that "To die is different from what
anyone supposed, and luckier." Indeed, they went Whitman one better:
to survive was to be *un*lucky, because it revealed that one's sanctification
was not complete. Anxious to transform the shame of survival into a
source of hope, elegists repeatedly fashioned the dead into neobiblical
guides to the mourner's spiritual betterment. As John Danforth
confirmed in his poem on Peter Thatcher and Samuel Danforth II, what
mattered was that the poem reveal the "Usefulness" of the dead as
models of "Piety and Charity," thereby ensuring that "Their precious
useful *Memory* remains" (Meserole 312, 314). This salvific "Usefulness"
resided chiefly, as Samuel Willard insisted, in "the remembrance that
they were *Saints*." It was their piety that "makes their loss greater than
any other Relation doth or can" (16). By stressing the deceased's permanence as a "noble Soul refin'd, all bright," as Taylor called David Dewey
("Edward Taylor's Elegy" 83), elegy fashioned the reader into a witness
to the spiritual success of a community capable, for all its faults, of preparing souls for heaven. Recently freed from carnal snares that continued to plague survivors, the dead embodied the successful outcome of
an inner drama that was still unfolding within the living.

Peter Sacks, commenting on the English elegiac tradition, observes
that "even in elegies that call themselves 'monodies,' such as 'Lycidas,'
the voice of the elegist seems to work through several moments of
extreme divisiveness or multiplicity" (35). Torn between a desire to
accept the loss and a persistent feeling that it is unfair, the elegist con-
fronts a "reality he might otherwise refuse" (36). Early New Englanders
configured this confrontation as self-struggle, thereby equating the divisiveness of mourning with the expected dichotomies of redeemed experience. To be made *aware* of the struggle against sin was to re-engage in
it. Elegists encouraged the good fight by proclaiming its cessation in the

deceased, whose sinful and saintly tendencies had just been separated by death. Edward Johnson thus foregrounds the dichotomizing of Thomas Hooker into carnal dust and an "Angell bright, by Christ for light now made": "Although in dust thy body mouldering fade; / Thy Head's in Heaven, and hath a crown for thee" (Meserole 150). The Indian student Eleazar articulates the same division in Reverend Thomas Thatcher: "You indeed lie buried," he tells the deceased, "but you lie among the glorious stars " ("jaces tu, / sed stellas inter gloriae nempe jaces") (Kaiser 34). And when Urian Oakes laments that Thomas Shepard is "gone alas! Down in the Dust must ly / As much of this rare Person as could dy" (Meserole 214), what he actually memorializes is the *rest* of Shepard, the deathless part that could continue to edify those who wished to follow him. Taylor's elegy on Dewey makes explicit this association of death's separation of soul from body with the opposition of saintly and sinful dimensions of Puritan experience. Dewey performed his duties as church deacon "Untill thy Person was dichotomiz'd / By death's sharp Sword, and by the same surpriz'd." Dewey is "both parted, and departed," and his soul and body now "standeth part from part" "As doth the *Zenith* from the *Nadir* stand" ("Edward Taylor's Elegy" 83). Only in the latter days, when Dewey's body would rise, purified and "Transcending brightest Gold," would Dewey's physical element be worthy of reuniting with his spirit.[6]

The elegist's concentration on the saint's "Zenith" is especially poignant in poems written for family members, as when Taylor bears witness to death's division of his wife Elizabeth: "Thou Summond hast her Noble part away: / And in Salt Tears I would Embalm her Clay" (*Minor Poetry* 110). Taylor underscores Elizabeth's dissolution by dividing his elegy into three parts. In the first he confesses his need to express sorrow, to write the poem as "this little Vent hole for reliefe" (110). In the second he receives admonitory guidance from the celestial Elizabeth, who gently chides his compulsion to weep: "Will Griefe permit you at my Grave to Sing?" (111). After begging her for permission to write – to "Spare me thus to drop a blubber'd Verse / Out of my Weeping Eyes Upon thy Herse" – Taylor defends his attempt to perpetuate Elizabeth's "Vertuous shine" by citing a sacred "Dutie" not to nail her virtues into her coffin but to preserve them for "thy Babes, & theirs." Part 3 is the longest section of the poem because it performs the real work of Puritan elegy. In it, Taylor shifts to a more impersonal mode demanded by a consideration not of Elizabeth's "Clay," but of her "Noble part." Elizabeth's depiction in this final section is virtually indistinguishable from other

elegiac portraits. As Norman Grabo observes, Taylor creates "an idealized portrait of the Puritan wife – one to be emulated rather than
known" (*Edward Taylor, Revised Edition* 77). Through elegy, Taylor
confirmed Elizabeth's translation into a saintly ideal: it was from that
process that he sought solace, and it was in that form that he commemorated her.

This was performable work. We have heard Oakes voicing the
common lament that he is "Hopeless" to praise Shepard sufficiently:
"They that can *Shepards* goodness well display, / Must be as good as he:
But who are they?" (Meserole 217). They, of course, were the writers and
readers of elegy. Because the deceased's removal from the body modeled
a subjective separation of sinful tendencies from the living, readers
found themselves opposing their own carnality in the very act of praising the saint's spirit. Although Kenneth Silverman correctly points out
that the heroic portrayals of the dead discouraged direct imitation of
their deeds (126), the subjective division enacted by the dead, together
with their abstract portrayal, made them fully imitable in a broader
sense as models of salvific experience. When Daniel Henchman warned
his readers, at the death of Governor Phips, that "thy Fate shows in his
Funeral. / Write now his Epitaph; 'twill be thy own" (Silverman 162),
their response would not have been exclusively or even primarily negative. That Phips was dead seemed to spell their doom, but Phips's apotheosis foreshadowed ultimate glory for those capable of assimilating his
dichotomized example. By placing Shepard among "the sweet Quire of
Saints and Seraphims," Oakes similarly presents the deceased as the
blazer of a trail that beckoned to speaker and reader alike: "Lord! look
on us here, clogg'd with sin and clay, / And we, through Grace, shall be
as happy as they" (Meserole 220).

The projected reconstitution of community in heaven gave the elegy
considerable force as a vehicle of collective comfort. Donne remarked
that "We can sin alone, and suffer alone, but not repent, not be absolved,
without another" ("Devotions" 69). Donne's "another," of course, was
Christ, the unifying center of an Invisible Church that defined how New
Englanders saw their collective ideal.[7] Mere private grief, based on
human rather than gracious ties, threatened to undermine this unity
because it did not speak to the foundational assumptions of a community defined by belief. By encouraging mourners to seek refuge within
this community, elegy strengthened their sense of participation in a
"society," as Charles Lloyd-Cohen describes it, "that conceived itself as
the embodiment of God's love" (161). Taylor thus made it clear that
Deputy Governor Francis Willoughby was one of "us." Had not death

intervened, "[H]e yet had stood within our garden, pal'd. / [H]e was our Chiefest Deputy for all / And now is Deputie in Glory's Hall" (*Minor Poetry* 24). Though Willoughby was gone, his piety – the quality that united survivors with the dead and with each other – remained. Oakes similarly insists that although Shepard was dead, his survivors remained securely situated in a "Huddling Crowd" united by divine love (Meserole 220).

The very God who took the dead away also stood ready to offer solace. "Blest be my Rock! God lives," Oakes proclaims, "Oh let him be, / As He is All, so All in All to me" (Meserole 220). Grindall Rawson asks the survivors of John and Martha Saffin to remember that "Though John and Marth're Dead yet God's alive" (Meserole 478). In an elegy for Hannah Sewall, John Danforth affirms that although Judge Sewall has offered up "Whole *Hecatombs*. . .in ONE" at the loss of his wife, "JESUS Remains; You cannot be Undone" (Winslow 31). Danforth makes the same point, though more obliquely, when he confirms that the deceased Mary Gerrish is fully "satisfy'd" that her "Relatives" will not "be Undone, / By the departure of a star, / while they enjoy the *Sun*" (Meserole 318). The living God who had authored the sanctity of the dead was poised to fill the space created by their leaving. Ultimately, elegy reconstituted the dead as pointers to the divine, as place markers for the one source of the faith that they and their commemorations jointly articulated. With death's transformation of one of "us" into a gracious lure to heaven, the ritual progression from sinful sorrow to saintly comfort was complete. Grief exposed the sin of survivors; praise for the dead shifted the focus of mourning from fallen self to saintly pattern; and finally, the dead deflected the mourner from their divine example to divinity itself. As Danforth visually shouted to Gerrish's survivors, "You want her Much: SEEK HER IN CHRIST / AND YOU WILL FIND HER THERE" (Meserole 319). Gerrish "has Attained now, with Advance, / what she desir'd below" (Meserole 317), and what she "desir'd below" was precisely what her survivors sought for themselves. As a repeatable proclamation that faith had prevailed, elegy culminated in a reassertion of the redemptive hope invoked by Danforth in his celebration of Anne Eliot as heaven's latest arrival, "th' New come welcome Company / of a *Bright Soul*, but lately flown" to her "happy State" (Meserole 320).

Eulogized as pioneers who, in Oakes's phrase, had "gone before" (Meserole 220), the Puritan dead intensified the possibility of an identical though inchoate self developing within the living. The frequent roll calls of the holy dead reinforced this possibility. We have seen William

Bradford put this convention to dehortative use in "A Word to New England," which laments the loss of Hooker, Winthrop, Cotton, and "many precious ones beside" (Meserole 387). But the passing of saints also held consolatory significance as an ongoing transfer of the spiritual community from earth to heaven. E. B., for instance, proclaims Samuel Stone's joyous reunion with the brotherhood of departed ministers: "Heaven is the more desireable (said he) / For *Hooker*, *Shepard*, and *Haynes* Company" (Silverman 143). Ichabod Wiswell places Samuel Arnold beside Josiah Winslow and Thomas Bourne in the "Trine" of celestial saints who had nurtured the church at Marshfield (Winslow 14). And in his poem for John Allen, Taylor confirms that the great "Spirituall Gamesters" are leaving in alarming numbers:

> Are Norton, Newman, Stone, Thompson gone hence?
> Gray, Wilson, Shepherde, Flint, & Mitchell since?
> Eliot, two Mathers Fathers first, then th' Son,
> Is Buncker's, Woodward's, Rainer's hourglass run? (*Minor Poetry* 31)

The immediate response to such heavy losses, of course, is panic. But on a deeper level, these epic rolls suggested that New England's "Quondam Glory" had a future as well – that it was simply being channeled to its proper destination. Despite the apparent disruption posed by death, the mission was succeeding because of a faith shared by all saints, living and dead. In his lament for the first-generation stalwarts, Bradford thus confirms that New England still contains "some. . .who mourne and weep, / And their garments they unspotted keep" (Meserole 387). As a script that both encouraged and effected redemptive mourning and weeping, elegy assured readers not only that salvation had just been won by someone who was recently among them, but that it was still being freely offered by a merciful God.

Not surprisingly, elegists depicted ministers as the clearest embodiments of gracious ties between the living and the dead. Benjamin Woodbridge thus asserts a continuation of John Cotton's pastoral efficacy through his ministerial successor, John Norton:

> Though *Moses* be, yet *Joshua* is not dead:
> I mean Renowned *NORTON*; worthy hee
> Successor to our *MOSES* is to bee,
> O happy Israel in *AMERICA*,
> In such a *MOSES* such a *JOSHUA*. (Meserole 411)

Oakes records a similar passing of the torch in Cambridge from Shepard to John Leverett: "*Harvard!* where's such a fast Friend left to thee! /

Unless thy great Friend, LEVERET, it be" (Meserole 218). Oakes further underscored the continuity of redemptive work by reporting that Shepard had received his charge from the venerable John Wilson: "Sure Father *Wilsons* genuine Son was he, / *New-England's Paul* had such a *Timothy*" (Meserole 217). Although *"Lot's* leaving *Sodom"* "to the *Fire,"* Francis Drake lamented at the death of Jonathan Mitchell, Sodom's sin would not go unchecked: "Tis true, the *Bee's* now dead, but yet his *Sting* / Death's to their *Dronish Doctrines* yet may bring" (Meserole 459). Ministers, of course, were not the only persons whose faith could be preserved and passed on through commemoration. As we have seen, one reason why Taylor writes an elegy for first wife Elizabeth Fitch is to teach "thy Babes, & theirs, thy Vertuous shine" (*Minor Poetry* 111). The venting of emotion, however necessary it was for Taylor the grieving husband, would not stop a ritual of didactic preservation performed by Taylor the dutiful elegist.

In giving their dead this kind of earthly immortality, New England's elegists modified the classical trope of inheritance and succession, in which the living replace the dead. Although these poems indeed prepared readers to take the place of the deceased, this would occur only if the spirit of the dead infused the living. Only through the survivor's genuine assimilation of the deceased's sanctity could the "gap" be filled. As mentioned above, Mather embalms Oakes by placing himself squarely within a succession of embalmers who absorbed and then passed along the godliness of those who went before:

> *Cotton* Embalms great *Hooker; Norton* Him;
> And *Norton's* Herse do's *Poet-Wilson* trim
> With Verses: *Mitchel* writes a Poem on
> The Death of *Wilson;* and when *Mitchel's* gone,
> *Shepard* with fun'ral Lamentations gives
> Honour to Him: and at his Death receives
> The Like from the (*like-Maro*) Lofty Strain
> Of admirable *Oakes.*   (*Verse* 51)

Although the nineteen-year-old Mather protests that "Pride / Ne'er made mee such an *Icharus,"* he had no need to fly, at least not as a poet. At issue was a lineage of grace, not of art. What forged Mather's elegiac chain was not the poems themselves but the faith that prompted their writing. By turning the performance of elegy into a metaphor for belief, Mather invokes a gracious succession that was thought to encompass all true saints. Oakes inserts Shepard into this legacy by alluding to the deceased's more famous father:

> To be descended well, doth *that* commend?
> Can Sons their Fathers Glory call their own?
> Our *Shepard* justly might to this pretend,
> (His Blessed Father was of high Renown,
>   Both *Englands* speak him great, admire his Name.)
>   But his own pers'onal worth's better claim. (Meserole 214)

Even though the younger Shepard's "pers'onal worth" was what
sanctified him, he was also a true heir to his father. As Oakes ambigu-
ously suggests, it was "A double portion of his Fathers Spirit" – perhaps
his own *and* his father's – that "Did this (his Eldest) Son, through Grace,
inherit" (Meserole 215). Taylor more decisively traces Mehetabel
Woodbridge's piety back to her "Grandsires Hains, & Willis, Brightsom
Stars / Connecticuts first" and "their Choice Mates, thy Grandams,"
who shone "Bedeckt with beams of Grace, & Life Sublime" (*Minor Poetry*
124).[8]

Gracious inheritance was a spur to piety, not an excuse for spiritual
laziness. Although Taylor congratulates Samuel Hooker's children as
"Plants of a Noble Vine, a Right, Right Seed," he warns that the legacy
would be revoked if they strayed: "Oh! turn not to a Strange Wild vine
or Weed." Hooker's family were, in this regard, no different from anyone
else. They, too, had to heed their father's lessons as a redemptive
example if they hoped to be saved. Indeed, as Taylor confirms, to do
otherwise would be to abuse that example horribly:

> Be n't like such babes as parents brains out pull
> To make a Wassill Bowle then of the Skull.
> That Pick their Parents eyes out, & the holes
> Stuff up with folly, as if no braind Souls. (*Minor Poetry* 123)

Taylor's warning applied equally to all of Hooker's "babes," whether
physical or spiritual – and it invoked a terrifying alternative to a proper
embalming. Survivors could either apply the deceased's piety to themselves or sink into a willful desecration of his memory. In the clarity of
this directive, elegy offered no middle ground, no room for a lukewarm
response to a saint's passing. As Taylor's framing of the choice suggests,
however, elegy made the wrong decision unthinkable, as did the more
positive inducements issuing the idealized portraiture central to these
poems. Who could fail to cherish a soul who was, as Oakes portrays
Shepard, "Lovely, Worthy, Peerless," "Precious, Pleasant," "Learned,
Prudent, Pious, Grave, and True," and "a Faithful Friend" (Meserole
213)? What's more, who could resist the chance to become such a self?
As Benjamin Tompson declares, he has "penned" his elegy on sister-in-

law Mary "for the imitation of the living" (Murdock 3). Samuel
Danforth similarly offers Thomas Leonard for pious imitation: "GOD
grant that all of his Posterity / May imitate his Virtues, and may say /
His GOD shall be our GOD" (Meserole 490). The *imitatio Christi* at the heart
of each poem is encouraged through a more immediate *imitatio sancti*, a
call to emulate a believer who was once fully human and thus provided
less intimidating precedent. Paul had pioneered this use of a holy life by
offering himself as access to the Savior: "Be ye followers of me, even as
I also am of Christ" (1 Cor. 11:1). Elegists attributed similar benevolence
to the Puritan dead. Like Lycidas, Fiske's John Cotton extends support
from beyond the grave as a guide to the treacherous "passage" though
the "worlds ocean": "now grant O G[od that we] / may follow afte[r
him]" (Meserole 188). Indeed, the ritual of elegy made it seem that
heaven was filling up with well-wishers. With each saint's death, the path
to bliss became more worn; with each commemoration, the trackless
wilderness of the world was offset by yet another clearly marked trail to
glory.[9]

Elegists frequently made the dead speak this comfort directly. In this,
the poets joined redemptive historians like Edward Johnson, who, as
Jesper Rosenmeier notes, "wrote of the dead as having the power to
'speak' to the living from beyond the grave" (160). These otherworldly
voices also parallel Milton's "Saints above," whose singing dries
Lycidas's tears (164), and their message echoes the heavenly call –
perhaps from Michael and perhaps from Lycidas himself – to "Weep no
more, wofull shepherds" (163). Benjamin Tompson has Edmund Davie
assert his status as heavenly pathfinder with typical directness: "I'm now
arriv'd the soul desired Port," Davie asserts; "I've hitt the very Place I
wisht at heart, / I'm fixt for ever: Never thence to part" (Meserole 223).
John Wilson has Joseph Brisco, a drowning victim, offer his death as a
catalyst for reconsidering, from the perspective of faith, what it really
means to be delivered:

> What if I was so soon in Waters drown'd,
> And when I cry'd to men, no help I found:
> There was a God in Heaven that heard my cry
> And lookt upon me with a gracious eye. . . (Meserole 384–85)

Saffin's John Hull advises his mourners to "Watch chearfully untill your
Lord shall call" (Meserole 202). Cotton Mather has schoolmaster Ezekiel
Cheever "dart his Wishes" for teachers to instill piety in their pupils so
"That you like me, with joy may meet them here" (*Verse* 92). Taylor's

Samuel Hooker extends the same hope: "In Faith, Obedience, Patience, walk a while / And thou shalt soon leape o're the parting Stile, / And come to God, Christ, Angells, Saints, & Mee" (*Minor Poetry* 122). As legible maps to bliss, the dead became celestial comforters who urged mourners, as Hooker advises his widow, to "Stay thy Sorrow: bless my Babes. Obey. / And soon thou shall with mee enjoy good day." Mary Gerrish, John Danforth affirms, only "craves, by Friends here left / for to be Visited," and "would Rejoyce to see them all / at th' Heav'nly Table fed" (Meserole 318).

Readers of elegy found themselves being coaxed to glory not only by Christ and the clergy, but by an ever-increasing company of souls with whom they had once shared life's trials. By presenting the dead as spiritual encouragers of the living, elegists ensured their continued usefulness on earth as recapitulations of Paul's willing martyrdom: "Yea, and if I be offered upon the sacrifice and service of your faith, I joy, and rejoice with you all. For the same cause also do ye joy, and rejoice with me" (Phil. 2:17–18). Elegy, in effect, kept the textualized dead within a community that would continue to benefit from their piety. In so doing, the poem strengthened the reader's sense of an ongoing dialogue with heaven. Elegists frequently underscored this exchange by addressing the poem directly to the dead, and Cotton Mather gave it explicit form by dropping the usual one-way speech in favor of a dialogue between Nathanael Collins and his survivors, including "an *Elect Lady*, there / Grov'ling in Ashes, with dishev'led Hair" – none other than "*the Church of* Middletown. . .*Set in the* midst of *swoons and sobs and shrieks*" (*Verse* 64–65). Invoking a constant exchange of piety between heaven and earth, elegy encouraged readers in their struggle against grief and sin with foretastes of a joy that only the dead could know. Collins himself speaks the comfort that such words from beyond the grave could bring: "Be *glad* that I am here, and after hye" (73).

The death of every saved soul was a good death. John Wilson proclaimed such peace even for the melancholic William Tompson of Braintree, who voices his own reward "Of joys & Consolations / Unspeakably posest" (Murdock 17). By relocating the *locus amoenus* of pastoral elegy from this world to the next, Puritan elegy proclaimed the deceased's translation from a physical state construed as illusory, and thus profoundly "fictive," to a spiritual dimension construed as "real." For Puritan readers, these poems confirmed celestial apotheoses that were taken as literal fact: even if elegists used recognizable metaphors to describe the saint's victory, the resulting poem was not read metaphorically. The elegist ensured that death had no more dominion over the poem than it would presumably have in fact (Rom. 6:9). And because the paradigmatic self commemorated in all elegies was potentially nascent in survivors, the dead who spoke directly in the poems offered something more than good advice from beyond the grave. At root, they offered *selves* from beyond the grave, completed versions of the mourner's hoped-for identity. As we have seen, when Taylor proclaimed David Dewey's division from zenith to nadir, he was confirming what Ames called the "double form" of the true believer: "that of sin, and that of grace, for perfect sanctification is not found in this life" (170). By celebrating the dichotomized dead, elegy encouraged mourners to claim the saintly duality for themselves. On the most immediate level, the fact of death confronted survivors with the unreliability of their own dust, the sinful dimension of selfhood that constantly impeded sanctification. But to hear words like those uttered by Mather's Collins – "Souls, follow me" (*Verse* 73) – was to be reminded, once again, of *another* dimension of the self that echoed, however faintly, Collins's glory. After praying for God to "Save ev'ry soul that reads this Elegy," Mather revealed, as directly and concisely as possible, how the prayer would come true: "Like COLLINS let us live, like COLLINS dy" (74).

Saving faith could not be mimicked, but it could be encouraged through a kind of reverse mimicry, in which the deceased's earthly experience was shown to have been similar to the reader's. When elegists described the process by which such saints achieved glory, they often took pains to point out that the dead had struggled, too. If the reader's anxious present could be equated, however tentatively, with the deceased's earthly past, then the deceased's celestial present could be recast as a hopeful harbinger of the reader's future. Taylor thus assures his readers that Samuel Hooker, for all his glory, was once beset by spiritual turmoil as difficult as theirs. The earthly Hooker's inner life had been "A Stage of War, Whereon the Spirits Sword / Hewd down the Hellish foes that did disturb" (*Minor Poetry* 117). Like the pastoral "Saint" who counsels "Soul" in Taylor's *Gods Determinations*, the dead offer comforting testimony: for all the doubts that plague Soul, "'Twas so with me" (*Poems* 436). Taylor records the presence of exemplary turmoil in the saintly Dewey, whose carnal element was nonetheless "A Seat of Sin, Corruption's nest" ("Edward Taylor's Elegy" 83) – a self that was, by theological and experiential definition, "True only to Untruth, and truthless view, / Unfaithfull, Stubborn, truly all Untrue: / Backward to

Good" (84). It was "easier," Taylor confirms, "to bring / Bears to the Stake" than to make the carnal self "cease to Sin" (84).[10] William Tompson's chronic depression provided an especially vivid example of the exemplary struggle with doubt. John Wilson exploited the opportunity to the fullest when he had Tompson confess that "sumtimes I did think, / In midst of my temptacions / I utterly should sink." It was only through God's help, Tompson concedes, that "with violenc / My self i did not kill" (Murdock 14). Troubled readers could take heart from Tompson's victory. If so tortured a believer could persevere in the faith, they could surely sustain the sorrow prompted by his death. Wilson's Tompson seemed to provide first-person proof that children of "Light" whose "state is very good," as Wigglesworth confirmed in "Riddles Unriddled," often walk "in sadness, in the night, / Till this be understood" (*Poems* 146). Such darkness, Wigglesworth made clear, was frequently the product of an excess of humility felt by "poore distressed Souls" (148). It was this distress that elegists sought to ease at the particularly humbling moment of loss.

Such comfort had to be provisional. Edward Pearse proclaimed that "Death, when ever it comes, will be the Death of all your Sins, and the Perfection of all your Graces; and will not that be a kindness?" (157). A complete end to the holy sin of grief could not be expected beforehand, and accordingly, elegists did not represent sorrow as a state that could be overcome in this life. The closure normally associated with elegy was consistently deferred, projected onto the next life and fully available only to those gracious figures whose obsequies were being performed. Sorrow, after all, was a manifestation of the sin that defined the human condition, and while the natural tendency to grieve could be confessed and forgiven, it could not be conquered. In the Puritan view, merely to exist in the world was to be in a state of mourning: ultimately, sorrow had less to do with loss than with the mere fact of being alive. This is why New England's elegies, like all Puritan writing, are pervaded with a sense of futurity: even as the poem reviewed a saintly life, its predominant mode was one of expectation. It was the future that would see the reunion of body and soul, and it was the future that held forth the promise of a full recovery for mourners rent by grief. Elegy thus redirected the mourner's search for comfort toward an anticipation of the larger healing of a self that was, like Taylor's Dewey, *already* "spoild" and rent "asunder" by sin ("Edward Taylor's Elegy" 83).

But while elegy reasserted the line between earth and heaven, it also blurred that line through its stress on the dead as models of salvific hope.

Such hope could be illustrated not just through holy living, but through holy dying. Many of these poems contain brief, stylized accounts of peaceful deaths that posed a sharp contrast to the grief-stricken panic of the living. Pearse stated the widespread belief that "in a Dying Hour the Devil is most fierce and terrible in his Assaults and Temptations upon the Soul" (10). The elegist's report of a "good death," which proved that the deceased had withstood this final onslaught, was sufficiently common to find its way into Silence Dogood's recipe as "last Words" and "dying Expressions" (22). In depicting Mehetabel Woodbridge's passing, Taylor presents just the sort of utterance that Franklin satirized:

> Come, one more Pray're, & Then. – said shee as tho'
> She should be where she would bee. Ending so.
> At last while all by, sunke in Sorrows deep,
>   She entred in Death's Chariot in a Sleep. (*Minor Poetry* 126)

Whether they spoke at the point of death or from the lofty perspective of heaven, the dead were made to demonstrate their fluency in the "New Words" that Taylor anticipated at his own death and glorification (*Poems* 49). As an anonymous elegist has Lydia Minot confirm, "New Light, new Love, new Joy me now do fill, / New Robes I have, new Company, new Skill / To sing th' new Song" (Winslow 7). Deathbed utterances dramatized the saint's transition to a celestial way of speaking. Taylor records Dewey's response to a storm as evidence of his pious readiness to leave the world: "*The Wind is high,* quoth thee, / *But by to Morrow I'st above it be!*" Taylor provides similar witness to the final hours of Samuel Hooker, whose otherworldly perspective emerges well before he dies:

> And holy Counsill on them he would shoure
> With Death Bed Charges till his dying hour.
> But seing Death Creep on his Fingers ends,
> And on his Hands, and Arms, bespake his Friends
> Thus, saying, They are Dead, you see, and I
> Have done with them: warm cloaths thereto apply
> But Death admits no check mate. Out he poures
> His Soul on Christ. On him they, weep in showers. (*Minor Poetry* 119)

Appropriating the subjective stance of self-elegy, the deceased models the fruits of a lifelong and efficacious preparation for death. By calmly presiding over the body's decline, the dying saint articulates a peaceful end to the turmoil of earthly existence.[11]

Nicholas Noyes's poem for Abigail Mather clarifies the didactic function of the good death as an *ars moriendi* performed for the benefit of survivors. After thirty weeks of illness and "*Fervent Pray'r*," Mather's "*Faith* and *Patience* t'was to Try, / And Learn *Us* how to *Live* and *Dy*" (Meserole 284). This gracious manner of dying – the embrace of an identity that is already "dead" – invested deathbed speech with prophetic status. Cotton Mather took immense comfort from Abigail's final words: "I faint, till thy last words to mind I call; / Rich Words! Heav'n, Heav'n will make amends for all" (*Verse* 44). In a headnote to John Wilson's anagram on William Tompson, William's son Joseph claims that his father's dying words were "love the lamb, love, love the lamb" (Murdock 12). Elizabeth Tompson's last words, as recorded by Benjamin Tompson, provide equal witness to a gracious leave-taking: "Sweet mother, close mine eyes & turn aside, / My Jesus sends for me" (Murdock 11). And we have already seen John Cotton attribute comforting words to his daughter Sara: "Pray, my Dear Father, Let me now go Home!" (Meserole 382). These vignettes of deathbed stoicism, even joy, offered anticipatory templates for the survivor's preparation for what Philip Pain called "So great a Change" (Meserole 290). Thomas Hinckley described Thomas Walley's passing as the easeful culmination of just such a process:

> Christ Jesus the same yesterday,
> To day for ever and for aye.
> As on his Death Bed he did find,
> When his past life he call'd to mind. . . (Jantz 148)

The preservation of such tranquil passings brought obvious comfort. With deep feeling and evident pride, the elder Thomas Shepard recorded in his diary that his second wife "continued praying until the last hour of her death," clear evidence that "she was fit to die long before she did die." Joanna Shepard's last words, as Shepard preserved them, were "Lord, though I unworthy; Lord, one word, one word" (*God's Plot* 71). When Simon Saffin died of smallpox at thirteen, his father ended an elegy that he entered into his commonplace book with the assertion that what "Crowneth all the Rest" of Simon's gifts was better expressed in "his own language" (21). What follows is a record of Simon's conversation with the doctor, who asked him, near the end, "how he did." The boy replied, "never better in all my life." When asked why, he answered, "Because I shall be blessed to all Eternity." When asked how he knew this, Simon replied that "Jesus Christ hath told me so." John Saffin took considerable assurance from his son's final days, when Simon "continued with Soul-Ravishing Expressions till his speech faild him" (22). An anonymous poet confirmed similar peace at the end for John Alden, who "with St. *Paul*, his *course* now *finished*, / Unclothed, is quietly put to bed":

"His Family and Christian friends he blest / Before he did betake himself to rest" (Winslow 13). The link with Paul, who proclaimed that "I have finished my course, I have kept the faith" (2 Tim. 4:7), reflects a death-bed conflation of personal and biblical subjectivities that was common in Puritan elegies. A striking example of this appears in Taylor's poem for Zecharia Symmes. Referring to "this aged Nazarite," the poet recounts a stylized deathbed scene in which Symmes cries out "my Head! me head!" (*Minor Poetry* 22). At first glance, these words hardly constitute an affirmation of peace. Yet Taylor could not have missed their precise echo of the words spoken by the Shunammite's son, who was stricken in the fields and then raised by Elisha (2 Kings 4:19). It is impossible to know whether Symmes actually spoke words that Taylor quoted for their biblical overtones, or whether the poet assimilated Symmes's words to the biblical text. Taylor's readers, however, would not have worried about it. They would have thought that the poet had gotten the biblical significance of the passing exactly right.

Symmes's last words underscore the ambiguous relation between the "real" and the "fictive" in these poems. The issue emerges with particular clarity in elegies written entirely in the deceased's voice. In Wilson's poem for William Tompson, for instance, the poet effaces himself completely, stepping aside to permit the celestial perspective to be conveyed through an authoritative voice represented as issuing directly from heaven. "Do not acount me lost," Tompson proclaims, "in his righteousness i stood / Before my father just" (Murdock 15, 17). To frame an elegy as the deceased's self-elegy was, of course, a device that no reader would have taken literally. But Puritan mourners would not have regarded Wilson's poem as a "fiction" either, at least in the modern sense of the word. They would have read it as a real message from the real Tompson – words he would surely say if they hear could him. Ironically, the credibility of the poem was enhanced by its frank artifice, the ploy of a dead man talking. The monitory advantage of having the dead speak their own obsequies was clear, as suggested by the anagram that Wilson teases from "Johannes Harvardus": "If [this does] not [fall] – alas – on deaf ears" ("Si non – ah! – surda aure") (Kaiser 11). The words of the dead carried too much weight to fall on deaf ears. As souls who had successfully prepared for the great change, they offered guidance that could not be ignored.[12] The dead articulated, above all, the salvific reversal of "life" and "death" that we saw in Wilson's treatment of Joseph Brisco's drowning as a deliverance from earthly afflictions. Samuel Torrey embodies this gracious inversion in the figure of William Tompson, who

> . . .did outlive his life; twas time to dye,
> He shall out live his death eternally.
> Wele not lament his timely Death, for why
> Twas death to live, his life to dye. . . (Silverman 144)

Paul insisted that it was the saved soul for whom death had no sting and the grave no victory (1 Cor. 15:55). Edward Pearse affirmed that for the redeemed, death was transformed utterly, from the "King of Terrors" to a "King of Comforts" (149). Taylor, who owned a copy of Pearse's treatise, dramatized this perceptual shift by calling the terrifying images on tombstones and broadsides a sham. While the skull retained its appropriateness for an unregenerate understanding of death, the elect soul saw death as "Tamde, Subdude, Washt fair" by the power of Christ's sacrifice:

> The Painter lies who pensills death's Face grim
>   With White bare butter Teeth, bare staring bones,
> With Empty Eyeholes, Ghostly Lookes which fling
>   Such Dread to see as raiseth Deadly groans,
>   For thou hast farely Washt Deaths grim grim face
>   And made his Chilly finger-Ends drop grace. (*Poems* 55)

In the same poem Taylor proclaims the grave to be "a Down bed now made for your clay," an image recalling Bradstreet's image of the grave in "As Weary Pilgrim" as the "bed Christ did perfume" (295). Readers of elegy who could agree with this perspective – and the poem helped them do so – found that their thinking had already moved closer to that of the commemorated dead. This was the perspective of someone, as Pearse confirmed, who "has all things ready for a dying hour." Such a person "sees Death to be a conquered Enemy, an Enemy conquered by the Death of Christ; and so is carried above the fear of it" (22).

Death's terror to the natural sensibilities was invoked easily enough, and elegists fostered repentance by exploiting the fear shared by all earthly pilgrims. Philip Pain underscored a key point in all Puritan treatments of mortality. "Could I in greatness farre surmount the skie," he attests, "Great, Fair, Rich, Wise, all in Superlatives: / Yet if I were still mortal, there would be / A debt still to be paid to death by me" (Meserole 289). Pain's list of "Superlatives," an echo of elegiac portraiture, reconfirmed the curse accruing to even the best of humanity. Not even the saintly Thomas Shepard, Oakes proclaims, could avoid paying his debt to the law:

If Holy Life, and Deeds of Charity,
If Grace illustrious, and Virtues tri'ed,
If modest Carriage, rare Humility,
Could have brib'd Death, good *Shepard* had not di'ed.
   Oh! but inexorable Death attacks
   The best Men, and promiscu'ous havock makes.
                     (Meserole 214)

Death and sorrow provided an unavoidable occasion for considering the most telling quality of the sinful self that elegy exposed for indictment: the mere fact of mortal existence. As Taylor's Hooker consoles his widow, "When we did wed, we each a mortal took; / And ever from that day for this did look / Wherein we parted are" (*Minor Poetry* 122). "All things on Earth do fall alike to all," John Wilson reiterated at the passing of Joseph Brisco, "To those that do Blaspheme his Holy Name, / And unto those that reverence the same" (Meserole 385). In this lay the urgency of elegy. "The Raising-Day hastens apace," John Danforth proclaimed in his poem for Mary Gerrish, and although Danforth concedes that Gerrish's death was unexpected, "Yet ben't surpriz'd to see that Dead, / you always knew was Dying" (Meserole 318). Elegy presented the saint's death as a proto-eschatological event, a situational precursor of doomsday. Pain voices the temporal urgency constantly reaffirmed in the elegies:

We have no License from our God to waste
One day, one hour, one moment, that do haste
So swiftly from us in our sinful pleasures,
But rather to lay up for lasting treasures.
Lord, spare me yet a little, that I may
Prepare for Death, and for the Judgement-day.
               (Meserole 290)

The permanence and ubiquity of elegies ensured that death's looming presence would not be forgotten, at least for long. Taylor, who confessed to having to relearn the lesson at the death of a second infant daughter, conceded that his resignation to the first loss was not transferable to the second but had to be achieved anew: "as I said, I say, take, Lord, they're thine" (*Minor Poetry* 107). This was a lifelong lesson – *the* lifelong lesson – in Puritan culture. When Saffin wrote a new elegy for his wife Martha twenty-five years after her death, he kept alive not only her memory and his love, but the continuing example of "Her Awefull fear of God" (84).

It was in the nature of carnal selves to be surprised by loss. Grindall

Rawson thus began his elegy on John Saffin Jr. with a rousing call similar to the openings of Bradstreet's house-fire poem and Wigglesworth's *Day of Doom*:

> Awake Sound Sleeper! hark, what Dismal knells,
> Arrests thy drowsie sences, and compells,
> Unbiden Tears to flow, from such a Source
> As doth deny Nature her freer Course. (Meserole 476)

At the death of Elizabeth Tompson, Benjamin Tompson similarly drives home the possibility of unexpected death. Since "none Can tell who shall be next," "Then surely it Concerneth all, / Their time not to neglect" (Murdock 6). The chilling force of the deceased's objectification as a *memento mori*, however, was softened when survivors grasped the divine mercy inseparable from the fact that *they* had not yet died. The greatest consolation of elegy lay in its reaffirmation that there was still time to prepare. Here, as everywhere in Puritan literary culture, texts helped instill the very attitudes they promoted. As a scripted performance in watching and praying, elegy projected a textual deliverance onto an audience whom death had spared. That they were still alive proved God's indulgence in extending them additional time to get their houses in order.

Elegy concentrated and intensified the three great Puritan lessons regarding life in the world. The first was the importance of a lifelong preparation for death. "His life was nothing but of death / a daily meditation," Wilson says of John Norton, "And to his happy end, at last, / a solemn preparation" (Murdock 94–95). The second was the convicting power of sorrow in exposing the vast gulf between human wishes and divine will. The third was the related disparity between earth and heaven, dramatized by another saint's departure from a world fit only for leaving. Taylor insists that Increase Mather "chose not the World to seeke / But didst resolve a better game to keep; / Didst rather choose to run a better race" (*Minor Poetry* 247). "O what Soul Ravishing Communion," Saffin says of John Hull, "he / Had Dayly with the Blessed Trinity" (Meserole 201). Oakes similarly extols Shepard's view of earth as merely a staging area for the assault on heaven. Shepard was "No Slave to th' Worlds grand *Idols*; but he flew / At *Fairer Quarries*, without stooping down / To Sublunary prey" (Meserole 217). Consistent with their status as a "Loan / Of Heaven" (212), the dead had lived their lives in full awareness that their real home lay above. As we have seen, these poems constructed sorrow as a smarting at God's ways. But grief also had value as an indispensable catalyst for the mourner's realignment, however tentative and partial, with God's will. Oakes does not minimize the fact that "'twas God" who took Shepard away, "To give him great Reward, and punish us" (Meserole 216). At the death of granddaughter Elizabeth, Bradstreet similarly concludes that the loss is "by His hand alone that guides nature and fate" (235).[13] New England's elegists repeatedly confirmed not only that losses were God's doing, but that his reasons for inflicting them had to remain beyond human understanding. As in all elegy, to respond to a death with calm assurance was a nearly insurmountable challenge. Full resignation necessarily had to remain out of reach – and yet, the attempt had to be made. As Oakes declared,

> We must not with our greatest Soveraign strive,
> Who dare find fault with him that is most High?
> That hath an absolute Prerogative,
> And doth his pleasure: none may ask him, why? (Meserole 218–19)

Despite human notions of fairness, "We're Clay-lumps," Oakes declares, "Dust-heaps, nothings in his sight: / The Judge of all the Earth doth always right" (219). In convicting all humanity to the grave, it indeed seemed, as Elihu proposed to Job, that God "respecteth not any that are wise of heart" (Job 37:24). So facile a summary of the divine intention, of course, prompted the terrifying voice from the whirlwind: "Who is this that darkeneth counsel by words without knowledge?" (Job 38:1). Job responds by acknowledging the sin inherent in the fact of being human, of not being God: "Wherefore I abhor myself, and repent in dust and ashes" (Job 42:6). Bradstreet forced Job's lesson upon herself after losing her third grandchild: "With dreadful awe before Him let's be mute, / Such was His will, but why, let's not dispute" (237).

Reacting to Christ's confirmation that God "maketh his sun to rise on the evil and on the good, and sendeth rain on the just and on the unjust" (Matt. 5:45), Puritan elegists encouraged mourners to accept what they could not understand. What faith "requires" at the death of "Urania's" child, Colman states, "is to resign, / To Heaven's own Act, and make it thine / By Silence under Discipline" (Meserole 338). Colman's advice to embrace such losses as "blest Acts" is echoed in poem after poem. Elegists challenged readers not simply to accept God's harsher dispensations but to turn them to spiritual advantage by using the dead as "Aurifick-Stones," as John Danforth called Peter Thatcher and Samuel

Danforth – holy touchstones for gauging their own piety (Meserole 314).
Since affliction fell upon the just and the unjust alike, the only visible distinction was one's response to it. This is why elegists frequently concede
that while some mourn the loss, some do not. Daniel Henchman por-
trays those whom he sees as enemies of the mission, French Catholics
and pagan Indians, as feeling unholy joy at the passing of Governor
Phips: "Rejoyce, Messieurs; Netops, Rejoyce; 'Tis True; / Ye Philistines,
None will Rejoyce, but you" (Silverman 160). We have already seen
Bradstreet make a similar distinction between those who loved her father
and those who feared him (203). And Thomas Hinckley embalms
Thomas Walley as a touchstone of orthodoxy by castigating those "poor
Deceived Quakers, who rejoice / At Death of him and such as he"
(Jantz 147). Nothing separated the sheep from the goats like the death of
a saint. "Envy and Malice," Samuel Danforth II asserts in a poem on
Thomas Leonard, "must be reigning Vices / In those who will not bear
to hear his Praise" (Meserole 489). Indeed, such a death forced survivors
to decide whether to embalm the deceased's virtues or to align themselves with the godless. Colman generalizes from Samuel Willard to
describe any "just" soul as a barrier between good and evil: "A *Name
imbalm'd* shall be the *Just* Mans lot, / While Vicious *Teeth* shall *gnash*, /
and *Names* shall *rot*" (Meserole 344).

Although Colman does not pose the choice too subtly, the clarity of
his moral stance strengthened the poem's consolatory impact. Colman's
readers were *not* gnashing their teeth, but were passing the test that
Willard's death posed in the very act of reading the poem. Oakes demonstrates the experience-shaping power of elegy when, in his final
stanza, he shifts to a more personal tone:

> My Dearest, Inmost, Bosome-Friend is Gone!
> Gone is my sweet Companion, Soul's delight!
> Now in an Huddling Crowd I'm all alone,
> And almost could bid all the World *Goodnight*. . . (Meserole 220)

Given the sense of collective loss voiced throughout the poem, the gracious Shepard has by this point become the reader's "Bosome-Friend"
as well. Oakes's "I" encompasses speaker and reader alike, bound in a
"Huddling Crowd" of mourners who cherish Shepard not just as one
of their own, but as a superior version of their very selves. By fostering
such high regard for the serene faces gazing back from the other side of
the potent fence, New England's elegies enacted a performance that
spoke well to the spiritual future of those who participated in it. While

discussing signs of relief during spiritual "desertions," John Weemse confirmed that if a man "hath ever loved the Saints of God" simply because they *were* saints, "it is a sure note that he loves God, *and is passed from death to life*" (295). It was this love – and this consolation – that elegy helped bring about.

All elegy, as Sacks has observed, seeks to absorb the "unique death" into "a natural cycle of repeated occasions" (24). Although Puritan elegists invoked spirit rather than nature, they indeed ushered particular losses into familiar – and thus comforting – cycles of fear and hope, sin and repentance, death and resurrection. Nor was Puritan elegy unique in connecting grief with culpability. As Jahan Ramazani has said of modern elegy, "the ego avoids outwardly venting its sadism and hate by turning its rage onto the inner substitute for the lost object" (29). By equating the body of the deceased with the fallen dimension of the living, New England's elegists directed sorrow's "rage" toward the survivor's sin. Proper mourning was, in essence, an attempt to beat death at its own game, to devalue carnal identity before death had its way with it. Mourners thereby strengthened their sense of what Mather called the believer's *"Better Part"* (*Cure of Sorrow* 24), the saintly aspect of identity capable of being edified by the loss. Elegists fostered this subjective realignment by means of conventions that served, in their very predictability, to make sorrow seem more manageable: interchangeable portraits of the dead, standard biblical parallels, rigidly formulaic language, endless calls for repentance. For Puritan readers, the very sameness of these poems only enhanced their power to instill hope just when God's face seemed darkest. Verbal and experiential patterns enacted in poem after poem reassured mourners that the death of a saint, however disruptive it seemed, only hastened the fulfillment of the redemptive plan. Saints died, but sanctity seemed stronger with each poetic witness to another glorious passing.

The hundreds of funeral elegies written in early New England constitute an extended incantation on this theme. The individual poem, like the individual death, was not construed in isolation from other poems and other deaths. Each elegy took its place within a relentless celebration of continuities uniting earth with heaven, the living with the dead, the past with the future, and the human with the divine. The stylized embalming of the deceased strengthened the mourner's ability to internalize these continuities. The pious dead, who made the limitations of earthly experience painfully obvious, also proved what faith could do for survivors. Mather, adapting a poem by Paulinus of Nola to conclude his elegy on the seven young ministers, dramatized this dichotomy of conviction and consolation by suspending himself between two different but mutually supportive self-readings enabled by salvific turmoil. "Gratuler an Doleam?" Mather asks at the close of the poem: "Should I rejoice or grieve?" (*Verse* 87). The Puritan answer, of course, was both: grieve for the sinful self mired in this world, but rejoice for the saintly self perfected in the dead and nurtured through their example within the living. Bradstreet voices the same paradox in her poem for grandson Simon. Suspended by grief between the sinful and saintly tendencies of all worldly pilgrims, she trusts that Christ will "return, and make up all our losses, / And smile again after our bitter crosses" (237).

Like all Puritan poetry, elegy existed not as a finished product but as stimulus and record of a meditative process. Despite their militant logocentrism, Puritans saw language as a temporary expedient, an imperfect vehicle by which eternal truths could be expressed within the fallen world of time and substance. In its relentless stress on process and response, Puritan discourse mimicked the provisional and mediatory nature of the Word and the Sacraments as divine ordinances which, however indispensable to earthly pilgrims, would be transcended in heaven. As Wilson's Abigaill Tompson confirmed, the pious dead were thought to enjoy an unmediated experience of God, free from the dark glass of fleshly perceptions. In heaven, Tompson proclaims, "i no longer need / Or word or seale my feeble soul to feede, / But facc to face i do behould the lamb" (Murdock 9). In the meantime, mourners had to rely, as elegy repeatedly reminded them, on faith and not vision – and on such "texts" as God had provided in Christ as *Logos*, the Bible, the deceased's example, and the poem itself as signposts along life's pilgrimage. All these texts worked to generate the redemptive hope that lay at the intersection of fear and joy. Such hope, Puritans believed, was fully capable of generating meditative glimpses beyond the wall that guilt and sin had erected between the dead and the living. In a poem for her brother, poet Benjamin Tompson, Anna Hayden tells the deceased that

> I hope that you'e attaind that rest
> Where nothing there will you molest,
> Where i do hope ere long to be,
> Wheres better times & Company. (Murdock 21)

As Hayden's longing for "better times & Company" suggests, elegy countered the sting of loss by reasserting a faith-based equation of reading present and celestial future. In its presentation of the deceased's *then* as the mourner's *now*, elegy unified time within a redemptive framework that seemed to counter death's apparent rupture.

Death, Edward Pearse assured his readers, "will turn your Conflict into Victory; this *Aceldama*, or field of Blood, (for such is the World,) into a Mount of Triumph, and a Throne of Glory" (153). Puritan readers did not feel elegy's relentless proclamation of this transformation as an imposition. On the contrary, the celebration of the holy dead helped them attain the calm anticipation that Pearse called "a more ready posture for my Death and Dissolution, which seems to be near at hand" (4). In a verse character of "The Happy Man," John Saffin wistfully observed "how did Gods Saints of old: / With Joyfull hearts, Approaching Death Behold" (124). The Bible provided many such examples of holy dying. Consider, Saffin asks his reader, "How sweetly Jacob gather'd up his feet, / When he by Death did his Redeemer meet." Joseph, too, looked toward his death "unconcern'd" and "famillierly"; Moses "meekly" climbed a mountain to die; David sang a "Swanlike Song"; Simeon prayed "that he might Cease." And how strong was Paul's "Desire to be with Christ, as best of all"? Surely, Saffin declares, the biblical story of these leave-takers "Was written for, our Constant Imitation" (124). New England's elegists figured that they could follow no better lead. Applying the death of a saint to the survivor's self-examination as a saint-in-the-making, elegy generated a response to loss that corresponded to a warm hearing of the Word. "This hearing," as Ames described it, "must come from the hope by which we embrace what God has promised as the word of life and from it also expect life" (255–56).

"As *Death* is a *Sleep*," Mather proclaimed in a funeral sermon for Mary Higginson, "so the Death of the Faithful, will be an Hopeful Sleep, yea a Joyful Sleep" (*Awakening Thoughts* 21). In the work of negotiating heartfelt sorrow with this view of death, Puritan elegy invoked a reading dynamic that can be visualized as a series of concentric circles. At the periphery, encompassing all else, was the Bible as an accessible point of entry. The next circle was occupied by Christ as the theanthropic embodiment of biblical truth. Next came the deceased, whom death and grace had refashioned into a Christic self in heaven. Next came the poem itself, a textualized embodiment of the objectified saint whose sanctity was being commemorated. At the very center of these circles stood the reader, challenged by elegy to imitate the dead and thereby to reconceptualize the inner life as a localized figuration of each larger circle. Then as now, accepting the death of a loved one posed a difficult challenge. But for Puritan mourners, recovery seemed possible through a renewed grasp of their own position within larger patterns that embodied God's design.

Speaking to a paradoxical identity defined by the turbulent interplay of sin and grace, elegy scripted an equally paradoxical performance: the active pursuit of passivity. Elegy was something to *do* that nonetheless left recovery entirely in divine hands. As Nathaniel Pitcher asked at the drowning of Isaac Stetson, "What though his Mortal Body Serve as Dishes / Instead of Feeding Worms, to feed the Fishes: / And all his dust be Scattered up and down"? God will "Easily" "Re-unite them into Form Compleat, / When Soul and Body at the last shall Meet" (Winslow 32). While Pitcher's images will no doubt strike the modern reader as comically repugnant, Puritan readers were convinced that the flesh deserved no better. For Isaac Stetson, the old war of flesh and spirit was over, and his peace dramatized an inner eschatology that cast all such turmoil, including the turmoil of grief, into tolerable and even comforting light. Although the war waged on in Stetson's survivors, their chances of achieving his victory seemed strengthened by the elegist's call for a vigorous and aggressive anticipation of divine deliverance. When God demands Ezekiel's reaction to the vision of the valley of dry bones, the divine question and the human answer describe the Puritan response to the challenge of writing resurrections for the dry bones of the holy dead. "Son of man, can these bones live?" Ezekiel replies, "O Lord God, thou knowest" (Ezek. 37:3). It was an answer on which early New Englanders built not just a poetics of commemoration, but an entire faith.

Epilogue: Aestheticizing loss

The summer of 1708 saw the passing of Ezekiel Cheever, the ninety-four year old headmaster at Boston Latin. Cotton Mather, Cheever's most prominent former student, undertook the duty of embalming this "*Christian Terence*" with thanks for what Cheever had given to his "Almighty *Tribe* of Well-instructed Youth":

> All the *Eight parts of Speech* he taught to them
> They now Employ to Trumpet his Esteem.
> They fill *Fames Trumpet*, and they spread a Fame
> To last till the *Last Trumpet* drown the same. (*Verse* 88)

Cheever's *Latin Accidence: An Elementary Grammar* had become the standard text in New England, and Mather found it appropriate to mourn his old teacher in elaborate figures recalling the subject he had taught for seven decades. Nor was Mather the only poet to do so. Another tribute, entitled "The Grammarian's Funeral," made Mather's application of wit seem positively restrained. Benjamin Tompson, who had actually written the elegy four decades earlier at the death of another schoolmaster, published it in broadside at Cheever's death.[1] The poem was unusual, to say the least. Instead of the usual celebration of faith, Tompson centers an impressive display of poetic ingenuity around Cheever's calling. After dressing the "Eight Parts of *Speech*" in "*Mourning Gowns*," the poet shows the modal verbs reacting to the loss: "*Volo* was willing" to mourn and "*Nolo* some-what stout," Tompson writes, "But *Malo* rather chose, not to stand out": "*Possum* and *Volo* wish'd all might afford / Their help, but had not an *Imperative Word*." The standard elegiac disorientation finds expression in a trope of grammatical chaos: "What *Syntax* here can you expect to find" when each element of speech "bears such discomposed mind" (Winslow 25)? This is surely the most linguistically controlled depiction of linguistic breakdown in any New England elegy. But as Tompson declares, the firm hand of poetry can save the day by forcing the stunned bits of grammar to work together: "That such a Train may in their motion *chord*, / *Prosodia* gives the measure Word for Word."

Like Milton in his playful pieces on Hobson the coachman, who "di'd for heavines that his Cart went light" (102), Tompson separates elegy from the work of mourning as Puritans usually defined it. Both Mather and Tompson, as we have seen, penned other elegies in the old style. It may well have taken a grammarian's death and the linguistic self-consciousness it prompted to produce these anticipations of the new grammar of mourning that emerged during the first quarter of the eighteenth century, as the Puritan grip on the culture weakened and neo-classical modes of thought and taste gained ground. For some, the old order could not pass quickly enough. A month before Silence Dogood's elegiac recipe appeared, Franklin blasted Harvard, the seat of Puritan orthodoxy, as a place where "every Beetle-Scull seem'd well satisfy'd with his own Portion of Learning, tho' perhaps he was *e'en just* as ignorant as ever" (12). Four years later, Mather warned young ministers against "harlot" muses as a frivolous distraction from more serious studies. His famous advice to "Be not so set upon *Poetry*, as to be always poring on the *Passionate* and *Measured* Pages" reveals an uneasy response to a growing number of poets who seemed to forget that the main goal of verse was spiritual edification (*Manuductio* 42). Mather's was a losing cause. By midcentury Benjamin Church's idyll of the good life included quiet hours reading not just "Britain's Genius, *Milton*," but "awful *Pope*," "copious *Dryden*," and "Nature-Limning *Thompson*" (Silverman 245, 246).

With the waning of biblical authority, nature and not Scripture began to provide the chief inspiration for poetry, including elegy – and it was not a nature construed as fallen. In 1713, a year after Taylor conceded that David Dewey's natural self had been "rebellion's Kennel, Disobediences Chest" ("Edward Taylor's Elegy" 83), Richard Steere celebrated how

> The chirping notes of winged *Choresters*,
> And Purling Murmurs of Gliding *brooks*,
> Modulate Accents of a *well Tun'd voice*,
> Joyn'd with the Sweet *Allurements* of the *Lute*. . . (Silverman 212)

Unlike Bradstreet, who demonstrated in "Contemplations" how a sin-dazed soul might resist such seductions, Steere kept his eyes and ears open to them. As this delayed introduction of pastoral themes in New England suggests, the natural realm was no longer seen as a barrier

through which the poet strained to discern God's ways. Even though
Steere's encomium of "Earth Felicities" and "Heavens Allowances" promotes "a kind of happiness in Crosses" for the "virt'ous man" whose
"way to Heaven seems a pleasant path," the world has become a stage
of contentment, not a wilderness of error from which true believers
longed to escape (Silverman 210, 214).

A poet's ability to perceive the "sublime" in the natural landscape –
precisely the sort of revelation that failed to satisfy Bradstreet – became
the only revelation worth seeking. This was the world that Freneau
described in "The Universality and Other Attributes of the God of
Nature": "All that we see, about, abroad, / What is it all, but nature's
God?" (Eberwein 248). Rehabilitated as a source of vision rather than a
site of mutability, nature stood poised as a ready source of consolation to
readers and mourners alike. At the beginning of the nineteenth century,
Bryant would proclaim a belief that had come to be shared equally in the
Lake District, the Hudson Valley, and New England: to the soul laboring
under melancholy prompted by thoughts of death, nature speaks "with
a mild / And healing sympathy, that steals away / Their sharpness, ere
he is aware" (Eberwein 271). As nature went, so went the nature-gazing
subject. It was the individual sensibility that was capable of grasping the
beauty of a world released from sin, and the new individualism fostered
by rationalist and romantic tendencies inevitably influenced verbal commemoration. Elegy, at least in its "literary" variety, no longer focused on
what was exemplary about a death. On the contrary, the elegist wrote to
confirm the irreducible uniqueness of the loss. Paradoxically, elegy began
to emphasize the particularity of the dead by citing their reintegration
with universal cycles that effaced their unique identities. With the absorp-
tion of the dead into Wordsworth's "diurnal course," the poetry of
mourning begins to sound familiar. It remains, by and large, our sense of
what is appropriate to say and think at times of loss. Modern mourners,
who generally share the romantic ideal of sustaining loss without
recourse to specifically religious compensations, understand the comforts
of a confirmation of the deceased's unique identity. We, too, seek comfort
from natural cycles that seem to invest death with a measure of rightness
and meaning. We also take comfort from art given and taken *as* art – from
the apparent permanence of poems on the page as enduring monuments
to the fragility of particular lives.[2]

Puritan elegies bear ample witness that standards of art and conventions
of mourning change over time, sometimes to the point of intelligibility.
Not everything, however, changes beyond recognition. I suspect that the

loss of a loved one was as hard for Puritans to accept as it is for us, and
if they hit upon a textual vehicle, however formulaic, that helped them
deal with it, we would be guilty of historical and critical arrogance to
dismiss the results. Beneath the stylized surface of Puritan elegy are
questions that are still familiar. Why has this death occurred? What does
it mean? Or, more darkly, does it mean anything at all? What words can
be spoken to express and thus relieve sorrow? How do we make peace
with the loss and go on? Broader structures find their modern parallels
as well. The Freudian distinction between mourning and melancholia,
for instance, provides a context for examining Puritan grief. Mourning
is situational: arising from a specific occasion, it usually fades as the
mourner adjusts to the loss. Melancholia, by contrast, is linked not to a
particular event in the world but to perceptions regarding the very
nature of the world. We see melancholia as pathology, and might indeed
spot its presence in the Puritan elegist's call for mourners to move from
the situational response – what we would call "healthy" mourning – to
something larger and more systemic. We would be correct, from a
modern point of view, in finding a theological equivalent of melancholia in the Puritan notion that sin was pervasive in the world and the self.
But Freud's model, however useful, obscures the degree to which pathology is culturally defined. To diagnose melancholia as a problem among
seventeenth-century New Englanders is to ignore the contrasting structures of normality in their society and in ours. Puritan elegy encouraged
a transcendence of the specific occasion through a conviction in sin that
was considered to be – and thus experienced as – spiritually therapeu-
tic. Elegists sought to replace "natural" reactions to loss with extrasitua-
tional patterns that Puritan culture equated with health, not sickness.
Although the redistribution of sanctity demanded a transcendence of
the merely personal, the resulting consolation was felt as personal. By
diffusing the deceased's piety throughout the community, elegy helped
mourners diffuse their own grief into a wider space equated not just with
a religion or a society, but with the very architecture of heaven and earth.
If mourners found themselves shaken by the inscrutable act of a merciful God, elegies told them that they were not alone in reacting this way.
Indeed, all people reacted this way. Puritans were convinced that there
were ample reasons to weep, and those reasons went beyond specific loss
to the very heart of what it meant to be human.

Puritan elegy also left room for the anger of loss. Unable to escape the
conclusion that God was responsible for taking beloved souls, Puritan
mourners deflected their bitterness from the Author of all things to the

one thing that humans had authored by themselves: depravity. Although the doctrine of original sin seemed to justify this deflection, the Puritan negotiation of anger was more complex than a mere recognition of dogma. Although the deceased's division into body and soul prompted survivors to distrust their own corporeality, they drew comfort from imagining the same subjective division within themselves. Death proved, once again, the unreliability of flesh, and mourners directed their anger toward the death-bound aspect of identity: not simply the flesh, but its relentlessly sinful proclivities. To repent was to acknowledge death's sway over *that* self and to cling to another self altogether, a saintly identity that mirrored the portion of the deceased which had *not* died. It is a paradox central to Puritan mourning that the deaths of saints made it easier for survivors to imagine their own immortality. In their belief that repentance would lead them to the same victory that the deceased now enjoyed, Puritans framed a profoundly optimistic reading of the traditional epitaph: "As I am, so you shall be."

Like all elegy, New England's poems of loss gave mourners something to *do* – activity as a counter to the shock of loss. Moreover, the work that the poems both encouraged and enacted was seen as the only activity that would do any good, not just in coping with this death but in grasping the inevitability of one's own. There was also, of course, the hoped-for reunion with the dead in heaven. To be sure, powerful redirection was at work here – a distracting of the mourner's attention from present to future, from current loss to deferred gain, from helpless passivity to significant action. But distraction is central to all elegy: some things simply cannot be faced head-on. We moderns also indulge an impulse to translate the stasis of grief into actions that will help us escape "the civil wars of a self-divided mind" that W. David Shaw finds in modern elegy (*Elegy and Paradox* 170). In its determined restlessness, as Jahan Ramazani points out, elegy resists consolation (xi). The loss of a loved one not only hurts: it is *expected* to hurt. The elegist thus, as Shaw notes, "transgresses norms by trying *not* to make the reader feel that art is totally coherent and controlled" (224). This resistance to complete control finds its equivalent in the deliberate artlessness of the New England elegy and the speaker's role as poetic amateur. It also emerges in the Puritan conviction that the cessation of sorrow in its deeper, convicting sense would not come until one's own death. To live on earth was, by definition, to live in turmoil. The power of loss to remind us of this is one point, at least, on which seventeenth-century and twentieth-century mourners could agree.

Because death is both a local event and a fact of life, elegy inevitably invokes a tension between the specific and the general, the unique and the representative. Modern mourners do not usually translate our particular loss completely into broader structures or general truths: our experience of the people we love is too intense and private to allow it. We resist the recognition that dying, for all its cultural and psychological charge, contains an embarrassing banality as the one thing that we will all do. Walking a difficult line between the unique impact of *this* death and the universality of death as a fact of existence, elegy seeks a way, as Peter Sacks observes, to fold the particular death back into cycles suggestive of order and continuity (36). This is a tricky negotiation, and poets use whatever tools they have to effect it. Modern elegists, and modern mourners generally, invoke cycles amenable to our time: the passing of an era, the changing of the seasons, the stages of a life, the continuity of generations, the redistribution of biochemical energy or genetic material or cosmic spirit – whatever works for us. Puritans found their consolatory cycles in religion, in the salvific pattern of death and rebirth that lies at the heart of Christianity. They saw the pattern everywhere, most immediately in the ongoing oscillation between sinful and saintly tendencies that defined their meditative lives. The great Plot of good versus evil was also unfolding in cosmic history, in the progress of the created universe toward eschatological fulfillment with – and within – a God who had set the wheels in motion. This was a vast stage, large enough to contain the heartbreak of loss. Although Puritans frankly acknowledged their fear of dying, they were convinced that death was contained, too – and that elegy made its presence easier to bear. In this lies a recognizable impulse, one that the alien surfaces of these poems don't quite conceal.

Notes

1 Despite recent attempts to forge a literary historiography answerable to poststructuralist critiques, I agree with Fox-Genovese that history cannot do without causation, and that writing it is inherently "structural" in the sense that historians "must disclose and reconstruct the conditions of conscious- ness and action" (217). The chief difference between the "old" and the "new" historicisms resides in the former's innocent claims for the objectiv- ity of causal structures on which all history relies. As Patterson observes, lit- erary history has never been able to abandon the notion of a *Zeitgeist* expressing itself through specific texts, and has thus always relied on "'his- torical' materials to construct an account of period consciousness that was then read back onto the 'literature'" (251). This is, of course, one form of the hermeneutic circle that David Perkins identifies in the historian's ongoing movement between taxonomy and text (113). All historiographies reenact it, including the varied forms of "new historicism," "cultural poetics" (Greenblatt's preferred term), and "literary anthropology" (see Iser, *The Fictive and the Imaginary*), by alternating between categories equivalent to what Geertz calls "local detail" and "global structure" (*Local Knowledge* 69).

2 A concise survey of the critical history of the Puritan poem appears in Daly's *God's Altar* (201–23). This reception history illustrates the tendency to read older texts in light of current preoccupations, to see the past merely as a precursor to the present (Jauss, *Toward an Aesthetic* 109). Among historians of early America this tendency has manifested itself in what Hall has called a "fusion of modernism and nativism" resulting from the combined agendas of formalist aesthetics and nationalist pride ("On Native Ground" 325). For critiques of the persistent impact of presentism on American literary historiography, see Colacurcio ("Does American Literature Have a History?"), Spengemann ("Discovering the Literature of British America"; *Mirror for Americanists* 31–33, 142), McWilliams (129), Hammond (*Edward Taylor* 121–23), Grabo ("Ideology"), and De Prospo ("The Latest Early American Literature"; "Marginalizing Early American Literature").

While modernist aesthetic preferences continue to encourage the formal- ist objectification of texts as the "matter" of literary study, the impact of nationalistic impulses on the development of literary history has been even more obvious. Appiah cites Herder, Carlyle, and Taine as foundational framers of German, British, and French literary historiographies that served "the ends of nation-building" (284). This goal was evident in early constructions of "American literature," where the chief concern was to show that Americans could write as well as the British, with English canonical literature becoming, in Lease's term, a normative "prison" for American writers (xiv). This strategy later reversed itself, with critics lionizing "American" roughness and crude strength as evidence of growing independence from British standards and polish; classic formulations of this latter approach include the enormously influential work of Vernon Louis Parrington and F. O. Matthiessen.

3 As Perkins observes, "in any act of interpretation, the borders between the textual and the contextual are drawn by convention" (122). By deemphasizing the canonical "classic" construed as a product of individual genius, the newer historiographies assume the existence, in Greenblatt's terms, of "very little pure invention in a culture" (*Shakespearean Negotiations* 13), and thus base the analysis on such extrapersonal rubrics as Foucault's *épistème* as an articulation of discursive and subjective order, anthropological notions of "culture" (Geertz and Turner), a pervasive "ideology" (Althusser), a "political unconscious" (Jameson), or a combination of these. Greenblatt, for instance, describes his "poetics of culture" as the "study of the collective making of distinct cultural practices and inquiry into the relations among these practices" (*Shakespearean Negotiations* 5). Within this formulation, culture is itself a text, and "thick description," to use Geertz's term, begins once that text becomes readable (*Interpretation of Cultures* 29). Iser has recently proposed a literary anthropology that focuses on the process by which "the fictionalizing act," a simultaneously constructive and transgressive gesture, "endows the imaginary with an articulate gestalt" (*The Fictive and the Imaginary* 3).

I follow these critics in seeing "intention" in texts as a product of forces larger than an author's seemingly deliberate choices. Because writing embodies impulses and influences that transcend the writer's immediate motives, "the moment of inscription," as Greenblatt states, is "a social moment" (*Shakespearean Negotiations* 5). Greenblatt clarifies how "social energy" is exchanged by means of literary representation: art arises not from "spontaneous generation" or individual "genius" but from cultural and historical forces; there can be no "timeless or unchanging representation" that transcends those forces; and finally, there are no "autonomous artifacts" but socially situated texts, each of which has an "origin and an object, a *from* and a *for*" (12). Reacting against the privileging of what Montrose calls "a unified and autonomous individual – whether an Author or a Work" ("Professing the Renaissance" 18), proponents of the newer historicisms follow Foucault in focusing on the discursive "subject" and "subjectivity" encoded in texts rather than the traditionally conceived "author" and canonical "authority." Concerned with reading all systems of representation as texts, including systems of human subjectivity, such historical models assume an intertextuality by which all expressive acts are bound up with other "texts," including material practices. The newer focus, in Montrose's now-famous phrase, is on "the historicity of texts and the textuality of history" ("Renaissance Literary Studies" 8).

4 As Ziff observes, within Puritan "culture's overwhelming commitment to the centrality of words over commitment to ambiguous images, to the dominance of the pulpit over the altar, was a folk belief in the animism of language" (*Puritanism in America* 119). Because of the coherence and pervasiveness of Puritan logocentrism, Puritan texts are especially amenable to a repositioning of "the axis of intertextuality" that Monstrose describes as a "substituting for the diachronic text of an autonomous literary history the synchronic text of a cultural system." This involves a shift "from the formal analysis of verbal *artifacts* to the ideological analysis of discursive *practices*" ("Professing the Renaissance" 17, 26). Sharing with reader-response criticism a stress on the reactions of readers positioned within historically specific ideologies (Jauss, *Toward an Aesthetic* 36), this approach rejects the timeless masterpiece central both to traditional literary historiography and to what Patterson calls the New Critical "essentializing of literature," which rendered truly historical readings impossible (256). Jauss has called this notion a persistent "metaphysics of supratemporal beauty" (*Toward an Aesthetic* 62), an ideal that prompted the increasing isolation of literary works from the socioeconomic conditions of their production and reception as professional criticism developed during the eighteenth and nineteenth centuries (Raymond Williams). The implicit denial that taste varies with time and place created a profoundly ahistorical bias embodied in what Fish has called a cult of "appreciation" (*Is There a Text* 353). Accounts of evolving professional constructions of "English literature" include Eagleton and Graff (*Professing Literature*); for similar developments in American literary studies, see Leitch, Vanderbilt, and Reising.

5 Whatever the methodology, all history writing is probably incapable of avoiding such condescension. Lentricchia, for instance, cites Taine as the source of a historical mode still prevalent, "a satirical historicist rhetoric, a debunker's style shared by old and new historicists alike" (231). More generally, the critic's superior position is couched in the very language of historical and literary analysis. As Eagleton remarks, "'ideology' is always a way of describing other people's interests rather than one's own" (211). Such denigration of the "other," deliberate or otherwise, can occur anywhere on the political spectrum. Montrose, for example, accuses conservatives alarmed by what they see as a growing politicization of the humanities of reserving "the term 'ideology' for the disapprobation of other people's 'social stances'" ("Professing the Renaissance" 28). Graff observes similar thinking in the opposing camp: "As a colleague of mine recently put it, when we call something 'subversive' nowadays we mean little more than that we *like* it" ("Co-optation" 173).

6 On the highly selective treatment of Taylor's poetry, see Hammond ("Diffusing All by Pattern" 153–54). This inequity of attention, based on modern assessments of what constituted Taylor's best poems, illustrates that literary history has always been – and will probably always be – shaped by the fact that "while we attempt to reconstruct a past horizon," as Perkins confirms, "we stand within our own" (26). An excellent example of this interaction of present with past within early American studies is the debate, when Taylor's work was rediscovered, over what kind of poet he was. He certainly did not seem typically "Puritan," and whether his poems were called "metaphysical" or "baroque" depended largely on whether formal unity could be found in them (see Brown for the metaphysical case, Warren for the baroque). Critics who found the poems disunified tended to call them "baroque," a term which, as Jantz later observed, suffered under the enormous prestige of "metaphysical" verse in the wake of Eliot and the New Critical rehabilitation of Donne and Herbert ("Baroque Free Verse" 270). The flurry of classification that marked early Taylor studies is described in Hammond (*Edward Taylor* 1–21).

7 As we shall see in chapter 1, the rejection of traditional Christian discourse in favor of structures more palatable to a secular "science" of criticism has had a profound effect on the reception of Puritan poetry generally. A common metanarrative of literary history centers on the gradual emancipation of the artist – and "artist" here has a decidedly romantic, individualistic cast – from such authoritarian structures as religion represents. Underlying the secularist bias, of course, is a progressivist historiography in which literary development is thought to culminate in the values of the historian's own era. Assumptions of literary progress take political as well as aesthetic form: the very term "early American literature," containing as it does an embedded futurity, has always encouraged a search for national precedents at the expense of originating contexts. Progress, a notoriously difficult notion to resist, can seduce even those critics who question traditional constructions of literary history. Perkins notes the historian's fundamental preference for "change" (163), a bias that Holub accuses the Konstanz school of indulging through their privileging of the innovative work (63). Jauss clearly recognized the prevalence in earlier eras – and this was certainly the case in Puritan New England – of "preautonomous" art, which told readers what they "already knew" by offering the "charm" of a game whose rules they understood ("Alterity" 184–85). Still, he called such texts "'culinary' or entertainment art" (*Toward an Aesthetic* 25) and dismissed them as objects for serious literary study. Shaw comes close to committing this critical anachronism in his view that successful elegy "tests the conventions" of the genre and avoids traditional consolations (*Elegy and Paradox* 246–47). "Innovation" and "testing," of course, are inherently diachronic concepts: we cannot identify what is innovative within a particular historical moment without knowing what prevailed later. More tellingly, we usually don't call a text "innovative" unless we approve of it. As Stock points out, the distinction between "tradition" and "modernity" is arbitrary to begin

with, not only because the concepts are "mutually interdependent" but also because their definition hinges on the historian's attitude toward the writing of his or her own era (163).

8 These questions, basic as they are, have not often been asked about the funeral elegy, English or American. Indeed, the cultural and historical contexts that such questions engage are antithetical to the aestheticism that has dominated literary history. Building on Perkins's conclusion that "historical contextualism tends to suppress critical intelligence" (128), Shaw cites opposing emphases on form and function in the scholarship dealing with English elegy: "The more historical context a scholar provides, the less opportunity to be critically reflective, and vice versa" ("Elegy and Theory" 11). Stock defines the conflict even more basically, as a clash between the synchronic concerns of criticism and the diachronic concerns of history (90). Form and function, however, need not be mutually exclusive categories. Like Shaw, I find possibilities for reconciliation – and thus for a viable blend of critical relevance and historical engagement – in Todorov's notion of genre as a meeting point of culture and poetics. My emphasis on genre, of course, risks making Puritan elegies look even more alike than they already seem. In addition, my approach does not encourage artistic distinctions within the genre. Although I will suggest some variations in poems written for men and for women, for adults and for children, and for deceased who practiced certain occupations, particularly the ministry, this study concentrates on those textual and experiential traits which most elegies have in common. A fruitful possibility for future work lies in extending and clarifying the varieties of elegy, including differing degrees of artistic achievement among these poems.

9 By rejecting, as much as possible, broad structures imported by the observer in favor of "local knowledge" operant within the culture being observed, we become more aware of the metanarrative that drives our own historical methods. The readings offered in this book consistently, though usually implicitly, counter a typically "modern" response to the New England elegy with a "Puritan" response constructed from the poems themselves and from such extratextual materials as the Bible, commentaries, sermons, spiritual journals, and theological treatises. Of the four discursive modalities – metaphor, metonymy, synecdoche, and irony – that Hayden White proposes as interpretive structures that underlie and enable the writing of history (*Metahistory*, *Tropics* 128), my approach is thus predominantly "ironic," a mode that Perkins describes as drawing on the "historical circumstances" of the critic (43) through an ongoing contrast between past and present literary practices.

10 The inability to escape the reductive effects of "narrative" is the chief target of the poststructuralist critique of historicism, new as well as old. Although Greenblatt tries to accede to the theorists' demands by attempting to "resist the integration of all images and expressions into a single master discourse" (*Shakespearean Negotiations* 2–3), "textuality" in any form, as Fox-Genovese points out, inevitably leads to just this sort of "totalization" (218). Stock sim-

ilarly concedes that a "fully coherent historical picture is a police state: the weapons have merely been concealed" (88). Lentricchia agrees that the newer historicisms convey a "feeling, usually just invoked, almost never argued through, that all social life is organized and controlled down to its oddest and smallest details" (234). Patterson questions an anthropological view of culture in which "material forces" are "wholly absorbed by symbolic needs," with a resulting model so static that change could not possibly occur (261), while Pecora criticizes a tendency in Geertz-based historicism to reduce "local knowledge" to "anthropological abstraction in spite of its claims to greater specificity" (266). Such abstraction cannot avoid reflecting the historian's position: Thomas cites a conflict in Jane Tompkins's *Sensational Designs* between the "poststructuralist critique of representation" and Tompkins's attempt "to redress past political inequities by giving representation to those previously excluded" (184, 185). In their decentering of "an 'American character' or 'the New England mind,'" Thomas concludes, poststructuralists "fall prey to the very totalization which they claim to abhor" (198, 200). Stock agrees that poststructuralists "are indeed rejecting old myths, but they are also creating new ones" (74).

Shaw describes the theory/history dilemma with admirable succinctness: "If the critical histories of some New Historicists require knowledge that seems too political, too local and place-specific, to be genuinely critical, some post-structuralist histories assume the validity of critical models that are too obviously a reflex of the historian's own mentality and biasses to be genuinely historical" (*Elegy and Paradox* 238). White sees the conflict between historicism and poststructuralism as insoluble because it reflects "a conflict between different theories of textuality" ("New Historicism" 297); Perkins identifies an even more basic crux between "description" and "explanation" (48). Here, as in all things human, imperfection and partiality are the result of doing business with language, especially other people's language. A purely "textualist view of history," as Fish reminds us, "cannot yield an historical method: it demands from a wholly situated creature a mode of action or thought (or writing) that is free from the entanglements of situations and the lines of demarcation they declare" ("Commentary" 311). Put more simply, historians will continue to tell stories in accordance with how they read them – and how they read them cannot be divorced from who they are. Because one cannot read without constructing "a reading," even the best history, as Jauss concedes, will produce "only a semblance of precision" (*Toward an Aesthetic* 63). Or as Fish affirms, "meaning is human," and "interpretation is the only game in town" (*Is There a Text* 96, 355).

1 MONUMENTS ENDURING AND OTHERWISE

1 Davis, "Edward Taylor's Elegy"79. This sketch of Dewey's burial draws on accounts of Puritan funerary practices in Stannard (109-22) and Geddes (103-53). Davis's commentary on the elegy is my source for details of

Dewey's life; my reconstruction of Taylor's thoughts is based chiefly on Davis, *A Reading of Edward Taylor*.

2 Taylor's theological conservatism, particularly his vehement and longstanding opposition to Stoddard in the Lord's Supper controversy, is discussed fully by Grabo ("Introduction," *Treatise*) and Davis ("Introduction," *Edward Taylor vs. Solomon Stoddard*; "Introduction," *"Church Records" and Related Sermons* xviii–xxx). I have drawn details of Taylor's life from Donald Stanford and from Davis (*A Reading*).

3 Numerous studies, correcting the intellectual cast of Perry Miller's Puritans as set forth in the two volumes of *The New England Mind*, have argued for the vitality of Puritan affective and ritual experience: they include Morgan, Pettit, Watkins, Holifield, Bercovitch (*Puritan Origins*), Greven, Leverenz, Hambrick-Stowe (*Practice of Piety*), Caldwell, King, Cohen, Kibbey, Stout, Hall (*World's of Wonder*), and Delbanco. A parallel development has been a fuller recognition of the richness and complexity of Puritan aesthetic structures. Scheick demonstrates the conceptual and imagistic complexity of Puritan verbal emblems (*Design*); while Grabo (*Edward Taylor* and *Edward Taylor Revised Edition*), Rowe (*Saint and Singer*), Hambrick-Stowe ("Introduction"), Gatta, and Hammond (*Sinful Self*) argue for the artistic complexity of Taylor's verse in terms of an interiority defined by salvific ritual. These studies, all of which build upon Grabo's early call for a revaluation of Puritan affective and symbolic structures ("Veiled Vision"), are consistent with the recognition that Puritan iconophobia, as the Tashjians (3–12) and Daly ("The Danforths" 148) point out, has frequently been overstated. Brumm, for instance, claims that Taylor "burst the confines of Puritan sobriety" in his late meditations on Canticles, succumbing "to the charm of biblico-Oriental word pictures." For Brumm, Taylor's "poetry ultimately led him to a sort of allegorical interpretation of the Scriptures, which Puritans rejected as Catholic and medieval" (*American Thought* 82, 57). Haims similarly suggests that Taylor's *Gods Determinations* succeeds despite the Puritan milieu in which it was written, and that Taylor's vivid imagery resulted from expressive needs suppressed by the dictates of a theological from which his "imagination found a partial outlet in the rich visual imagery of scripture" (96).

4 For a survey of the critical reception of New England's elegies, see Schmitt-von Mühlenfels (*Die "Funeral Elegy"* 9–16). Passing comments on the New England Puritan funeral elegy continue to be widespread but generally dismissive, with the elegy usually serving as a foil to other Puritan verse with greater appeal to twentieth-century tastes, such as Taylor's meditations and Bradstreet's personal lyrics. Sustained discussions of the elegy are rare; the fullest treatments include Draper (*Funeral Elegy* 155–77), Henson, Pearce (24–41), Silverman (121–32), Bowden, Hahn, Tashjian and Tashijan (39–44), Daly (*God's Altar* 113–17, 147–51, 162–76), Scheick ("Standing in the Gap," "Tombless Virtue," *Design* 80–88), Schmitt-von Mühlenfels (*Die "Funeral Elegy,"* "John Fiske's Funeral Elegy," "Puritan Society"), Elliott ("Development of the Puritan Funeral Sermon" 152–56), Peter White

(39-48), Sargent, Hammond ("Puritan Elegiac Ritual," "Diffusing All by Pattern"), Schweitzer (41-74), and Rowe ("Mourning my Dove"). Most of these discussions stress the elegy's sources and themes, and assess the poems in accordance with traditional standards of poetry. As we shall see, however, Puritans wrote and read elegies for reasons quite different from aesthetic appreciation, and instead put them to what is best described as ritual use; the fullest discussions of this dimension of the Puritan elegy include the Tashjians, Scheick, and Hammond, cited above. Lewalski (*Donne's Anniversaries* 174-215) and Madden describe simular ritual in the textualizing of the deceased in English and New English funeral sermons; on the ritual dimension of Puritan preaching generally, see Edward Davidson.

Most assessments of the Puritan elegy reflect the fact critics have consistently described Puritan public and didactic poetry in terms of artistic failure. Keller, for instance, remarked that the *Metrical History of Christianity* was "written by a different Taylor from the Taylor of the Meditations," which makes the poem "all the less interesting" (*Example* 143). Keller suggested, in reference to *Gods Determinations*, that Taylor's view of public verse was "too low, too issues-oriented, quite provincial" (137). Among the few critics who comment at all on Taylor's elegies, Grabo (*Edward Taylor: Revised Edition* 71, 77) and Keller (*Example* 71) agree on their artistic inferiority to the *Preparatory Meditations*. Although such assessments are consistent with a blend of postromantic and formalist critical standards (textual unity, direct feeling, vivid imagery, original expression), Puritan elegies, including Taylor's poem for Dewey, appear in a different light when read as ritual scripts designed to provoke a specific mourning process among historically positioned mourners, as opposed to a purely aesthetic response within ahistorically positioned "readers." As Sacks point out, because elegiac conventions reveal "the actual project of mourning" in an anthropological and psychological sense, elegies demand attention "not so much to the figures of language as to the workings of the mind that uses them" (22). Pigman takes a similar approach in his study of the English Renaissance elegy "as part of the process of mourning rather than the poetry of praise" (46). Ramazani, in his study of modern elegy, similarly comments that "insofar as the elegy is a mimesis of mourning, psychoanalysis offers a more useful framework" than genre theory (28).

5 Draper, *Funeral Elegy* 57. Kay discusses the elegies of Churchyard and Whetstone (17-26); for Donne's influence on the early seventeenth-century elegy, see Kay (91-123) and Lewalski (*Donne's Anniversaries*). Other studies of the English funeral elegy include Wallerstein, Bennett, Hardison, Pigman, and Scodel. The popularity of the funeral elegy is supported by the fact that Draper identified almost three hundred seventeenth-century examples published as broadsides, a figure that does not include poems circulated in manuscript or published in commemorative volumes, widespread practices in the late sixteenth and early seventeenth centuries (Kay 219-23.). A selection of English broadside elegies appears in Draper, *Century*.

While the emergence of demonstrative forms of mourning added to the growing popularity of elegies, the more subdued decorum of grief was consistent with the Protestant dismissal of Purgatory and the attendant practice of offering prayers for the dead (Stannard 99). William Ames stated the case succinctly: "We should not pray specially for the dead because such prayer has no precept or commended example in the Scripture nor any use or end" (264). Commenting on funerary pomp, Hugh Latimer similarly argued that "Those that die in the favour of God are well; those that die out of the favour of God, this can do them good" (Kay 3). It was thus a Protestant impulse that prompted old Lafew to insist that "Moderate lamentation is the right of the dead, excessive grief the enemy to the living" (*All's Well That Ends Well* I.i.55-56). More fully, though less honorably, Claudius offers Hamlet similar advice: "Final obligation" indeed demands "obsequious sorrow," "But to persever / In obstinate condolement is a course / Of impious stubbornness, 'tis unmanly grief, / It shows a will most incorrect to heaven, / A heart unfortified, or mind impatient, / An understanding simple and unschool'd" (*Hamlet* I.ii.92-97).

6 Classical precedent encouraged this thematic versatility: as Hardison observed, because the "pagan" elegy offered no theological explanation of death, it "tends to move away from the central idea rather than toward it" (120). Among classical poets, the term "elegiac" referred simply to a particular metrical form – alternating dactylic hexameters and pentameters – that proved amenable to a wide variety of reflective and satirical themes. Although those themes included the lament, classical "elegies" could contain social and political satire as well as more general philosophical or moral reflections. Among the *loci classici* for the elegy of mourning are Theocritus's first idyll, Bion's poem for the dying Adonis, a lament for Bion attributed to Moschus, and Vergil's fifth and tenth eclogues, the former a poem for Daphnis and the latter a dirge for the lovesick Gallus, famous for its claim that "omnia vincit Amor." Perhaps the most moving classical expression of loss was not technically an "elegy" at all: Catullus's famous "ave atque vale" to his brother epitomized an emotional restraint that would prove congenial to Christian mourning, in which excessive grief was checked by ascetic ideals and the compensatory belief in eternal life. During the Middle Ages, poetic laments usually followed Boethius in blending Stoic decorum with Christian edification, either by invoking the homiletic tradition of the *ubi sunt*, as in Geoffrey de Vinsauf's poem for Richard I, or by taking a more allegorical turn in confirming earthly transience and vanity, as in *The Pearl*. The Christian lament offered a more direct model for the Renaissance funeral elegy than did the classical pastoral; for a brief description of the classical and late medieval *consolatio*, see Curtius (80-82). Chiefly because the classical poem and its pastoral successors privileged art over actual grieving, studies of English elegy have centered largely on the pastoral variety. The amount of commentary is enormous, particularly when compared with the relatively few studies of funeral elegies of the period.

Representative recent scholarship on the Renaissance pastoral elegy includes Sacks, Pigman, and Schenck. Sacks and Pigman relate the form to psychological models of grieving; Pigman, who also discusses nonpastoral elegies, stresses Renaissance attitudes toward mourning, while Sacks stresses transhistorical patterns of loss and recovery. Schenck, tracing the panegyric impulse through the "ceremonial" genres of epithalamium and elegy, discusses the poetic "careerism" central to the pastoral tradition (33-53).

7   Scheick warns against overstating the uniqueness of the New England elegy prior to the Restoration ("Tombless Virtue" 287-88). Hall comments on the compensatory reinscription of ritual in early New England: "Hostile to the magic of the Catholic System, these people reinstated ritual practice at the heart of their religion" (*Worlds of Wonder* 167). On the growing elaboration of funerary customs in late seventeenth-century New England, see Stannard (122-26) and Bosco (xii-xiii). Bosco, citing the funeral sermon as a precursor to developing funerary rites and the proliferation of elegies, notes the growing popularity of jeremiad themes in funeral sermons as the century progressed (xv-xvi); on this point, also see Silverman (129). On the jeremiad as a response to the perceived decline in piety in the late seventeenth century, see Miller (*The New England Mind: From Colony to Province* 1-39, *Errand* 1-15), Minter, and Bercovitch (*American Jeremiad*).

8   Despite the widespread assertion that "An elegy may be a good work of art but a flawed work of mourning, and vice versa" (Shaw, *Elegy and Paradox* 51), it is of course impossible to separate form from function in elegy except as a matter of emphasis. As Ramazani points out, "the 'fiction' and 'grief'" that Johnson "tried to distinguish are as intertwined in elegy as are 'ritual' and 'mourning' in traditional lamentation – ritual that not only contains but produces feeling, feeling that not only produces but emulates ritual" (31). Still, it is the ritual dimension that is usually slighted in the criticism, the acknowledgment that elegy can, in Shaw's words, "comprise a kind of liturgy, releasing emotion even while controlling it" (*Elegy and Paradox* 229). Noting a longstanding formalist bias in historical scholarship dealing with the elegy, Strickland claims that the impact of New Criticism accounts for the consistent inability to deal with its noncanonical, popular, and more situational forms. An example of this can be seen in Schenck, who argues that Milton's Latin poem on Charles Diodati fails as a "literary gesture" in part because of its narrowly "contemporary horizon" (102-3), an assessment that dismisses the poem for being what it is and for doing what it was written to do. Draper, writing at the very start of the New Critical influence, invoked a similar privileging of aesthetic form over cultural function when he remarked that in their elegies Puritans were religiously sincere but aesthetically insincere, trapped within "a melancholy cast whose Pegasus could not soar beyond the details of immediate realism" (*Funeral Elegy* 91, 119). Classic studies of the funeral elegy, English as well as American, have been repeatedly marked by such condescension toward its realistic – that is, "nonliterary" – agenda. On the American side, Tyler wryly applauded the fact that

"divine intervention" had caused so many poems of the era to be lost (231), and even a sympathetic critic like Wright, working forty years later, remarked that the "lowest ebb" in early American poetry, the years from 1670 to 1700, would seem less bleak if the funeral elegies were ignored (159, 86). Draper assessed English funeral elegies in simular terms: "If half the elegists who unhappily found a printer had only been content to waste their sorrows on the desert air, the present study had been much mitigated, and the general average of English poetry much advanced" (*The Funeral Elegy* vii). Wallerstein later began her study by assuring readers that of the elegies she was examining, "almost all are literary in the sense of being formal literary celebrations and not merely of that class of admonitory consolation which Mr. Draper describes among his mortuary elegies" (5).

9 It is easy nowadays to recognize the metanarrative underlying Tyler's formulation, a progressive story of national identity and artistic betterment. This overarching plot, central to traditional constructions of American literary history, resulted from what Hall calls a "fusion of modernism and nativism" ("On Native Ground" 325). Consistently backreading features of a later America and later literature onto earlier texts, critics saw the past as prologue – and all too often, *only* as prologue. As De Prospo aptly states, historians of American writing have frequently labored under a "cult of continuity" based on a "presentist marginalizing of the past," a procedure that cannot avoid distorting the text in its time ("Marginalizing" 235). I prefer De Prospo's "presentism" to Hall's "modernism," since *our* present is already postmodern; most reinscriptions of the past in terms of the present are now poststructural in nature.

10 Schmitt-von Mühlenfels notes the impact of the romantic bias against the didactic poem on critical discussions of the Puritan elegy (*Die "Funeral Elegy"* 35-36). On the shift from preromantic to postromantic notions of texts and reading, see Eagleton (17-22) and Tompkins (201-32). On the novel's implicit concern with romantic individualism and its interrogation of cultural norms, see Iser (*Implied Reader* xii), Watt, Hall ("Uses of Literacy" 38-47), and Cathy Davidson. Poetry underwent similar changes; Philip Freneau offers a poignant example of a poet who straddled this line but went against the historical tide by shifting from a lyric to a political mode. As Elliott notes, "The argument that the change is a degeneration . . . rests upon adherence to aesthetic principles of judgment formulated in a post-Romantic age" (*Revolutionary Writers* 132).

11 On the familiarity of educated New Englanders with classical and English poets, see Wright (24-61, 110-51). Bookseller invoices, library holdings, and literary quotations are included in Morison (*Intellectual Life* 113-51) and Wright's "Appendix" (219-95). On poets read at Harvard in the seventeenth century, see Morison (*Harvard College* 125-27, 141, 146, 154, 197-99). The literary isolation of early New England has consistently been overstated in large part because of the nationalistic search for proto-American traits in Puritan culture. On this point see Spengemann (*Mirror, New World*), De Prospo ("The

Latest," "Marginalizing"), McWilliams, and Colacurcio ("Does American Literature Have a History?"). Studies of transatlantic exchange in early modern times include Cressy (*Coming Over*), Selement, Bremer (*Puritanism, Shaping New Englands*), Foster, and Allen.

12 On this more democratic conception of texts and reading in early New England, also see Hambrick-Stowe (*Practice of Piety* 157-61). Hart, judging from signatures, once estimated that literacy among free males in seventeenth-century Massachusetts and Connecticut was 90 percent, but this figure is surely too high, since the ability to sign one's name is no guarantee of functional literacy (8). Lockridge countered that in the middle of the seventeenth century, about half of adult males could read (*Literacy* 13), a figure that has since been challenged as too low. Cressy has called seventeenth-century New England "a partially literate society" in transition "to a widespread literacy" ("Literacy" 150). Hall agrees that New Englanders "were very largely literate," though many who could read could not write, which was a separate skill in the era ("Uses of Literacy" 20). Monaghan similarly argues that more women could read than is commonly supposed (22-25), and Hall points out that basic literacy rates were probably higher in New England than old (*Worlds of Wonder* 30-37). In contrast to the reading habits of literary London, New Englanders practiced what Hall has called "traditional literacy," the close and repeated use of texts as powerful devotional inducements; this form of literacy, which "engaged every social group," did not wane until the elite and popular reading habits began to diverge in the eighteenth century ("World of Print" 174, 177).

2 TOWARDS AN ANTHROPOLOGY OF PURITAN READING

1 Cremin points out that *The Day of Doom* was part of a body of popular literature that "was read and reread, often in groups and almost always aloud; much of it was memorized and thus passed into the oral tradition, where it influenced many who could not themselves read" (131). Hall comments similarly on the "intermingling of the oral and the printed" in early New England ("Readers and Reading" 348), while Ziff notes that books were "continuous with the oral culture of the entire society" ("Upon What Pretext" 302). For a classic study of orality, see Ong; on the symbiosis of literacy and orality in medieval culture, see Stock.

2 The "textual attitude" that Madden describes as central to Puritan experience (232) can scarcely be overstated, and serves as a valuable check on the tendency to use current models of subjectivity "to explain seventeenth-century self-interpretation" (Hoopes 10). Pious texts were indispensable vehicles for disseminating and absorbing ideal patterns of self-experience. Watkins notes that for Puritans the "inner landscape had already been mapped by experts. A man knew what he ought to find, because everyone was alike" (231). King, asserting a similar relation between individual experience and textual paradigm, argues that patterns of self-perception set forth

in spiritual autobiographies helped Puritan readers "build experience out of the innate confusion of sensation" (43). Individual believers, King explains, sought "spiritual peace through the narration of their own psychological experience, narrations that build experience according to formulas established in the Puritan generation of John Bunyan" (7). Cohen agrees that "Cultural systems teach people how to perceive, and theology among Puritans had a major impact in shaping experience." Consequently, the individual experience of the faith "acquiesced in the ministry's paradigm of grace" and "ratified the cultural definition of conversion experience" (21, 147). On the role of texts in helping New England Puritans achieve and maintain a sense of self consistent with theological expectation, see Hambrick-Stowe (*Practice of Piety* 157–61), Clark ("Subject of the Text"), Hall ("World of Print"; "Uses of Literacy"; *Worlds of Wonder* 21–70), King (13–82), Caldwell, and Hammond (*Sinful Self* 3–36).

3 Although "Puritanism" was a far more diverse and fragmented movement than is commonly thought, the theology of death transcended these differences. Whatever one's stand on polity and practice and regardless of one's position within the matrix of society, death's lessons were the same. Death-texts – elegies, funeral sermons, manuals on preparing for death – encouraged social cohesion and a perceptual leveling of social differences by stressing a broad redemptive message on which everyone could agree.

4 On Protestant attempts to counter secular verse with a popular poetry of devotion, see Fraser. Murdock once remarked that for New Englanders "the real power of a piece of writing" came not from the pleasure it provided but from "the truth it contains and the divine efficacy of that truth." The Puritan writer was to avoid "anything, however appealing, that he thought might make men's hearts stray from theological truth and self-forgetful devotion toward pleasantly sensuous reveries on this world." Indeed, Puritans may have had "more liking than they dared to confess, or their principles allowed them to indulge, for the literary flights which they professed to scorn" (*Literature and Theology* 51, 37, 47). Pearce similarly observes that "The Puritan never hated literature – or, for that matter, the arts in general. Rather, he feared that he might like them too much and that he might therefore veer from the strait path he knew he must follow" (18).

5 Grabo reminds us that in early America a great deal of behavior, "then as now, was attitudinal rather than ideational, and probably operated below any level of articulation" ("Ideology" 276–77). Jauss agrees that for the participant in a culture, "the ambient institutional world of intersubjective behavior is generally so self-evident or so opaque that he does not become conscious of its norms and rules until a malfunctioning occurs" (*Aesthetic Experience* 268). The unconscious workings of ideology are reflected in the split between the Puritan theory and practice of poetry noted by Grabo ("Veiled Vision"), Ludwig (21–64), and Daly (*God's Altar*). On the complexity of Puritan logocentrism and its relation to verbal emblems, see Scheick (*Will and the Word* 93–149; *Design*).

6 In their ongoing reenactment of Paul's promise that "with the mouth
confession is made unto salvation" (Rom. 10:10), Puritan expressions of
unworth, in elegies and elsewhere, display a marked similarity that should
caution us against reading them as strictly "confessional" or "personal" in a
modern sense. Fish once warned against similarly confessional readings of
Herbert: "rather than being a sincere report of a mind in the act of changing, the poem is a sincere effort on the part of the poet-catalyst to change
his reader-pupil's mind" (*Living Temple* 26). Given the Puritan desire to be
saved, Montrose's reminder that collective structures "may enable as well as
constrain individual agency" is instructive ("Professing the Renaissance" 21).
The didactic element in Puritan autobiographical expression was inseparable from a preromantic construction of personal identity that Pearce once
summarized as follows: "Whereas the Puritan community was made up of
individuals whose sense of identity told them that they were nothing except
as God made them so, the 'Romantic' community was made up of individuals who could acknowledge God only to the degree that their ideas of the
godhead demonstrated that they were nothing except as their individuality
made them so" (41). Jauss finds such impersonality in preromantic didactic
texts generally. "Edification," he maintains, originally meant a "preparation
for the imitation of Christ which was to be achieved by a depersonalization
whereby the individual as part of a community becomes an 'edifice of
belief' through a movement of his soul. What the term emphatically did not
mean was a turning back to subjective inwardness" (*Aesthetic Experience* 99).
    As Jauss observes, the critical presumption of an "expressive" text has
prompted literary historians to seek not only sources and influences but the
"lives" behind literary works (*Toward an Aesthetic* 46–47), an approach that has
always figured prominently in treatments of Puritan poetry. But while biographical contexts shed important light on the genesis and motivation of
these poems, readings that are based on them tend to impose inappropri-
ately postromantic subjectivities onto preromantic texts. This is why the
sharp distinction between the "private" and the "public" in Puritan verse
argued by Salska, and by Silverman in regard to the elegies (123), is problematic. Inseparable from its role as a script of individual reorientation,
Taylor's elegy strengthened the reader's sense of community with other
souls knit together in a "society that conceived itself," as Cohen describes it,
"as the embodiment of God's love" (161). Such poems were, as Edward
Davidson has remarked concerning the Puritan sermon, embodiments of
what anthropologist Jane Harrison once called "fear felt together": they
were "spoken and heard as a form of the community's subjectivity. It was
what a people felt and believed together" (506).
    Grabo's early call for an "aesthetic" reading of early American writing
anticipated current views of Puritan subjective and symbolic structures by
countering the naive assumption "that a work of art is a symptom of the
artist's predominant emotion at the time of creation" ("Veiled Vision" 23).
Clark, for example, describes Taylor's language as a "grammar of grace"

that serves to "situate the individual within a broad framework of social relations and theological hierarchies" ("Subject of the Text" 129), while Keller
stresses the role of redeemed psychological paradigms, especially the self's
utter worthlessness stemming from the Fall, in giving Taylor a sense of
verbal freedom, even playfulness, that was fully compatible with the serious-
ness of purpose informing his *Preparatory Meditations* ("Edward Taylor, The
Acting Poet"). The Puritan obsession with self-examination in relation to
texts locates seventeenth-century New Englanders squarely within the
growing Renaissance awareness of self noted by Greenblatt, who argues
that "in the sixteenth century there appears to be an increasing self-consciousness about the fashioning of human identity as a manipulable, artful
process" (*Renaissance Self-Fashioning* 2). In their belief that God had authored
the inner "text" of the saved soul, however, Puritans experienced "self-fashioning" as discovery rather than creation – and they felt it as a process that
was in no way fictive. One could not simply "adopt" a graced identity cyn-
ically or deliberately. As King affirms, "No sense of hypocrisy exists in
speaking or in writing of oneself in terms of former scripts." "It is not a
question," he observes, "of choosing between words and experience, or
between a language of conversion and conversion itself" (48, 49).

7 In addition to Calamy's manual, which first appeared in 1667, other popular
guides to meditation included Richard Rogers, *Seaven Treatises Containing Such
Directions as Is Gathered Out of the Holie Scriptures* (London: 1603); Joseph Hall,
The Art of Divine Meditation (London: 1607); and Richard Baxter, *The Saint's
Everlasting Rest* (London: 1650). The methods suggested in such manuals
support Cohen's assertion that believers could enjoy a greater certainty of
their salvation than is generally assumed (101), an optimism based on the
doctrine of the "perseverance of the saints" – the assumption that a genuine
conversion would not be revoked. Because conversion, as Cohen observes,
restored "some of the spiritual potency lost in the Fall" (46), the saint could
now feel true remorse for his or her carnal leanings and consequently
oppose them. On the influence of meditative traditions on seventeenth-
century verse, see Martz (*Poetry of Meditation*), Lewalski (*Protestant Poetics*
147–78), Brumm ("Meditative Poetry"), Ann Stanford ("Anne Bradstreet as
a Meditative Writer"), Hambrick-Stowe ("Introduction"), and Gatta. On
meditative attempts to recover the intensity of the initial conversion experience, see Cohen (76, 103–8), Hambrick-Stowe (*Practice of Piety* 198–203), and
Schuldiner.

8 As King observes, "Without the always real presence of conversion made
sensible through the spoken word, no conversion was real" (44). Cohen
agrees that narratives of the inner life served to connect redemptive
morphology with the felt experience of individual believers, who naturally
"ratified the cultural definition of conversion experience" because they had
been so carefully trained in recognizing the signs of that experience (147,
101). This was as true of poems as it was of personal narratives, as Pearce
suggested when he remarked that "the paradigmatic case for the best

Puritan poetry is the diary entry, with its emphasis on 'special providences,' through which the diarist explores and expounds his sense of the events whose appropriate expression he has invented" (35–36). McGiffert similarly observes that keeping a record of inner activity was "itself a means of assurance," and that "the regulating of the exercise may itself have contributed to the diarist's composure" (18).

On the homiletic and psychological applications of the legal and evangelical dispensations in Puritan thought, see Cohen (47–74, 104–8), Hall (*Faithful Shepherd* 18–19, 63–66, 163–65), Knott (11, 133, 142–44), Levy (25–27), Pettit (17–18), Watkins (8–9, 12–14, 228), Woolf, McGiffert (4, 19–26), Bercovitch (*Puritan Origins* 15–25), Hambrick-Stowe (198–203), and King (15, 41–42). Because sin had to be confronted before it could be opposed, a primary function of all autobiographical texts was to expose the writer's corrupt nature. As Shea notes in his discussion of Thomas Shepard's diary, "the diary would fail in its purpose if the writer could not bring himself to view his most abhorrent self" (142). The Puritan psychomachia as an internalizing of the two dispensations is New England's counterpart of the "split reader" that Fish finds in *Paradise Lost*, a reader "who is continually responding to two distinct sets of stimuli – the experience of individual poetic moments and the ever present pressure of the Christian doctrine – and who attaches these responses to warring forces within him, and is thus simultaneously the location and the observer of their struggle" (*Surprised by Sin* 42).

9 As Edward Davidson notes, such response was just as essential to the "true sermon," which "did not exist until it was created by the hearer." "There could be no 'words delivered,'" Davidson comments, "until the reader was involved and convinced. What mattered was that the sermon did something, performed an act of suasion and leading, whereby the hearer could respond and be able to live by it" (504). If, as Iser argues, every reader searches for the "unknown" in a text (*Act of Reading* 43), the great Unknown for the Puritan reader was the future of his or her soul: reading invariably pointed toward a single underlying "meaning" that was inseparable from the reader's standing with God. This manner of reading echoed the deliberately "unfinished" quality that Fish attributes to *The Temple* as a reflection of the ongoing nature of the spiritual processes that Herbert promotes (*Living Temple* 157). Keller invokes the satisfactions arising from feeling an identity clarified in accordance with spiritual expectation in his discussion of the "mythic self" of Taylor's *Meditations* (*Example*, 74–78, 230–36), where he suggests that "Poetry as a *liberating* art in Puritan culture may be an important, neglected idea. In Taylor's hands it became a way of extending the range of the myth that bound him. The ideology was perhaps livable without such a device, though perhaps not yet alive in *him* until he wrote" (*Example* 236). Gatta agrees that Taylor was deeply animated by the "festival frame of spirit" of the assured soul (*Gracious Laughter* 94). Keller posits a similar role for writing in making possible Bradstreet's "liberation via piety, via Puritan allegiance" (*Only Kangaroo* 16). As these recognitions of the enabling dimension of Puritan verse suggest, even the supposedly gloomy

funeral elegy gave textual shape to the spiritual "potency" that Cohen has identified as a consequence of belief (5, 210). On similarly consolatory forms in the Puritan sermon, see Madden.

10 As Henson observes, the elegy's "conventionality was reinforced by the ever-present, elder example of the funeral sermon application and its offshoot, the religious biography" (24). Silverman attributes the conservatism of New England's elegies to a cultural lag between Old World and New (130), while Sacks links the poems to a "severe rationalization" marking the Puritan attitude toward grief and evidenced in a need for "justifying bereavement and in the practice of such rigidly formal schemes as those of the anagram and acrostic" (363). Although Stannard (147–63) and Elliott ("Development" 153–56) identify a shift in the elegies toward sentimentalism around the turn of the eighteenth century, this evolution was minor compared to the broader and more rapid movement in English elegy toward neoclassic and sentimental modes (Draper, *Funeral Elegy* 178–206). Wallerstein once summarized this development as a shift from meditating on death toward "solving the problems of the active life." As Wallerstein noted, in many English elegies "the temper of the solution is closer to a dependence upon Stoic poise and judgment than to Christian conversion, such a feeling as will in the end come to depend on human order more than divine. And to the models of poetry which had in the past expressed such human order, to classical models rather than to metaphysical, mid-seventeenth century poetry will turn" (95). For a discussion of developments in English elegy that led to romantic and Victorian forms, see Shaw (*Elegy and Paradox* 10–48).

11 Scheick notes that the Puritan elegy was "funerated" in the reader's assimilation of the biblical perspective that the text set forth ("Tombless Virtue" 298). Edward Davidson posits a similar response to the biblicism of the sermon: "A sermon and the sermon's form were like Scripture and history – part of a prior arrangement, all parts in a single design which held everything together. It was a design which had already been traced through Scripture: the Bible was a mosaic of citations, a resonance of meanings; thus one text led to another and to any number of corollary and supporting ideas" (510–11). The impact of the Bible as a text that subsumed all pious discourse cannot be overstated. Ziff observes that although Puritans "distrusted wit and metaphorical elaboration, they could quite consistently leap to metaphor so intense as to be allegorical for in so doing they were relating their experiences to the patterns in the Bible" ("Literary Consequences" 42). The process of internalizing the discourse of Scripture lay at the heart of all Puritan reading. Rosamond Rosenmeier observes, for example, that Bradstreet's poems were meant to be "lived through": the poem "would become, like the law, a 'mere shadow' as the spiritual condition which the poem was to engender became a reality" ("Wounds Upon Bathsheba" 139, 138). Daly comments similarly regarding Bradstreet's elegies: "Each poem is a part of the difficult process it records, a method for achieving the resignation it expresses" (*God's Altar* 117). This manner of reading promoted, as Iser describes it in *The Pilgrim's Progress*, "self-examination through experience"

(*Implied Reader* 24) – a subjective relation to texts that Fish demonstrates more generally in seventeenth-century English devotional writing (*Self-Consuming Artifacts*). As Fish elsewhere notes regarding the sermons of Lancelot Andrewes, "The experiential point is realized only through the agency of the structure it subverts, which becomes, in effect, the vehicle of its own abandonment" (*Is There a Text* 194).

12 Although Henson correctly describes the elegy as a "deliberate social gesture" (11), Scheick confirms that its experiential significance was as much private and psychological as it was communal and sociological ("Tombless Virtue" 287). Despite the soteriological function of all Puritan texts, reconstructions of the probable responses of early New Englanders to their poetry are rare. Colacurcio's study of audience in Taylor's *Gods Determinations* was pioneering ("*Gods Determinations*"), but see also Gatta (101–40) and Hammond (*Sinful Self*).

3 WEEP FOR YOURSELVES: THE PURITAN THEOLOGY OF MOURNING

1 In keeping with the image of Sheol as a place of oblivion, the point of these rites was not to intercede for the dead, but to perpetuate their memory among the living. The importance of leaving behind a good name is reflected in the central role of moral commentary in the Old Testament lament, which usually took the form of a catalog of the deceased's virtues exemplified by David's poem to Saul and Jonathan (2 Sam. 1:19–27). The opposite significance of a death – the legacy of a bad name – was reflected in the prophets' device of applying the language of mourning to the denunciation of the living, as in Isaiah's promise of Babylon's destruction: "Thy pomp is brought down to the grave, and the noise of thy viols: the worm is spread under thee, and the worms cover thee" (Isa. 14:11). Isaiah, Ezekiel, and Jeremiah all frame ironic inversions of the funeral lament in mock elegies for enemy nations such as Babylon (Isa. 46), Tyre (Ezek. 27), and Egypt (Ezek. 32:1–16, Jer. 46:12). Prophets also mourned the "death" of a virtuous Israel, as in Ezekiel's lament for a captive Judah (Ezek. 19:1–14) and Jeremiah's grief for the death of righteousness, not only in the "Lamentations" but in his call for "mourning women" to "take up a wailing for us, that our eyes may run down with tears, and our eyelids gush out with waters": "For death is come up into our windows, and is entered into our palaces, to cut off the children from without, and the young men from the streets" (Jer. 9:17–18, 21). As we will see, the prophetic use of mourning tropes in social commentary anticipated the Puritan elegist's linking of grief with repentance. "Cut off thine hair, O Jerusalem," Jeremiah urges, "and cast it away, and take up a lamentation on high places; for the Lord hath rejected and forsaken the generation of his wrath" (Jer. 7:29).

2 Ramazani comments on the resurgence of public commemorative forms like the Vietnam Memorial and the AIDS Quilt, which "may finally be prodding our society beyond denial and embarrassment and toward

affirmation of the human work of mourning" (365). Far from denying death, Puritans moved it to the very center of consciousness as an ongoing goad to repentance. Preparing for death was institutionalized through countless sermons, meditations, poems, journals, and manuals such as William Perkins's *A Salve for a Sicke Man: A Treatise Containing the Nature, Difference, and Kindes of Death as also the Right Manner of Dying Well* (Cambridge, 1595), Jeremy Taylor's *The Rules and Exercises of Holy Dying* (London, 1651), Cotton Mather's *Awakening Thoughts on the Sleep of Death* (Boston, 1712), and Edward Pearse's *The Great Concern, or, A Serious Warning To a Timely and Thorough Preparation for Death* (Boston, 1705), which had gone through over twenty editions by 1705. On the importance of the *ars moriendi* tradition in Protestant culture, see Martz (*Poetry of Meditation* 135–44), Beaty (108–56), Stannard (15–28), Slater (15–90), Geddes (57–81), Ariès (*Hour of Our Death* 298–305), and Hambrick-Stowe (*Practice of Piety* 219–41). On death's varied significations in early New England, see Hall (*Worlds of Wonder* 197–210).

3 As Vinovskis points out, precise mortality rates in early New England are difficult to determine because of the paucity of evidence and problems in interpreting the data ("Mortality Rates"). Nevertheless, it seems certain that death rates were higher in Boston and the coastal towns than in the small inland villages ("Mortality Rates" 186). In the first three-quarters of the eighteenth century, Vinovskis cites a rate of 30–40 per 1000 in Boston, and 15–25 per 1000 in rural communities ("Angels' Heads" 278). Lockridge proposed a rate of 24 to 27 deaths per 1000 in seventeenth-century Dedham, Massachusetts, as compared to 30 to 40 deaths per 1000 in Europe ("Population," *New England Town* 67). Those who survived to adulthood could expect to live reasonably long lives; shorter life expectancies were due chiefly to that fact that child and infant mortality rates were far higher than today (Greven 26; Vinovskis, "Angels Heads" 282), though probably lower than in England and Europe (Hall, *Worlds of Wonder* 293 n. 3; Vinovskis, "Mortality Rates" 200). Demos estimates mortality prior to age twenty-one in seventeenth-century Plymouth at around 25 percent (66). Vinovskis estimates 115 deaths per 1000 for children in seventeenth-century Andover, Massachusetts, and averages of 202 (for males) and 313 (for females) per 1000 in seventeenth-century Salem; 10 to 30 percent of infants did not survive their first year ("Angels' Heads" 286). High as these numbers seem, the powerful cultural construction of death in early New England may have produced an exaggerated perception of its frequency. Vinovskis maintains that while death rates in early New England were no higher than in England and Europe, the intimacy of funerary rites and the Puritan tradition of the *memento mori* made death seem more frequent than it actually was ("Angels' Heads" 300–2). On the comparably healthy conditions in early Andover, see Greven (25–26); for similar conclusions regarding Dedham, see Lockridge (*New England Town* 66–68).

4 Funerary practices in early New England are described in Stannard (108–29), Ludwig (58–62), Tashjian and Tashjian (20–30, 34–48), Bosco,

Geddes (103–53), and Davies (195–205).

5 In aim and function, funeral sermon and poem were virtually identical. The latter was ancillary to the former, serving as its more private and permanent reinscription. While poem and sermon both occupied the middle ground between speech and text, the sermon was more insistently oral and the poem "textual": what one proclaimed, the other preserved. An elegy was, in this sense, the written essence of a funeral sermon – a physical memento to have and to hold in commemoration of the deceased and as a permanent reminder of pulpit lessons.

6 The martyr tradition set forth in Acts and updated in Foxe's *Acts and Monuments* reinforced the close relation of history and biography in Puritan thinking. Within this version of "great man" historiography, the overall progress of God's people in the world could be seen as the story of the saved soul writ large (Haller 131–32). This explains why Foxe's stories, far from being objects of terror, gave children a sense of control in the face of "apparent helplessness" and offered "a positive means of self-creation" (Rosen 227, 228).

4 THIS POTENT FENCE: THE HOLY SIN OF GRIEF

1 The extrapersonal dimension of the speakers in Puritan poetry has been noted by several scholars. King observes that "Like Taylor, Bradstreet could write in verse of cleansing a body of sin without conceiving that hers figured as a character abnormally described" (57). Rosamond Rosenmeier calls Bradstreet's speaker a "prophetic self" who invokes a biblical voice at the expense of mere particularity ("Wounds upon Bathsheba" 133–34, *Anne Bradstreet Revisited* 142–43). What Rosenmeier says of Bradstreet's poetry applies to Puritan autobiographical verse generally: it "is not primarily a retelling of the events of her life so much as it is a re-creation of afflictions so that her children may be changed by reliving them" ("Wounds" 140). Other discussions of Bradstreet's voice as shaped by biblical, meditative, and didactic imperatives include Ann Stanford ("Meditative Writer"), Hammond ("Make Use of What I Leave"; *Sinful Self* 83–141), Steiner, Doriani, and Craig. On the discursive underpinnings – chiefly biblical and soteriological – of Taylor's voice, see Mignon ("Decorum of Imperfection"), Lewalski (*Protestant Poetics* 388–426), Scheick (*Will and the Word* 161–62), Keller (*Example* 74–75; "Edward Taylor, The Acting Poet" 190), Lowance (91–96), Rowe ("Sacred or Profane?"; *Saint and Singer* 22, 148, 163, 223), Gatta (76), Fithian, and Hammond ("Puritan *Ars Moriendi*"; "Who Is Edward Taylor"; *Sinful Self* 213–35).

Because the extrapersonal patterns enacted by Puritan speakers run counter to the modern preference for "expressive" rather than didactic texts, twentieth-century subjectivities tend to get played out in readings that overstate a "rebellious" quality in the verse. The conservative Taylor, for example, has been called a theological as well as artistic rebel in his use of biblical imagery (Brumm [*American Thought* 57], Haims); the spiritual turmoil recorded in his verse has also been reinscribed as post-Freudian psychic turmoil (Hughes). Wigglesworth has also been read anachronistically, in terms of post-Freudian psychology (Hughes, Cherniavski). Feminist scholarship sometimes modernizes Bradstreet by reading the struggle voiced in her poetry as evidence of un-Puritan leanings (Ann Stanford [*Anne Bradstreet: Worldly Puritan*], Martin). Such an approach encourages a highly selective reading of her verse: didactic poems and poems affirmative of her religion tend to be ignored except as evidence of her self-censorship or capitulation (Schweitzer 127–80).

While such approaches can be insightful and can enhance the relevance of these texts for modern readers, they tend to retroject current experience onto seventeenth-century New Englanders, and thus reinscribe the past in terms of the present. While Cheryl Walker, for instance, correctly points out that John Fiske's elegy on Anne Griffin stresses merely her significance as "a pattern of piety for all" (113), her view that the poem evidences the marginality of women overlooks the fact that all deceased believers, male as well as female, were commemorated as idealized types rather than particular individuals: for men and women alike, sainthood and not selfhood was the elegist's real subject. Gender issues often lie at the heart of such debates, but as Thickstun points out, discussions of women in Puritan texts "must also eschew contemporary theories about psychology and gender, which sidestep the problem of why these authors thought about women the way they did" (*Fictions* 159). Readings based on current cultural or psychological models frequently define gender in terms that are at once essentialist and arbitrary, a problem that emerges in the disagreement among feminist critics over whether Puritan subjectivity enacted a "subsumption of feminine virtues into a male ideal" (Thickstun, *Fictions* 2) or fostered the opposite process, resulting in "a male spirituality feminized" (Schweitzer 44). Puritans themselves would probably cite Paul's claim that "There is neither Jew nor Greek, there is neither bond nor free, there is neither male nor female: for ye are all one in Christ Jesus" (Gal. 3:28). Such a view squares well with Madden's observation that the "influence of 'textual attitude'" in early New England "transcends gender" (243). On feminine paradigms as spiritual models for all Puritans, male as well as female, see Thickstun (*Female Piety* 3–13).

2 As Sacks observes, the testing of survivors is central to the elegiac tradition generally and to the mourning process that elegy both mirrors and generates. The repetitive forms of elegy, Sacks argues, provide vehicles by which "the mourner brings his loss into language, testing how it feels to speak *and hear* of it in words" (25). Scheick, describing early New England's version of the elegiac trial, has observed that the Puritan elegy "transfers its text to the soul, the reason and will, of each member of its audience." As Scheick notes, the text of the elegy was "funerated" as the reader internalized salvific traits exemplified by the dead ("Tombless Virtue" 296, 298). The salvific decision forced by grief and the otherworldly figures commemorated in Puritan

elegy support Clark's observation that "Like death, art was a liminal event poised at the limit of human experience and defining that limit in the act of transcending it. Fixed between the failure of human language and the Puritans' rejection of disembodied revelation, their art mirrored the divine translation of death by disrupting its own integrity as sign even as it made the collative gesture that would bind the world to the Word" ("Honeyed Knot" 81). Clark argues elsewhere that the ambiguous nature of Puritan signs as pointers that both reveal and conceal the unseen realm gave Puritans "a sense of the meaning of things and of their persistent refusal to make sense" ("Crucified Phrase" 291). The perceptual instability of the created world, including the ephemeral status of human lives, constantly pushed Puritans toward the textual certainties of the Word as an overarching discursive frame for efficacious mourning.

3 On the classical and scientific origins of astronomical imagery in almanac verse, see Daly ("The Danforths" 149–54) and Secor. On classical images in New England's elegies generally, see Schmitt-von Mühlenfels (*Die "Funeral Elegy"* 102–11) and Hahn.

4 The fullest discussions of the social dimensions of New England elegy include Schmitt-von Mühlenfels (*Die "Funeral Elegy"* 24–31; "Puritan Society"), Silverman, Elliott ("Development"), Henson, and Scheick ("Tombless Virtue").

5 Schmitt-von Mühlenfels identifies the main biblical sources for these images (*Die "Funeral Elegy"* 62–64): stars, candles, and lights from Matt. 5:14 and John 5:35; fallen pillars from Jer. 1:18, Gal. 2:9, and Rev. 3:12; and damaged temples from 2 Kings 25:13–17 and Jer. 52:20–21.

5 LORD, IS IT I?: CHRISTIC SAINTS AND APOSTOLIC MOURNEN

1 On this point see Henson (11), Silverman (127–29), and Scheick ("Tombless Virtue" 297).

2 This was the primary function of what Silverman has called "portraits of the Saved Soul" and the "idealized great man" (123, 127), the communal self that Scheick finds at the center of the elegiac process ("Tombless Virtue" 290–94).

3 Draper's observation that "Puritanism, by intensifying both heaven and hell, made wickedness infinitely bad, and goodness correspondingly good" (*Funeral Elegy* 191) is mirrored in the contrastive strategies of New England's elegies, particularly the division of both the deceased and the survivor into sinful and saintly dimensions of redeemed subjectivity. This internal struggle explains the Puritan fondness on both sides of the Atlantic for debate poems. Marvell penned a typical dialogue between the body and "A Soul hung up, as 'twere, in Chains / Of Nerves, and Arteries, and Veins" (15). Wigglesworth exploited the form in "Riddles Unriddled" through a series of debates that feature a self split into "Distressed Conscience" and "Rectified Judgment," "Unbelief" and "Faith," and "Flesh" and a "Spirit" who recognizes her twin as "a treacherous Thief, / That robs me of my Faith, and then

/ Condemns for Unbelief" (*Poems* 161). Taylor's *Gods Determinations* includes debates between a distressed "Soul" and a persistent Satan who accuses the nascent believer of mere "Lip Love" (*Poems* 412), while Bradstreet dramatizes the inner duality in her debate between "Flesh" and a "Spirit" who finally commands her carnal twin to "Disturb no more my settled heart" (216).

4 On Puritan attitudes toward hyperbole in elegy, see Schmitt-von Mühlenfels ("John Fiske's Funeral Elegy" 52–53) and Silverman (125–27).

5 Henson comments on the impact of character writing on New England's elegies (15); on its influence on Puritan biography generally, see Piercy ("The 'Character' in the Literature"; *Literary Types* 168–75). The character also found satirical uses in New England, as it did in English character books. Taylor created character-like portrayals, both satirical and exemplary, in such early polemics as his dialogue with "a Maypole Dresser" and his "Laymans Lamentation" for the godly ministers silenced at the Restoration. Taylor's depiction of the conformist preachers, "Blinde Leaders of the blinde," echoes Milton's complaint in "Lycidas" against the clerical abuses committed by "Blind mouths! that scarse themselves know how to hold / A sheephook, or have learn't ought els the least / That to the faithfull herdsmans art belongs!" (162). John Saffin also dabbled in the genre, entering into his notebook brief "charracters" of "a Pernicious Backbiter" and "a Proud man," "a true description of a meek Spirited Peace Maker," and two versions of a "Charracteristicall Satyre on a proud upstart" (150–52, 82). A related influence on elegiac portraiture, especially in poems for ministers, was Herbert's *A Priest to the Temple*, with its depiction of a "Country Parson" who "is exceedingly exact in his Life, being holy, just, prudent, temperate, bold, grave in all his wayes" (227). Schmitt-von Mühlenfels points out the popularity of collective biographies of the pious, such as Samuel Clarke's *Lives of the Emminent Divines* (London: 1662) (*Die "Funeral Elegy"* 58). The stylized portrayal of the dead in New England's elegies has been noted in Silverman (123, 127), Schmitt-von Mühlenfels ("John Fiske's Funeral Elegy" 54–55; *Die "Funeral Elegy"* 68–92), Elliott ("Development of the Funeral Sermon" 152), Peter White (*Benjamin Tompson* 43–44), Scheick ("Tombless Virtue"), Hammond ("Puritan Elegiac Ritual"), and Schweitzer (47). Bosco discusses similarly idealized portraiture in the New England funeral sermon (xxvi–xxviii), while Breitwieser relates such stylized depictions to "exemplification" as the central trope of Puritan mourning (53–70). On the role of such depictions in the English funeral sermon, see Lewalski (*Donne's Anniversaries* 174–215); on similarly generalized portraits in the English funeral elegy, see Bennett (110–14).

6 The Puritan elegy exemplifies the larger fact that salvific discourse cut across all levels of New England society, defusing social tensions by uniting popular and elite conceptions of spiritual experience (Allen, Selement). As Hall points out, the circulation and devotional use of such texts as elegies reinforced this unity ("World of Print" 172–77; *Worlds of Wonder* 68). On the fundamental agreement of private experience, as recorded in spiritual journals

and conversion narratives, with models of that experience presented by the ministers, see Cohen (162–200), Caldwell, Schweitzer (1–39), and Hammond (*Sinful Self* 3–36).

7 Johnson's memorials had the effect of collapsing all time into a single redemptive moment. Of George Phillips of Watertown, dead nearly ten years at the publication of the history, Johnson writes: "Though thou thy days hast ended on this Earth, / Yet still thou livest in Name and Fame alway; / Christ thee poore dust doth crowne with lasting Mirth" (75). Johnson gives old Governor Dudley, who was about to die, a pre-elegy that sets forth the same promise: "Wearied with yeares, it plaine appeares, Dudley not long can last, / It matters not, Christ Crown thee got, its now at hand, hold fast" (81). And John Wilson of Boston, still hale at sixty-five and destined to live another fourteen years, receives almost identical commemoration: "Estate and person thou spends liberally; / Christ thee and thine will Crown with lasting Blisse" (68). The ever-charitable Johnson even extends to Stephen Batchellor of Lynn, excommunicated for misconduct, the possibility of his reward by issuing a brief warning to "teach thy selfe with others thou hast need": "Run to the end, and crowned thou shalt be" (74).

8 Mayer discusses the popularity of stories about "dying children who tell of their path to salvation" (216). On Puritan patterns of grieving for dead children, see Slater (15–48). The elegiac convention of having deceased children speak as mature souls finds an infernal parallel in *The Day of Doom*, when Wigglesworth has the "Reprobate Infants plead for themselves" as fully responsible, though misguided, souls (*Poems* 52).

9 Israel/New England parallels pervade Puritan discourse, and accordingly, typology has been the most closely studied dimension of the impact of the Bible on Puritan thought and writing. See, for example, Brumm (*American Thought*), Bercovitch (*Typology and Early American Literature*), Miner, Lewalski (*Protestant Poetics* 111–44), Lowance (57–88, 96–111), Rowe (*Saint and Singer*, "Prophetic Visions,"), Mignon ("Introduction"), and Davis (*A Reading* 145–62).

6 DIFFUSING ALL BY PATTERN; THE READING OF SAINTLY LIVES

1 On the transformation of the Puritan dead into pious texts, see Scheick ("Tombless Virtue"), Hammond ("Puritan Elegiac Ritual"), and Schweitzer, who observes that the elegist was able to perform the commemorative duty by "giving up writing altogether, to become the reader of divine grace," a shift that offered Puritans "a practical method, consistent with their theology, for the apparent production, rather than the creation, of discourse" (70, 58).

2 As Jeffrey Walker points out, Puritans took pleasure in the discovery of anagrams, though that pleasure did not contradict their serious uses in funerary texts. As the Tashjians note, "both the spiritual and playful aspects of puns

and anagrams gained Puritan approval. The one aspect did not deny or pre-
clude the other" (43). Such devices were by no means limited to funerary
texts. Panegyrics for the living often featured anagrams, acrostics, and puns,
as illustrated by John Saffin's acrostic encomia to Elizabeth Hull and
Winifret Griffin, by Edward Taylor's youthful acrostics to his brother and
sister-in-law, and by Taylor's elaborate courtship acrostics to Elizabeth
Fitch. Anagrams were also applied to the living. Grindall Rawson celebrated
the publication of the *Magnalia Christi Americana* by teasing a Latin anagram
from Cotton Mather's name: "Tuos Tecum ornasti" ("you have adorned you
and yours") (Meserole 478). John Wilson extolled the anti-Quaker zeal of
Claudius Gilbert of Limerick, Ireland, by turning his name into "Tis Braul
I Cudgel" (Meserole 385). And an anonymous poet, possibly Nathaniel
Ward, devised two anagrams in praise of Anne Bradstreet. The first – "Deer
neat *An Bartas*" – alluded to the similarity of her work to that of Guillaume
Du Bartas, while the second offered more general praise: "Artes bred neat
An" (Silverman 69). Anagrams for the living, however, could also yield
lessons associated with their more common use in funerary texts, as in a
poem sent anonymously to Bradstreet's father, Thomas Dudley: "Ah! old
must dye" (Meserole 505).

3 On the parallel between the anagram and the biblical "text" of a sermon,
see Schmitt-von Mühlenfels (*Die "Funeral Elegy"* 54). The threefold structure
of anagram, poem, and textualized deceased supports the Tashjians' statement that the anagram produced "a verbal correlative to the spiritual metamorphosis" of the saint: "In his discovery of the anagram the poet was
simply recreating that which had already occurred spiritually, by demon-
strating the iconic power perceived in words" (44). Commenting on Fiske's
elegy for Cotton, Schweitzer similarly observes that anagram gives the
deceased "the status of an object rather than a subject" (63). For additional
discussions of anagrams, see Bray, Schmitt-von Mühlenfels ("John Fiske's
Funeral Elegy" 58–59; *Die "Funeral Elegy"* 113–16), Daly (*God's Altar* 150–51),
and Jeffrey Walker.

4 As with anagrams, the pious truths revealed by puns were not limited to the
dead. While Samuel Stone was still living, John Cotton saluted him by
declaring "How well (dear Brother) art thou called *Stone*? / As sometimes
Christ did *Simon Cephas* own." Cotton also invoked Samuel's Ebenezer and
David's sling stone, which, in the guise of the living Stone, wounded the
head of "that huge Giant-Church, (so far renownd) / Hight the Church-
Catholicke" (Meserole 381–82). Some of these figures also appear in
Nicholas Noyes's pre-elegy for James Bayley as elaborate puns on Bayley's
illness, the "stone" that was destroying his kidneys and bladder. However
bizarre it might seem to pun on a dying man's malady, especially when he is
still alive and suffering, Noyes offered his witty exercise as a gesture of consolation, assuring Bayley that could he anticipate manna "In which no gritt,
nor gravel are" and an eternal "*White Stone*, / With a *New Name* engrav'd
thereon" in heaven (Winslow 21).

5 Mather's self-consciously visual images of the celestial dead contrast sharply with an older iconography consisting of medieval images of decay and corruption, especially winged skulls, which continued to appear on broadsides and tombstones. While these older images stressed the decay of the physical body, elegies underscored the saint's victorious apotheosis. This disjuncture between the verbal and the pictorial can be seen in early broadsides, as a 1667 sheet for Lydia Minot illustrates. A prominent cut at the top features twin skull-and-crossbones and hourglasses, a funeral procession, crossed pick and shovel, and a skeleton with a scythe; also prominent, on either side of the text, are larger hourglasses and shovels. The three anagram-based poems printed on the sheet, however, tell a different story, and speak to Minot's embrace by "Happy Death" and her passage to "Life indeed": "O pleasant Lines that thus are fall'n to me! / To make that *Day my Lot* which aye shall be" (Winslow 7). In tone and message, it is the text and not the graphics that anticipates the stylized cherubs and angels that would replace death's heads on tombstones in the early eighteenth century. Indeed, the optimism of elegy may have stimulated the development of corresponding optimism in the visual representation of death. Dethlefsen and Deetz graph the shift to an iconography more consistent with the optimistic thrust of elegy in the cemeteries of Cambridge, Concord, and Plymouth (505). For photographs of stones illustrating this change and insightful discussions of its significance, see Ludwig and the Tashjians. On Taylor's dissatisfaction with the gloom associated with the traditional iconography of death, see Hammond and Davis.

Despite such changes on the tombstones, later broadsides, such as those for Jonathan Marsh in 1708, Rebekah Sewall in 1710, Hannah Sewall in 1717, and Nathanael Baker in 1733, continued to feature the older iconography (Winslow 23, 27, 31, 36). This conservatism may lie in the broadside's closer visual link with the tombstone, a link reinforced by the broadside's visual design as a stone rendered as a printed text. Later broadsides stressed the *idea* of the gravesite rather than its actual, literal imagery, and while the stones changed, these printed representations that functioned in the absence of the burying ground did not. Despite their grim images, however, broadside elegies functioned like other elegies: what they marked was not the place of interment but the *response* to interment, fixing the redemptive significance of the loss in time. Epitaphs and tombstone verses, which grew more prominent as the burying ground became a popular site of meditation in the late seventeenth and early eighteenth centuries, reconnected the *memento mori* to the actual place of burial. Such verses served as abbreviated elegies, permanently posted for the reflection of passersby.

These subgenres reveal that Puritan funerary texts, in all their variety, offered mutual reinforcement of a message that transcended genre. In its underlying aims, the elegy differed little from the funeral sermon, of which it was a more permanent reinscription. Functioning as the written essence of a sermon, the poem offered a physical artifact that preserved the deceased's faith and the lessons of death. Sermon and poem both occupied a middle ground between orality and literacy. Although the funeral sermon was explicitly oral and the elegy was explicitly "textual," sermons constantly appealed to the written text of Scripture and were frequently printed. Elegies, for their part, made constant reference to the preached Word; moreover, they were frequently read aloud and were thus experienced as oral performances.

6 In light of the eschatological reunion of body and soul, Puritans did not harbor a totally negative view of the flesh. To be sure, a shedding of the corrupt flesh (*sarx* in the New Testament) at death was a necessary prelude to the saint's purification. As Paul affirmed, "they that are in the flesh (*en sarki*) cannot please God" (Rom. 8:8). For the redeemed, however, the sinful body – the "body of this death" (*soma tou thanatou toutou*) (Rom. 7:24) or the "natural body" (*soma psychikon*) – was destined to be revived as a "glorious body" (*soma tes doxes*) (Phil. 3:21) or "spiritual body" (*soma pneumatikon*) (1 Cor. 15:44). The anticipated reunion of glorified soul and purified body figures prominently in Puritan writing, and not just in elegy. Bradstreet, for example, looks toward the cessation of struggle between her own flesh and spirit at the final resurrection, when "soul and body shall unite." In so doing, she paraphrases the transformation of the body lined out by Paul in 1 Corinthians 15:44: "A corrupt carcass down it lays, / A glorious body it shall rise. / In weakness and dishonour sown, / In power 'tis raised by Christ alone" (295).

7 As Pearce maintains, "the poet and his subject have their highest value as they are members of this special community with its special sense of its special mission" (28). The strength of collective purpose invested Puritans with what Bercovitch has called "the assertion of a *social*-divine selfhood which certifies their calling as introspection alone could never do" (*Puritan Origins* 120).

8 At first glance, Taylor might appear to ignore the Puritan insistence on individual salvation. As Robert Henson notes, New England's elegists could not pose a literal genealogy of grace without violating the primacy of personal conversion (19). Still, the expectation that a pious legacy would bear gracious fruit proved irresistible, and the theological justification for it was twofold. First, the New England mission was predicated on the belief that piety could indeed be nurtured by a godly society. To be raised in the faith thus vastly increased one's chances of ending in it. Second, elegists routinely retrojected a presumption of election onto the deceased's entire life. The happy conclusion of the saint's pilgrimage was thus frequently connected to promising beginnings.

There are clear parallels between the New England elegist's proclamation of a gracious spirit transmitted from generation to generation and the claims to artistic succession voiced in English pastoral elegies. As Sacks notes, the pastoral speaker asserts his status as a "true heir to a poetic legacy," seizing this role by invoking "ancient funeral games," in which "the winners exemplify and seem to immortalize the qualities of the deceased, or at least those virtues deemed important for the community's survival" (36).

9 Rowe comments on a similar role played by Old Testament personal types in Puritan histories and elegies, in which New England's antitypical relation to ancient Israel "allows the contemporary Christian to emulate the *exemplum fidei* without feeling self-defeated by the *exemplum exemplorum* of Christ Himself" (*Saint and Singer* 87).

10 Although Taylor gives it extreme form in the Dewey poem, this was the same struggle that Bradstreet articulates in her letter "To My Dear Children." Hoping that her readers "gain some spiritual advantage by my experience," Bradstreet states that she has "not studied in this you read to show my skill, but to declare the truth, not to set forth myself, but the glory of God" (240). Casting her "experience" into a catalogue of "sinkings and droopings" relecting the afflictive phases of the cycle of belief, she confirms that "Many times hath Satan troubled me concerning the verity of the Scriptures." She even admits that she wondered "many times by atheism how I could know whether there was a God" (243). Bradstreet's confessions echo the inner lives of the eulogized dead, objectified as helpful reminders of the salvific significance of trials, especially the current trial of sorrow.

11 The good death was also a standard feature in English elegies (Bennett 117). On the cultural importance of the exemplary death in early New England, see Schmitt-von Mühlenfels (*Die "Funeral Elegy"* 60–61, 88–92) and Hall (*Worlds of Wonder* 206–9).

12 As Schmitt-von Mühlenfels points out (*Die "Funeral Elegy"* 98), biblical precedent for the voices of the Puritan dead came from Hebrews 11:4. By offering a more acceptable sacrifice than Cain, Abel "obtained witness that he was righteous, God testifying of his gifts: and by it he, being dead, yet speaketh." In the *Magnalia* Mather incorporated this text as a subtitle to his "Book of God-Fearers" ("Liber Deum Timentium"), the second part of his collection of lives of prominent New England clergy: "Dead Abels yet speaking, and spoken of" (1:353).

13 As Daly observes, Bradstreet's statement is "not a sudden abdication to the will of God by a rebellious poet," but "the best argument that can be made, the best consolation for the survivors – that the child's untimely death is a clear act of providence, not merely a regrettable part of the order of nature" (*God's Altar* 112). On the tension between doubt and faith in Bradstreet's grandchild elegies, see Mawer, Hammond ("Make Use of What I Leave" 12–17; *Sinful Self* 132–35), and Clark ("Honeyed Knot" 78).

EPILOGUE: AESTHETICIZING LOSS

1 Robert Woodmancy, who died in 1667, was probably the original subject of Tompson's poem. Tompson had been in competition with Cheever to succeed Woodmancy, and Peter White suggests that he published the poem at Cheever's death "to achieve a kind of gentle vengeance upon his competitor" ("Benjamin Tompson" 324). Schmitt-von Mühlenfels comments on the poem as a transitional text in the movement from piety to wit in New

England's commemorations during the early eighteenth century (*Die "Funeral Elegy"* 125).

2 For a discussion of the impact of Milton and neoclassicism on the newer style of elegy in New England, see Schmitt-von Mühlenfels (*Die "Funeral Elegy"* 125–38). Elsewhere Schmitt-von Mühlenfels comments on Franklin's satire as "conclusive evidence for a society that has lost a strict theological frame of reference and frankly luxuriates in pathos" ("Puritan Society" 32). Draper traces a corresponding shift to more sentimental modes in the English elegy (178–201). For later developments in American elegy, see Elliott and Stannard (147–63); Silverman surveys the transition to neoclassical and romantic modes in American poetry generally (202–9).

Works cited

Abernethy, Julian W. *American Literature.* New York: Maynard, Merrill, & Co., 1903.

Allen, David Grayson. "Both Englands." In *Seventeenth-Century New England.* Ed. David D. Hall and David Grayson Allen. Boston: The Colonial Society of Massachusetts, 1984. 55–82.

Ames, William. *The Marrow of Theology.* Trans. John D. Eusden. Boston: The Pilgrim Press, 1968.

Angoff, Charles. *A Literary History of the American People.* 4 vols. Vol. 1: *From 1607 to the Beginning of the Revolutionary Period.* New York: Alfred A. Knopf, 1931.

Appiah, Kwame Anthony. "Race." In *Critical Terms for Literary Study.* Ed. Frank Lentricchia and Thomas McLaughlin. Chicago: University of Chicago Press, 1990. 274–87.

Appleton, Nathanael. *A Great Man Fallen in Israel.* Boston, 1724. In *New England Funeral Sermons.* Vol. 4 of *The Puritan Sermon in America.* Ed. Ronald A. Bosco. Delmar, NY: Scholars' Facsimiles and Reprints, 1978. 175–212.

Ariès, Philippe. *Western Attitudes toward Death: From the Middle Ages to the Present.* Trans. Patricia M. Ranum. Baltimore: Johns Hopkins University Press, 1974.

  The Hour of Our Death. Trans. Helen Weaver. New York: Vintage Books, 1982.

The Bay Psalm Book: A Facsimile Reprint of the First Edition of 1640. Ed. Zoltan Haraszti. Chicago: University of Chicago Press, 1956.

Beaty, Nancy Lee. *The Craft of Dying: A Study in the Literary Tradition of the Ars Moriendi in England.* New Haven: Yale University Press, 1970.

Bennett, A. L. "The Principal Rhetorical Conventions in the Renaissance Personal Elegy." *Studies in Philology* 51 (1954): 107–26.

Bercovitch, Sacvan. *The Puritan Origins of the American Self.* New Haven: Yale University Press, 1975.

  The American Jeremiad. Madison: University of Wisconsin Press, 1978.

  ed. *Typology and Early American Literature.* Amherst: University of Massachusetts Press, 1972.

Blake, Kathleen. "Edward Taylor's Protestant Poetic: Nontransubstantiating Metaphor." *American Literature* 43 (1971): 1–24.

Bloomfield, Morton W. "The Elegy and the Elegiac Mode: Praise and Alienation." In *Renaissance Genres: Essays on Theory, History, and Interpretation.*

Ed. Barbara Kiefer Lewalski. Cambridge, Mass.: Harvard University Press, 1986. 147–57.

Bosco, Ronald A. "Introduction." *New England Funeral Sermons.* Vol. 4 of *The Puritan Sermon in America 1630–1750.* Ed. Ronald A. Bosco. Delmar, NY: Scholars' Facsimiles and Reprints, 1978. ix-xxviii.

Bowden, Edwin T. "Urian Oakes' Elegy: Colonial Literature and History." *Forum* 10 (1972): 2–8.

Bradstreet, Anne. *The Works of Anne Bradstreet.* Ed. Jeannine Hensley. Cambridge, Mass.: Harvard University Press, 1967.

Bray, James. "John Fiske: Puritan Precursor of Edward Taylor." *Early American Literature* 9 (1974): 27–38.

Breitwieser, Mitchell Robert. *American Puritanism and the Defense of Mourning: Religion, Grief, and Ethnology in Mary White Rowlandson's Captivity Narrative.* Madison: University of Wisconsin Press, 1990.

Bremer, Francis J. *Shaping New Englands: Puritan Clergymen in Seventeenth-Century England and New England.* New York: Twayne, 1994.

ed. *Puritanism: Transatlantic Perspectives on a Seventeenth-Century Anglo-American Faith.* Boston: Massachusetts Historical Society, 1993.

Bridenbaugh, Carl. *Cities in the Wilderness: The First Century of Urban Life in America, 1625–1742.* London: Oxford University Press, 1971.

Brown, Wallace Cable. "Edward Taylor: An American Metaphysical." *American Literature* 16 (1944): 186–97.

Brumm, Ursula. *American Thought and Religious Typology.* Trans. John Hoaglund. 1963. Rpt. New Brunswick: Rutgers University Press, 1970.

"Meditative Poetry in New England." In *Puritan Poets and Poetics: Seventeenth-Century American Poetry in Theory and Practice.* Ed. Peter White. University Park: Pennsylvania State University Press, 1985. 318–36.

Caldwell, Patricia. *The Puritan Conversion Narrative: The Beginnings of American Expression.* Cambridge: Cambridge University Press, 1983.

Cherniavski, Eva. "Night Pollution and the Floods of Confession in Michael Wigglesworth's Diary." *Arizona Quarterly* 45 (2) (1989): 15–33.

Clark, Michael. "'The Crucified Phrase': Sign and Desire in Puritan Semiology." *Early American Literature* 13 (1978/79): 278–93.

"The Honeyed Knot of Puritan Aesthetics." In *Puritan Poets and Poetics: Seventeenth-Century American Poetry in Theory and Practice.* Ed. Peter White. University Park: Pennsylvania State University Press, 1985. 67–83.

"The Subject of the Text in Early American Literature." *Early American Literature* 20 (1985): 120–30.

Coffin, Mark Tristram. *American Narrative Obituary Verse and Native American Balladry.* Norwood, Pa.: Norwood Editions, 1975.

Cohen, Charles Lloyd. *God's Caress: The Psychology of Puritan Religious Experience.* New York: Oxford University Press, 1986.

Colacurcio, Michael. "*Gods Determinations* Touching Half-Way Membership: Occasion and Audience in Edward Taylor." *American Literature* 39 (1967): 298–314.

"Does American Literature Have a History?" *Early American Literature* 13 (1978): 110–32.

Colman, Benjamin. *A Devout Contemplation On the Meaning of Divine Providence, in the Early Death Of Pious and Lovely Children*. Boston, 1714. In *New England Funeral Sermons*. Vol. 4 of *The Puritan Sermon in America*. Ed. Ronald A. Bosco. Delmar, NY: Scholars' Facsimiles and Reprints, 1978. 21–50.

The Prophet's Death. Boston, 1723. In *New England Funeral Sermons*. Vol. 4 of *The Puritan Sermon in America*. Ed. Ronald A. Bosco. Delmar, NY: Scholars' Facsimiles and Reprints, 1978. 139–73.

Craig, Raymond A. "Singing with Grace: Allusive Strategies in Anne Bradstreet's 'New Psalms.'" *Studies in Puritan American Spirituality* 1 (1990): 148–63.

Cremin, Lawrence. *American Education: The Colonial Experience, 1606–1783*. New York: Harper and Row, 1970.

Cressy, David. "Literacy in Seventeenth-Century England: More Evidence." *Journal of Interdisciplinary History* 8 (1977): 141–50.

Coming Over: Migration and Communication between England and New England in the Seventeenth Century. Cambridge: Cambridge University Press, 1987.

Curtius, Ernst Robert. *European Literature and the Latin Middle Ages*. Trans. Willard R. Trask. New York: Pantheon Books, 1953.

Daly, Robert. *God's Altar: The World and the Flesh in Puritan Poetry*. Berkeley: University of California Press, 1978.

"The Danforths: Puritan Poets in the Woods of Arcadia." In *Puritan Poets and Poetics: Seventeenth-Century American Poetry in Theory and Practice*. Ed. Peter White. University Park: Pennsylvania State University Press, 1985. 147–57.

Davenport, John. *The Saint's Anchor-Hold*. In *Salvation in New England*. Ed. Phyllis M. Jones and Nicholas R. Jones. Austin: University of Texas Press, 1977. 147–52.

Davidson, Cathy N. *Revolution and the Word: The Rise of the Novel in America*. New York: Oxford University Press, 1986.

Davidson, Edward H. "'God's Well-Trodden Foot-Paths': Puritan Preaching and Sermon Form." *Texas Studies in Literature and Language* 25 (1983): 504–27.

Davies, Horton. *The Worship of the American Puritans, 1629–1730*. New York: Peter Lang, 1990.

Davis, Thomas M. "Introduction." *Edward Taylor vs. Solomon Stoddard: The Nature of the Lord's Supper*. Ed. Thomas M. Davis and Virginia L. Davis. Boston: Twayne, 1981. 1–57.

"Introduction." *Edward Taylor's "Church Records" and Related Sermons*. Ed. Thomas M. Davis and Virginia L. Davis. Boston: Twayne, 1981. xi–xl.

"Edward Taylor's Elegy on Deacon David Dewey." *Proceedings of the American Antiquarian Society* 96, Part 1 (1986): 75–84.

A Reading of Edward Taylor. Newark: University of Delaware Press, 1992.

Dean, John Ward. *Sketch of the Life of Rev. Michael Wigglesworth. A. M., Author of the Day of Doom*. Albany: J. Munsell, 1863.

Delbanco, Andrew. *The Puritan Ordeal*. Cambridge, Mass.: Harvard University Press, 1989.

Demos, John. *A Little Commonwealth: Family Life in Plymouth Colony*. London: Oxford University Press, 1970.

De Prospo, R. C. "The Latest Early American Literature." *Early American Literature* 24 (1989): 248–56.

"Marginalizing Early American Literature." *New Literary History* 23 (1992): 233–65.

Dethlefsen, Edwin, and James Deetz. "Death's Heads, Cherubs, and Willow Trees: Experimental Archaeology in Colonial Cemeteries." *American Antiquity* 31 (1966): 502–10.

Donne, John. *The Complete Poetry of John Donne*. Ed. John T. Shawcross. Garden City, NY: Doubleday & Co., 1971.

"Devotions upon Emergent Occasions." In *Seventeenth-Century Prose and Verse*. Ed. Alexander M. Witherspoon and Frank J. Warnke. New York: Harcourt Brace Jovanovich, 1982. 60–69.

Doriani, Beth M. "'Then Have I. . .Said with David': Anne Bradstreet's Andover Manuscript Poems and the Influence of the Psalm Tradition." *Early American Literature* 24 (1989): 52–69.

Douglas, Ann. *The Feminization of American Culture*. New York: Knopf, 1977.

Draper, John W. *The Funeral Elegy and the Rise of English Romanticism*. New York: New York University Press, 1929.

ed. *A Century of Broadside Elegies*. London: Ingpen and Grant, 1928.

Drayton, Michael. *The Works of Michael Drayton*. Ed. J. William Hebel. 5 vols. Oxford: Shakespeare Head Press, 1931.

Eagleton, Terry. *Literary Theory: An Introduction*. Minneapolis: University of Minnesota Press, 1983.

Eberwein, Jane Donahue. "Anne Bradstreet." In *Early American Poetry: Selections from Bradstreet, Taylor, Dwight, Freneau, and Bryant*. Ed. Jane Donahue Eberwein. Madison: University of Wisconsin Press, 1978. 3–13.

Edwards, Jonathan. *Jonathan Edwards: Representative Selections*. Ed. Clarence H. Faust and Thomas H. Johnson. Revised edition. New York: Hill and Wang, 1962.

Elledge, Scott, ed. *Milton's Lycidas*. New York: Harper and Row, 1966.

Elliott, Emory. "The Development of the Puritan Funeral Sermon and Elegy: 1660–1750." *Early American Literature* 15 (1980): 151–64.

Revolutionary Writers: Religion and Authority in the New Republic, 1725–1810. New York: Oxford University Press, 1986.

Empson, William. *Collected Poems*. New York: Harcourt Brace Jovanovich, 1935.

Milton's God. London: Chatto and Windus, 1961.

Fish, Stanley. *Surprised by Sin: The Reader in Paradise Lost*. Berkeley: University of California Press, 1967.

The Living Temple: George Herbert and Catechizing. Berkeley: University of California Press, 1978.

Is There a Text in This Class? The Authority of Interpretive Communities. Cambridge, Mass.: Harvard University Press, 1980.

"Commentary: The Young and the Restless." In *The New Historicism*. Ed. H. Aram Veeser. New York: Routledge, 1989. 303–16.

Fithian, Rosemary. "'Words of My Mouth, Meditations of My Heart': Edward Taylor's *Preparatory Meditations* and the Book of Psalms." *Early American Literature* 20 (1985): 89–119.

Ford, Paul Leicester. "Introduction." *The New-England Primer*. Ed. Paul Leicester Ford. 1897. Rpt. New York: Teachers College, Columbia University, 1962. 1–53.

Foster, Stephen. *The Long Argument: English Puritanism and the Shaping of New England Culture, 1570–1700*. Chapel Hill: University of North Carolina Press, 1991.

Fox-Genovese, Elizabeth. "Literary Criticism and the Politics of the New Historicism." In *The New Historicism*. Ed. H. Aram Veeser. New York: Routledge, 1989. 213–24.

Franklin, Benjamin. *Writings*. Ed. J. A. Leo Lemay. New York: The Library of America, 1987.

Fraser, Russell. *The War Against Poetry*. Princeton: Princeton University Press, 1970.

Gatta, John. *Gracious Laughter: The Meditative Wit of Edward Taylor*. Columbia: University of Missouri Press, 1989.

Geddes, Gordon E. *Welcome Joy: Death in Puritan New England*. Ann Arbor: UMI Research Press, 1981.

Geertz, Clifford. *The Interpretation of Cultures*. New York: Basic Books, 1973.
 Local Knowledge: Further Essays in Interpretive Anthropology. New York: Basic Books, 1983.

The Geneva Bible: A Facsimile of the 1560 Edition. Intro. Lloyd E. Berry. Madison: University of Wisconsin Press, 1969.

Grabo, Norman S. *Edward Taylor*. New York: Twayne, 1961.
 "Introduction." *Edward Taylor's Treatise Concerning the Lord's Supper*. Ed. Norman S. Grabo. East Lansing: Michigan State University Press, 1966. ix–li.
 "The Veiled Vision: The Role of Aesthetics in Early American Intellectual History." 1962. Rpt. in *The American Puritan Imagination: Essays in Revaluation*. Ed. Sacvan Bercovitch. Cambridge: Cambridge University Press, 1974. 19–33.
 "Ideology and the Early American Frontier." *Early American Literature* 22 (1987): 274–90.
 Edward Taylor: Revised Edition. Boston: Twayne, 1988.

Graff, Gerald. *Professing Literature: An Institutional History*. Chicago: University of Chicago Press, 1987.
 "Co-optation." In *The New Historicism*. Ed. H. Aram Veeser. New York: Routledge, 1989. 168–81.

Greenblatt, Stephen. *Renaissance Self-Fashioning: From More to Shakespeare*. Chicago: University of Chicago Press, 1980.
 Shakespearean Negotiations: The Circulation of Social Energy in Renaissance England. Berkeley: University of California Press, 1988.

Greven, Philip. *The Protestant Temperament: Patterns of Child-Rearing, Religious Experience, and the Self in Early America*. New York: Knopf, 1977.

Hahn, T. G. "Urian Oakes's *Elegie* on Thomas Shepard and Puritan Poetics." *American Literature* 45 (1973): 163–81.

Haims, Lynn. "Puritan Iconography: The Art of Edward Taylor's *Gods Determinations*." In *Puritan Poets and Poetics: Seventeenth-Century American Poetry in Theory and Practice.* Ed. Peter White. University Park: Pennsylvania State University Press, 1985. 84–98.

Hall, David D. *The Faithful Shepherd: A History of the New England Ministry in the Seventeenth Century.* Chapel Hill: University of North Carolina Press, 1972.

"The World of Print and Collective Mentality in Seventeenth-Century New England." *New Directions in American Intellectual History.* Ed. John Higham and Paul K. Conklin. Baltimore: Johns Hopkins University Press, 1979. 166–80.

"On Native Ground: From the History of Printing to the History of the Book." *Proceedings of the American Antiquarian Society* 93 (1983): 313–36.

"The Uses of Literacy in New England, 1600–1850." *Printing and Society in Early America.* Ed. William L. Joyce, David D. Hall, Richard D. Brown, and John B. Hench. Worcester, Mass.: American Antiquarian Society, 1983. 1–47.

"Toward a History of Popular Religion in Early New England." *William and Mary Quarterly* 41 (1984): 49–55.

Worlds of Wonder, Days of Judgment: Popular Religious Belief in Early New England. New York: Knopf, 1989.

"Readers and Reading in America: Historical and Critical Perspectives." *Proceedings of the American Antiquarian Society* 103, Part 2 (1994): 337–57.

Haller, William. *The Elect Nation: The Meaning and Relevance of John Foxe's Book of Martyrs.* New York: Harper and Row, 1963.

Hambrick-Stowe, Charles E. *The Practice of Piety: Puritan Devotional Disciplines in Seventeenth-Century New England.* Chapel Hill: University of North Carolina Press, 1982.

"Introduction." *Early New England Meditative Poetry.* Ed. Charles E. Hambrick-Stowe. New York: Paulist Press, 1988. 7–62.

Hammond, Jeffrey A. "A Puritan *Ars Moriendi*: Edward Taylor's Late Meditations on the Song of Songs." *Early American Literature* 17 (1982/83): 191–214.

"'Make Use of What I Leave in Love': Anne Bradstreet's Didactic Self." *Religion and Literature* 17 (1985): 11–26.

"Where Are We Going, Where Have We Been? Puritan Poetics Reconsidered." *Early American Literature* 22 (1987): 114–32.

"Who Is Edward Taylor?: Voice and Reader in the *Preparatory Meditations*." *American Poetry* 7 (3) (1990): 2–19.

"The Puritan Elegiac Ritual: From Sinful Silence to Apostolic Voice." *Studies in Puritan American Spirituality* 2 (1991): 77–106.

Edward Taylor: Fifty Years of Scholarship and Criticism. Columbia, SC: Camden House, 1993.

Sinful Self, Saintly Self: The Puritan Experience of Poetry. Athens: University of Georgia Press, 1993.

"Diffusing All by Pattern: Edward Taylor as Elegist." In *The Tayloring Shop: Essays on Edward Taylor in Honor of Thomas M. and Virginia L. Davis*. Ed. Michael Schuldiner. Newark: University of Delaware Press, 1997. 153–92.

Hammond, Jeff, and Thomas M. Davis. "Edward Taylor: A Note on Visual Imagery." *Early American Literature* 8 (1973): 126–31.

Hardison, O. B., Jr. *The Enduring Monument: A Study of the Idea of Praise in Renaissance Literary Theory*. Chapel Hill: University of North Carolina Press, 1962.

Hart, James D. *The Popular Book: A History of America's Literary Taste*. New York: Oxford University Press, 1950.

Henson, Robert. "Form and Content of the Puritan Funeral Elegy." *American Literature* 32 (1960): 11–27.

Herbert, George. *The Works of George Herbert*. Ed. F. E. Hutchinson. Oxford: The Clarendon Press, 1941.

Holifield, E. Brooks. *The Covenant Sealed: The Development of Puritan Sacramental Theology in Old and New England, 1570–1720*. New Haven: Yale University Press, 1974.

Holub, Robert C. *Reception Theory: A Critical Introduction*. London: Methuen, 1984.

Hooker, Thomas. *The Application of Redemption: The first eight Books*. 1657. Rpt. New York: Arno Press, 1972.

Hoopes, James. *Consciousness in New England: From Puritanism and Ideas to Psychoanalysis and Semiotic*. Baltimore: Johns Hopkins University Press, 1989.

Hughes, Walter. "'Meat Out of the Eater': Panic and Desire in American Puritan Poetry." In *Engendering Men: The Question of Male Feminist Criticism*. Ed. Joseph A. Boone and Michael Cadden. New York: Routledge, 1990. 102–21.

Iser, Wolfgang. *The Implied Reader: Patterns of Communication in Prose Fiction from Bunyan to Beckett*. Baltimore: Johns Hopkins University Press, 1974.
  The Act of Reading: A Theory of Aesthetic Response. Baltimore: Johns Hopkins University Press, 1978.
  The Fictive and the Imaginary: Charting Literary Anthropology. Baltimore: Johns Hopkins University Press, 1993.

Jantz, Harold S., ed. *The First Century of New England Verse*. Worcester, Mass.: The American Antiquarian Society, 1944.
  "Baroque Free Verse in New England and Pennsylvania." In *Puritan Poets and Poetics: Seventeenth-Century American Poetry in Theory and Practice*. Ed. Peter White. University Park: Pennsylvania State University Press, 1985. 258–73.

Jauss, Hans Robert. "The Alterity and Modernity of Medieval Literature." *New Literary History* 10 (1979): 181–229.
  Aesthetic Experience and Literary Hermeneutics. Trans. Michael Shaw. Minneapolis: University of Minnesota Press, 1982.
  Toward an Aesthetic of Reception. Trans. Timothy Bahti. Minneapolis: University of Minnesota Press, 1982.

Johnson, Edward. *Johnson's Wonder-Working Providence*. Ed. J. Franklin Jameson. New York: Charles Scribner's Sons, 1910.

Johnson, Thomas H. "Poetry." In *The Puritans*. Ed. Perry Miller and Thomas H. Johnson. 2 vols. 1938. Rpt. New York: Harper and Row, 1963. 2:545–52.

"A Seventeenth-Century Printing of Some Verses of Edward Taylor." *New England Quarterly* 14 (1941): 139–41.

Jonson, Ben. *The Complete Poetry of Ben Jonson*. Ed. William B. Hunter, Jr. New York: W. W. Norton, 1968.

Kaiser, Leo M., ed. *Early American Latin Verse 1625–1825: An Anthology*. Chicago: Bolchazy-Carducci, 1984.

Kaiser, Leo M., and Donald E. Stanford. "The Latin Poems of 'Edward Taylor.'" *Yale University Library Gazette* 40 (1965): 75–81.

Kay, Dennis. *Melodious Tears: The English Funeral Elegy from Spenser to Milton*. Oxford: Clarendon, 1990.

Keller, Karl. *The Example of Edward Taylor*. Amherst: University of Massachusetts Press, 1975.

The Only Kangaroo among the Beauty: Emily Dickinson and America. Baltimore: Johns Hopkins University Press, 1979.

"Edward Taylor, The Acting Poet." *Puritan Poets and Poetics: Seventeenth-Century American Poetry in Theory and Practice*. Ed. Peter White. University Park: Pennsylvania State University Press, 1985. 185–97.

Kibbey, Ann. *The Interpretation of Material Shapes in Puritanism: A Study of Rhetoric, Prejudice, and Violence*. Cambridge: Cambridge University Press, 1986.

King, John Owen, III. *The Iron of Melancholy: Structures of Spiritual Conversion from the Puritan Conscience to Victorian Neurosis*. Middletown, Ct.: Wesleyan University Press, 1983.

Knott, John R., Jr. *The Sword of the Spirit: Puritan Responses to the Bible*. Chicago: University of Chicago Press, 1980.

Lambert, Ellen Zetzel. *Placing Sorrow: A Study of the Pastoral Elegy Convention from Theocritus to Milton*. Chapel Hill: University of North Carolina Press, 1976.

Lease, Benjamin. *Anglo-American Encounters: England and the Rise of American Literature*. Cambridge: Cambridge University Press, 1981.

Leitch, Vincent B. *American Literary Criticism from the Thirties to the Eighties*. New York: Columbia University Press, 1987.

Lentricchia, Frank. "Foucault's Legacy – A New Historicism?" In *The New Historicism*. Ed. H. Aram Veeser. New York: Routledge, 1989. 231–42.

Leverenz, David. *The Language of Puritan Feeling: An Exploration in Literature, Psychology, and Social History*. New Brunswick: Rutgers University Press, 1980.

Levy, Babette May. *Preaching in the First Half Century of New England History*. 1945. Rpt. New York: Russell and Russell, 1967.

Lewalski, Barbara Kiefer. *Donne's Anniversaries and the Poetry of Praise: The Creation of a Symbolic Mode*. Princeton: Princeton University Press, 1973.

Protestant Poetics and the Seventeenth-Century Religious Lyric. Princeton: Princeton University Press, 1979.

Lockridge, Kenneth. "The Population of Dedham, Massachusetts, 1636–1736." *Economic History Review*, 2nd Series, 19 (1966): 318–44.

A New England Town: The First Hundred Years, Dedham, Massachusetts, 1636–1736. New York: W. W. Norton, 1970.

Literacy in Colonial New England: An Enquiry into the Social Context of Literacy in the Early Modern West. New York: W. W. Norton, 1974.

Lowance, Mason I., Jr. *The Language of Canaan: Metaphor and Symbol in New England from the Puritans to the Transcendentalists*. Cambridge, Mass.: Harvard University Press, 1980.

Ludwig, Allan I. *Graven Images: New England Stonecarving and its Symbols, 1650–1815*. Middletown, Ct.: Wesleyan University Press, 1966.

Madden, Etta. "Resurrecting Life through Rhetorical Ritual: A Buried Value of the Puritan Funeral Sermon." *Early American Literature* 26 (1991): 232–50.

Martin, Wendy. *An American Triptych: Anne Bradstreet, Emily Dickinson, Adrienne Rich*. Chapel Hill: University of North Carolina Press, 1984.

Martz, Louis L. "Foreword." *The Poems of Edward Taylor*. Ed. Donald E. Stanford. New Haven: Yale University Press, 1960. xiii-xxxviii.

The Poetry of Meditation: A Study in English Religious Literature of the Seventeenth Century. New Haven: Yale University Press, 1962.

Marvell, Andrew. *The Poems of Andrew Marvell*. Ed. Hugh Macdonald. Cambridge, Mass.: Harvard University Press, 1952.

Mather, Cotton. *Ornaments for the Daughters of Zion*. Ed. Pattie Cowell. Boston, 1692. Rpt. Delmar, NY: Scholars' Facsimiles & Reprints, 1978.

Magnalia Christi Americana; or, The Ecclesiastical History of New England. London, 1702. Ed. Thomas Robbins. 2 vols. 1852. Rpt. New York: Russell and Russell, 1967.

The Cure of Sorrow. Boston, 1709.

Bonifacius: An Essay upon the Good. Boston, 1710. Ed. David Levin. Cambridge, Mass.: Harvard University Press, 1966.

Awakening Thoughts on the Sleep of Death. Boston, 1712.

A Christian Funeral. Boston, 1713.

An Essay on the Consolations of God. Boston, 1714. In *New England Funeral Sermons*. Vol. 4 of *The Puritan Sermon in America*. Ed. Ronald A. Bosco. Delmar, NY: Scholars' Facsimiles and Reprints, 1978. 51–94.

Hades Look'd Into. Boston, 1717. In *New England Funeral Sermons*. Vol. 4 of *The Puritan Sermon in America*. Ed. Ronald A. Bosco. Delmar, NY: Scholars' Facsimiles and Reprints, 1978. 95–138.

Psalterium Americanum. Boston, 1718.

Manuductio ad Ministerium. Boston, 1726.

Cotton Mather's Verse in English. Ed. Denise D. Knight. Newark: University of Delaware Press, 1989.

Mather, Increase. *The Life and Death of that Reverend Man of God, Mr. Richard Mather*. Cambridge, Mass., 1670.

Mawer, Randall R. "'Farewell Dear Babe': Bradstreet's Elegy for Elizabeth." *Early American Literature* 15 (1980): 29–41.

Mayer, Howard A. "Puritan Triumph: The Joyful Death Books of Cotton Mather and James Janeway." In *Triumphs of the Spirit in Children's Literature.* Ed. Francelia Butler and Richard Rotert. Hamden, Ct.: The Shoe String Press, 1986. 209–20.

McGiffert, Michael. "Introduction." *God's Plot: The Paradoxes of Puritan Piety.* Ed. Michael McGiffert. Amherst: University of Massachusetts Press, 1972. 3–32.

McWilliams, John. "Writing Literary History: The Limits of Nationalism." *Resources for American Literary Study* 13 (1983): 127–33.

Meserole, Harrison T., ed. *American Poetry of the Seventeenth Century.* 1968. Rpt. University Park: Pennsylvania State University Press, 1985.

Mignon, Charles W. "Edward Taylor's *Preparatory Meditations*: A Decorum of Imperfection." *PMLA* 83 (1968): 1423–28.

"Introduction." Edward Taylor, *Upon the Types of the Old Testament.* Ed. Charles W. Mignon. 2 vols. Lincoln: University of Nebraska Press, 1989. 1: xix–lxxvii.

Miller, Perry. *The New England Mind: The Seventeenth Century.* 1939. Rpt. Boston: Beacon Press, 1961.

The New England Mind: From Colony to Province. 1953. Rpt. Boston: Beacon Press, 1961.

Errand into the Wilderness. New York: Harper and Row, 1964.

and Thomas H. Johnson, ed. *The Puritans.* 2 vols. 1938. Rpt. New York: Harper and Row, 1963.

Milton, John. *The Complete Poetry of John Milton.* Ed. John T. Shawcross. Garden City, NY: Doubleday, 1971.

Miner, Earl, ed. *Literary Uses of Typology from the Late Middle Ages to the Present.* Princeton: Princeton University Press, 1977.

Minter, David. "The Puritan Jeremiad as a Literary Form." In *The American Puritan Imagination: Essays in Revaluation.* Ed. Sacvan Bercovitch. Cambridge: Cambridge University Press, 1974. 45–55.

Mitford, Jessica. *The American Way of Death.* New York: Simon and Schuster, 1963.

Monaghan, E. Jennifer. "Literacy Instruction and Gender in Colonial New England." *American Quarterly* 40 (1988): 18–41.

Montrose, Louis A. "Renaissance Literary Studies and the Subject of History." *English Literary Renaissance* 16 (1986): 5–12.

"Professing the Renaissance: The Poetics and Politics of Culture." In *The New Historicism.* Ed. H. Aram Veeser. New York: Routledge, 1989. 15–36.

Morgan, Edmund S. *The Puritan Dilemma: The Story of John Winthrop.* Boston: Little, Brown, 1958.

Morison, Samuel Eliot. *Harvard College in the Seventeenth Century.* Cambridge, Mass.: Harvard University Press, 1936.

The Intellectual Life of Colonial New England. 1936. Rpt. Ithaca: Cornell University Press, 1960.

Morton, Thomas. *New English Canaan of Thomas Morton.* Ed. Charles Francis Adams, Jr. 1883. Rpt. New York: Burt Franklin, 1967.

Murdock, Kenneth B. *Literature and Theology in Colonial New England*. Cambridge, Mass.: Harvard University Press, 1949.

ed. *Handkerchiefs from Paul*. Cambridge, Mass.: Harvard University Press, 1927.

The New-England Primer. Ed. Paul Leicester Ford. 1897. Rpt. New York: Teachers College, Columbia University, 1962.

Ong, Walter J., S.J. *Orality and Literacy*. London: Methuen, 1982.

Otis, William Bradley. *American Verse, 1625–1807: A History*. 1909. Rpt. New York: Haskell House, 1966.

Patterson, Lee. "Literary History." In *Literary Terms for Critical Study*. Ed. Frank Lentricchia and Thomas McLaughlin. Chicago: University of Chicago Press, 1990. 250–62.

Pearce, Roy Harvey. *The Continuity of American Poetry*. Princeton: Princeton University Press, 1961.

Pearse, Edward. *The Great Concern: or, A Serious Warning To a Timely and Thorough Preparation for Death*. Boston, 1705.

Pecora, Vincent P. "The Limits of Local Knowledge" In *The New Historicism*. Ed. H. Aram Veeser. New York: Routledge, 1989. 243–76.

Perkins, David. *Is Literary History Possible?* Baltimore: Johns Hopkins University Press, 1992.

Perkins, William. *The Workes of. . .Mr. William Perkins*. 3 vols. London, 1613.

Pettit, Norman. *The Heart Prepared: Grace and Conversion in Puritan Spiritual Life*. New Haven: Yale University Press, 1966.

Piercy, Josephine K. "The 'Character' in the Literature of Early New England." *New England Quarterly* 12 (1939): 470–76.

Studies in Literary Types in Seventeenth Century America (1607–1710). 1939. Rpt. Hamden, Ct.: Archon, 1969.

Pigman, G. W., III. *Grief and English Renaissance Elegy*. Cambridge: Cambridge University Press, 1985.

Puttenham, George. *The Arte of English Poesie*. E. Gladys Doige Willcock and Alice Walker. Cambridge: Cambridge University Press, 1936.

Ramazani, Jahan. *Poetry of Mourning: The Modern Elegy from Hardy to Heaney*. Chicago: University of Chicago Press, 1994.

Reed, Michael. "American Puritanism: The Language of Its Religion." *American Imago* 37 (1980): 278–333.

Reising, Russell. *The Unusable Past: Theory and the Study of American Literature*. New York: Methuen, 1986.

Rosen, Barbara. "John Foxe's 'Book of Martyrs' and Its Value as a Book for Children." In *Triumphs of the Spirit in Children's Literature*. Ed. Francelia Butler and Richard Rotert. Hamden, Ct.: The Shoe String Press, 1986. 223–29.

Rosenmeier, Jesper. "To Keep in Memory: The Poetry of Edward Johnson." In *Puritan Poets and Poetics: Seventeenth-Century American Poetry in Theory and Practice*. Ed. Peter White. University Park: Pennsylvania State University Press, 1985. 158–74.

Rosenmeier, Rosamond R. "The Wounds Upon Bathsheba: Anne Bradstreet's Prophetic Art." In *Puritan Poets and Poetics: Seventeenth-Century American Poetry in Theory and Practice*. Ed. Peter White. University Park: Pennsylvania State University Press, 1985. 129–46.

Anne Bradstreet Revisited. Boston: Twayne, 1991.

Rosenwald, Lawrence. "*Voces Clamantium in Deserto*: Latin Verse of the Puritans." In *Puritan Poets and Poetics: Seventeenth-Century American Poetry in Theory and Practice*. Ed. Peter White. University Park: Pennsylvania State University Press, 1985. 303–17.

Rowe, Karen E. "Sacred or Profane? Edward Taylor's Meditations on Canticles." *Modern Philology* 72 (1974): 123–38.

"Prophetic Visions: Typology and Colonial American Poetry." In *Puritan Poets and Poetics: Seventeenth-Century American Poetry in Theory and Practice*. Ed. Peter White. University Park: Pennsylvania State University Press, 1985. 47–66.

Saint and Singer: Edward Taylor's Typology and the Poetics of Meditation. Cambridge: Cambridge University Press, 1986.

"Mourning my Dove: Epithalamiums and Elegies in Edward Taylor's Poetry." Forthcoming in *Early American Literature*.

Sacks, Peter M. *The English Elegy: Studies in the Genre from Spenser to Yeats*. Baltimore: Johns Hopkins University Press, 1985.

Saffin, John. *John Saffin His Book*. Ed. Caroline Hazard. New York: The Harbor Press, 1928.

Salska, Agnieszka. "Puritan Poetry: Its Public and Private Strain." *Early American Literature* 19 (1984): 107–21.

Sargent, Ritamarie. "Poetry and the Puritan Faith: The Elegies of Anne Bradstreet and Edward Taylor." *A Salzburg Miscellany: English and American Studies 1964–1984*. Ed. Wilfried Haslauer. Salzburg: Institut für Anglistik und Amerikanistik, Universität Salzburg, 1984. 1:149–60.

Scheick, William J. *The Will and the Word: The Poetry of Edward Taylor*. Athens: University of Georgia Press, 1974.

"Standing in the Gap: Urian Oakes' Elegy on Thomas Shepard." *Early American Literature* 9 (1975): 301–6.

"Tombless Virtue and Hidden Text: New England Puritan Funeral Elegies." In *Puritan Poets and Poetics: Seventeenth-Century American Poetry in Theory and Practice*. Ed. Peter White. University Park: Pennsylvania State University Press, 1985. 286–302.

Design in Puritan American Literature. Lexington: University Press of Kentucky, 1992.

Schenck, Celeste Marguerite. *Mourning and Panegyric: The Poetics of Pastoral Ceremony*. University Park: Pennsylvania State University Press, 1988.

Schmitt-von Mühlenfels, Astrid. *Die "Funeral Elegy" Neuenglands: Ein gattungsgeschichtliche Studie*. Heidelberg: Carl Winter, Universitätsverlag, 1973.

"John Fiske's Funeral Elegy on John Cotton." *Early American Literature* 12 (1977): 49–62.

"Puritan Society Reflected in the New England Elegy." *The Origins and Originality of American Culture.* Ed. Tibor Frank. Budapest: Akademiai Kaidó, 1984. 21–33.

Schuldiner, Michael. *Gifts and Works: The Post-Conversion Paradigm and Spiritual Controversy in Seventeenth-Century Massachusetts.* Macon, Ga.: Mercer University Press, 1991.

Schweitzer, Ivy. *The Work of Self-Representation: Lyric Poetry in Colonial New England.* Chapel Hill: University of North Carolina Press, 1991.

Scodel, Joshua. *The English Poetic Epitaph: Commemoration and Conflict from Jonson to Wordsworth.* Ithaca: Cornell University Press, 1991.

Secor, Robert. "Seventeenth-Century Almanac Verse." In *Puritan Poets and Poetics: Seventeenth-Century American Poetry in Theory and Practice.* Ed. Peter White. University Park: Pennsylvania State University Press, 1985. 229–46.

Selement, George. "The Meeting of Elite and Popular Minds at Cambridge, New England, 1638–1645." *William and Mary Quarterly* 41 (1984): 32–48.

Shaw, W. David. *Elegy and Paradox: Testing the Conventions.* Baltimore: Johns Hopkins University Press, 1994.

"Elegy and Theory: Is Historical and Critical Knowledge Possible?" *Modern Language Quarterly* 55 (1994): 1–16.

Shea, Daniel, Jr. *Spiritual Autobiography in Early America.* Princeton: Princeton University Press, 1968.

Shepard, Thomas. *The Sincere Convert.* In *The Works of Thomas Shepard.* Ed. John A. Albro. 3 vols. Boston: Doctrinal Tract and Book Society, 1853. 1:1–109.

The Sound Believer. In *The Works of Thomas Shepard.* Ed. John A. Albro. 3 vols. Boston: Doctrinal Tract and Book Society, 1853. 1:111–284.

God's Plot: The Paradoxes of Puritan Piety. Ed. Michael McGiffert. Amherst: University of Massachusetts Press, 1972.

Sibbes, Richard. *Spiritual Mourning* (orig. numbers 14 and 15 of *The Saint's Cordials* [London, 1629]). In *Works of Richard Sibbes.* 7 vols. Ed. Alexander B. Grosart. 1862. Rpt. Edinburgh: The Banner of Truth Trust, 1983. 6:265–92.

Silverman, Kenneth, ed. *Colonial American Poetry.* New York: Hafner, 1968.

Slater, Peter Gregg. *Children in the New England Mind: In Death and in Life.* Hamden, Ct.: Archon, 1977.

Smith, Eric. *By Mourning Tongues: Studies in English Elegy.* Ipswich: The Boydell Press, 1977.

Spengemann, William C. "Discovering the Literature of British America." *Early American Literature* 18 (1983): 3–16.

A Mirror for Americanists: Reflections on the Idea of American Literature. Hanover, NH: University Press of New England, 1989.

A New World of Words: Redefining Early American Literature. New Haven: Yale University Press, 1994.

Stanford, Ann. *Anne Bradstreet: The Worldly Puritan.* New York: Burt Franklin, 1974.

"Anne Bradstreet as a Meditative Writer." *Critical Essays on Anne Bradstreet.* Ed. Pattie Cowell and Ann Stanford. Boston: G. K. Hall, 1983. 89–96.

Stanford, Donald E. *Edward Taylor*. Minneapolis: University of Minnesota Press, 1965.

Stannard, David E. *The Puritan Way of Death: A Study in Religion, Culture, and Social Change*. New York: Oxford University Press, 1977.

Stedman, Edmund Clarence. *Poets of America*. Boston: Houghton, Mifflin and Company, 1890.

Steiner, Dorothea. "Anne Bradstreet – Poet of Communication." *Arbeiten aus Anglistik und Amerikanistik* 10 (1985): 137–53.

Stock, Brian. *Listening for the Text: On the Uses of the Past*. Baltimore: Johns Hopkins University Press, 1990.

Stone, Lawrence. *The Crisis of Aristocracy, 1558–1641*. Oxford: Clarendon, 1965.

Stout, Harry S. *The New England Soul: Preaching and Religious Culture in Colonial New England*. New York: Oxford University Press, 1986.

Strickland, Ronald. "Not So Idle Tears: Re-Reading the Renaissance Elegy." *Review* 14 (1992): 57–72.

Tashjian, Dickran, and Ann Tashjian. *Memorials for Children of Change*. Middletown, Ct.: Wesleyan University Press, 1974.

Taylor, Edward. *The Poems of Edward Taylor*. Ed. Donald E. Stanford. New Haven: Yale University Press, 1960.

Edward Taylor's Christographia. Ed. Norman S. Grabo. New Haven: Yale University Press, 1962.

Edward Taylor's Minor Poetry. Ed. Thomas M. Davis and Virginia L. Davis. Boston: Twayne, 1981.

"Edward Taylor's Elegy on Deacon David Dewey." Ed. Thomas M. Davis. *Proceedings of the American Antiquarian Society* 96, Part 1 (1986): 75–84.

Thickstun, Margaret Olofson. *Fictions of the Feminine: Puritan Doctrine and the Representation of Women*. Ithaca: Cornell University Press, 1988.

Female Piety in Puritan New England. Oxford: Oxford University Press, 1992.

Thomas, Brook. "The New Historicism and other Old-fashioned Topics." In *The New Historicism*. Ed. H. Aram Veeser. New York: Routledge, 1989. 182–203.

Todorov, Tzvetan. "The Origin of Genres." *New Literary History* 8 (1976): 159–70.

Tompkins, Jane. "The Reader in History: The Changing Shape of Literary Response." In *Reader-Response Criticism: From Formalism to Post-Structuralism*. Ed. Jane Tompkins. Baltimore: Johns Hopkins University Press, 1980. 201–32.

Torgovnick, Marianna. *Crossing Ocean Parkway: Readings by an Italian American Daughter*. Chicago: University of Chicago Press, 1994.

Tucker, Samuel Marion. "The Beginnings of Verse, 1610–1808." In *The Cambridge History of American Literature*. Ed. William P. Trent, et al. 4 vols. New York: G. P. Putnam's Sons, 1917–21. 1:150–84.

Twain, Mark. *The Adventures of Huckleberry Finn*. In *Mississippi Writings*. Ed. Guy Cardwell. New York: The Library of America, 1982. 617–912.

Tyler, Moses Coit. *A History of American Literature, 1607–1765*. 1878. Rpt. Ithaca: Cornell University Press, 1949.

Vanderbilt, Kermit. *American Literature and the Academy: The Roots, Growth, and Maturity of a Profession.* Philadelphia: University of Pennsylvania Press, 1986.

van Gennep, Arnold. *The Rites of Passage.* Trans. Monika B. Vizedom and Gabrielle L. Caffee. Chicago: University of Chicago Press, 1960.

Vinovskis, Maris A. "Mortality Rates and Trends in Massachusetts Before 1860." *Journal of Economic History* 32 (1972): 184–213.

"'Angels' Heads and Weeping Willows': Death in Early America." *Proceedings of the American Antiquarian Society* 86, Part 2 (1977): 273–302.

Waggoner, Hyatt. *American Poets from the Puritans to the Present.* Boston: Houghton Mifflin, 1968.

Walker, Cheryl. "In the Margin: The Image of Women in Early Puritan Poetry." In *Puritan Poets and Poetics: Seventeenth-Century American Poetry in Theory and Practice.* Ed. Peter White. University Park: Pennsylvania State University Press, 1985. 111–26.

Walker, Jeffrey. "Anagrams and Acrostics: Puritan Poetic Wit." In *Puritan Poets and Poetics: Seventeenth-Century American Poetry in Theory and Practice.* Ed. Peter White. University Park: Pennsylvania State University Press, 1985. 247–57.

Wallerstein, Ruth. *Studies in Seventeenth-Century Poetic.* Madison: University of Wisconsin Press, 1950.

Warren, Austin. "Edward Taylor's Poetry: Colonial Baroque." *Kenyon Review* 3 (1941): 355–71.

Watkins, Owen C. *The Puritan Experience.* London: Routledge and Kegan Paul, 1972.

Watt, Ian. *The Rise of the Novel: Studies in Defoe, Richardson, and Fielding.* Berkeley: University of California Press, 1957.

Weemse, John. *The Christian Synagogue.* London, 1623.

Wendell, Barrett. *A Literary History of America.* 4th edition. New York: Charles Scribner's Sons, 1907.

White, Hayden. *Metahistory.* Baltimore: Johns Hopkins University Press, 1973.

Tropics of Discourse: Essays in Cultural Criticism. Baltimore: Johns Hopkins University Press, 1978.

"New Historicism: A Comment." In *The New Historicism.* Ed. H. Aram Veeser. New York: Routledge, 1989. 293–302.

White, Peter, ed. *Benjamin Tompson, Colonial Bard: A Critical Edition.* University Park: Pennsylvania State University Press, 1980.

"Benjamin Tompson." In *American Colonial Writers, 1606–1734.* Ed. Emory Elliott. Vol. 24 of *Dictionary of Literary Biography.* Detroit: Gale Research, 1984. 322–26.

White, Trentwell Mason, and Paul William Lebmann. *Writers of Colonial New England.* Boston: The Palmer Company, 1929.

Wigglesworth, Michael. "The Prayse of Eloquence." In *The Puritans.* Ed. Perry Miller and Thomas H. Johnson. 2 vols. 1938. Rpt. New York: Harper and Row, 1963. 2:674–78.

The Poems of Michael Wigglesworth. Ed. Ronald A. Bosco. Lanham, Md.: University Press of America, 1989.

Wilkins, John. *Ecclesiastes; or, A Discourse concerning the Gift of Preaching as it falls under the rules of Art.* London, 1646.

Willard, Samuel. *The High Esteem which God hath for the Death of his Saints.* Boston, 1683. In *New England Funeral Sermons.* Vol. 4 of *The Puritan Sermon in America.* Ed. Ronald A. Bosco. Delmar, NY: Scholars' Facsimiles and Reprints, 1978. 1–20.

Williams, Raymond. *Marxism and Literature.* Oxford: Oxford University Press, 1977.

Williams, Stanley T. *The Beginnings of American Poetry (1960–1855).* Uppsala: Almqvist and Wiksells, 1951.

Wilson, Thomas. *Arte of Rhetorique* (1560). Ed. Thomas J. Derrick. New York: Garland, 1982.

Winslow, Ola E., ed. *American Broadside Verse.* 1930. Rpt. New York: AMS Press, 1974.

Winthrop, John. "A Modell of Christian Charity." In *The Puritans.* Ed. Perry Miller and Thomas H. Johnson. 2 vols. 1938. Rpt. New York: Harper and Row, 1963. 1:195–99.

Woolf, Cynthia Griffin. "Literary Reflections of The Puritan Character." *Journal of the History of Ideas* 29 (1968): 13–32.

Wright, Thomas Goddard. *Literary Culture in Early New England 1620–1730.* 1920. Rpt. New York: Russell and Russell, 1966.

Ziff, Larzer. *Puritanism in America: New Culture in a New World.* New York: Viking, 1973.

"The Literary Consequences of Puritanism." In *The American Puritan Imagination: Essays in Revaluation.* Ed. Sacvan Bercovitch. Cambridge: Cambridge University Press, 1974. 34–44.

"Upon What Pretext?: The Book and Literary History." *Proceedings of the American Antiquarian Society* 95 (1985): 297–315.

Index

Rosen, Barbara, 230 n. 6
Rosenmeier, Jesper, 189
Rosenmeier, Rosamond R., 227 n. 11, 230 n. 1
Rosenwald, Lawrence, 34–5, 36, 37
Rowe, Karen E., 217 n. 3, 218 n. 4, 230 n. 1,
    234 n. 9, 238 n. 9

Sacks, Peter M., 81, 143, 182, 201, 210, 218 n. 4,
    220 n. 6, 227 n. 10, 231 n. 2, 237 n. 8
Saffin, John I, 47, 112, 143, 160, 203, 233 n. 5,
    235 n. 2
  poem on Charles Chauncy, 111, 160
  poem on Thomas Danforth, 112, 136–7, 153
  poem on Grace Ellsworth, 174
  poem on John Hull, 116, 124, 125, 131, 161,
    164, 179–80, 189, 198
  poem on Samuel Lee, 145, 160, 170, 172
  poem on Sarah Leverett, 150–1
  poem on Jonathan Mitchell, 119, 145, 174
  poem on John Saffin II, 34, 152
  poems on Martha Saffin, 85, 151, 170, 174,
    197
  poem on Simon Saffin, 34, 152, 194
  poem on John Wilson, 139, 146–7, 160, 174
Saffin, John II, 102, 119, 131, 185, 198; *see also*
    Saffin, John I
Saffin, Martha, 185; *see also* Saffin, John I
Saffin, Simon, 194; *see also* Saffin, John I
Salska, Agnieszka, 224 n. 6
Sargent, Ritamarie, 218 n. 4
Scheick, William J., 23, 35, 50, 58, 67, 141, 155,
    217 n. 3, 217 n. 4, 220 n. 7, 223 n. 5, 227
    n. 11, 228 n. 12, 230 n. 1, 231 n. 2, 232
    n. 4, 232 n. 1, 232 n. 2, 233 n. 5, 234 n. 1
Schenck, Celeste Marguerite, 220 n. 6, 220
    n. 8
Schmitt-von Mühlenfels, Astrid, 40, 217 n. 4,
    221 n. 10, 232 n. 3, 232 n. 4, 232 n. 5, 233
    n. 4, 233 n. 5, 234 n. 1
Schuldiner, Michael, 225 n. 7
Schweitzer, Ivy , 218 n. 4, 231 n. 1, 233 n. 5,
    234 n. 6, 234 n. 1, 235 n. 3
Scodel, Joshua, 218 n. 5
Scottow, Joshua, 88
Secor, Robert, 232 n. 3
Selement, George, 222 n. 11, 233 n. 6
self-elegies, 102–7
selfhood, Puritan
  and elegiac performance, 137–9, 163–8
  and reading, 58–9, 63–8, 226 n. 9
  duality of, 52, 61–2, 86, 89, 102, 169, 182–4,
    191–2, 202, 226 n. 8, 232–3 n. 3, 238 n. 10
  extrapersonal nature of, 58–63, 104–8,
    179–81, 224–5 n. 6, 230–1 n. 1

Sewall, Hannah, 236 n. 5; *see also* Danforth,
    John
Sewall, Rebekah, 236 n. 5; *see also* Tompson,
    Benjamin
Sewall, Samuel, 47, 103–4, 130, 131, 139, 148,
    185
Shakespeare, William, 219 n. 5
Sharpe, Samuel, *see* Fiske, John
Shaw, W. David, 41, 209, 214 n. 7, 215 n. 8, 216
    n. 10, 220 n. 8, 227 n. 10
Shea, Daniel, Jr., 226 n. 8
Shelley, Percy Bysshe, 19
Shepard, Joanna, 194
Shepard, Thomas I, 61, 100, 105, 128, 155–6,
    175, 187–8, 194, 226 n. 8; *see also* Wilson,
    John
Shepard, Thomas II, *see* Oakes, Urian
Sibbes, Richard, 90–1, 92, 95, 120, 122
Sidney, Sir Philip, 20, 54
Silverman, Kenneth, 138, 184, 217 n. 4, 220 n.
    7, 224 n. 6, 227 n. 10, 232 n. 4, 232 n. 1,
    232 n. 2, 233 n. 4, 233 n. 5, 239 n. 2
Slater, Peter Gregg, 229 n. 2, 234 n. 8
Smith, Eric, 140
Snelling, Margaret, 174
Snelling, William, 174
Spengemann, William C., 211 n. 2, 221 n. 11
Spenser, Edmund, 20, 54
Stanford, Ann, 225 n. 7, 230 n. 1
Stanford, Donald E., 217 n. 2
Stannard, David E., 87–8, 216 n. 1, 220 n. 7,
    227 n. 10, 229 n. 2, 229 n. 4, 239 n. 2
Stedman, Edmund Clarence, 27
Steere, Richard, 206–7
Steiner, Dorothea, 230 n.1
Stephen, 73, 76, 99
Stetson, Isaac, 85, 173, 204
Stock, Brian, 10, 214–15 n. 7, 215 n. 8, 215–16
    n. 10, 222 n. 1
Stoddard, Solomon, 12, 217 n. 2
Stone, Lawrence, 20
Stone, Samuel I, 113, 114, 137, 150, 156–7, 176,
    186, 235 n. 4
Stone, Samuel II, 110–11, 113, 119, 129–30, 172,
    173
Stout, Harry S., 217 n. 3
Strickland, Ronald, 220 n. 8
survivors
  biblicizing of, 159–64
  culpability of, 89–90, 92, 115–20, 139–40,
    164, 201
  textualizing of, 38–41, 58–9, 140–1, 162–4,
    167–8, 171–2, 177, 182, 191–2
Symmes, Zecharia, *see* Taylor, Edward